VICTORIANS ON BROADWAY

VICTORIANS ON BROADWAY

LITERATURE, ADAPTATION,
AND THE MODERN AMERICAN MUSICAL

Sharon Aronofsky Weltman

UNIVERSITY OF VIRGINIA PRESS

Charlottesville and London

University of Virginia Press
© 2020 by the Rector and Visitors of the University of Virginia
All rights reserved
Printed in the United States of America on acid-free paper

First published 2020

1 3 5 7 9 8 6 4 2

Library of Congress Cataloging-in-Publication Data
Names: Weltman, Sharon Aronofsky, 1957– author.
Title: Victorians on Broadway : literature, adaptation, and the modern American musical / Sharon Aronofsky Weltman.
Description: Charlottesville : University of Virginia Press, 2020. | Includes bibliographical references and index.
Identifiers: LCCN 2020017314 (print) | LCCN 2020017315 (ebook) | ISBN 9780813944319 (cloth) | ISBN 9780813944326 (paperback) | ISBN 9780813944333 (ebook)
Subjects: LCSH: Musicals—United States—20th century—History and criticism. | Musical theater—United States—History—20th century. | English literature—19th century—Influence. | Musicals—Stories, plots, etc.
Classification: LCC ML1711.5 .W45 2020 (print) | LCC ML1711.5 (ebook) | DDC 792.60973—dc23
LC record available at https://lccn.loc.gov/2020017314
LC ebook record available at https://lccn.loc.gov/2020017315

Cover art: "Victorians on Broadway," cartoon by Ethan Gilberti, June 2019 (author's private collection); stage curtains, iStock/farakos

For Jerry
Because there's nowhere else on earth that I would rather be
Than here on the street where you live.

CONTENTS

Acknowledgments ix

Introduction 1

1 · Broadway, Victorian Venus, and the Middlebrow 25

2 · *The King and* Who? Race, Dance, and Home 55

3 · Performing Jewishness in *Oliver!* 79

4 · Dickens, Cultural Anxiety, and Victorianness in *Sweeney Todd* 108

5 · The Meta-*Mystery of Edwin Drood* 132

6 · *Goblin Market,* Performance, and Sexuality 161

7 · "Bring on the Men" and Women: Melodrama and Gender Performance in *Jekyll and Hyde* 182

8 · Broadway's "Jane! Jane! Jane!" 210

Conclusion 227

Notes 233

Bibliography 263

Index 295

ACKNOWLEDGMENTS

When I was a little kid, the dining room floor of our split-level Connecticut home was just enough higher than the living room to form a stage. Virtually every evening while my mother cooked dinner, I'd dance there in the twilight, singing along with the cast albums my parents had brought home from special evenings at a Broadway show, with no other audience than the empty furniture and the light reflecting off the snow outside the curved mid-century bay window. I memorized all the melodies and lyrics, no matter how inappropriate for an elementary school child: "One pair of arms is like another / . . . I'll go with you or with your brother," "Two ladies, and I'm the only man, *ja*," "Krup you!" My first debt in writing this book (as in all else) is to my beloved parents, Molly and Julius Aronofsky, whose enjoyment of Broadway long ago molded mine.

My older sisters and brother—who never appear in my memories of performing for the empty living room at dusk because they were off doing whatever teens and big kids do between school and dinnertime—nevertheless kept musical theater cool with backyard theatricals, home puppet shows, and songfests on cross-country road trips: so loving thanks to Wayne Aronofsky, Ellen Cole, and Barbara Latham. I wish I could share this book with my parents and oldest sister. My glamorous cousin Sharon Ruben's spectacular singing of standard repertoire introduced me to all sorts of styles and songs early on; my aunt Gladys and her sister, my honorary aunt Selma, danced their girlhood routine from the Yiddish theater at every wedding and bar mitzvah, piquing my curiosity about theatrical dance. My New York–area cousins Matt (who took me at age sixteen to my first Broadway show), Nancy, and Stu Ruben and Kathy Shwiff have continued to steer me toward and accompany me to many a musical; my niece Becky Stone clued me in early to *Hamilton,* and my niece Laura Riley (gorgeous-voiced) introduced me to the joys of duets from *Wicked.* The Palmers, Ordiways, Weltmans, Shwiffs, Lichtensteins, and Nadelmans already know how our family parody skits at decades of rehearsal dinners and birthdays have provided innumerable opportunities to think about and play with Broadway classics; particularly, I would like to recall to loving memory Marianne Lichtenstein, my dear mother-in-law, the engine behind every production, and Abe Lichtenstein, my father-in-law and her cherished "golf club baby."

I have worked on this book for so long, with so many other important projects intervening, that I cannot thank here all those who heartily deserve acknowledgment. These include my brilliant writing partners and colleagues whose insights over the years have made this book and those that went before so much better: Dan Novak, Pallavi Rastogi, Chris Rovee, Isiah Lavender, Chris Barrett, Sunny Yang, Robin Roberts (who urged me to consider this an academic study), Les Wade, Jennifer Jones Cavanaugh, Solimar Otero, Carolyn Ware, Angeletta Gourdine, Carol Mattingly, and of course Elsie Michie, who read the whole manuscript again to make crucial suggestions just before I initially submitted it. I owe a hearty debt to my incredible series of smart and resourceful research assistants: Doris Raab Frye, Katie May, Zach Keller, Lindsey LaFleur, Jordan LaHaye, Christina Welsch (who assisted on my Rowan Atkinson interview, now a professor at the College of Wooster), and the multitalented Ethan Gilberti, who has not only provided top-notch annotated bibliographies but also is the marvelous cartoonist responsible for the cover art. My gratitude goes to students in my Victorians Performed courses and to confrères in the Works in Progress series at Louisiana State University. The editorial, production, and marketing staff at the University of Virginia Press deserve my deep appreciation, including Eric Brandt, Helen Chandler, Mark Mones, Colleen Romick Clark, and my anonymous expert readers whose reviews were so generous and helpful. Thanks also to Linda Dubois for jogging my memory of shows at the Saenger and to June Pulliam for an excellent index.

Thank you to my dazzling Dickens Project colleagues and Friends whose presence each summer at the Dickens Universe makes everything better and whose thoughts improved two chapters that began as lectures there. I know I am forgetting people I should mention in this representative sampling: Adam Abraham, Murray Baumgarten, John Bowen, Jim Buzard, Ryan Fong, Renee Fox, John Glavin, Marty Gould, Juliet John, Gerhard Joseph, Prithi Joshi, Melisa Klimaszewski, Lorraine Kooistra, Kate Newey, Teresa Mangum, Carol McKay, Helena Michie, Daniel Pollack-Pelzner, Catherine Robson, Cathy Waters, with special gratitude to John Jordan (the Master of the Universe) and George Levine (to whom I owe so many other debts). Also in Santa Cruz, in 2014 I directed an NEH Summer Seminar for College and University Teachers, "Performing Dickens: *Oliver Twist* and *Great Expectations* on Page, Stage and Screen"; the sixteen Summer Scholars who participated helped me to rethink adaptation theory: Kirsten Andersen, Daniel Brown, Patrick C. Fleming, Joshua Gooch, Taryn Hakala, Carrie Sickmann Han, Mary Isbell, Rob Jacklosky, Doug Kirshen, Rebecca O'Neill, Becky Richardson, Julianne Smith, Mary-Antoinette Smith, Adina Spingarn, Linda Willem, and Steve Willis. They also became my friends, as did the extraordinary speakers: Jacky Bratton, Gilli Bush-Bailey, Tracy Davis, and the indefatigably astute Carolyn Williams—also an essential Dickens Project colleague—whose incisive and generative reading and commentary on this manuscript and others has made all the difference.

The Nineteenth Century Theatre Caucus (19CTC) has provided unending inspiration and support. I have presented material from every chapter of this book at North American Victorian Studies Association (NAVSA), Research Society for Victorian Periodicals (RSVP), the Victorians Institute, and Interdisciplinary Nineteenth Century Studies (INCS); all have given me phenomenal opportunities and exceptional feedback. Let me thank my co-editors at *Nineteenth Century Theatre and Film*—Jim Davis, Janice Norwood, and Pat Smyth—from whom I have learned so much, just as I have learned much from David Mayer, former *NCTF* editor. Thanks go all the way back to theatergoing friends from my PhD program at Rutgers, Hildegard Hoeller, Anne Sobel, and Jonathan Levin; Jon once asked me as he drove into New York from New Brunswick with me and my husband to see a show why I wasn't writing about musicals.

I must express deep gratitude to the Louisiana Board of Regents for the ATLAS grant (Awards to Louisiana Artists and Scholars), without which this project might never have come to fruition. Likewise, I want to thank the LSU College of Humanities and Social Sciences and LSU Department of English, including a series of supportive chairs whose tenure spanned the years of this project's gestation and birth (Jerry Kennedy, Malcolm Richardson, Anna Nardo, Rick Moreland, Elsie Michie, and Joseph Kronick), as well as various LSU committees whose decisions to award me research leaves, sabbaticals, and travel grants have been so essential. Many thanks also to my colleague Andy Burstein, who reached out to the University of Virginia Press to ask if they might be interested in publishing on Broadway, and to Molly Buchman, who directed the LSU in London program for several years and invited me along as the English professor, which meant I was on the spot both for the city's rich archives and for the London theater scene. There Molly and I went together to many a musical, including Sondheim's *Road Show*.

The libraries and archives providing a cornucopia of extraordinary material helpful here include the Alley Theatre Archives (with special thanks to Lauren Pelletier), New York City Library of Performing Arts at Lincoln Center, the NYPL Theatre on Film and Tape Archive, the Paley Center for Television in New York, the British Library, the Kurt Weill Foundation Archive, University of California–Santa Cruz Library Special Collections, the Victoria and Albert Theatre Collection at Blythe House, the Templeman Library at the University of Kent, and the Library of Congress online collections. Most of all, I heartily thank the amazing librarians at Hill Memorial Library at Louisiana State University, where the special collections staff are incredibly helpful: Germain Bienvenu, Amanda Hawk, John Miles, and Melissa Smith. Likewise, the Interlibrary Loan staff at LSU deserve thanks for years of satisfying far-flung requests. Thanks also go to Kevin Duffy of LSU's Digital Media Services, who generously assisted with high-quality digital imaging of privately held materials.

I greatly appreciate my fantastic interviewees and interlocutors (Stephen Sondheim, Rowan Atkinson, Polly Pen, Frank Wildhorn, and Victoria J. Liberatori) for their generous donation of time and thought. Thanks also go to the wonderful choreographer Larry Fuller, who shared a DVD of his work with me. Chapters 2, 3, 4, and 6 include revised and much expanded portions previously published, appearing here with my gratitude: "The King and Who? Dance, Difference, and Identity in Anna Leonowens and *The King and I*" in *Conflict and Difference in Nineteenth Century Literature*, edited by Dinah Birch and Mark Llewellyn (Palgrave Macmillan, 2010), reproduced with permission of Palgrave Macmillan; "Boz versus Bos in *Sweeney Todd:* Dickens, Sondheim, and Victorianness," *Dickens Studies Annual* 42 (2011): 55–76; "'Can a Fellow Be a Villain All His Life?': *Oliver!*, Fagin, and Performing Jewishness," *Nineteenth-Century Contexts* 33.4 (September 2011): 371–88; and "Performing *Goblin Market*" in *Essays on Transgressive Readings: Reading over the Lines*, edited by Georgia Johnston (Edwin Mellen Press, 1997).

There are some debts I can't squeeze into a litany, no matter how heartfelt each statement of gratitude in the list above. I owe whole-hearted and earnest thanks to my kids, Alex and Elizabeth Weltman, who gamely listened to numerous albums, trouped to a multitude of shows, and even let me try out my PowerPoints on them. Their good-natured open-mindedness let them enjoy not only Victorian literature (and, yes, they have read or listened to *Great Expectations, Jane Eyre, Goblin Market* . . .) but also this glorious medium of musical theater that is not to every younger millennial's taste. Their imagined Broadway in which any magical thing could happen—even a show to be called *Whales on Broadway* ("they're whales, not snails / they leave no slimy trails")—made my research not just fun but possible. It is thrilling to think that now, grown up and going to musicals on their own, they might even want to read this book when I give them each an inscribed copy.

Finally, always and forever, there is my husband, Jerry Weltman, whom I met at a party where he was playing show tunes on the piano and I was singing them. He likes Victorian literature, too. Beginning with grad school, we went together to almost all the musical theater I discuss here. For decades he has encouraged me to continue with this project when intervals of working on something else threatened to go on too long. He urged me to do the interviews and bolstered my courage in requesting them. When I saw STEPHEN SONDHEIM in my email inbox, it was to Jerry that I ran, hyperventilating, after I picked myself up off the floor. Whenever I needed to think hard about a song (to analyze rhythm or harmony), he played it for me or we sang it together and brainstormed. I tested my ideas on him as they developed, and he read the manuscript top to bottom. It is no exaggeration to say that this book exists because of him.

VICTORIANS ON BROADWAY

Introduction

PROLOGUE: THE LIVENESS OF LIVE THEATER

In July 2011, I saw Stephen Sondheim's *Road Show* at London's Menier Chocolate Factory theater, where something happened that I have never seen before or since. In the middle of a scene, the conductor of the small orchestra stood and stopped the show: she alerted us that a man on the first row urgently needed medical attention. All eyes fixed on a white-haired fellow slumped in his seat.

Instantly the entire cast gathered round him. One brought water. One called an ambulance. The man, now somewhat revived, walked tentatively across the traverse stage toward the exit, helped by two women who might have been his wife and daughter. In the next few seconds, the cast conferred; an actor announced that the show would resume, but slightly earlier in the interrupted scene.

What fascinated me about all this (besides admiring the actors' swift and caring response to an audience member's health emergency) was how the performance of precisely the same lines differed when delivered moments apart. I was curious to see which iteration would be better. There is no doubt adrenaline heightened the actors' delivery. They spoke more fervently. They touched one another more tenderly.

This incident reminded me again (it bears repeating and repeating) that theater is a live, embodied experience, with minute or significant alterations every time. It is very different in this respect from films or print culture, which—barring new editions and director's cuts—largely stay the same. But in theater, there is no pretense of a fixed, final product. Thus, the notion of detailed textual analysis of theatrical texts carries challenges even if one pores over a libretto and score or attends multiple performances of a single production. The brief emergency at the Menier Chocolate Factory intensified the actors' performances. But it also heightened the audience's acuity:

the episode made us hyper-attentive, watching the actors' subtle modifications with strengthened interest. In this sense performance is like life, or like Heraclitus's river of life, because the actors, audiences, and performance environments change as time moves on.

LITERARY CRITICISM/THEATER HISTORY

Victorians on Broadway is about live stage musicals adapted from Victorian books. Examining musical dramatizations of works by Charles Dickens, Charlotte Brontë, and others, I consider how Broadway musicals from the second half of the twentieth century depict Victorian culture. I examine what ideological work adaptations such as *The King and I* (1951) and *Jekyll and Hyde* (1997) accomplish in 1951, 1997, and now. It is a critical commonplace to demonstrate that a film adaptation reflects the aesthetic and social concerns of its own time, no matter when its source text was written. Movies pervasively and persistently influence both audience and reader perception of their sources: *Dracula* (1931) and *Frankenstein* (1931) come to mind, cinema classics whose images haunt the preceding novels whenever we read them. Yet few scholars view live musical theater in this way, even though Broadway music, lyrics, drama, dance, and spectacle also shape both popular and critical interpretations of the past, as we have seen with the widespread interest in Lin-Manuel Miranda's *Hamilton* (2015).[1]

In examining these musicals and their sources, I ask several key historical, theoretical, and interpretive questions. How does researching musical theater adaptation require an expansion of adaptation theory that is often grounded in a novel-to-film model, as the titles of George Bluestone's seminal *Novels into Film* (1957) and Brian McFarlane's influential *Novel to Film* (1996) make abundantly clear? There is, for example, no book yet entitled *Novels into Musicals*. What is the relationship between the embedded musical-theatricality of a print narrative and its realization on stage? How do each musical and its original negotiate the performance of identity: nationality, race, class, sexuality, and gender? What cultural work does musical theater accomplish by appropriating and re-creating a sense of Victorianness, which often boils down to a sense of the Dickensian? What do we learn by excavating the strata of adaptation from source to incarnation on Broadway? How do Victorian-based musicals fit within the trajectory of Broadway's development, and how does that arc fit into intellectual trends beyond the theater? How much does the Broadway musical depend upon its precursor genre, the Victorian melodrama? And then there are the usual adaption-study questions: How does each adaptation interpret its source? And, simultaneously, how does each comment on its own contemporary culture?

Victorians on Broadway interprets Victorian literature and culture *through* the Broadway musical, focusing on the reciprocal illumination of both source text and adaptation that inheres in studying them closely, side by side. Each chapter explores the adapters' choices in understanding the originals, using the adaptations as critical lenses to see the Victorian texts more fully. Examining adaptations uncovers elements in the literary sources that we would not otherwise notice: for example, dramatizations of the incident in *The Mystery of Edwin Drood* (1870) in which Rosa Bud sings, such as Rupert Holmes's musical of the same name (1985), expose the inherent musical-theatricality of Charles Dickens's scene. Conversely, our understanding of each musical gains from investigating the selection, excision, emphasis, and rendering into a new medium that occurs in the creation of a completely new work of art out of the Victorian raw materials. For instance, Lionel Bart rewrote *Oliver Twist* (1837–39) with a less anti-Semitic and more lovable Fagin in *Oliver!*, sublimating the Jewishness of the novel's character into the Judaic qualities of the music and making his identity as a Jew entirely a matter of performance.

I interpret these twentieth-century musicals as drama, as Scott McMillan advocates, exploring how each musical play uses song and dance to tell a story, reveal character, and advance themes.[2] I analyze intermediate plays, films, and illustrations within the often long genealogy of adaptations between the Victorian original and its musical-theater descendant, tracing the path of inheritance, reading the significance of such intertexual borrowings. An adaptation that we experience now is, as Thomas Leitch points out, really an adaptation of multiple sources ("Twelve Fallacies" 164), a fundamentally overdetermined artifact. A case in point is the 1997 Frank Wildhorn and Leslie Bricusse musical *Jekyll and Hyde*. It not only adapts the 1886 novella by Robert Louis Stevenson, but also the 1887 Thomas Russell Sullivan melodrama, the 1920 silent film starring Lionel Barrymore that steals whole scenes from Oscar Wilde's *The Picture of Dorian Gray*, two other Hollywood movies, and a made-for-TV musical, all of which had already borrowed elements from Dickens. This abundance forms what Sarah Cardwell names the *meta-text*, the gradual development and accretion of all versions starting with the source and including its many offspring; the significance of the story shifts with each new iteration (25). Grasping the complex heritage of these musicals—now often classics in their own right—helps us to understand what subtle or not so subtle cultural or ideological work they do when we enjoy or consume them.

Comprehending the impact of any art object means understanding its historical context. Dianne Sadoff points out that film adaptations "can never be theorized apart from cultural and historical situations, production and distribution regimes, and the careers of dramatizers, directors, and screenwriters" (51), and the same is true of musical theater. *The King and I* responds to the Cold War. *Goblin Market* (1985) responds to the AIDS crisis. Whether contemplating the source or the adaptation, our insights mature when enhanced by probing into historical landscapes, not only the cultural context of both Victorian books and the mid- to late twentieth-century musicals, but also their literary and theatrical history.

Victorians on Broadway moves chronologically, reflecting the major developments in American musical theater. Chapters 1 through 3 read Victorian-sourced Broadway musical adaptations from the time dubbed the Golden Age of Broadway (Swain 8).[3] Chapter 1 outlines the first half of the twentieth century in a very brief history of American musical theater, describing the shift from *musical comedy* as the dominant Broadway genre to what we now call the *integrated musical*. In musical comedy, songs and dances exist as independent and often interchangeable sites of pure entertainment within the show; the integrated musical incorporates dance and song fully into the plot, innovated most fully by Rodgers and Hammerstein in the 1943 *Oklahoma!*[4] The musical *One Touch of Venus* (1943) exhibits characteristics of both kinds of musical entertainment. It serves as an ideal jumping-off point to consider musical theater adaptations of Victorian literature in the second half of the twentieth century in terms both of musical theater history and of intellectual history. Chapters 2 and 3 concentrate on *The King and I* (1951) and *Oliver!* (1963) respectively; both fully integrate music and dance into the storytelling. The book's next section, consisting of chapters 4, 5, and 6, investigates musical theater experiments of the 1970s and 1980s that focus as much on concept as story; such *concept musicals* are most associated with Stephen Sondheim, but other composers and lyricists also wrote in this genre. These chapters examine *Sweeney Todd* (1979), *The Mystery of Edwin Drood* (1985), and *Goblin Market* (1985). Chapters 7 and 8 enter the era of pop megamusicals with *Jekyll and Hyde* (1997) and *Jane Eyre* (2000). These shows reveal the Broadway musical's debt to melodrama, always a precursor genre but now explicitly acknowledged by critics. They also constitute musical theater's corollary to the late twentieth-century emergence of the Neo-Victorian movement in fiction: re-creating a Victorian sensibility while uncovering current issues implicit in Victorian culture. Organizing these chapters chronologically situates the adaptations within the history of musical theater and focuses attention on how they fit into aesthetic and intellectual movements, such as the mid-century critical reappraisal of Victorian literature after its earlier rejection by Modernism.

The field of Victorian literary studies often neglects drama, privileging the novel (Weltman, "Theater" 68). The pattern of dismissal by literary critics of the supposed dramatic wasteland between Richard Brinsley Sheridan and George Bernard Shaw parallels many theater scholars' opinion of Broadway musicals, which are often scorned as too commercial, too escapist, too artificial, and too middlebrow or *midcult,* to borrow Dwight MacDonald's term. As David Savran explains, since musical theater was "long derided and ignored by university theatre and music departments," it is hardly surprising that other literary critics also ignored it. In addition, "for many theater scholars and musicologists, the musical is embarrassingly commercial and too closely linked to high school drama clubs" ("Class and Culture" 243). And perhaps there is, even today, even in the United States, a residue of the old British hierarchy that privileged prestigious theaters like Drury Lane—the ones that held royal patents—above all the rest. Patent houses were legally permitted to mount spoken drama, such as Shakespeare. The others (the vast majority) did not have such licenses and would thus perform melodramas and other entertainments that included music to get around the law forbidding them from performing purely spoken drama. I still hear people making plans to see a "legit" play, meaning "legitimate" or spoken drama, placing the genre as the binary opposite of musical theater, denominated "illegitimate" in the nineteenth-century London theater context.

Rigorous academic analysis of Broadway musicals is relatively new, in the grand scheme; as a "viable academic field," it is "not much more than a decade old," said Stacy Wolf in 2016 ("Musical Theatre Studies"). But it is a vibrant growth industry, and many splendid books analyze musical theater history. Several offer an overview or analyze a specific decade.[5] Others focus on particular composers such as Richard Rodgers or Stephen Sondheim or investigate particular musical theater genres, such as the musical comedy, the adult musical, the rock musical, or the megamusical.[6] A few consider musicals' importance for specific audiences (African American,

LGBTQ+, Jewish, female, Latinx, etc.) or offer social histories that draw connections between the art on stage and the political or historical issues confronting the authors and audiences in the moment of the production.[7] Some investigate the representation of Victorian culture in contemporary media.[8] Other theater historians have looked with interest at how a particular musical reworks a particular source text, and other Victorianists have studied individual musical adaptations on film as interpretations of particular Victorian literary works.[9] But none before this book has investigated a pattern of adaptation to the musical stage across time and nationality or has focused on how temporal and geographical distance enables a particularly vivid kind of cultural work. No previous book focuses on musical theater's attraction to literary artifacts of the past as a vehicle for mediating present concerns. *Victorians on Broadway* is the first to study how musicals revise and interpret Victorian literature for the American musical stage or to study how Victorian texts—or texts of any time—routinely contain inherently musical-theatrical tropes, opening a new area of inquiry.

Current adaptation theorists defend adaptations from the charge that they are merely derivative and inevitably inferior transmutations of the original masterwork to a new medium. Critics who advocate this reconsideration of adaptation argue that the supposedly secondary text—the adaptation—forever changes how we experience the primary text, which we can never read in complete isolation from its descendants. In this introduction, I next consider how the application of these theories to musical theater disrupts the typical page-to-screen model, continuing the process of broadening adaptation theory. I then turn to understanding the Broadway musical as a middlebrow entertainment and to advocating a joyful recuperation of its middling status. This brings me straight to Dickens, who functions as a touchstone for everything we think of as Victorian as well as for the middlebrow artist who creates for all brows of consumer. Finally, I offer a detailed summary of each chapter that follows.

ADAPTATION THEORY: LITERATURE, FILM, AND MUSICAL THEATER

One effect of the liveness of musical theater is the delighted encore moment, the spontaneous expression of approval from an audience that insists on hearing the song or seeing the dance again, immediately. Conventions of musical theater and opera permit this kind of interruption and celebration of the performers' skill in a way that films do not. No one asks the film actor, who isn't present, to stop for applause.[10] Thinking about showstoppers and other artifices of live musical theater brings home how very different a film adaptation is from a musical theater adaptation. Considering live performances of song and dance when analyzing adaptation shifts the theoretical equation. These issues matter because often adaptation theory struggles with issues of hierarchy and authenticity: How faithful is the film to the novel it adapts? How convincing is its interpretation of its source? How successful is its translation to in a new medium? These concerns are grounded in what is known as *fidelity theory*.[11] A significant body of adaptation theory since the late 1990s revolves around overcoming our very common reliance on fidelity theory; for example, Imelda Whelehan articulates the aim of her co-edited collection *Adaptations: From Text to Screen, Screen to Text* (1999) as one that "further destabilizes the tendency to believe that the origin text is of primary importance" (3). Even using terms such as *source* and *original* implies for some a pecking order in which the adaptation is a mere copy, necessarily inferior. Paul Naremore points out that most film adaptations are considered "belated, middlebrow, or culturally inferior" (6). Current adaptation theorists work hard to pry our thinking away from such binaries, critiquing fidelity theory. Because musicals do not conform to the same expectations, more fully including musical theater in the calculation will help.

Contending that "most formal adaptations" of books to film to a large degree "carry the same title as their source" (22), Julie Sanders observes that such movies depend "upon the audience's awareness of an explicit relationship to a source text" (22). Diane Sadoff gives examples of filmmakers Franco Zeffirelli and Peter Kosminsky, who boast of their films' fidelity to the Brontës' novels. She points out that Zeffirelli thanks the Brontë Society for advice and archival expertise, to "warrant his film's authenticity" in his 1996 *Jane Eyre*; likewise, Kosminsky's film is entitled *Emily Brontë's Wuthering Heights* (1992), which "brands his film as genuine" (81). Francis Ford Coppola's *Bram Stoker's Dracula* (1992) and Kenneth Branagh's *Mary Shelley's Frankenstein* (1994) are two more examples. Musicals do not claim this kind of genuineness, not even *Hamilton*, which at times quotes directly from the best-selling biography *Alexander Hamilton* by Ron Chernow (2005). Far from titles that proclaim themselves authentic versions of a novel or biography, musicals' titles often assert their identity as not-the-book. *Hamilton*'s shortened name signifies poetic divergence from historical accuracy just as

Fiorello! (1959) is not a biography of Fiorello LaGuardia and *Oliver!* is not *Oliver Twist*. In the 1990s, when movie adaptations were busily declaring their fidelity to their sources by appropriating the literary authors' names, a fashion in musical theater went the other way, using the original title (or a shortened version of it) along with the subtitle "The Musical." Appending "The Musical" to a title recalling the source text is a proud declaration of difference from the genre of origin rather than a signifier of similarity.[12]

While audience members, after seeing a film based on a beloved novel, often continue to make the century-old assessment that "the book was better," that statement rarely applies to a musical theater adaptation.[13] Musicals *can't* be faithful because the experience of reading narrative in the form of novels, poems, nonfiction, and so on, simply does not include characters abruptly singing and dancing their stories. Novels can narrate musical-theatrical moments; musicals often take advantage of such diegetic scenes. But reading a narrative about a performance has a different effect from watching and hearing in real time—perhaps with wonder and delight—as live performers sing and dance in choreographed and orchestrated splendor, enjoying the show in physical proximity to other members of the audience simultaneously reacting energetically to the moment's lived experience. Even when musical numbers move the plot forward, as they do in an integrated musical, they nonetheless generally interrupt spoken dialogue (the exception is a *through sung* musical, like opera). This anti-realistic convention of characters that normally communicate in speech bursting into song annoys many people for whom there is no willing suspension of disbelief regarding this artifice, just as it thrills others.[14]

Live musical theater renders the notion of fidelity nonsensical in another way. In performance, a perfectly faithful adherence even to the musical itself, let alone to the source, is illusory. Each new production differs significantly from those that have gone before, often using not only different choreography, sets, costumes, actors, and directors but also at times different songs, like the 2013 revival of *Jekyll and Hyde,* or an updated *book* (meaning the plot, dialogue, and characterization), like the 2016 London revival of *Half a Sixpence.* In addition, even within the run of a single production, each actor's performance alters slightly every night, as is always true in live theater. The formats of novel and musical theater are so very different (and so different from film) that theorizing adaptation to musical theater means rethinking the theoretical apparatus to accommodate the particularities of this genre. Musical theater adapters themselves understand this. For example, the creators of *One Touch of Venus* were quick to distance themselves from any requirement that their artwork be faithful to its source: Ogden Nash and S. J. Perelman state at the outset of the published libretto that their play is merely "suggested by F. Anstey's story 'The Tinted Venus'" (front matter), just as Lionel Bart includes a disclaimer, both on *Oliver!*'s theatrical program and in the film's opening credits, that each is "freely adapted" from *Oliver Twist* (Dianne Brooks 117). And because fidelity does not apply to musicals to begin with, the concerted effort to distance adaptation theory from adherence to a fidelity model is largely irrelevant when applied to them.

Sanders's *Adaptation and Appropriation* (1999) briefly theorizes how musical theater adapts source texts, discussing *West Side Story* (1957) and *Kiss Me Kate* (1948), two musicals drawn from Shakespeare (27–29). Though it is a short section, her distinction between adaptation and appropriation accommodates the differences between various genres' expectations of fidelity. She also uses musical terms for theorizing adaptation generally, borrowing the notions of theme and variation, jazz, improvisation, and even hip-hop sampling as metaphors for adaptation and appropriation. Likewise, Linda Hutcheon—who has written several books on opera, medicine, and cultural history—glances at adaptations to opera and musical theater throughout her influential *A Theory of Adaptation* (2006), particularly when she discusses forms and the selection of scenes or lines for musicalization (44–47). Her widely known definition of adaptation as "repetition with variation" seems plucked straight from music theory (4). These paradigms provide excellent ways to think beyond fidelity, reminding us that, as Walter Pater says, all art aspires to the condition of music (90).

The notion of "musicalizing" a scene or dialogue is a basic feature of adaptation to musical theater. It is a term practitioners employ frequently, a word Sondheim, for example, uses repeatedly in his autobiographies. He remembers that he and Mary Rodgers considered "adapting Frank Stockton's story 'The Lady or the Tiger?'" which they "had tried to musicalize in the early 1950s for a proposed television show" (Sondheim, *Look* 298). And he later regrets not musicalizing a scene in *Sweeney Todd* exactly as Christopher Bond had written it in the play that was Sondheim's immediate source (Sondheim, *Finishing* 371). Musicalizing a scene or setting words to music is a form of adaptation limited, obviously, to musical performance genres. The technique serves to distance the scene or song from the source even as it may emphasize meaning, intensify emotion, or otherwise reveal features of the original text that might be excised in some other way. Music could serve to accentuate the dialogue's rhythm. A high note might literally heighten the significance of a word. Characters who could never be understood speaking overlapping dialogue can sing in counterpoint with perfect clarity, revealing their separate thoughts simultaneously for extra dramatic tension. Folkloric music can reveal or underscore a character's ethnicity. None of this is possible without musicalizing the adapted text.

In a similar vein, musicologists and composers, particularly of operas, who work on adaptions from literary texts talk about the musical composition as "ornamenting" the libretto, by which they mean the insertion of trills, arpeggios, melismas, extra repetitions, and other sonic delights that might augment or distract from the text.[15] Both these commonly used technical terms, *musicalizing* and *ornamenting,* can be misleading. They imply to a non-musicologist that musical theater and opera simply add tunes to dialogue or fancy vocals to individual words, as though the music were merely auxiliary to the experience. But music is not merely a decorative supplement. Certainly, the composers themselves do not think it is merely supplemental, and for many—and this is so transparent it's hardly worth saying—the whole point of a musical is the music. For much of the twentieth century, musicals functioned much like music videos from the 1980s on: to sell popular songs, earlier as sheet music and later as musical recordings. But no matter what aspect of a show critics most laud, the ensuing marriage of music and words is surely—again obviously—a completely new artwork. The result is different from either the words or music alone. The effect multiplies when the element of dance also enters the equation. Perhaps the clearest example is *Cats* (1982), with lyrics that were not purpose-written for the show but were a book of preexisting poems by T. S. Eliot, *Old Possum's Book of Practical Cats* (1939), worlds apart from the immersive experience of hearing Andrew Lloyd Webber's swelling music while surrounded by cats skillfully slinking and pouncing, not only on stage but also in the aisles and precariously on the ledge of the balcony.

Movies often described as costume dramas, that is, *heritage film,* bear directly on theorizing the ideological work performed by Broadway musicals that adapt many of the same Victorian novels. Heritage film and television have generated their own body of criticism, including detractors who see the genre as neoconservative, as packaging upper-class privilege for middle-class viewers who find themselves "applauding private ownership of stately mansions" as part of a kind of patriotism or as compensation for their own lack of material wealth (Sadoff xvii).[16] Sadoff and Robert Hewison critique British heritage television for promoting nostalgia for a past that, were it suddenly present, would deprive most of its contemporary viewership of many rights, including the vote (all women, all working-class viewers, most middle-class viewers, etc.). They point out that these series uphold a view of the ruling class as essentially warm-hearted, civic-minded, and inclusive, and of the servant class as generally industrious, respectful, devoted, and contented with their station. Though there are musicals that romanticize the past (*Jane Eyre: The Musical,* for example), the conventions of musical theater, even when dramatizing some of the same novels as heritage TV and film, tend also to undercut idealization and to encourage an ironic view of the class system. There is always hovering at the edge of a portrayal of a singing aristocrat an incipient element of camp. Even when Broadway shows include musical moments that seem to validate upholding past and present inequities, other moments (often production numbers and humorous songs) reset the show's import by injecting obvious artifice that counters the conservative effect. When the whole cast bows together on stage while the orchestra continues to play and the audience applauds, recognition of craft and artistry of the whole show—from the actors and musicians to the creative team—is built into the experience. No fuzzy feeling that this was a long-lost but beloved reality lingers after multiple curtain calls with dripping actors smiling under the stage lights and people all around cheering and egging them on for one last whirl through the spectacular dance of the finale.

Sadoff argues that the 1943 classic *Jane Eyre* with Orson Welles and Joan Fontaine is just one example of heritage film that feeds into Hollywood's legitimation of heteronormativity. Screenwriters "trimmed and telescoped narrative to focus on the heterosexual couple" (Sadoff 83). Musicals, however, even when they draw directly from earlier films that have already done exactly this, add considerable material that must distract from the lead heterosexual couple. This material may take the form of large-scale song and dance sequences such as the opener, the finale, the "eleven o'clock" number in the second act that is supposed to wake everyone back up again, when audience attention has started to lag. Such traditional spectacles do not operate in every musical (certainly not in every musical I discuss in this book), but the point remains that musical theater has built into the genre expectations that work against the heteronormative. And here is a sharp distinction. For all that adaptations of Victorian texts to the musical stage maintain the same characters and plots as the film adaptations, a claim that Broadway musicals, no matter what their subject matter, help to maintain the heteronormative status quo would immediately run into problems. Several books have appeared in recent decades documenting how important the medium has been for the gay and lesbian communities;[17] others argue for gay and lesbian readings of particular shows.[18] In other words, even with identical plots as their Victorian sources and with intervening non-movie-musical film adaptations as additional sources, Broadway musicals do not come across to fans as heteronormative to the same degree as film or television, which—as mass entertainment, unlike theater—targets a much broader audience.[19] And this point takes us straight to a discussion of the Broadway musical as middlebrow.

MIDDLEBROW CULTURE AND THE BROADWAY MUSICAL

So middlebrow is the mid-century integrated Broadway musical that Dwight MacDonald denounced both *Oklahoma!* and Rodgers and Hammerstein's *South Pacific* (1949) as defining examples of the insidious midcult in his influential 1960 essay "Masscult and Midcult." "Midcult is the transition from Rodgers and Hart to Rodgers and Hammerstein," MacDonald writes, invoking Lorenz Hart, whose 1943 death necessitated Rodgers's seeking a new lyricist. He continues the sentence, praising Rodgers and Hart's smart and satirical musical *Pal Joey* (1940), deriding the move "from the gay tough lyrics of *Pal Joey*, a spontaneous expression of a real place called Broadway, to the folk-fakery of *Oklahoma!* and the orotund sentimentalities of *South Pacific*" (36–37). The transition that MacDonald seizes upon is also precisely the shift from the domination of the musical comedy to the modern integrated musical that is the focus of chapter 1 of this book.

Like MacDonald's, French sociologist Pierre Bourdieu's dislike of middlebrow proclivities is clear. Bourdieu locates highbrow and middlebrow tastes within higher and lower classed elements of the bourgeoisie. He aligns the *culture moyenne* or middlebrow culture pejoratively with the petite bourgeoisie in their pretentions toward the haute bourgeoisie's preference for what he calls "legitimate culture," which is akin to Rodgers and Hammerstein's aspiration for a more cohesive aesthetic accomplishment. Bourdieu does not address the Broadway musical specifically, other than mentioning in his preface to the English-language edition of *Distinction* that bourgeois New Yorkers will seek "undemanding entertainment" there (xii). But, as that statement implies, American musical theater fits squarely within the domain of his critique. Bourdieu offers a set of contrasts that delimit middlebrow tastes cultivated through variety TV like *The Ed Sullivan Show:* "television programmes uniting jazz and symphonic extracts, music-hall and chamber music, string quartets and gypsy orchestras, violinists and fiddlers, bel canto and cantata, prima donnas and songsters, the 'Pas de deux' from *Swan Lake* and Rossini's 'Cat Duet'" (326). This catalogue seems a veritable recipe for musical theater—even down to singing in imitation of cats. The petite bourgeoisie values "minor forms of legitimate culture, like light opera" and prefers "'accessible' (*moyen*) or 'declasse' works," with primary examples being "*Scheherazade, Rhapsody in Blue, La Traviata,*" and so on (327). Musical theater—including the Broadway composer of *Rhapsody in Blue,* George Gershwin—fully matches the parameters Bourdieu sets out here.

Both Bourdieu and MacDonald refer to Broadway as a physical space. The physical existence of this location matters in understanding Broadway as a middlebrow genre and how it troubles not only adaptation theory but also theories of the middlebrow. Bourdieu and MacDonald recognize the central relationship between Broadway as the canon of American musical theater and Broadway as the street in Manhattan that comprises New York's theater district: a wide avenue and those roads intersecting it between 42nd Street and 49th, give or take a few blocks, and technically referring only to those theaters that seat five hundred patrons or more. Yet most American theater happens beyond Broadway's tight geographical ambit. I include in my extra-Broadway calculations all the regional, semiprofessional, amateur, school, house-of-worship, community center, and camp productions that feed Savran's point about the musical's too-close-for-comfort arrogation by drama clubs. Thus some of my performance examples come from theater beyond Broadway. This preponderance of regional American theater—the only live theater most Americans ever see—should be valued; significant theatrical innovation occurs there, perhaps never to move from the periphery to the theatrical center and only experienced in local circumstance.

Nevertheless, regional theaters and schools largely choose from a canon established by Broadway performance. Broadway confers cachet. And while great performers, crew, and musical theater creators of every kind work in theaters all over the country, there is no question that the superior budgets and enormous talent pool in New York count, particularly with the larger scale of production that musicals often require. In other words, fabulous performances of *A Streetcar Named Desire* are performed in New Orleans, where Tennessee Williams wrote the play. But those productions do not hire the hundreds of dancers, singers, musicians, and so on needed for the kinds of labor-intensive spectacle many musicals relish, just for starters. Excellent big productions are certainly both doable and done in the Big Easy, but it simply is not as easy without the apparatus already in place in the Big Apple. The classic American "legitimate" play (think not only Tennessee Williams but also Lillian Hellman, Sam Shepard, Lorraine Hansberry, Edward Albee, August Wilson, Wendy Wasserstein, David Mamet, Tony Kushner, etc.) does not have a moniker associated with New York City. But the Broadway musical most certainly does.

In this respect, as in so many others, the Broadway musical does not quite fit the parameters of other middlebrow genres set up by critics and theorists of the middlebrow, which Susan Hegeman associates not only with the middleclass but also quite convincingly with the Midwest (141–45). Most middlebrow commodities that Joan Rubin and Hegeman study are distributed in affordable mass-produced formats—Book of the Month Club memberships, for example—that might not have the circulation of pop music but are procurable in Middletown, USA. In contrast, large theater districts simply require large populations and throngs of visitors to support the thousands of live performers in multiple venues with the colossal budgets involved in simultaneous productions. The Broadway musical is an art form grounded in the big metropolis. But that does not raise its "'brow'-elevation level," in part because of another paradox (Sedgwick, *Between Men* 12): as Savran explains, the Broadway musical survives not only because New Yorkers help to make up the audiences, but also because it "continues to epitomize a middle-class, middlebrow form beloved of suburbanites and tourists" ("Class and Culture" 243). In other words, it needs both the center and the periphery to survive.

Bourdieu's analysis of middlebrow palates depends upon a population "inspired by a concern to rehabilitate and ennoble" (326) middlebrow tastes. Historically, American theater—excepting the most Modernist, the most avant-garde—is middlebrow in precisely this way. Savran points out that, until 1964, the Pulitzer Prize for drama, first given in 1918, was "explicitly charged with uplifting the stage" ("Class and Culture" 243).[20] This brings us right back to MacDonald's dismissal of Rodgers and Hammerstein's aspirations for creating in the Broadway musical a fully integrated art form, like Gluck's vision of opera. Stacy Wolf makes a related point that the "formal quality of integration also became tied to musical theatre's aspirations to be high art and to espouse progressive social messages" (*Changed*

248n18). Aiming for high seriousness (a Victorian concept, coined by Matthew Arnold) is the hallmark of a middlebrow aesthetic.

Although in her essay "Middlebrow" (1942) Virginia Woolf included Dickens in her list of highbrow authors (right between Shakespeare and Byron) and although F. R. Leavis allotted Dickens's novel *Hard Times* a sort of postscript in the final section of *The Great Tradition* (1948), adaptations of Dickens to any other medium, let alone the musical stage, ratchet quickly down the forehead to the middle of the brow. Heritage film studies grounded in the middlebrow, such as Sadoff's *Victorian Vogue* (2010), concentrate significant energy on films adapted from the novels of Dickens. But it is not just the adaptations that are understood to be middlebrow: Dickens himself is. We feel this in Leavis's barely including him in literature's "great tradition." Indeed, the definitions of middlebrow we see in Joan Rubin's *The Making of Middlebrow Culture* (1992), Janice Radway's *A Feeling for Books: The Book-of-the-Month Club, Literary Taste, and Middle-Class Desire* (1999), Hegeman's *Patterns for America: Modernism and the Concept of Culture* (1999), Bourdieu, and so on, feed directly into Dickens's own upwardly mobile trajectory from Warren's Blacking Factory to worldwide literary phenomenon. We have seen Bourdieu emphasizing the petit bourgeois's longing for the cultural capital of the haut bourgeois. Radway and Rubin focus on cultural uplift through reading selections from the Book of the Month Club. Hegeman defines the cultural aspirations of the genteel midwesterner as middlebrow. As Philip Cox points out, Dickens's biography tallies with this portrait, seeing the author himself in one of the *Sketches by Boz* depicting a "shabby-genteel" gentleman who reads all day at the British Museum, improving himself through a publicly available means of study (122). That same script of uplift appears in many of Dickens's books, most famously in the autobiographical *David Copperfield*. Accessible, sentimental, melodramatic, advocating the acquisition of high culture by the middle class: how could these novels *not* be considered middlebrow? Yet they are at the same time brilliant, moving, inventive, and fiercely original, so that while in 1914 the Modernist magazine *Blast* blasted them, Modernists such as Woolf cherished them.

Simultaneously highbrow and middlebrow, Dickens occupies a space similar to the Broadway musical, which Savran proclaims is "*both high and low at the same time*" (emphasis original; "Class and Culture" 243). A bit too esoteric for some, the object of fanatical devotion by others, scorned by many intellectuals as "undemanding" (to quote Bourdieu), escapist, and bourgeois, the Broadway musical troubles the notions of the middlebrow. That's Trouble with a capital T that rhymes with D and that stands for Dickens.

DICKENSIAN

When I asked Stephen Sondheim what he thinks of—what he pictures or hears—when he thinks of Victorian literature and culture, he replied, "I just hear Dickens, I think Dickens. Dickens movies I've seen, and the couple of novels of his I've read" (personal correspondence with author). For the Broadway musical generally as well as for Sondheim specifically, *Victorian* equals *Dickensian*. This refers not to just any Dickens, but to the mediated Dickens of earlier film and theatrical adaptation, reconfirming the importance of adaptation as a vehicle for shaping later reception of canonical literature. That the musicals discussed in this book tend to represent Victorian culture in ways that are largely understood as Dickensian raises questions about the notion of Victorianness itself and what it stands for on the American musical stage. And this is of course because Dickens has been so very often adapted to all media.

There is, as Sanders points out, an important reciprocal relationship between source texts and their many adaptations in any format. On the one hand, we enjoy repeated adaptations of *A Christmas Carol* because it is a classic, and we want to see it made anew, so long as we can see connections to the source. On the other hand, as Dickens already knew when he worked with stage adapters in his own lifetime, adaptations prolong the afterlife of the source text, because new potential readers are first introduced to the material in the transmediated form. Some works, and *A Christmas Carol* is the best example, have been adapted so many times that they have become what Paul Davis calls a *culture text* (6), one which is so pervasive that we recognize it without ever having read the original. As Sanders explains, adaptation works "to require and to perpetuate the existence of a canon" (8). Far from being an indication of disrespect for the source, repeated "adaptation becomes a veritable marker of canonical status; citation infers authority" (9). Dickens is an excellent case in point.

Immediately upon publication—in fact, even before the final installments appeared in print—dramatizations of Dickens's fiction hit the stage. Three different adaptations of *Pickwick Papers* (1836–37) opened in London before it completed its serial publication. Although such piracy chagrined Dickens (no copyright protection for theatrical adaptation of novels meant no royalties for novelists whose work was dramatized by other authors), the shows expanded his already enthusiastic fan base while he was alive and further preserved his popularity after his death.[21] By 1897, just two years after the invention of the motion picture, Dickens began his long posthumous history of adaptation to film with a short depicting Nancy's murder by Bill Sikes from *Oliver Twist* (Zemka 30). Dickens and adaptation of Dickens inaugurated both filmmaking's narrative triumphs and the advent of film theory, with the early director D. W. Griffith and the early theorist Sergei Eisenstein each specifically acknowledging Dickens's influence on storytelling techniques in their emergent medium.[22] Griffith ascribes his creation of montage to Dickens's parallel action in fiction, when scenes depicting concurrent incidents are intercut successively, one after the other.[23] Grahame Smith goes further, arguing in *Dickens and the Dream of Cinema* (2003) that Dickens's writing is incipiently cinematic (47).[24]

Dickens tracks throughout *Victorians on Broadway*. Two of the major musicals I discuss are adaptations of Dickens, *Oliver!* and *Drood*. The first is taken from *Oliver Twist*, written early in the novelist's career, being his first prose narrative generally acknowledged as a fully fledged novel, and the second comes from his final, incomplete novel, *The Mystery of Edwin Drood*.[25] Besides the musicals adapted directly from Dickens, all the other Victorian-sourced musicals are influenced by him. They include characteristics and even characters that appear not in their ostensible source texts but in Dickens or in prior adaptations of Dickens. For example, the sonorous villain Beadle Bamford of *Sweeney Todd* finds a counterpart in Mr. Bumble, the large singing beadle from *Oliver!*; the earliest source text of the *Sweeney Todd* story barely has a beadle at all. To account for the Victorian mise-en-scène created by Harold Prince for *Sweeney Todd*, a story originally set in the eighteenth century, we need turn only to Dickens as social critic with his concern for the urban poor and we find the source of Broadway's sense of the Victorian. Similarly, if we mine all the way back through decades of preceding adaptations leading to the musical *Jekyll and Hyde*, we find the prostitute Lucy springs not from Stevenson's novella *The Strange Case of Dr. Jekyll and Mr. Hyde* but at least in part from the character of Nancy from, again, *Oliver Twist* via the musical *Oliver!* The gritty London that Stevenson himself describes is already indebted to Dickens, multiplying the Dickensian influences on later adaptations.

Theater mattered importantly to several of the Victorian authors covered in this book, particularly Dickens; perhaps one reason Dickens is so easily performed on stage and screen is that he composed in front of a mirror, acting out all the characters as he wrote, laughing aloud along the way (Mamie Dickens 49–50). Critics profitably engage in metaphors of theater, theatricality, and performance in analyzing Victorian novelists.[26] David Kurnick argues that "theater is a condition of the text" for certain Victorian novelists (7). I agree and further point out ways in which the source texts are already musical-theatrical, ripe for musical dramatization. The exuberant song and dance "You've Got to Pick a Pocket or Two" from *Oliver!* highlights that even in Dickens's anti-Semitic portrayal of Fagin as a consummate villain, Oliver laughs (perhaps for the first time?) as he watches the antics; thanks to the musical we see how fit for choreography and song the novel's brief paragraph describing the pickpocket game really is. Such scenes are proleptically musical-theatrical.

WHAT FOLLOWS

All the chapters of *Victorians on Broadway* examine Broadway musicals based on Victorian books, considering their complex network of prior adaptations and affiliations as well as the contemporary cultural milieu in which each premiered and continues to be performed and re-performed.[27] After providing a brief history of the Broadway musical up to 1943, chapter 1 discusses the Modernist rejection of the Victorians and delves more deeply into Virginia Woolf's essay "Middlebrow." It then investigates the 1943 musical *One Touch of Venus,* by Kurt Weill, Ogden Nash, and S. J. Perelman, which explicitly pokes fun at middlebrow aesthetics, in the context of the new movement among literary critics to reappraise and revalue the Victorians. It opened just a few months after *Oklahoma!* (1943), widely recognized as revolutionizing musical theater by integrating songs and dances fully into the plot. Being almost exactly contemporaneous with the show that caused such a sea change, *One Touch of Venus* serves not only as a foil to showcase the cultural work that adaptations of Victorian literature were about to do on stage in the second half of the twentieth century, but also to demonstrate how it fits into the swelling interest in reclaiming Victorian literature after its dismissal by the Modernists. The show is based on F. Anstey's comic novel *The Tinted Venus: A Farcical Romance* (1885), with its own connections to drama and exhibition, to a series of now forgotten interceding adaptations, and to a complex web of cultural connections. The show is set in the current moment of the 1940s, and in New York

City rather than London in the 1880s. By abandoning its Victorian setting, *One Touch of Venus* participates in the earlier part of the century's reaction against the Victorians just as it lingers in the musical comedy format that entertained Broadway audiences throughout the 1920s and 1930s. Yet like the Victorian-based musicals that follow, it seizes upon a Victorian source, incorporates some integrative features, demonstrates that the novel is already musical-theatrical, and performs important work in connecting the musical stage with its intellectual and aesthetic context.

Chapter 2 analyzes Richard Rodgers and Oscar Hammerstein's *The King and I* (1951), based on earlier fiction and film adaptations of Anna Leonowens's *The English Governess at the Siamese Court* (1870) and *The Romance of the Harem* (1873). The power dynamics between the King and Anna have long generated scholarly discussions about colonialism and gender.[28] Yet Leonowens's accounts of her experiences in Thailand often reveal a far more varied vision of women's roles than the 1950s musical does. Instead, the musical deflects the books' concept of slippery gender identity onto the intricate series of multiple race performances in the ballet "The Small House of Uncle Thomas." This play-within-a-play, choreographed by Jerome Robbins, is itself an adaptation of *Uncle Tom's Cabin* (1852) as envisioned through a long and complex stage history of melodrama and blackface minstrelsy, in productions that helped at once to end slavery and to perpetuate damaging stereotypes. In this ballet, dancer-actors of any race (every race, when worldwide performances are considered) perform Thai court dancers performing fictional African American slaves imagined by a white woman, Harriet Beecher Stowe. The performers depicting both black and white characters in the ballet wear whiteface, as is typical of traditional Japanese classical drama, or elaborate masks, a convention in traditional Thai dance drama. These techniques distance the ballet from racist traditions and allow the musical to comment on contemporary issues of civil rights, American imperialism, and women's roles through a hyperextension of identity performance.

Chapter 3 examines Lionel Bart's *Oliver!* (London 1960, Broadway 1963), a successful and enormously influential work, not only in musical theater history but also in subsequent adaptations and interpretations of Dickens's *Oliver Twist*. No single adaptation of Victorian literature has had a greater impact than this musical on the public's understanding of Dickens, of "Victorianness," or of the imaginary space that is Victorian London, although in aggregate the many adaptations of *A Christmas Carol* far exceed it. Bart transforms the novel's Fagin from a stock anti-Semitic villain drawn from a long stage tradition into a lovable comic scamp, from a corrupting criminal who incites brutal murder to a naughty but nurturing substitute mother to his band of little thieves. The novel insists on identifying Fagin's wickedness with his Jewishness, labeling him "the Jew" hundreds of times in the original serial publication. Early adaptations on stage and screen took their iconography directly from George Cruikshank's racially charged illustrations. But the musical recuperates Fagin's Jewishness in part by never mentioning that Fagin is Jewish. Instead, the show sublimates Fagin's Jewish identity into the music (Fagin's songs are full of klezmer instrumentation and cantorial vocal riffs), which makes it entirely a matter of performance. Bart also emphasizes Fagin's Cockney culture, integrating him more fully into his class. As a Jewish East-Ender himself, Bart revised Fagin partly in response to David Lean's 1948 film *Oliver Twist*, which aroused public outrage against the anti-Semitism of Alec Guinness's portrayal, including a giant prosthetic nose. Actors create the musical Fagin's Jewish identity a variety of different ways; I interviewed Rowan Atkinson about his portrayal of Fagin in the 2009 London revival at Drury Lane, which provided me firsthand testimony about the performance process and what an actor might do in the twenty-first century to embody Jewishness without risking an insulting caricature—or worse.

Chapter 4 begins a new section of the book that treats the concept musical and other innovations of the 1970s and 1980s. It looks at *Sweeney Todd,* Stephen Sondheim and Hugh Wheeler's brilliant 1979 thriller and revenge tragedy. With its plot about abuse of power by the state and justice system and their nemesis in the form of a murderous barber in cahoots with a cannibal pastry chef, the musical reflects disgust with and distrust of the government in the 1970s and 1980s generated by worries such as Watergate, the beef boycott, and scandals about food safety. Following Sondheim's concept musicals *Company* (1970) and *Follies* (1971), *Sweeney Todd*'s Brechtian elements include a chorus commenting on the story and characters breaking frame. Despite their great differences, *Sweeney Todd* owes a debt to Bart's *Oliver!* in grafting onto the traditional Sweeney Todd narrative such characters as a large singing beadle and Mrs. Lovett, a beautiful ice queen in the original tale, but in Sondheim's version a comic, fast-talking, manipulative, lusty middle-aged woman, like *Oliver!*'s Mrs. Bumble. The musical derives from the anonymously published serial novel *The String of Pearls* (1846–47), written in imitation of Dickens, but without his powerful cultural critique; yet Sondheim's musical reintroduces Dickensian concern for reform.

Chapter 5 examines the 1985 Rupert Holmes musical adaptation of *The Mystery of Edwin Drood,* Dickens's last novel, unfinished at his death in 1870. The musical's unique construction capitalizes not only on the novel's musicality but also on the narrative's unfinished state. *Drood* is a play within a play, set in the fictional Music Hall Royale in 1895. At the point in the unfolding story at which Dickens died and was unable to go on writing, the action stops, the music grinds to a halt, and the actors and even the orchestra appear flustered. Then the audience votes on who killed Edwin Drood and other unfinished business. This meta-theatrical device interrogates conventions of the mystery genre and drives home the importance of creating the sense of an ending, particularly when the unfinished novel ends mid-narrative.[29] *Drood,* as the musical is often called, helps us to recognize that this novel is already musical-theatrical, employing music and gesture when language becomes insufficient for characters to converse; they are integral to the novelist's storytelling. For example, the scene in the novel in which the villain Jasper plays the piano while his beautiful pupil Rosa sings before a drawing room full of friends is key to understanding the relationships among characters as they struggle for control of the music, themselves, and one another. It is only in a narrative of musical performance that this crucial scene can undertake so much, and it is no wonder that virtually every adaptation, even nonmusical ones, performs it. I compare it to the same moment in an 1871 melodrama by Walter Stephens entitled *Lost,* the first British production adapted from *The Mystery of Edwin Drood,* and to the corresponding scene in Holmes's musical. The incomplete state of the novel fosters the musical's self-reflexive and playful jockeying for control among Dickens, Holmes, the performers, and the audience.

Chapter 6 analyzes *Goblin Market,* a musical by Polly Pen and Peggy Harmon adapted from Christina Rossetti's powerful 1859 poem of the same name about two sisters—Lizzie and Laura—who encounter goblin men. Like *Drood,* this experimental chamber opera opened in 1985. Like *Sweeney Todd* and *Drood, Goblin Market* helps us to rethink the work accomplished by musical theater, scrutinizing the relationships among poetry, performance, and audience. The poem *Goblin Market* has provoked an astonishing array of contradictory interpretations, such as addiction, incest, prostitution, fairy tale, sexual desire, the divided self, feminism, sisterly affection, and Christian allegory.[30] A rich history in visual culture offers a kind of interpretative chronology, from the lush Pre-Raphaelite illustrations by the poet's brother Dante Gabriel Rossetti in 1862 to the 1973 *Playboy* spread provided by artist Kinuko Craft's pornographic revision of Arthur Rackham's famous 1933 drawings, bearing on the poem's dramatization, reminding us that theater is also a visual art form.[31] A striking change from the poem to musical is that, in the decade of Gay Pride and AIDS activism, this show excises important lines commonly used to support a lesbian reading of the poem and adds lyrics that instead emphasize a conventional sibling rivalry. Nevertheless, in a sort of theatrical return of the repressed, homosexual desire ultimately reenters the show through the addition of cross-gender performativity. Because in the play men are embodied only as women (by an all-female cast playing sisters who are remembering or fantasizing the goblins), heterosexuality appears only in the guise of same-sex encounters. By having each sister play the very sexual male goblins in turn, Pen and Harmon metaphorically accentuate the lesbian content their other changes in staging and lyrics elide. In September 2013, Polly Pen confirmed to me that the musical was seen by some as a response to the 1980s AIDS crisis, which seems clearest in the musical's depiction of Laura's near death and Lizzie's courage in bringing back the antidote to her mysterious illness (personal interview).

Chapter 7 takes us to the megamusical. Stylistically, *Jekyll and Hyde* (1997) by Frank Wildhorn and Leslie Bricusse incorporates previous Broadway shows imported from London and set in nineteenth- or early twentieth-century France that rely on lavish spectacle and a pop sound to tell a tale grounded in melodrama; *Les Misérables* came to Broadway in 1987, and *Phantom of the Opera* arrived on Broadway in 1988. But rather than a French novel, Robert Louis Stevenson's 1887 *The Strange Case of Dr. Jekyll and Mr. Hyde* is the source text for the Wildhorn-Bricusse show, which became a popular phenomenon. While Hyde's crimes in the novella deal primarily with nonsexual violence, the show adds seamy love interests for Jekyll and Hyde. The genealogy for this show is particularly complex, not only including earlier musicals and previous adaptations of the novel, but also incorporating elements from Dickens and Oscar Wilde. The doubled women (the prostitute and the fiancée) resemble characters from Dickens's *Oliver Twist,* Nancy and Rose Maylie; the emphasis on first Jekyll and then Hyde's slumming derives in part from the nighttime outings of Dorian Gray.[32] The Broadway show imagines that, for the Victorians, respectability is always a façade, exemplifying late twentieth-century

American fascination with Victorian sexual hypocrisy. Sexual and ethical misconduct committed by leading citizens motivates Hyde to punish them by serial murder, suggesting a debt to *Sweeney Todd* as well. Choreography in key dance numbers highlights the instability and illegibility of gender and other categories of identity, a theme present in the novel and highlighted in the earliest serious stage adaptation written by Thomas Russell Sullivan as a virtuoso vehicle for the actor Richard Mansfield. By 1997, at a time in which the biggest American news stories involved the revelation of sex scandals in high places and media hype about exposure of serial killers, this musical's concentration on universal deceit is topical. Nevertheless, focusing on the sordidly sexual tames the terror of Stevenson's vision of the double self.

Chapter 8 concludes the book's readings, considering *Jane Eyre: The Musical* (2000) by Paul Gordon and John Caird. Like *Jekyll and Hyde*, it fits into the late twentieth-century pop tradition of spectacular Broadway adaptations of Victorian Gothic. Charlotte Brontë's *Jane Eyre* (1847) has inspired no end of adaptation, not only many films, television, and radio series but also symphonies and ballets.[33] It has bred prequels, such as Jean Rhys's acclaimed *Wide Sargasso Sea* (1966), itself a classic, and web phenomena such as a Brontë superheroes action figure video.[34] Patsy Stoneman has published eight dramatizations before the twentieth century in her *Jane Eyre on Stage, 1848–1898* (2007). With such an irresistibly adaptable text (complete with musical performance embedded within important scenes, as in *The Mystery of Edwin Drood*), it is no wonder that it had been musicalized before.[35] An elegant technique that sets this play apart from some of its predecessors is the shadowing of the child Jane by the actress playing the adult Jane, who sings narration to the audience while the child Jane acts; this creates a stage manifestation of the "double I" in fictional autobiography, in which the adult narrator (Jane or, in *Great Expectations*, Pip) tells the story of the child protagonist, with the narrative voice slipping between the two personae.[36] In a return to the sexual politics we saw in *The King and I*, this musical play presents a feisty heroine challenging a domineering hero. Also like *The King and I*, the play is in several ways less progressive in terms of gender politics than the Victorian original. Because it transforms Jane's famous feminist speech from the lonely roof of Thornfield Hall where she works as a governess into a lecture she sings first to her pupils at Lowood and then to the audience as she leaves—still singing—for her job at Thornfield, the musical suggests that Jane has *already* won her freedom by leaving the repressive school and striking out on her own, to find love with Rochester. The result individualizes Jane's rebellion and loses the novel's protest against a systemic Victorian patriarchy. It also Americanizes Jane's longing for liberty in the lyrics' word choice "of sweet liberty I sing," bringing the use of the Victorian back to the Americanization of F. Anstey's novel in *One Touch of Venus* and the use of a Victorian setting to address American issues as in *The King and I*. A brief conclusion returns readers to a discussion of adaptation theory and middlebrow culture with a brief glance at twenty-first-century American musical theater.

1
Broadway, Victorian Venus, and the Middlebrow

To set the stage for my focus in the coming chapters on Victorian-sourced musicals from 1951 to 2000, I offer a brief history of American musical theater (including an explanation of some introductory terminology) from the mid-nineteenth century up to the mid-twentieth. I place the lively period of American musical theater in the early decades of the twentieth century into an intellectual context insufficiently considered in relation to musical theater: the Modernist rebellion against the Victorian culture of their parents' generation. Occurring at the same time as the foundational rejection of Victorian authors by the Moderns was American theater's assertion of its independence from British and European dominance in the 1920s to 1940s, a time when musicals were in general self-consciously American in theme, music, and setting. But just as the Modernists rebuffed the Victorians, the subsequent generation snubbed the Modernists' anti-Victorian stance. I situate Broadway's mid-century turn toward nineteenth-century British source material within a broad shift in extra-theatrical culture in which academics also began seriously to reexamine Victorian writers, reacting against their Modernist forebears. An extended case study of the musical comedy *One Touch of Venus* (1943) and its neglected source text, the Victorian novel *The Tinted Venus* (1885), exemplifies the tension in the 1940s between the contradictory desires to reject and to recover the Victorians.

One Touch of Venus is a pivotal specimen for talking about how adaptations of Victorian texts fit into the history of musical theater for several reasons. It was created and produced in 1943, just months after the revolutionary *Oklahoma!* But *One Touch of Venus* absorbs only some of the groundbreaking elements that distinguished *Oklahoma!* (such as a ballet that propels plot), retaining older, soon-to-be-outdated features as well. While it anticipates the other shows analyzed in this book in recognizably adapting a Victorian text (unusual for a successful Broadway musical from the 1920s to 1940s), it differs from Victorian-sourced shows produced in the second half of the twentieth century in that it retains almost no vestige of its Victorian origin (in setting, costuming, dialogue, and so on). Instead, it transposes the 1885 British novel into a modern, stylish American milieu. In its overt Americanness, *One Touch of Venus* resembles the musical comedies that preceded it more than the musicals that followed. Moreover, by adapting a British novel from 1885, *One Touch of Venus* joins an important mid-twentieth-century intellectual trend beyond musical theater: that of revaluing Victorian literature. It marks a transition between American shows that refuse Victorian settings and those that relish them.

A VERY BRIEF HISTORY OF BROADWAY TO 1943

The Broadway musical has a wonderful origin story. In 1866 a Parisian company set to perform the *féerie* extravaganza *La Biche au Bois* (the doe of the forest) in New York found itself suddenly deprived of a theater because the Academy of Music burned down. Meanwhile, *The Black Crook*, a melodrama by Charles M. Barras with a similar plot involving forests, fairies, and shepherds (with shepherd's crooks, hence the title), was about to open at New York's Niblo's Garden. *The Black Crook* absorbed the ballet troupe (Knapp, *Formation* 21), resulting in an innovative, plot-driven, five-and-a-half-hour spectacular display, alternating drama, music, and dance (Preston 21). Its fabulous sets, elaborate costumes, innovative stagecraft, and one hundred shapely ballet dancers—wearing so little that ministers preached against the show—ensured success. Mark Twain reviewed it in 1867 for San Francisco's *Daily Alta*: "Beautiful bare legged girls . . . dressed with a meagerness that would make a parasol blush . . . with more tights in view than anything else.[1] They change their clothes every fifteen minutes for four hours, and their dresses become more beautiful and more rascally all the time" (80). Thus the first *book musical* was born. In contrast to a revue, a book musical tells a story while including a significant number of songs and dances. *The Black Crook* boasted thematically connected singing and dancing and a parade of visual delights, running for a phenomenal 474 performances (Knapp, *Formation* 23), the first show in New York to play for over a year (Bordman 18). So good is this origin tale that in 1954, it became its own Broadway musical, *The Girl in Pink Tights*.[2] In this musical, the two very different performance troupes blend their talents, leading to conflict and blossoming romance between melodrama actors and ballet divas. Running for 115 performances, the show did not come near the success of *The Black Crook*.

Despite its place in the annals of musical theater history, the runaway hit *The Black Crook* is not really in the same genre as the Broadway musical, as we currently think of it. One reason is its exorbitant length, but there are many other differences. The ballet and melodrama elements complemented each other but were not designed to be part of a cohesive entertainment. This creation story does not account for the multitude of generic influences on the modern Broadway musical; in addition to melodrama, these include European operetta, English comic opera, minstrelsy, vaudeville, jazz, and spectacular revues such as Ziegfeld's Follies. Many other shows have vied just as legitimately for the title of first Broadway musical, including George M. Cohan's "aggressively American" 1904 *Little Johnny Jones* (Hirsch 9), featuring the songs "Give My Regards to Broadway" and "The Yankee Doodle Boy." Tired of the European dominance of the American stage, Cohan created his musical comedy about an American jockey who goes to England for the Derby, using American styles of music, dancing, colloquial dialogue, and a plot celebrating American values.

But like *The Black Crook*, Cohan's *Little Johnny Jones* did not achieve the kind of lasting influence needed to make it the germ of a new American genre. It could not permanently unseat imported European operetta, such as Franz Lehár's unprecedented success *The Merry Widow* (1907). An *operetta* is "customarily set in exotic or fabled" locations, "using operatic voices, contrapuntal duets and choruses, and more elaborate and frequent sections with continuous music" (Block, "Melody" 139). Operetta remained immensely popular, as did Gilbert and Sullivan's English comic operas. This situation began to shift only with the patriotism endemic to fighting in World War I, when "fondness for Central European operetta fell dramatically among English speaking audiences" (Everett 99). But even after the war, operetta still thrived on Broadway; in fact, seven of the ten most popular shows in the 1920s were operettas (Block, "Melody" 141). The difference was that these were more likely to be something like *Rose-Marie* (1924), set in the American West, or *Rosalie* (1928), which starts out in the fictional

European country of Romanza but swiftly moves to the state of New York, at West Point, a geographical allegory for the Broadway operetta in general. Like so many evolutionary tales, the origin of the Broadway musical is a process of innovation and influence rather than a single creation *ex nihilo*.

The most popular form of Broadway entertainment at the beginning of the 1920s was the *revue*. A musical revue or variety show is a series of unrelated or vaguely related acts, including music and dance numbers that follow one another to make up an evening's entertainment. Particularly successful were those composed by homegrown talents Irving Berlin, George Gershwin, and Cole Porter (Block, "Melody" 141). Often with the word "Follies," "Scandals," or "Revue" in the title, these spectacular amusements sported constellations of beautiful (and largely undressed) chorus girls, a series of song-and-dance numbers, comic sketches, and other bits strung together visually and sonically, without telling a story. Also often appearing in the title were words that identified the producer or location of the revue in a particular theater or neighborhood (such as "Ziegfeld," "George White," "Music Box," "Greenwich Village"), which emphasized not only the revue's American but also its New York identity.

Musical comedies also abounded in the 1920s and were the most popular genre of the austere 1930s. Unlike operettas of this period, they "normally utilised contemporary American urban settings with matching dialogue and music (e. g. ragtime, blues, jazz and, after 1930, swing)" (Block, "Melody" 139). Cole Porter's brilliant but utterly farcical *Anything Goes* (1934) quintessentially represents musical comedy. Nevertheless, despite the often silly plots, in the 1930s American musical comedies with "overt political themes and musicals with social commentary proliferated" (Block, "Melody" 137).[3] Madcap, yes, but many musical comedies at this time remarked directly and acerbically on American issues in shows with titles such as George and Ira Gershwin's Pulitzer Prize–winning *Of Thee I Sing* (1931),[4] satirizing American political campaigns, and Kurt Weill and Maxwell Anderson's *Knickerbocker Holiday* (1938), mocking Peter Stuyvesant's government of colonial New York, with clear links to contemporary politics.[5]

But what exactly is a *musical comedy*? First, it is a book musical rather than a revue; it tells a story—even though that story is sometimes a flimsy one, just an excuse to connect songs—with a recognizable plot, characters, themes, and so on. Musical comedies in the 1920s and 1930s (and after) were often written for specific comedy teams with their improvisational talents or shticks in mind rather than for operatic voices. With vernacular comic and musical tastes, they targeted a broader audience than opera or operetta. The point was to produce hit songs that would sell outside of the dramatic context of the show. Many of these musical comedy songs—the love songs in particular—could be plucked out and replaced by another thematically similar song with no harm done to the storytelling, so that they typically "interrupt rather than continue the action" (Block, *Enchanted Evenings* 147). Proof? Revivals of musical comedies from this era often substitute other songs by the same composer/lyricist. For example, the 1962 Broadway revival of *Anything Goes* ransacked the cache of Cole Porter hits to replace "Where Are the Men?" with "Heaven Hop" from *Paris* (1928), also the source for "Let's Misbehave"; it swapped "All through the Night" with "Delovely" from *Red, Hot, and Blue* (1936); it also injected "Friendship" from *DuBarry Was a Lady* (1939), "Let's Step Out" from *Fifty Million Frenchmen* (1929), and "Take Me Back to Manhattan" from *The New Yorkers* (1930)—a veritable frenzy of Portermania unrelated to the original score.[6] Notwithstanding Block's reminder that musical comedy composers and lyricists such as Kern, the Gershwins, Rodgers and Hart, and Porter typically wrote their songs with the show's characters and storyline in mind ("Melody" 139), it is also simply true that these entertainments do not integrate their musical numbers into their plots to the degree that we see after Richard Rodgers and Oscar Hammerstein's 1943 *Oklahoma!*

The 1920s and 1930s also gave birth to American shows that blur lines between opera, operetta, and musical theater while emphasizing American issues, sources, and music. One important example is *Show Boat* (1927), adapted from Edna Ferber's 1926 novel of the same name, with music by Jerome Kern and book and lyrics by Oscar Hammerstein.[7] With its setting on a Mississippi riverboat and its plot centering on racial passing and miscegenation, it exposes the cruelty of American racism through the use of important American musical theater idioms such as blackface minstrelsy, the incorporation of the ubiquitous form of melodrama, and the blending of European and African musical influences: the "sometimes quite fluid grouping of spirituals, blues, ragtime, waltz, and standard light Broadway styles" are incorporated into Tin Pan Alley conventions (Knapp, *Formation* 186). While the young white lovers' songs could fit stylistically into any operetta, signifying the failed fantasy of their future together, the black characters' songs generally derive from spirituals or the blues, signifying the untenable position these characters hold in an American culture that oppresses them and anyone who crosses the race line.

Show Boat was a revolutionary artifact in a number of ways: its music, its themes, its weightiness, even its casting. It is arguably the first Broadway book musical in which black and white actors performed together.[8] In addition to integrating the cast, it also integrated many of its extraordinary songs fully into the plot. Most obviously, "Can't Help Loving Dat Man" is crucial to several story twists, but most importantly revealing Julie's mixed racial status, making her marriage illegal, and forcing her and her white husband to flee. The anthem "Ol' Man River" powerfully relays three major themes: racial inequality, the fluidity of racial interconnectedness, and the centrality of the river as a symbol of time and movement. Like *Show Boat*, the shows that constitute the focus of *Victorians on Broadway* tell their stories not only through dialogue but also through song and dance, as do all *integrated musicals*—that is, musicals that integrate songs and dances into the storytelling process. But, despite its enthusiastic reception, *Show Boat*'s innovations didn't stick; it took Hammerstein's second go at creating an integrated musical, this time with Rodgers, to change audiences' and critics' expectations about musical theater's capacity for tightly crafted dramatic storytelling through music and dance.

That effort was *Oklahoma!* Many innovations distinguished it from the contemporary musical comedy scene: instead of a high-energy, fully orchestrated opening number featuring a large chorus of glittering dancing girls, the curtain rises to reveal an old woman churning butter and a solitary man's voice coming from offstage, singing the slow ballad "Oh, What a Beautiful Mornin'" without any instrumental accompaniment. Like its precursor *Show Boat*, this is a story steeped in American issues and folk music, whose plot is serious, involving the dramatic death of a character onstage. The setting is the Oklahoma territory around 1900 (Oklahoma became a state in 1907), when cowboys and farmers were still fighting over land use. Disputes raged about the shift from the open grazing ranges for cattle to the inexorable enclosure of fields for crops; in the musical, cowboys and farmers need to learn to get along and to govern themselves in preparation for the young soon-to-be state to grow up and join the Union. The costumes were "rather homespun" and the characters ordinary people (Sears 151). Curley is a cowboy; Laurey is a farm girl, their marriage uniting the two factions; Jud Fry is Laurey's hired farmhand; and Ali Hakim is a traveling salesman.[9]

Oklahoma! premiered in 1943, barely past the horrors of the Dust Bowl and its Black Blizzards that rampaged throughout the 1930s, with the last miserable drought of the decade still going strong in 1940. The Dust Bowl caused 3.5 million people to abandon their blighted homes and farms throughout the American plains in desperate migration, primarily to California. Although most were from other affected states, many were from the panhandle of Oklahoma, spawning the derogatory term "Okie" and inspiring John Steinbeck's novel *The Grapes of Wrath* (1939).[10] Perhaps the perennially humanitarian Hammerstein saw that in 1943 the recovery of the state of Oklahoma should have its own celebratory musical, its own title song, and its own lyrics with the reassuring line "You're doing fine, Oklahoma" and the exuberant proclamation, "Oklahoma, OK!" For a long time, this profound, wholly integrated musical was seen as a clear watershed moment in musical theater history. Although historians now point out that *Show Boat* and other musicals (particularly those by Rodgers and Hart) had already begun incorporating songs and dances into the storytelling process more thoroughly, there is no question that *Oklahoma!* struck contemporaries as something remarkable, with "a dramatic unity and momentum that had hardly been present in American musical theatre before 1943" that "announces the arrival of the 'musical play'" (Sears 152). Critics understood that the whole package (songs, lyrics, dialogue, and music) was one art object. In 1944, it became only the second musical to win a Pulitzer Prize (a special citation for Letters rather than Drama), awarded to both Hammerstein *and* Rodgers to indicate that the music, book, and lyrics form a single prize-winning entity.

Although the choreographer, Agnes de Mille, was not included in the Pulitzer, her revolution in the use of dance in storytelling in many ways made the crucial difference in fashioning the integrated musical. Just as it is necessary to temper claims that Rodgers and Hammerstein created the new form by mentioning antecedents, it is important to note that de Mille was not the first choreographer to incorporate ballet dramatically into a Broadway musical: George Balanchine had already done that for Rodgers and Hart's musical comedy *On Your Toes* (1936). But that show is *about* a ballet company, with all its intrigues, jealousies, and artistic struggles as it fits more contemporary dance styles into its repertoire. An important distinction between *On Your Toes* and *Oklahoma!* is that in the earlier show, the characters dance diegetically as part of the story rather than telling the story through dance. For example, a lead male character performs at the fictional Cosmopolitan Opera House in a new ballet the company is premiering, *Slaughter on Tenth Avenue;* a gangster in the audience tries to shoot him during the performance (he is in cahoots with the male lead's rival in love). Dance matters crucially in that the intended victim evades the bullet by comically dancing faster and faster. Yet this device is a very different kind of integration into the plot than choreography that is itself a mode of storytelling. So entirely separate an entity from *On Your Toes* is the stand-alone choreography Balanchine created as the fictional ballet *Slaughter on Tenth Avenue* that it entered the actual repertoire of the New York City Ballet (albeit in revised form, danced tragedy with no comic speeding up at the end).

Because Agnes de Mille had just set the ballet *Rodeo* to music by the classical composer Aaron Copland (famed for using American folk motifs in orchestral compositions) for the Ballet Russe de Monte Carlo, the producers of *Oklahoma!* knew she could create brilliant dances that appropriated American folk movements, forging them into a distinguished ballet. Paul R. Laird explains that the ballet "Laurey Makes Up Her Mind" at the end of *Oklahoma!*'s act 2 "changed Broadway history"; de Mille's choreography depicts—entirely through dance—a character making an important choice, with all the psychological and emotional nuance of such a dramatic moment made abundantly clear without words or vocalization. De Mille insisted on professional dancers (rather than actors who could dance a little), scheduling separate rehearsals for them and substituting them for the acting leads to portray the main characters during the dream ballet (266). She innovated the use of sophisticated choreographic elements in Broadway dance sequences that represent psychological states and relationships; an example is counterpoint, "with characters doing different movements at the same time," adding "visual appeal" as well as relaying interiority and the emotional complexity of relationships (Laird 266).

Opening six months after *Oklahoma!,* the musical *One Touch of Venus* was also choreographed by de Mille, who supplied fully integrated, innovative dances. It was composed by Kurt Weill with lyrics by Ogden Nash and book by Nash and S. J. Perelman, best known as a screenwriter for the Marx brothers.[11] Whereas *Oklahoma!* broke ground with its seamless incorporation of old-fashioned folk elements,[12] *One Touch of Venus* revels in urbane wit, more reminiscent of the past accomplishments of Rodgers and Hart than the present and future of Rodgers and Hammerstein. In 1943 *One Touch of Venus* was already becoming outmoded not only in that it is a musical comedy with fewer integrative elements, but also—and here is the paradox—in its self-conscious modernity. But it also bridges the Modernist rejection of the Victorians (and of middlebrow culture), laying the groundwork for their mid-century reclamation, at least on the Broadway stage.

THE MODERN, THE MIDDLEBROW, AND RECUPERATING THE VICTORIANS

One way in which the Modernists signified their modernity was in rejecting the Victorians who immediately preceded them. In the 1910s and 1920s, the Modernists rebelled (and continued thereafter to rebel) against their Victorian parents and defined themselves as *not*-Victorian in reaction to their nineteenth-century antecedents in literature, art, and theater. An example mentioned in the introduction is the June 1914 Vorticist manifesto in *Blast,* signed by both Ezra Pound and Wyndham Lewis, who in a *Daily News and Leader* interview explaining the manifesto called for the "blowing away of dead ideas and worn-out notions" (M.M.B., quoted in Hoen 106).[13] The manifesto identified Dickens, Wilde, Gissing, and Tennyson, as well as the aesthete, the realist, several theaters, and both the "Victorian Vampire" and the "Victorian Bourgeois" among those to 'blast" or "curse" in the formation of a new aesthetic movement (11–18). Another obvious instance is Lytton Strachey's 1918 *Eminent Victorians,* a witty experiment in group biography skewering Victorian moral hypocrisy and deploring the political policies leading to World War I.

Even more germane to later chapters of *Victorians on Broadway* is Virginia Woolf's talk to the Women's Service League in 1931 called "Professions for Women," urging them to kill the Angel in the House (a concept from Coventry Patmore's 1854 poem of that name), who once haunted every Victorian home and who still lurked within themselves. No everkind and supportive angel can adequately critique a book (critics require the freedom to be negative); therefore, to take on the task of writing book reviews or anything else of importance, modern women must strangle their Victorian inner angels. The cultural work of blasting the Victorians continued throughout the 1940s. In addition to her feminist position, which is inextricable from her Modernism, part of Woolf's rebellion against the Victorians is linked to her dismissal of the middlebrow. In the same volume in which "Professions for Women" appeared, *The Death of the Moth, and Other Essays* (1942), Woolf's 1932 essay "Middlebrow" was also published. Written as an unsent letter to the editor in response to a review of her work in the *New Statesman,* she comically extolls the highbrow and the lowbrow, excoriating the brow in the middle, those who are betwixt and between. The quality of the highbrow is obvious, and the lowbrow has at least the advantage of authenticity. "At random," Woolf lists "Shakespeare, Dickens, Byron, Shelley, Keats, Charlotte Bronte, Scott, Jane Austen, Flaubert, Hardy or Henry James" as examples of "highbrow" authors ("Middlebrow" 177).[14] She mentions no lowbrow or middlebrow authors by name. A primary perpetuator of the middlebrow is the chief purveyor of Victorian radio dramatizations, the British Broadcasting Company (BBC), which she calls the "Betwixt and Between Company."

F. R. Leavis addresses middlebrow BBC adaptations directly in *The Great Tradition* (1948).[15] Leavis values some Victorian novelists at the expense of others, drawing a highbrow/lowbrow dichotomy that depends on their adaptability to British radio performance: to isolate and elevate the few laudable Victorian authors, he disparages the public's "present vogue of the Victorian age" in fiction, naming "minor novelists" such as "Trollope" (he doesn't bother identifying which one), "Charlotte Yonge, Mrs. Gaskell, Wilkie Collins, Charles Reade, Charles and Henry Kingsley, Marryat, Shorthouse" (1). None of the authors that Virginia Woolf admires as highbrow appear on Leavis's disapproving list. He complains that they "are being commended to our attention, written up, and publicized by broadcast, that there is a marked tendency to suggest that they not only have various kinds of interest to offer but that they are living classics" (1). Leavis objects to inferior works being lumped together with novelists he considers genuinely worth distinguishing as the Great Tradition—Jane Austen, George Eliot, Henry James, and Joseph Conrad—a lineup that includes only one entirely Victorian author (George Eliot), with Dickens's *Hard Times* granted an ambivalent place in the afterword.[16] Besides Dickens, two of these authors also appear on Woolf's list. Leavis's recuperation of nineteenth-century English Literature (based on what is *not* easily dramatized for radio production) does not go very far beyond the Modernists' negative assessment.

Yet soon the tide of interest in thoughtful reappraisal of the Victorians began to swell. Hugely influential, Jerome Buckley's *The Victorian Temper* appeared in 1951.[17] Buckley identifies his own and others' motivation explicitly as reacting against the Moderns' negativity toward their progenitors: "I looked back at the anti-Victorianism of Lytton Strachey . . . as ill-considered and badly outdated. . . . I was, of course, not alone in my impressions, for I felt myself at the beginning of a newly sympathetic reappraisal of the Victorians, in which I should be glad to have some small share"

(Foreword 75). Kathleen Tillotson's groundbreaking *Novels of the Eighteen-Forties* came out in 1954. Another leading mid-century scholar to reassess the Victorians for serious criticism was Walter E. Houghton. In *The Victorian Frame of Mind* (1957), he addresses unequivocally his own critical impetus in reassessing the Modernist rejection of their immediate past: "It is now forty years since Lytton Strachey decided with a flourish that we knew too much about the Victorian era to view its culture as a whole. The truth was rather that in the full tide of reaction it was impossible to achieve a detached and broad perspective" (xiii).[18] That year, 1957, also brought Richard Altick's seminal *The English Common Reader* and the founding of the first and still major academic journal in the field, *Victorian Studies*.

The same cultural phenomenon that was occurring in literary criticism was also occurring in the choices musical theater creators made in materials and manner of adaptation. In the context of Woolf and Leavis, it is not surprising that the 1943 Weill-Nash-Perelman musical takes an ambivalent approach toward the Victorians. For the first time in decades, an American creative team chose a Victorian text—a British novel from 1885—as the source for what became a major Broadway musical comedy of enduring quality and popularity. But they eliminated all the Victorian elements from its setting and ambiance, inventing a musical just as Americanized as anything by George M. Cohan. Yet it was a bellwether, signaling a change: a mere eight years later, in 1951, exactly a half century removed from the death of Queen Victoria (1819–1901), the task of openly appropriating, appreciating, and identifying with the Victorians had begun, not only in academic literary-critical circles but also on Broadway, with the arrival of *The King and I*.

In maintaining the Modernist rejection of the Victorians by abandoning the nineteenth-century milieu of its source text (and by making merciless fun of middlebrow culture, so tied to Victorian culture in the Modernist mindset), *One Touch of Venus* fits seamlessly with the aesthetic outlook of the preceding Modernist decades. In its approach, it does not anticipate the reassessment and renewed regard of the Victorians that was to be a feature of the post–World War II attitude, both of literary critics and of theater practitioners. But at the same time, the source text *The Tinted Venus* also presents itself as entirely modern, particularly in spoofing its own moment: the aesthetic movement and the artistic classicism current in 1885. Because my method throughout this book is to examine the source text alongside the adaptation, the next section of this chapter is an extended reading of

The Tinted Venus, excavating its sources, analyzing its cultural critique, noting its inherent musical-theatricality, and considering how understanding both the novel and the musical provides reciprocal insights.

THE TINTED VENUS

One Touch of Venus grew from the 1885 novel *The Tinted Venus: A Farcical Romance* by F. Anstey, the pen name of the versatile and prolific Thomas Anstey Guthrie (1856–1934), a novelist, playwright, translator of Molière, and—from 1886 to 1930—a popular columnist for the satirical magazine *Punch*.[19] His most enduring novel is *Vice Versâ: A Lesson to Fathers* (1882), which inspired *Freaky Friday* (1972), Mary Rodgers's much-adapted novel for children (familiar now as the 2003 movie starring Jamie Lee Curtis and Lindsay Lohan).[20] A great success, *Vice Versâ* catapulted Anstey to fame and allowed him to abandon his fledgling career as a barrister to continue writing full time. In addition to being Anstey's most famous and most adapted book (made into many plays and films before *Freaky Friday*), it has the dubious distinction of being so hilarious that it caused Anthony Trollope to die laughing, literally. As Trollope's nephew explained, "After dinner my sister read 'Vice Versa' aloud to him and my father, also a great laugher. Uncle Tony roared as usual; suddenly my father and sister noticed that while they were laughing, he was silent: he had had a stroke from which he never recovered" (qtd. Merchant, Introduction 13).

While *The Tinted Venus* has not achieved *Vice Versâ*'s fame or fatal impact, it was adapted to stage and film before its musicalization by Weill for Broadway, as many as five times, according to Kurt Gänzl (1539). British actress and musical theater star Rosina Vokes and her company received Anstey's permission to perform a one-act farce also called *The Tinted Venus,* adapted by Willie Wilde (Oscar's older brother), on September 7, 1885, at the Prince of Wales in Liverpool (T. Allston Brown 568).[21] Anstey records annoyance at various pirated productions as well as his disappointment with Willie Wilde's adaptation. "[It] did not impress me as a good one or likely to be successful," he complained.[22] *A Vision of Venus; or, A Midsummer-Night's Nightmare,* an 1893 play by Harry Pleon performed at the Britannia and published in Dicks Standard Plays, was—as the title page explains—"partly inspired by Anstey's 'Tinted Venus.'" The fact that Pleon's play was published suggests that it was the most successful adaptation prior to *One Touch of Venus*. In 1921 the British silent cinema company Hepworth made a film entitled *The Tinted Venus,* with Cecil Hepworth directing and with Blanche MacIntosh as scenario writer (Simon Brown).[23]

Anstey's novel is itself an adaptation—or at least a comic revision and reversal—of the Pygmalion and Galatea myth, in which a sculptor falls in love with the beautiful ivory statue he has carved and wishes he could marry. In that myth, Venus grants Pygmalion's wish when he kisses the statue's lips and finds them warm with life. *The Tinted Venus* imagines what would happen to a hard-working, good-looking, complacent young man in the modern London of 1885 were he to find himself suddenly desired by a statue of Venus whom he had inadvertently animated. Largely forgotten, the novel needs more summary than the more canonical texts discussed later in this book.

Leander Tweddle, a successful barber-hairdresser, foolishly places the engagement ring he intends for his fiancée, Miss Matilda Collum (a pretty pillar of virtue), onto the finger of a sculpture tucked away in a suburban pleasure garden, where he has been walking with another young lady (a circumstance that will get him into trouble later), extolling the slenderness of his fiancée's fingers, just like the marble goddess's.[24] This act of slipping the love token onto the divinely sculpted digit causes Venus to inhabit the statue. She falls passionately in love with Tweddle, who never returns the immortal's affections; far from wanting to wed her, he wants to get rid of her. He spends the entire novel trying to figure out how to retrieve his ring without invoking her quite deadly wrath, all the while avoiding both the police and various gangsters who think he stole the priceless statue. In addition to worries that he will suffer the terrible fate awaiting most mortals whom Venus loves, he keeps digging himself into a bigger hole with his fiancée by explaining that he can't help it that the other woman in his life, the one wearing Matilda's engagement ring, is "a goddess." It is this sort of circumstantial distress E. V. Lucas meant when in 1903 he proclaimed F. Anstey to be "the best novelist of the tight place" (544).

What could be melodrama (with the powerful and statuesque older woman punishing the virtuous young lady beloved by the foolhardy but honorable young protagonist) or tragedy (with the goddess exacting colossal punishment for the hero's fatal mistake), here is farce. The fun, as Roger Lancelyn Green explains, is in the "fantastical treated as the actual" (178).[25] The story's charm is in its teasing out the humorous potential in a series of misunderstandings and misidentifications that grow from the goddess-inhabited statue's interfering in the life of a very practical-minded and not very classically educated young tradesman: he may know nothing of Greek and Roman mythology, but he prides himself on creating superior hair-dressing products. In short, the novel speculates on what might happen were Galatea to come to life to the dismay instead of the delight of a lower-middle-class Pygmalion of little imagination and strong work ethic. By the end, the young lovers make up and marry (unlike Leander Tweddle's namesake in the many retellings of Hero and Leander), Venus goes back to Olympus, the "stolen" statue is returned to the park, and Leander becomes the proprietor of a resplendent West End hairdressing "saloon" so successful that keeping the company's books "would prove too much for Matilda, even if more domestic duties had not begun to claim her attention" (281).

As with speculative fiction generally, it is partly realism that makes the fantasy work. For example, C. S. Lewis, in his foundational essay "On Science Fiction," points out that it is the *ordinariness* of Gulliver or Alice that makes them believable and interesting in their extraordinary circumstances (60). Brooks Landon explains that science fiction "relies on realist techniques to glove its fantastic elements with the rhetoric of rationality" (109). George Levine lists among "the primary conventions of realism . . . its deflation of ambition and passion, its antiheroism, its tendency to see all people and things within large containing social organizations and, hence, its apparently digressive preoccupation with surfaces, things, particularities, social manners" (15). Other constitutive elements of realistic fiction are characters that are middling sorts of people, the use of vernacular dialogue, and lots of quotidian details that provide the illusion of unmediated experience. *The Tinted Venus* employs all these features. The accuracy of both the setting in the familiar, navigable city of London and the satire in Anstey's depiction of his shop girls, lawyer's clerks, hairdressers, policemen, religious mothers, and doting aunts work to make the absurdity of Tweddle's situation in being beloved by Venus both funny and credible within the world of the novel.[26]

In his autobiography, *A Long Retrospect* (1936), Anstey identifies the inspiration for *The Tinted Venus* as "a story in Burton's *Anatomy of Melancholy* of a ring placed on the finger of a statue of Venus, which had long struck me as a possible subject for a modern fantasy" (201). But there were likely additional stimuli.[27] He lists W. S. Gilbert as well as William Thackeray and Charles Dickens as important influences on his writing (88–91).[28] Perhaps one inspiration for *The Tinted Venus* was Gilbert's *Pygmalion and Galatea, an Original Mythological Comedy*, which opened on December 9, 1871, for a successful run at the Haymarket of 184 performances. It had at least two revivals before the publication of Anstey's novella in 1885, including one at the Lyceum for the 1883–84 season that starred the great actress Mary Anderson. Decades later, in 1915, when Anstey co-authored a silent screen scenario for his own never-produced film adaptation of *A Tinted Venus*, he referred to this production specifically: "Drapery of statue might be copied from that worn by Miss Mary Anderson as 'Galatea'" (BL Millar Bequest, vol. 82, Add. MSS. 54308).[29] Gilbert's play was burlesqued in a *Galatea, or Pygmalion Re-Versed*, which opened on December 26, 1883, at the Gaiety.[30] Both the Gilbert comedy and its parody manipulate the myth in ways that could have piqued Anstey's imagination; so could the "unprecedented popularity" of the Pygmalion and Galatea legend among neoclassicists in the 1870s,[31] including two series of four paintings by Edward Burne-Jones (Alison Smith 200).[32] Anstey became friends with Burne-Jones when the publication of his 1882 novel *Vice Versâ* hurled him suddenly into a new social sphere populated by painters, authors, intellectuals, and bohemians. In his autobiography, he describes enjoying frequent dinners at this time with artists in the Pre-Raphaelite circle, including not only Edward and Georgiana Burne-Jones, but also William and Jane Morris and Edward and Agnes Poynter (123–24).

But there is another source to consider. The title *The Tinted Venus* is taken directly from a polychrome statue also called *Tinted Venus* (1851–56) by John Gibson, a member of the Royal Academy.[33] Gibson was a pioneer in using pigment on sculptures in the nineteenth-century restoration of ancient Greek practice. His coloration was subtle—in other words, merely a tint—so that it was not meant to depict accurately the colors of flesh or hair, but to represent an aestheticized ideal of beauty with a warmer tone than statues of cold, white stone normally offer. Nevertheless, the practice was controversial; the *Tinted Venus* caused a sensation when displayed at the London International Exhibition of 1862. Gibson's obituary in the *Athenaeum* decried his *Venus* as "representing a naked, impudent Englishwoman" with "enough vulgarity in it to destroy all alluring power, and every sign of the goddess" (172). The *Examiner* railed at it as a degradation of the sculptor's task of portraying pure form. Gibson's addition of such quotidian details as "painted eyes and little gold earrings" to the pristine and dignified plain marble moved the reviewer to state that "our condemnation of it is unqualified" (681). Even the critics who praised it also addressed the

Figure 1. "The Great Exhibition." Cartoon by John Leach. *Punch* 43 (October 25, 1862): 170. (Image courtesy of Hill Memorial Library, Special Collections, Louisiana State University, Baton Rouge)

reactions it provoked among the amazed and sometimes unsettled public; John Leach's October 25, 1862, cartoon in *Punch* shows two female spectators ogling the statue (fig. 1); in the caption, "Sarah Jane" exclaims to her companion, "Lawks, why it's exact like our Hemmer!" (*Punch* 43: 170). The ridicule cuts both ways: it mocks the lower-class, dialect-speaking Sarah Jane for alluding publicly (and loudly) to the naked appearance of Emma, apparently a member of her family, immodestly conjuring up Emma's physique for all who have overheard and broadcasting Sarah Jane's lack of critical distance and appropriate aesthetic appreciation in her reaction; it also pokes fun at the vulgarity of a sculpture so true to life that it evokes any actual flesh-and-blood relative rather than an idealized figure, let alone that of a live, working-class woman.

Although Victorian art critics agreed that the statue's coloration was not lifelike (nor meant to be) and indeed pointed out that the tint emphasized the sculpture's artifice, the response of viewers and critics to the spectacle of its display underscores that there is a theatrical undercurrent to *The Tinted Venus* long before Anstey's novel and the musical based on it. Victorian art exhibitions are shows, as Richard Altick reminds us.[34] A more direct connection between the statue and the theater—specifically a New York production of W. S. Gilbert's *Pygmalion and Galatea*—is made by an 1884 column in *Judy:*

> Mrs. Langtry has been announced to appear as Galatea in Mr. Gilbert's piece at Niblo's Garden. A reporter, we are told, who heard that she intended playing the part in pink in place of the usual white draperies, called upon her to ascertain her reason for making the change, and pointed out, rather unnecessarily, that Galatea is a statue and is supposed to be made out of marble. "Very true," answered the actress, "but we advance in everything." And then she told him that in the London Exhibition of 1862 there was a tinted Venus which gave rise to much discussion, the general conclusion of the critics being that "the marble might as well be tinted as remain white." "You can hardly imagine," she argued, "Pygmalion loving a pure white marble." She considered it an improvement to give the statue "the colours of life, the tints of youth, and the semblance of all human beauty." ("The Only Jones," *Judy,* May 14, 1884: 232)

Langtry's remark that one could not imagine the sculptor "loving a pure white marble" exposes how loaded is the word *tinted* (which I will discuss further, in relation to race, below), particularly in opposition to "pure," so that the question becomes to what extent is the Tinted Venus a *tainted* Venus? It emphasizes that the many-partnered Venus is always tainted—if not a scarlet woman, then just a little pink.

The novel's theatrical underpinning is apparent even in the subtitle "A Farcical Romance," since farce was the second-most common theatrical form in the Victorian period, after melodrama (Booth, *Plays* 1). Furthermore, ironizing references to the ubiquity of musical theater occur throughout the novel. Upon first realizing that Venus wants him as her lover, Tweddle recognizes his danger because "he had seen the operas of *Don Giovanni* and *Zampa,* and knew that any familiarity with statuary was likely to have unpleasant consequences" (51). A notable scene occurs when a gadabout friend of Tweddle's brags about how he'd gone to the Cosmopolitan to see a ballet called "Olympus," where he had spotted "a regular ripping little thing who comes on as one of Venus's doves.... I saw directly that I'd mashed her" (84). In horror, the goddess overhears the remark, which she interprets literally. She prepares to slay the masher (late Victorian slang for a seducer) to avenge her supposedly crushed dove; only Tweddle's hustling the roué out of this barbershop saves him from a painful death. Tweddle must explain music halls, dance spectaculars, and British vernacular to the Olympian; in turn, Venus must explain to the barber that doves and swans are sacred to her. The novel's musical-theatricality not only provides the backdrop and grist for the humor mill but also initiates its action. For example, to avoid continued waltzing with a persistent young lady who is not his fiancée, Tweddle meanders around the pleasure garden's secluded walkways with her, chatting and admiring the classical statues in the moonlight, ruefully aware that Matilda would hardly like this activity better than his dancing. The entire time he heartily wishes himself safe at the Adelphi Theater, a spectator rather than a performer in the evening's entertainment.

When Venus comes to life in the novel, she remains an animated statue, never metamorphosing into an actual flesh-and-blood woman. Her blank eyes have no color, and her marble hair stays stiff, being stone. Her odd appearance causes logistical problems for Tweddle, who must hide her identity when they are in public or risk danger from those on both sides of the law who suspect him of stealing her. When the goddess's spirit temporarily leaves the statue, de-animating it, Tweddle takes the opportunity to use his skill as a hairdresser and cosmetician: he paints on irises and he "penciled the eyebrows, laid on several coats of the 'Bloom', which he suffused cunningly with a tinge of carnation, and stained the pouting lips with his 'Conserve of Coral'" (108). After he "deftly fitted" a luxuriant wig of "light closely curled" human hair, he echoes the sentiment of many an observer of Gibson's *Tinted Venus*: "I don't know how it is, . . . she looks more natural, but not half so respectable" (108). He purchases the elegant coat his fiancée had admired in a shop window to cover most of Venus's classical drapery (another misstep with Matilda). Like a good theatrical costume designer and makeup artist (his kit even includes "grease paint"), he succeeds in hiding the goddess's marble skin, colorless eyes, and solid coiffure from view while they walk through the city (107). Performing the role of a human, made-up and stage-managed by Tweddle, she passes.

Thus Tweddle, like Gibson, has tinted Venus. Adding the "colours of life", as Lily Langtry put it, means darkening the marble's surface. *Punch* jokes racially about Gibson's *Tinted Venus* (then on display at the London International Exhibition) being a "coloured woman" ("A manufactured Article," *Punch* 43 [August 30, 1862]: 84).[35] In a sense, Anstey's fantasy about such a statue exposes the failure of both language and theatrical art to get at what it means to depict complexion on stage, as well as on sculpture. Although convention would suggest that Langtry's choice of makeup for the role of Galatea remained racially "white" (since there is no neutral makeup that is devoid of racial pigmentation), neither blackface, brownface, yellowface, or whiteface accurately gets at what Langtry seems to be thinking of as lifeface, when the contrast is not among human races but between playing a piece of marble and playing a live woman.[36]

But unlike Gibson, Tweddle tints his Venus not in an effort to make her more beautiful as an art object but—as we have seen Sarah Jane observe—to make her *less* extraordinary, less the goddess, more like an everyday Emma or Hemmer.[37] Anstey gently mocks the Victorian cult of beauty by diminishing John Gibson, Royal Academician, into a hairdresser, perhaps also poking fun at his friend Burne-Jones, aesthete, by making him into an aesthetician. In either case, Leander Tweddle, who most emphatically is not in love with his statue and only tints her in order ultimately to rid himself of her, is the anti-Pygmalion.

Tweddle is also the anti-Todd—that is, Sweeney Todd, the cutthroat barber. First appearing in 1846–47 in a serial novel that was pirated, rewritten, and reprinted in every decade of the nineteenth century, this favorite scoundrel enjoyed a long a success on the melodrama stage. Although it premiered in 1847, the play *Sweeney Todd: The Fiend of Fleet Street* by George Dibdin Pitt was published for the first time only in 1883, just two years before *The Tinted Venus* came out. The striking contrast between the main characters of *The Tinted Venus* and *Sweeney Todd* merits discussion. Unlike Todd, who murders his customers and chops them into meat pies, tender Tweddle would never hurt anyone on purpose, even scrupling to slight the feelings of Venus, who has repeatedly threatened to kill him and everyone he knows if he won't consent to become her lover. Unlike Sweeney's wild unkempt hair in which he stores his combs, Leander's handsome coiffure is always utensil-free.

But there are similarities between these Victorian barbers that go beyond both having successful businesses and a reputation for skill. The most interesting is the potential for damage that any barber can inflict, which *The Tinted Venus* recognizes explicitly.[38] When Tweddle tries to convince Venus that he is too far beneath her socially for a suitable match, he suggests she watch him at work in his barbershop, certain that once she realized that his job involves such intimate and messy service to others, she would relinquish all interest in him. To his dismay, she was more enamored than ever, declaring him "great amongst the sons of men":

"Do you not compel them to furnish sport for you? Have I not seen them come in, talking boldly and loud, and yet seat themselves submissively at a sign from you? And do you not swathe them in the garb of humiliation, and daub their countenances with whiteness, and threaten their bared throats with the gleaming knife...? Then, having in disdain granted them their worthless lives, you set them free; and they propitiate you with a gift, and depart trembling." (89)

Even the mild Tweddle can be pushed to invoke the tools of the most famous barber villain: in despair of regaining the love of his fiancée or extricating himself from Venus, Tweddle shaves with less than his usually impeccable dexterity. At first he endures upbraiding from an irate customer, but finally threatens, "I've a good deal of private trouble to put up with just now, without having you going on at me; so I just ask you not to 'arris me like this, or I don't know what I might do, with a razor so 'andy!" (231). But the emptiness of that threat only serves to demonstrate how far Tweddle is from the fiend of Fleet Street.

ONE TOUCH OF VENUS

Critics often read *One Touch of Venus* as a direct adaptation of the Pygmalion and Galatea myth without much thought about the novel that is its immediate source (Grant, *Rise* 75, 264). The musical inherits the novel's premise: a barber places his intended bride's ring on a statue of Venus, bringing it to life. But now the statue is in an art museum, the fiancée is pushy, the goddess is lovable, and the protagonist is a nebbish.[39] The musical emulates the novel as light entertainment with no tragic consequences and no heroic characters. It comments satirically on contemporary culture, including suburbia, consumerism, and a false aesthetic that blindly favors the modern over the ancient.

The stage musical's New York locale is emphatically modern, exhibiting no interest in sustained representation of Victorian culture (either British or nineteenth-century). This shift in setting was a calculated choice, attributed erroneously to S. J. Perelman, who wrote the musical's book. Mark Grant explains that the initial book writer, Bella Spewack,[40] was fired with unanimous agreement among the producer (Cheryl Crawford), composer, and lyricist; Nash's friend Perelman (a writer for the *New Yorker*) was hired as her replacement. Grant mistakenly attributes the modification in time and place to Perelman, saying Perelman's new book "jettisoned the Victorian setting and set the story in modern-day New York, adding highly sophisticated, not to say leeringly suggestive, dialogue" (Grant, "One Touch"). Yet the plan to move the action to 1940s New York precedes Spewack's ouster: the typescript of Spewack's draft held in the Kurt Weill Foundation archives (her third attempt) sets the play in contemporary Manhattan. No matter whose idea it was to situate the show in current times, the musical's Modernist objective in rejecting the Victorians is clear.

The opening chorus of the stage musical *One Touch of Venus* celebrates modernity: Whitelaw Savory, director of the Whitelaw Savory Foundation of Modern Art, stands in the Foundation's main museum gallery, teaching his students through a song of Socratic call and response. But before examining Savory's rejection of older forms of art, I want to consider his name. The character is invented for the stage play, having no antecedent in Anstey's novel. Whitelaw Savory becomes Whitfield Savory in the film version, relinquishing the many possible interpretations of the name "Whitelaw," including the irresistible reading that he represents the dominant law of the white establishment as a wealthy Englishman with an Oxford education and a penchant for picking up archeological treasures abroad, removing them from their countries of origin, and enshrining them in museums back home. This smacks not only of European and American booty-hunters stripping valuable artifacts from Asian, Middle Eastern, and African sites but also of another aural resonance to Whitelaw Savory's name: white law slavery and the seizing of Africans for the slave market in the Americas. But the effect of the name's racial satire is muddled. Although Elia Kazan would go on to make several progressive films focusing on passing, such as *Gentleman's Agreement* in 1947 and *Pinky* in 1949, neither the play directed by Kazan nor the 1948 movie version directed by William A. Seiter adopts the notion of tinting Venus so that she will pass more easily, with the potential to critique American racial politics in the 1940s. Unlike the novel's Tweddle, who is so concerned that the goddess should appear human that he paints, coifs, and dresses her, Rodney Hatch (Tweddle's counterpart in the stage musical) has no part in her passing as human. The musical's Venus amuses herself by fitting in, exerting very little effort other than taking some clothes from a department store window.

The show opens with Savory singing to his students that "New art is true art" (4). The set is hung with "an impressive group of the modern masters— Cezanne, Van Gogh, Gaugin, Picasso, Matisse, etc." (5). Picasso and Matisse were alive and well in 1943; only Van Gogh had died before the turn of the century. Praising their more conceptual vision, Savory and his students proclaim of the old masters, "They all learned how to draw, / But they painted what they thought they saw, / Instead of what they saw they thought, / As a liberated artist ought" (4). The chorus reverses the Victorian art critic John Ruskin's advice to painters that they paint accurately what they see, instead of what convention has taught them.

The song jumbles together all artists working before the Post-Impressionists, no matter what their actual period or how highly they are typically esteemed, with the seventeenth-century Dutch masters Van Dyck and Rembrandt and the great Victorian artist Millais tossed out along with "Gainsborough and Romney" because they're the "wrong Anno Domini" (5). These sallies ultimately carry forward to modern art movements, too. The gentle spoofing of Cubism is explicit: "The best of ancient Greece, / It was centuries behind Matisse, / Who has carried us beyond Renoir, / Till our bosoms are tri-an-gu-lar" (4)." Not only does Whitelaw Savory himself dismiss the old masters as part of his educational agenda, but he also campaigns militantly to spread good taste, which he opposes to middlebrow, middle-class Victorian preferences: he vows to fight on "until the hydra-headed monster of bad taste lies dead on the doily of every tea shoppe in the land!" (6).

These lines bash the bourgeoisie, the British (it is a "tea shoppe," after all), and the nineteenth-century predilection for lace doilies in terms that fit remarkably well with Woolf's acerbic remark that both highbrows and lowbrows "would rather sit in the coal cellar, together, than in the drawing-room with middlebrows and pour out tea" ("Middlebrow"). Another element in the ridicule here is affected cultural uplift, a hallmark of the middle-class middlebrow, both for themselves and for those lower on the educational and economic scale: Woolf makes fun of the middlebrow efforts to teach high culture such as *Hamlet* while they keep "bound volumes of the classics behind plate glass" ("Middlebrow"). To put it in Pierre Bourdieu's terms, "Middlebrow culture is resolutely against vulgarity" (326), but for Woolf such cultural aspirations are hopelessly vulgar. Nevertheless, the song's lyrics also mock Savory's Modernist agenda that throws out all the good art of preceding eras. Indeed, Savory himself is Victorian, both British and born in the nineteenth century. A graduate of Oxford, he echoes Oscar Wilde's *Importance of Being Earnest,* in which Miss Prism reveals the identity of the baby found in the cloakroom at Victoria Station. Savory admits, "I was born in the cloakroom during the Bachelor's Cotillion" (7), taking the allusion up a notch in salaciousness from discovery to childbirth. In some ways, *One Touch of Venus* reaches farther back into the nineteenth century than the Victorian farcical romance it adapts and the Victorian world in pretends to reject. As Ethan Mordden points out, the theme represented by the musical's Venus—sexy and uninhibited in the musical as compared to the imperious and threatening statue in the novel—is Goethe's last line in *Faust* (1808), "Eternal Woman draws us ever upward"; the goddess transforms the barber who does not even realize how unhappy and mistreated by his fiancée he has been, preparing him to be able to find love with a more suitable mortal woman at the musical's end (*Beautiful Mornin'* 150). Despite the musical's dropping its Victorian setting and establishing its identity as a thoroughly Modern musical, Victorian elements rematerialize and even intensify.

Notwithstanding his adherence to a cult of the Modern, and perhaps as a vestige of Paterian classical aestheticism, Savory displays an antique statue of Venus that he recently purchased on a trip to Europe—but only because it reminds him of an old flame. Rodney Hatch, the diffident hairdresser hired to attend to Savory's toilette, arrives at the museum and—like Tweddle before him—places on Venus's finger the engagement ring intended for his fiancée, Gloria. The plot diverges from the novel in that Gloria is an unpleasant, domineering person; we know from the outset that Rodney would be better off without her. He sings, "More than a catbird hates a cat, / Or a criminal hates a clue, / More than the Axis hates the United States, / That's how much I love you" (19). The topical allusion to World War II reminds us that we are in an America currently at war with Germany, from which the Jewish composer Weill had fled ten years earlier, in 1933. The lines get even more graphic in the next verse: "I love you more than a wasp can sting, / And more than a hangnail hurts" (19) and later "more than a hive can itch . . . more than a chilblain chills" (20), hinting that Gloria is an abusive mate, and that Rodney is ripe for picking by the newly awakened Venus, played by Mary Martin in the original Broadway production.

Unlike the novel's goddess, this Venus does not simply animate a cold stone statue; she has a soft, warm, attractive body, more like the Galatea of Greek myth.[41] Her personality is warmer, too: while still prone to occasional acts of divine vengeance, she mostly wants to promote amours. In "I'm a Stranger Here Myself," Venus observes that in this foreign world she has entered, people don't know how to enjoy romance anymore; they seem to prefer playing cards and skiing to making love. She complains that nowadays "gender is just a term in grammar"; she sings, "I can't believe that... passion is really passé" (26). Finally, bringing home the point that the musical's modernity, its open-minded sexuality, and its rejection of the Victorians (both of their art and of their repressed morality) are one and the same, she wonders why the engaged Hatch seems uninterested in her, asking, "Why these Victorian views?" (26).

As in the novel, much of the play's humor derives from misunderstandings due to her lack of experience in twentieth-century life (the rest comes from fast-paced, innuendo-laced repartee). A series of comic misadventures follow, which culminate in Hatch's being arrested for the fiancée Gloria's murder (Venus has sent her to the North Pole, later retrieved unharmed). Venus is incarcerated with her lover. In one moment of many that simultaneously emphasizes and mocks the play's modernity precisely when Freud is still modern, a Viennese-accented Doctor Rook attempts to psychoanalyze her:

> ROOK. How old are you?
> VENUS. Well, there's some doubt. Homer says one thing—Virgil says another.
> ROOK. How can I contact these people?
> VENUS. (*After a thoughtful pause—answering him with sweet helpfulness*). Go to Hell.

This dialogue layers the highbrow in-joke that requires one to know that Homer and Virgil provide contradictory birth stories for Venus (and lets the middlebrow audience feel complacently highbrow) while also confirming the troglodytic, Philistine middlebrow 1940s tendency to scoff at psychoanalysis, as when Gregory Peck's character in *Spellbound* (1945) calls Freud a bunch of hooey.

The play's frothiness fits the genre of musical comedy rather than the generally more serious storyline of the integrated musical. Even if the songs were removed, the play would still make sense. They are unnecessary to move the plot forward. Likewise, many of the songs could be inserted into other musical comedies and work well there, or they could succeed independently. Even the title song, "One Touch of Venus"—sung by Whitelaw Savory's smart, fast-talking, caustically funny secretary, Molly, about how every woman needs a "touch" of Venus within her to manipulate men—neither propels the plot nor develops her personality, which is a model of efficiency.[42] Nevertheless, the song matters in other ways. Molly sings,

> If you have a touch of Venus,
> Men of Iron turn to clay.
> Confidentially, between us,
> They are suckers in the hay.
> Look what Beatrice did to Dante,
> What du Barry did to France,
> Venus showed them that the pantie
> Is mightier than the pants. (11)

Though they do not advance the plot, the lyrics connect women's sexual dominance over men not only to European historical figures but also to a shift in Western women's underwear from open-crotched drawers made from bulky woven fabric designed with two separated legs tied together with a drawstring to closed-crotch, step-in, form-fitting, elasticized waist, knitted fabric panties. This transformation in undergarments in the 1920s and 1930s responded to women's fashion needs: slim silhouettes, trousers, and greater participation in sports (Carter 91). The word *panties* was first used in regards to women's closed knickers in 1908, according to the *OED*, and came generally to signify the knit brief by the mid-1930s. The word *panties* links directly to the Modernist rejection of Victorian morality, to dramatic reforms in fashion for women permitting a wider range of employment, and to the ascendancy of a movement toward women's rights.

The lyric also emphasizes the Americanness of the show in contrast to the Britishness of the source text in that the usage here of the words *pantie* and *pants* are resolutely Americanisms. Whereas in American English, *pants* are what the British call *trousers,* for the British, the word *pants* means (and meant in 1943) *underwear*—that is, what Americans mean by *panties*. In other words, the sentence "the pantie is mightier than the pants" only makes sense in American vernacular. Moreover, in an American context, the terms are gendered: *panties* are clearly feminine attire by the 1930s and 1940s; pants (while worn by both men and women) are associated with such expressions as who "wears the pants in the family," indicating a sometimes mobile authority generally ascribed to the man. Ogden Nash's play on these terms highlights how insistently *One Touch of Venus* is rewritten as an American rather than a British story, Modern rather than Victorian. However, no matter what these lyrics tell us about the sexual politics of 1943, they tell us virtually nothing about the musical's storyline, characters, or theme, other than setting a tone of risqué cleverness.

It is important to think of musicals on a continuum of integration rather than simply as integrated or not. Block points out that *One Touch of Venus* exhibits "integrative as well as non-integrative traits" (*Enchanted Evenings* 144). The show is integrated in its "thematic transformation in narrative ballets and the use of strong rhythmic profiles to reflect character" (151). For example, Block details the musical consistency in "Weill's recasting of Venus's... jazzy and uninhibited opening song, 'I'm a Stranger Here Myself' moments later in the ballet 'Forty Minutes for Lunch'" in which the goddess brings together lovers, and, likewise, "the reiteration of quarter note triplets from Venus's entrance music in Whitelaw Savory's love song 'West Wind'" (151). Mark Grant quotes Elia Kazan as explaining that Weill asked him to be the director (even though he had never directed a musical before) specifically to create the show more dramatically, with the "songs as a continuation of the dialogue" (*Rise and Fall* 243), a clear hallmark of integration.

Even more to the point, the choreographer Agnes de Mille's two ballets move the plot forward; they also provide psychological insight into the characters and satire on contemporary commercialism and the alienation of harried city life. In "Forty Minutes for Lunch," an extended dance sequence that occurs shortly after the statue has come to life, Venus wanders through the urban crowd at lunchtime, bringing strangers together for joyful romance; they part, better for the experience. Not knowing or caring about the silly bourgeois custom of purchasing merchandise before making off with it, Venus seizes haute couture clothing from a window display to dress appropriately in contemporary garb, rather than in her Grecian drapery. Knowing nothing of mortal concepts like modesty or using a private dressing room, she changes into her finery in plain sight, still in the shop window, like a live mannequin. The other fully integrated dance is a dream ballet, now a musical theater staple, as it has been ever since de Mille invented the form for *Oklahoma!*'s fifteen-minute finale to act 1. Laurey's dreamwork reveals to her that she loves the cowboy Curly and that Jud, the farmhand with whom she has promised to go to the ice cream social, is a sexually dangerous and murderous villain. In the ballet "Venus in Ozone Heights," de Mille gives us an equally revealing reverie in which the goddess realizes that despite their delightful love affair, she and Hatch are not suited to each other. Venus imagines herself married, a homemaker in Ozone Heights, Hatch's ideal neighborhood "where every bungalow is just the same" (94). The monotonous, prosaic, humdrum existence of suburban human life—with neighbors, children, lawn mowers, and newspaper comics—closes in on her; ancient Greece and the Olympian heavens open above as she disappears (98). When the curtain rises again, the scene has shifted back to the museum where the statue reappears, regal and inanimate, in her niche. In the original Broadway production, Mary Martin, who played Venus, is now a wholesome girl-next-door who lives in Ozone Heights and loves it there. She wanders into the museum and bumps into the heartbroken Hatch. Their eyes lock. They speak. The play ends.

Other than the two integrated ballets and some musical motifs, in most respects *One Touch of Venus* retains the musical comedy formula so popular throughout the 1920s and 1930s. Indeed, musical comedy remained the dominant form up until precisely this crucial moment of 1943, when *Oklahoma!* was changing audience expectations about musical theater's dramatic cohesion and potential to be a very serious art form. The *New York Times* commented, "In truth, 'One Touch of Venus' is not another 'Oklahoma!' although it may well be the best new musical show to have opened since that time" (Nichols). Although the generic shift from the dominance of musical comedy to the integrated musical did not happen quite as abruptly with the opening of *Oklahoma!* as is often suggested, *Oklahoma!*'s innovations had an enormous impact. Opening hard on the heels of *Oklahoma!*, *One Touch of Venus,* normally classified as a musical comedy, is really a hybrid, incorporating a few of the integrative characteristics that made *Oklahoma!* such an important milestone.

A feature at once eliminated and retained from the novel to *One Touch of Venus* is the barber-protagonist as an anti-Todd. In the Victorian tale of *Sweeney Todd,* the victims usually meet their end not by the razor but when the barber's trick chair flips them down through a trapdoor twenty feet into the cellar, onto their heads. The fall typically kills them; they are soon carved and baked into meat pies. In *One Touch of Venus,* Whitelaw Savory's henchmen lure the barber Hatch (a "hatch," he is a kind of trapdoor himself) into the cellar below his own shop. Then they conk *him* on the head while they seek the missing statue. Although Gloria's mother calls Hatch a "fiend" (70), no character is less like the "Fiend of Fleet Street," not even Hatch's amiable precursor, Leander Tweddle.

While *One Touch of Venus* plays down the possibility of a Sweeney Todd connection to its hero, one production number highlights a related serial killer. The song "Dr. Crippen" is choreographed as a series of tableaux performed in Edwardian costumes by the art students for Whitelaw Savory and assembled guests. This show-within-a-show tells the real-life story of

Dr. Hawley Harvey Crippen, "Britain's second most famous murderer," convicted of the horrific 1910 murder through poison and dismemberment of his wife, the actress Belle Elmore, to run off with his secretary, Ethel LeNeve (Early 209). The historical Crippen fled to Canada with LeNeve, who traveled in disguise as a boy. This sensational case reminded the press and the public of the serial killer Jack the Ripper, whose brutal murders of prostitutes in the Whitechapel area of London in 1888 riveted newspaper readers around the world and remained vividly in living memory. Unlike the perpetrator of the unsolved Whitechapel murders, Crippen was executed at Pentonville Prison in 1910 for killing his wife.[43] Whitelaw Savory plans the performance of "Dr. Crippen" by his students to trigger a reaction from Rodney in the supposed murder of Gloria.[44] Naturally Rodney remains unmoved, because he does not even know that Gloria has disappeared. He is an anti-Crippen and anti-Ripper as much as he is an anti-Todd. The musical establishes Hatch as an sanitized, wishy-washy, and significantly Americanized barber (utterly unlike the real and fictional British villains Crippen, Jack the Ripper, and Todd) by setting the only musical number taking place in his tonsorial parlor as an actual barbershop quartet—a quintessentially American genre originating in African American barbershops, which served as community gathering places—already a very old-fashioned musical style by 1943. Retaining the trade of the protagonist from novel to stage musical allows for them both to resonate as anti-Todds while, in a surprising twist, highlighting his American identity. The film adaptation *One Touch of Venus* (1948) changes Rodney's career from barber to window dresser (the statue is on display in a fancy Manhattan department store), emphasizing the protagonist's aesthetic connection to Venus's makeover and paving the way for yet another movie inspired by this tale, *Mannequin* (1987). But eliminating Rodney's tonsorial profession loses the *frisson* created between his characteristic nonviolence and the ruthlessness of his more famous colleague forever haunting the barber's persona.

Despite its backward generic glance to musical comedy, the original production of *One Touch of Venus* was in some ways as modern as could be. Critics praised the designers' "striking modernity." The *New York Post* specifically commented on Weill's "new and modern score" (qtd. Ronald Davis 81–82). And, as we have already seen, the show explicitly expresses in lyrics and dialogue the decades-old Modernist dismissal of the Victorians. Coming in 1943, at the very moment that musicals began to integrate music and dance in a systematic way, *One Touch of Venus* also participated in another recognizable shift in generations. The Modernists were still rebelling against the Victorians at the very transitional moment when the children of the Modernists began to defy *their* intellectual parents and reassess the Victorians more favorably. Meanwhile, in 1943 American theater was still vigorously freeing itself from earlier British dominance in comic opera and from European preeminence in operetta, with successful musicals from the 1920s through the 1940s insisting on American settings, characters, and sounds. Yet, in contrast, *One Touch of Venus* adapts a British Victorian novel, anticipating musicals from the 1950s onward that turn to Victorian, British sources.

Another feature of *One Touch of Venus* that looks both forward and backward is a subtext of empire. In both the novel *The Tinted Venus* and the musical, the statue of Venus hails originally from Anatolia, a part of modern Turkey where the ancient Greek civilization flourished and where Aphrodite was an important deity. The antique statue's presence in a London pleasure garden or a New York art museum can only happen in a world in which British or American travelers bring home beautiful objects from abroad, just as Lord Elgin took what we call the Elgin Marbles from the Acropolis in Athens (then part of the Ottoman Empire—in other words, under Turkish control). They were later installed in pride of place at the British Museum. In a tantalizing coincidence, Anatolia is also the region of Turkey from which the ethnically Greek family of the director of the stage musical *One Touch of Venus,* Elia Kazan, fled first to Istanbul (where Kazan was born) and then to the United States. In the musical, Orientalist vision goes so far as to have Venus's worshippers show up in vaguely Turkish folk-garb to beg her to return to her mythic realm and to destroy the American "infidel" who seems poised to profane her (85), conflating ancient Greek religion with current stereotypes about Turkey and Islam. This almost childish use of Orientalist tropes will undergo a sea change by 1951, with *The King and I,* a play that grapples not with what it means to be either an Anatolian immigrant or an object of imperialist booty but instead with how the United States, suddenly the dominant world power, deals with taking up the mantle of the British Empire in an effort to bring its culture and democratic institutions to the East, willy-nilly, with less armed conflict and more Americanization soft-pedaled as British inheritance.

In both genre and setting, *One Touch of Venus* is a precursor and an outlier, illustrating an important conjunction of intellectual and aesthetic changes occurring simultaneously in the 1940s and 1950s. The shift from the supremacy of musical comedy to the integrated musical coincided with American musical theater's beginning to adapt British Victorian materials. It also happened precisely while a new generation of scholars began to reevaluate and elevate Victorian literature, which had been snubbed by the previous generation of thinkers. By 1951, when *The King and I* appeared on Broadway, the artists and writers of the last generation who had been fully active during the final years of Victoria's reign were either dead or nearly so. Even the seemingly unstoppable George Bernard Shaw died in 1950, at the age of ninety. While twentieth-century adapters and their critics have seen Anstey's tale as quaint, as a novel that needs updating and resetting to suit contemporary audiences, the Victorian works adapted into the rest of the musicals I consider in this book were not usually dismissed by their adapters in this way. Set in the Victorian period (even the campy *Drood*), these later shows tell us what their creators understood as "Victorian" and what commonalities they saw between the Victorian culture and their/our own.

2

The King and Who?

Race, Dance, and Home

We have seen that *One Touch of Venus* looks both backward and forward in its choice of a British rather than American text for adaptation. From *Little Johnny Jones* to *Oklahoma!,* American theater in the first half of the twentieth century actively asserted its Americanness in reaction to European imports; the creative choice to drop the source's British setting for *One Touch of Venus* also links to the play's explicit stake in modernity. By the second half, as Continental operetta's sway over American musical theater had ebbed and the domination of Gilbert and Sullivan had dissipated, so too the need to aggressively affirm Americanness subsided. The prospect of no longer having to prove their independence from England opened the opportunity for American artists to musicalize British culture differently, to appropriate it *as British,* without needing to modify setting. We see this change occurring between *One Touch of Venus,* which in 1943 adapts a Victorian novel originally set in London as a contemporary New York story, and *The King and I,* which in 1951 retains the author Anna Leonowens's place (Siam), characterization (British governess), and time (1862). The Victorian-sourced musicals I discuss in the rest of *Victorians on Broadway,* all from the second half of the twentieth century, represent American cultural concerns not by relocating the material geographically and temporally but by allowing audiences to see themselves at once as Victorian and as not-Victorian.

The King and I works differently when revived in New York over the decades, as each iteration changes a play's meaning in relation to the time of its production. It also varies according to location: when produced in New York, London, Tokyo, Sydney, Tel Aviv, Nairobi, or Buenos Aires by performers of any race or nationality, embodied enactments are interpreted and experienced differently on stage and off. Variables in casting may change how audiences respond; variables in audience demographics or nationality may affect the cultural work any play accomplishes in any locale at any time. But as performed on Broadway, from 1951 on, while retaining the source texts' nineteenth-century settings, the musicals I analyze use their Victorian lenses to refract contemporary American concerns.

In 1951, when the Rodgers and Hammerstein musical *The King and I* premiered, the United States still occupied Japan and was already in Korea. Set in Siam (now Thailand), a Southeast Asian country that—unlike its neighbors Vietnam, Laos, Malaysia, Cambodia, and Burma (Myanmar)— was never colonized by a European nation, *The King and I* uses Leonowens's account of her experiences to negotiate the dilemma of twentieth-century American imperialism by displacing it onto a Victorian stage and imagining a route toward US global leadership that eschews violent takeover or direct control. In the process, the musical draws from Leonowens's travelogues to create fictional versions of the historical Anna Leonowens, King Mongkut, Lady Thiang, and Prince Chulalongkorn: now Anna, the Victorian English schoolteacher and advocate of human rights; King Mongkut, the forward-thinking monarch who (of his own free will) leads his kingdom to the brink of liberty; and the crown prince Chulalongkorn, educated in part by Mrs. Anna, completing the task of ending slavery in Siam.

The King and I presents an American worldview in which the modernization and democratization of less industrial nations occurs through friendly although uneven exchange with the United States, with Cold War rhetoric employing metaphors of anti-slavery to justify anti-communism (Klein 207). In *The King and I*'s mythologized Victorian milieu, the white British governess represents in part an idealized United States, in the ostensibly noncolonizing, nonmilitaristic role Americans generally find morally palatable, educating rather than conquering the East into Western democracy.[1] Another way of thinking about this is what Danielle Glassmeyer calls "sentimental orientalism." Arguing that the English schoolteacher Mrs. Anna is "functionally American," Glassmeyer claims that the governess "fulfills a fantasy of masculine maternity offered in the service of conquest without bloodshed: by nurture, education and emotional constancy, but never by force, she wins her charges to her democratic values" (107). The upshot is that *The King and I* helps convey to Americans the urgent need to incorporate Asian nations into an anti-communist alliance (Most 185).

Yet this is only part of the cultural work that *The King and I* accomplishes. Leonowens wrote two accounts of her experiences in Thailand: a memoir called *The English Governess at the Siamese Court* (1870) and a book of semi-fictional, quasi-historical tales called *The Romance of the Harem* (1873).[2] These autobiographical books written by a Victorian woman offer a significantly broader understanding of nineteenth-century gender roles than the twentieth-century play *The King and I*, which instead depicts stereotypes of the Victorian domestic angel often associated with Dickens. Broadway sees Victorian culture through a Dickensian lens, but the mid-twentieth-century musical's ideological thrust is not simply to flatten the exciting gender terrain provided by its Victorian source (which it does) but also to shift the more flexible gender differences from Leonowens's books—and their often-contradictory elements—onto race performance, a different but equally radical aim. Hints of this slippage already appear in Leonowens's writing: she describes the life of women in the Siamese harem as simultaneously more repressive and more open than life for Western women, using nineteenth-century American tropes of slavery and women's rights to analyze Siamese culture.

Clearly, race matters in a piece about an Englishwoman in Thailand confronting and adjusting cultural and religious difference. Likewise, the Jewish identity or heritage of the composer, the book writer/lyricist, the choreographer, and so on, matter when this show about racial and religious difference premiered in 1951, so soon after the Holocaust made clear the ultimate horrors of racial and religious persecution. Nevertheless, the most overt site of the musical's racial performativity is the musical's twenty-minute play-within-a play, "The Small House of Uncle Thomas." This is an adaptation of another nineteenth-century book, the American writer Harriet Beecher Stowe's *Uncle Tom's Cabin* (1852). The inclusion of this story ballet (instead of the dream ballets of prior Rodgers and Hammerstein shows) within the musical *The King and I* Americanizes the show even more while emphasizing Leonowens's abolitionist-feminist stance. Incorporating a ballet based on the quintessential American anti-slavery novel *Uncle Tom's Cabin* also draws attention to the budding civil rights movement in the United States, which in 1951 focused on integrating schools; Mrs. Anna's role as teacher in a mixed-race/nationality classroom is telling here: her son Louis learns with the Siamese children as do the wives from several Southeast Asian nations.

Further complicating the intersections of gender, race, class, and nationality is Leonowens's own presentation of herself as an English lady when, as had previously been hypothesized and as Susan Morgan has proven in *Bombay Anna: The Real Story and Remarkable Adventures of "The King and I" Governess* (2008), Leonowens was from a lower-class family, of mixed racial origin, born in Bombay rather than Wales, never even setting foot in England before her journey to Siam.

Certainly, the British actresses Gertrude Lawrence in the original Broadway production and Deborah Kerr in its movie incarnation (1956) presented an Anna every bit as English as the persona Leonowens not only invents for herself in her books but also successfully performed in real life. She passed as white, English, and middle-class from her third decade to her eightieth year, moving during that time from Singapore to Siam to the United States and finally to Canada (Morgan, *Bombay Anna* 7–10).[3] While Leonowens's personal performance of racial and national identity is masked in her own books, the musical makes the performative elements of these and other identity categories explicit in "The Small House of Uncle Thomas." With female Thai court dancers playing both African American slaves and slavers of both sexes, the play-within-a-play highlights race and gender performance even while it blends nineteenth-century American and British writing to negotiate 1950s American worries about race, religion, and world affairs.

SEX IN THE CITY OF WOMEN

Successful in America, particularly among post-abolitionist readers, Leonowens's two books about Thailand were less well received in England (Morgan, Introduction ix–x). In 1870 the *Athenaeum* regretted that her first book ever "saw the light," citing Leonowens's inaccuracies about the Siamese language and culture and her unseemly criticism of King Mongkut (836). In reviewing her second book, the *Athenaeum* accused her in 1873 of outright ingratitude to her royal employer (205–7), perhaps suggesting that a British subject ought to be more respectful of monarchy in general. Or perhaps the *Athenaeum* took exception to her quoting the Siamese ambassador's praise of Queen Victoria because her "eyes, complexion, and above all her bearing, are those of a beautiful and majestic white elephant" (Leonowens, *English Governess* 145). But the criticism has not been exclusively British or Victorian. Generations of Thai readers and later viewers of the books' screen adaptations have even more emphatically repudiated an unflattering picture of a revered king (Esterik 300-303).[4] Twentieth-century historians have also castigated Leonowens's books for numerous factual errors about Thai history.[5] Most recently, feminist and postcolonial critics have pointed out ways in which Leonowens's books participate in the patriarchal and imperial projects of her time.[6]

Yet remarkably Anna Leonowens did serve as the governess to King Mongkut's children, including the crown prince Chulalongkorn, from 1862 to 1867, until shortly before he became king in 1868. She was the only British subject (or self-identifying Westerner of any country) in the nineteenth century to gain intimate access to life in the Siamese harem and to write an account of it (Morgan, Introduction xvii). She received letters expressing esteem from both her employer King Mongkut and her former pupil King Chulalongkorn. Leonowens's Siam books, particularly the controversial *The Romance of the Harem*, focus largely on Thai women. In describing their lives—or rather inventing them, since this volume is entitled not the "*History*" of the Harem but the "*Romance*," a term denoting fictional narrative (Morgan, Introduction xvi)—Leonowens appeals to a readership of former abolitionists by declaring that in Siam "woman is the slave of man" (11). She details the harem women's sexual attractiveness and the misery it causes; the most famous is the story of the beautiful young Tuptim and the tragic result of efforts to "render her a fitter offering for the king" (15).[7] She links the plights both of the king's concubines and of their own female slaves to what American slaves had suffered. Portions of her books were first published as essays in the abolitionist magazine *Atlantic Monthly*, whose most famous contributor in the 1860s had been Harriet Beecher Stowe (Morgan, "Chinese" 243–56, 253). Situating herself within a long tradition of Western feminist Orientalism (which puts her in company with Mary Wollstonecraft, Harriet Martineau, Florence Nightingale, and Charlotte Brontë) and nineteenth-century British women travel writers (such as Isabella Bird, Mary Kingsley, and Mary Seacole, also a woman of color),[8] Leonowens relies on her audience's stereotypical expectations about tales of Oriental potentates to help them accept and organize her analysis as a feminist stance.[9]

Contemporary American reviews certainly received her books as feminist; for instance, in 1873 the *Princeton Review* praises *The Romance of the Harem*, commenting that "no recent book gives so vivid a description of the interior life, customs, forms and usages of an Oriental Court; of the degradation of women and the tyranny of man" (378), and in 1871 the

Overland Review pities the women in *An English Governess in the Siamese Court* "who languish out their lives in this splendid misery" (293). But they do not make the leap to compare Western and Eastern tyrannies. The same reviewer, far from making any connection between harem life and women's legal position in the United States, without the vote or many other basic rights, simply concludes with a self-complacent Orientalist relief that "we are heartily glad that we are not subjects of the Golden-Footed Majesty of Siam" (293). In contrast, Leonowens herself does not present polygamy as exclusively Eastern; in fact, she pointedly invokes Western polygamy when she derisively terms the Siamese prime minister's harem as "his Excellency's private Utah" (18).[10] While using erotic Orientalist motifs to promote a feminist agenda, Leonowens pushes her readers to recognize not only the differences between women's roles in America and Siam but also their troublesome similarities.

Despite the persona that she cultivates in her pages, Leonowens was not a white Westerner, nor was she a colonizer, coming from Bombay of mixed-race heritage and working in a country that was never colonized. Thus the influential templates provided by Anne McClintock's *Imperial Leather* and Malek Alloula's *The Colonial Harem* that help to put Leonowens in global perspective do not fit perfectly because of the very significant difference between Leonowens's depiction of the harem and those addressed by these scholars, who do not focus on Thai culture or consider countries that—like Siam—remained outside European imperial or colonial rule; the same is true for the groundbreaking work on nineteenth-century European women's travel writing by Mary Louise Pratt. Leonowens perhaps better fits the south-south migratory paradigm suggested by such postcolonial scholars as Pallavi Rastogi, whose *Afrindian Fictions: Diaspora, Race, and National Desire in South Africa* examines Indian migration and national identity within the global south. An important difference here is religion: Leonowens describes a Buddhist rather than Muslim harem. Harems in Muslim contexts more typically appear in postcolonial criticism than Buddhist harems (for example, Alloula focuses on Algeria), and they are far more often presented as quintessentially Other to Christian marriage in Victorian literature. Victorian poems and novels alluding to harems generally envision them to be like those of the Turkish sultans, frequently filtered through the lens of *Arabian Nights*. But perhaps the most important difference is that Leonowens is an employee of the king, hired to teach the children of the royal women she describes; her position is at once subservient and authoritative to the women of the august household. For all her pedagogical influence over their children and for all the appreciation the king expresses for her hard work and her success, for all her freedom to leave her employment and to leave Thailand, she is far beneath the harem wives and concubines in power, social hierarchy, and financial wherewithal.

Both *The English Governess at the Siamese Court* and *The Romance of the Harem* depict a much larger and more complex gender landscape than *The King and I* provides, focusing on the great variety of jobs women hold. Leonowens describes female armed guards in the Nang Harm or "City of Women," as the harem was called. She emphasizes their gender by referring to them as Amazons (the women warriors of Greek myth) and translating one kindly guard's title as "Great Mother of War." She tells of female judges who resolve conflicts involving women, such as the court that convicts and sentences to death Tuptim, the concubine who runs away from the harem to live in gender-bending disguise as a Buddhist monk for several weeks. These tasks are far more varied and more traditionally masculine than those to which nineteenth- or mid-twentieth-century Western women could aspire.

Furthermore, as Leonowens presents them (with historical accuracy), the king's wives and concubines are enormously wealthy. Wielding great power drawn both from their social status and from their money, their individual official relationships to the king create a vast diplomatic web of familial ties throughout Siam and Southeast Asia. The books depict them as living in the City of Women, a walled compound of many blocks, housing over nine thousand inhabitants (none male), boasting houses, shops, gardens, and streets. Women there fill virtually every social role, including many they could never hold in a contemporary Western society:

> This woman's city is as self-supporting as any other in the world: it has its own laws, its judges, policy, guards, prisons, and executioners, its markets, merchants, workers, teachers, and mechanics of every kind and degree; and every function of nature is exercised by women, and by them only. (*Harem* 13)

Susan Brown characterizes Leonowens's harem as what Nina Auerbach would term a community of women (587–614, 598);[11] communities of women are "emblems of female self-sufficiency" that "have haunted our literary imagination from the beginning" (Auerbach 5), granting women banded together without men "subtle, unexpected power" (3). Brown also points out that the Siamese harem is far from being the private feminine world of Western stereotypes, instead including public and very political activities; for Leonowens, "private and public, inside and outside, female and male spheres influence each other despite the walls, just as [her] representation of the harem as a city blurs the boundaries of domestic and non-domestic space" (600). This blurring of home and city, domestic and public, hidden and seen, serving and served, is part of Leonowens's effort to depict the complexity of a system in which the wives and concubines were simultaneously slave-owners and enslaved. The king's wives and concubines and their royal children were served by women of many classes as well as a multitude of female slaves, all within Nang Harm.

In *The King and I*, however, Thai women are generally depicted as enslaved: luxuriously pampered, but existing for the sole purpose of serving the pleasure of (and procreation with) the king. Because they are almost the only Thai women depicted, women appear to be without any rights at all, let alone opportunities to engage in a career as a judge or a shopkeeper. Female guards silently stand at the doors in many scenes but are generally unnoticed by the dialogue and action. They do not sing or dance even as supernumeraries in a chorus number. Many viewers would be unaware that these characters are women at all; both in the Broadway productions and the 1956 musical film, the costuming—while not unisex—is sufficiently different from the rest of the women's alluring attire and sufficiently like the men's that audiences could easily miss their gender altogether. There are no female judges in the musical. Far from successfully escaping and passing as a man for many weeks, in the musical play Tuptim is caught trying to flee with her beloved, Lun Tha. Her punishment is immediate and without trial: upon the king's order, she is about to be summarily whipped by male guards; the musical's king explains that this is what is usually done is such cases (125). No female-run system of justice operates here.

In direct contrast to the subservient position of the wives and concubines in *The King and I* is the governess Mrs. Anna, whose power struggle with the King to maintain her independence (figured primarily through her insistence on having a house of her own outside the palace) propels both the plot and the humor. Although the King repeatedly bests her through an appeal to her attachment to his children, she remains independent in an important sense. The musical play signals her freedom from the system of slavery or concubinage by emphasizing her profession as a schoolteacher, a role already wide open to nineteenth-century women; indeed, by 1888, women "constituted 63 percent of American teachers—90 percent in the cities"

(Grumet 34). A governess is certainly an identity that Broadway audiences in the 1950s (and now) recognize as viable for Victorian women through such novels as *Little Women* and *Jane Eyre*, both adapted many times to film and to the musical stage.[12] Indeed, *The King and I* makes the distinction between unpaid and paid labor explicit when Anna emphatically sings about *not* being a servant in "Shall I Tell You What I Think of You?":[13]

> Your servant! your servant!
> Indeed I'm *not* your servant,
> (Although you give me less than servant's pay)
> I'm a free and independent employé.

It is her paid work as a professional that distinguishes her from both the harem women and their slaves. The song continues to bring this point home:

> Because I'm a woman
> You think, like every woman,
> I have to be a slave or concubine—
> You conceited, self-indulgent libertine—. (54)

The musical unequivocally promotes an ideology of women's rights, but—like the self-complacent post-abolition review about eighty years earlier from *Overland*—the rights promoted are those that women in the mid-twentieth-century American audience already enjoyed of not being a "slave or concubine."

The comparison to slavery comes straight from Leonowens, who realizes that, despite her description of multiple roles in the City of Women and the fabulous personal wealth of the royal women, her Western readers will interpret the harem wives as de facto slaves. She gives her audience plenty of evidence. When she describes telling the prime minister that she wants her own house rather than chambers in the palace, a private home where she "might be free from intrusion, and at perfect liberty before and after school hours," she imagines that "he had doubts as to the use I would make of my stipulated freedom, and was puzzled to conjecture why a woman should wish to be free at all" (*Governess* 16). In this brief statement, she twice uses the word "free" along with "freedom" and "liberty." Leonowens hints that, despite their riches and high position, the king's wives and concubines—particularly the young ones—are prohibited from leaving the walled city even temporarily and are certainly not permitted to lead other kinds of lives or to choose their own husbands.[14] When the women of the harem ask why Anna would not want to marry the king or the prince, she gives two answers: first, that as a Christian, she would never marry a non-Christian; and second, that she is unlike the playful wives of the harem, because she must work to support herself and her children: "I am only here to teach the royal family. I am not like you. You have nothing to do but to play and sing and dance for your master; but I have to work for my children" (*Governess* 21–22). Susan Brown points out that

> in dissociating herself from marriage as a woman who must work Leonowens echoes English and American feminist critique of marriage and arguments in favor of remunerative employment for women. In so doing, the passage destabilizes the initial opposition between Christian and pagan marriage practices by implicitly aligning married Christian women whose only role is to please their husbands with women of the harem. (Brown 595)

While both halves of her answer demonstrate Leonowens's construction of herself within her books as a white Christian Englishwoman and a governess, they are not as contradictory as Brown suggests, in that the Buddhist harem women's playfulness is presented in contrast to Leonowens's Protestant work ethic. In other words, women's work in Western discourse is still called work, even if it is not paid. While "obey" is part of the Anglican marriage ceremony, "play" is not. On the one hand, it is because of their huge wealth, unconnected to their marriage or concubinage with the king, that the harem women can afford to play all day. Women are depicted as slave owners in Leonowens's books as often as they are depicted as slaves. But on the other hand, this description of their task in life, "to play and sing and dance for your master," resembles the job of many a slave as depicted in American anti-slavery writing. It is precisely the role of little Harry, Eliza's son in *Uncle Tom's Cabin,* who is asked to "show this gentleman how you can dance and sing" and whose sale immediately after that moment to the trader Haley in the first chapter throws the novel's plot into motion (15).

Yet Leonowens is careful to articulate differences between the position of the royal wives and that of actual slaves. Even when describing the tragic Tuptim, Leonowens takes care to present her as both slave owner and enslaved: the wayward young concubine to the king has a loyal slave of her own, Phim (*Romance* 32). In another example from the *Romance of the Harem,* Leonowens describes enjoying a dinner party with particularly good food, music, and service, given by one of the king's wives whom she had been teaching English, Sonn Klean (or "Hidden Perfume"): "When dinner was over, my friend, in concert with her sisters and slave-girls, performed on several musical instruments with wonderful effect. At last all Sonn Klean's slave-women with their children appeared in a group, one hundred and thirty-two in all, in nice new dresses, all looking particularly happy" (249). Leonowens then records her hostess's announcement that she has freed her slaves; Sonn Klean says she will "never buy human bodies again but only to let go free once more, and so I have now no more slaves, but hired servants. I have given freedom to all of my slaves to go or to stay with me as they wish. If they stay with me, . . . I will give them each four ticals every month after this day, with their food and clothes" (249). Her inspiration for emancipating her slaves is *Uncle Tom's Cabin:* Leonowens reports Sonn Klean's saying, "I am wishful to be good like Harriet Beecher Stowe" and even signing her name Harriet Beecher Stowe from that point on. Again, while detailing a range of differences in class and condition among Thai women, Leonowens appeals to American post-abolitionist readers who will delight in the success of her abolitionist message as a continuation of their own recent success in bringing about the end of slavery in the United States.

The musical shifts the complex, multidimensional, multiclass, multirole depictions of women's possible identities in Leonowens to a one-dimensional portrait in which all the women characters (other than the British schoolteacher Mrs. Anna) are slaves to the king; in fact, he is presented as the only slave owner. While Leonowens's text luxuriates in particularities and differences among women, the musical simplifies and essentializes them. For example, the musical retains Leonowens's description of how the Siamese prime minister and people in the palace address her as "Sir" (*Governess* 16, 70). While this could have been a way for the musical to incorporate the book's more nuanced treatment of gender, it becomes instead a way to reinforce the depiction of all the harem women as enslaved, a stark contrast to the free and voting American woman of 1951. In the musical, the King's head wife, Lady Thiang, explains that they call their new teacher "Sir" because Mrs. Anna is "scientific. Not lowly, like woman" (26). The musical Anna's response, that she does not think that "*all* women are more lowly than men," advocates some parity between the sexes (26). But it does not extend to expanding women's roles in the way that Leonowens's description of the City of Women does.

In "Shall We Dance," the King and Anna whirl in an electrifying polka, the closest their relationship gets to a romantic climax. An iconic moment in both play and film, it often appears in visual advertising and provides the cover art for the fiftieth anniversary edition DVD (Twentieth Century Fox). The scene emphasizes the differences between the King and Anna as they embrace in exuberant choreography: male and female, king and governess, East and West. Costuming enhances the difference. Confronting Anna in her revealing finery, the King speaks for his audience as well as himself when he indicates that, although Thai women's outfits generally display more skin than does the Victorian dress, her covering up everything below the exposed bust in a vast swath of shimmering silk magnifies the bareness of Anna's neck, shoulders, arms, and bosom. The voluminous, swirling skirt—beneath which not even her feet peek—emphasizes the tiny waist of her hourglass figure, no doubt corseted into shape, and the amplitude above. "Is different," the King says in his imperfect English (86), disturbed and admiring while withholding judgment, his reaction to many of the Western traditions Anna embodies. By "different," the musical means several things. The King finds the European costume exotic and thus erotically charged, as the Thai costumes may be for Western audiences; thus, "different" articulates the East/West dichotomy that the entire musical has investigated. But in a way Anna's dress is also exotically different for audiences, for whom, in 1951 or now, bare midriffs and close-fitting pants are not unusual, but tight-waisted, low-cut crinoline ball gowns are. This moment in which the audience sees Anna through the eyes of the Siamese king as "different" highlights the vast distance between mid-twentieth-century (and later) audiences and the Victorian world the play invokes: women no longer must wear corsets or hoop skirts, having long ago won the fight for what the Victorians called "rational dress." Thai pants and tops in midriff and bandeaux style seem far less exotic than the crinoline, which the Victorians themselves recognized as ludicrous.

The musical makes clear that Victorian dress is absurd and "different" in several earlier scenes. Mrs. Anna billows, ripples, and flows whenever she moves. Her enormous skirt puffs around her whenever she sits, almost as though she were surrounded and protected by the petals of an immense flower. Indeed it is so large that when she plops onto the floor in "Getting to Know You," the Thai royal children join her by sitting on the fabric surrounding their teacher. In the 1956 film, Jerome Robbins's choreography creates a kind of cultural exchange of dances during this song, so that the Thai court dancer mimics the absurdity of Mrs. Anna's dress by having four children create the twirling skirt's shape as they dance, encircling her. The mature and sensible Lady Thiang explains that the reason the foolish young women of the harem try to peek under Mrs. Anna's bell-like petticoats is to check if she is "shaped like that"; this line highlights not only the naiveté of the wives but also the absurdity of Western women's dress in the Victorian period.[15] That silliness is underscored when the wives don massive Western skirts for the banquet honoring British dignitaries but maintain the Thai practice of bowing to the ground, so that when the women prostrate themselves, their stiff hooped hems pop up, resulting in a comic peep show for the visitors, made even more salacious by Mrs. Anna's lamenting that in her haste to manufacture European styles for the women, she had neglected to provide undergarments. Lady Thiang, naturally, is far too dignified to abandon her Thai clothing. Her choice, a model of propriety, emphasizes *The King and I*'s respect for Thai customary dress and by extension for Thai identity.

RACE DANCING

Lady Thiang's phrase "lowly, like woman" echoes the subtitle to Harriet Beecher Stowe's novel *Uncle Tom's Cabin, or Life among the Lowly*. Complicating *The King and I*'s flattened understanding of possibilities for women is its depiction of race and slavery in its play-within-a-play, which retells the story of *Uncle Tom's Cabin*. Because the King has heard that a British diplomat plans to paint him inaccurately as a barbarous despot in order to provide England with an excuse to attempt seizing Siam as a protectorate, the King and Mrs. Anna prepare an elaborate banquet with entertainment that will display how civilized (in Western terms) the country and its ruler really are. This action reinforces Anna's advocacy of peaceful pedagogy in resolving potential conflict and Westernizing the East rather than violent imposition of colonial rule. Tuptim, the King's newest and most unhappy concubine, has written the script for the show's narration. To catch the conscience of a king à la *Hamlet*, Thai dancers present her dramatization of *Uncle Tom's Cabin*. This ballet, "The Small House of Uncle Thomas," serves both to provide an allegory justifying Tuptim's later attempted escape and to provide a teachable moment for the King. It also implies to *The King and I*'s audiences that the United States has much to offer other nations as a model in having recognized and ultimately—even though it required war—rejected the evil of slavery. It also glosses over the fact that slavery had already been abolished in British lands in 1833, which should have put British subject Mrs. Anna on an even higher moral high ground.

The dance operates on the assumption that everyone watching *The King and I* agrees that slavery is contrary to the basic democratic values that constitute American society. *The King and I* repeatedly alludes to the American Civil War and to King Mongkut's (historically accurate) support of President Lincoln; the musical's use of *Uncle Tom's Cabin* serves to highlight the King's blindness to his own status as a slave owner and monarch of a slave country. As Laura Donaldson points out about the movie musical, the insertion of "*Uncle Tom's Cabin* 'westernizes' the film's concept of freedom" (62).

Tuptim narrates the ballet herself. Her narration provides a representation of performativity as a method of achieving change. By describing an American slave running for freedom, Tuptim prepares for her own attempted escape from the King's harem to be with Lun Tha, the Burmese court functionary who had accompanied her to Siam, in a kind of Tristan and Isolde story. Whereas we have seen that Leonowens presents Tuptim as a royal concubine with devoted slaves of her own (*Romance* 20–21), in the play, introduced as a "gift from the prince of Burma," Tuptim is explicitly enslaved: when she first arrives, she sings bitterly about having to please her "lord and master" (17); when her lover Lun Tha urges her to flee with him, he says, "you have been a slave long enough" (94). Caren Kaplan argues that in *The King and I*, "the figure of Tuptim clearly equates North American slavery and Siamese concubinage, allowing the audiences to make the same ideological link without examining or questioning the historical accuracy" (Kaplan 42). Kaplan rightly points out that the institutions are very different; not only did the concubines own slaves (as Leonowens carefully details), but also their slaves could purchase their own freedom.[16]

It is through the elaborate layers of race performance in the ballet "The Small House of Uncle Thomas" that the play shifts often conflictual gender identity onto race. The cast of all female dancers of any ancestry portray Thai court dancers portraying African American slaves of both sexes.[17] Portrayal of Thai women as performers is true to Thai dance-drama tradition, as is the use of a narrator. But complicating the layers of race and gender representation, the Jerome Robbins choreography (retained in the film and in Broadway revivals)[18] suggests that the Burmese author Tuptim and royal Thai dancers have together created characters based not only on Stowe's novel but also on nineteenth-century blackface minstrels' representations of *Uncle Tom's Cabin*. In addition, while some of the dancers use large, elaborate masks that are authentically within Thai dance-drama conventions while also recalling Victorian pantomime "big heads," some dancers also wear whiteface makeup—in a kind of reverse blackface—to register the characters' racial difference from the performers, all understood within the drama as Thai.[19]

Robbins did not worry too much about scrupulous authenticity in creating a Thai dance-drama; like Richard Rodgers, he avoided what Oscar Hammerstein called "research poison" (Rodgers 274). Yet Robbins did investigate Thai, Cambodian, and Loation dance in choreographing the ballet. He hired Mara von Selheim, who had studied Cambodian dance at the court of Phnom Penh, to work with his dancers in establishing a vocabulary of movement that might approximate Thai style. Deborah Jowitt describes Robbins following "the Cambodian court-dance custom of an all-female cast in terms of the principal dancers, as well as making use of some of its flexible hand gestures, hyperextended elbows, crawls, and the 'celestial walk' (standing on one bent leg, the dancer raises the other bent leg behind her, flexed foot flat to the sky) or a similar pose kneeling" (181). He also borrowed from Japanese theatrical conventions in several facets of the ballet. For example, Kabuki drama uses symbolic props like the rippling fabric that represents water, as in Robbins's Ohio River. Visible but unobtrusive stage assistants wear black. Noh drama uses masks and introduces characters individually, as does "The Small House of Uncle Thomas" (Jowitt 183). Most significant is the whiteface.

These Japanese inflections to his Southeast Asian dance about African American slaves may have been partially influenced by two of Robbins's principal dancers, women of Japanese descent (and at least some upbringing in Japan) who studied a variety of Asian dance forms and served not only as principal dancers but also as consultants on this ballet: Michiko Iseri played the Angel from Buddha; Yuriko Kikuchi, Jerome Robbins's assistant, played Eliza. A Japanese American, she had been interned in the Gila River War Relocation Camp in Arizona during World War II. The Asian-fusion quality of Robbins's ballet heightens its artificiality in a way that highlights its theatricality. This has an important function, ensuring that *The King and I*'s audiences watching the play-within-a-play see it as a piece of theater that seems even more theatrically artificial than its frame play, even though the frame is a musical, a form that revels in artifice. But "The Small House of Uncle Thomas" also emphasizes identity performance. The musical's court dancers employed by King Mongkut are obviously all Siamese women playing every role in this abbreviated *Uncle Tom's Cabin* (focusing mostly on the sensational frozen river scene so popular in Victorian melodramas and early film versions of the story), including Liza, George, Topsy, Little Eva, and King Simon of Legree. As its fictional players cross multiple boundaries of gender, race, and nationality in each portrayal, its actual players (always understood by *The King and I*'s audience to be actors playing actors) double that performative experience. And there is one more gender element to consider: even the ballet's music was written not by Richard Rodgers but by his longtime arranger and dance composer, Trude Rittman, a woman uncredited on the published score until 1979 (Cavenaugh 85).

Changing the ballet's title to "The Small House of Uncle Thomas" defuses the negative connotations of an "Uncle Tom" lingering from decades of derogation clinging to the book's original title.[20] Despite the novel's pivotal role in promoting abolition and ending slavery in the United States, the self-sacrificing characteristics of the title character had become associated with servility. By 1951, indeed as early as the 1910s, "Uncle Tom" was considered a slur. Stage adaptations had similarly suffered from this association. The antislavery message of the novel was augmented by George L. Aiken's popular 1852 melodrama, a version of the play Harriet Beecher Stowe herself enjoyed; it and other versions were performed so often it was accurately billed as "The World's Greatest Hit" (Birdoff). But the play was soon co-opted for minstrel shows, a fraught genre. Sara Meer has shown that minstrelsy helped to pave the way for the abolitionist reception of *Uncle Tom's Cabin*. (11). While providing performance opportunities to African American actors, minstrel shows also provoked some of theatrical history's most egregious stereotypes; in particular, comic dance scenes involving the slaves became standard fare in "Tom shows" and other frankly racist entertainments. These were generally performed in blackface and continued on the vaudeville stage and film as mainstream entertainment into the 1940s and beyond. Some well-known twentieth-century blackface performers were African American, such as Bert Williams; others were Jewish, such as Eddie Cantor (whose early career included playing Bert Williams's son, in blackface). Both groups added an additional layer of racial performance to the history of blackface. Michael Rogin argues that in part blackface performance by Jewish actors, especially scenes in which they don the makeup and take it off again, demonstrated their not-blackness, and so partially constituted their identity in America as white. Blackface minstrelsy would be inescapably familiar to Rodgers, Hammerstein, Robbins, and their audiences in 1951.

Further complexity accrues to issues of racial or ethnic identity in *The King and I* through the fact that, as Andrea Most points out, all three of these men (composer, lyricist, and choreographer) were Jewish or of Jewish heritage.[21] She convincingly argues that they had in mind the American immigrant experience as much as anything else in creating *The King and I*, so that Anna's job in teaching English language and American values—but most significantly *not* Christianity, which her missionary predecessors had previously taught in the harem, much to the King's chagrin—resembles the task of "Americanization" teachers in the Jewish ghettos of New York's Lower East Side in the 1910s, part of a nationwide movement staffed by trained educators and sponsored by labor unions, YMCAs, the National Council of Jewish Women, the Hebrew Immigrant Aid Society, and charitable or fraternal organizations (Most 186). Seeing the musical's King in this context foreshadows the character of Tevye in *Fiddler on the Roof* (1964), whose effort to negotiate between the traditions of an Eastern European patriarchal past and a Western future in which women—his daughters—have the right to marry for love results in his crying out, "If I bend that far, I will break" (88). The King does break when, bending back to raise the whip he has grabbed from his secret service men to lash Tuptim for her escape and attempted infidelity, he crumples forward, finding that he can no longer bear to follow "tradition." The Jewish American experience must have affected *The King and I*'s creators in their sensitivity to the historical King Mongkut's stipulation of education without missionary baggage: in his initial letter of offer to Leonowens, the real-life King Mongkut states that he will employ Mrs. Leonowens for instruction in "English language, science, and literature, but not for conversion to Christianity" (*Governess* vi). Such a proviso would resonate for an immigrant religious minority weary of trying to find education with no religious strings attached.

By changing the name of his adaptation to "The Small House of Uncle Thomas" and by presenting it not in blackface but in whiteface, Robbins distances his ballet from the racist traditions that had grown up around theatrical presentations of *Uncle Tom's Cabin* while alluding to and subverting them. Furthermore, by resetting it in a pan-Asian milieu, by appropriating dance forms that recall both Eastern and Western traditions, and by mediating race performances through multiple layers (actual dancers of any race playing female Siamese dancers playing a white woman's fiction of male and female African American slaves of both sexes), Robbins undermines the inherited racist potential of "Tom shows." Instead, he reveals the ballet's performativity and refreshes the abolitionist point of Stowe's text. In this way it anticipates the more radical presentation of *Uncle Tom's Cabin* provided by Bill T. Jones's late twentieth-century interrogation of black and gay issues in his revolutionary modern dance "Last Supper at Uncle Tom's Cabin/The Promised Land" (Murphy 84–102).

Both in Leonowens's writing and in *The King and I*, Stowe's novel serves as a radicalizing agent, bringing women to resist their own positions as slaves or—much more prominently in the source text—as slave owners. As mentioned above, in *Romance of the Harem*, Lady Sonn Klean has already read Stowe's novel; she translates it, adopts Stowe's name, and frees her own slaves. But in the musical, it is Tuptim to whom Anna has lent *Uncle Tom's Cabin*. She writes the ballet for performance as a court event to agitate for her own release from bondage. Donaldson rightly points out that Leonowens's Tuptim is far more heroic and accomplishes a far more daunting task in successfully gaining her freedom for a time, living in disguise as a priest's male acolyte in a monastery; in contrast, the show's Tuptim's (although clever, talented, brave, and devoted) is captured almost immediately when she tries to escape with her lover.

Nevertheless, becoming an author of a play based on another female author's book makes the musical's Tuptim the only named female character other than Mrs. Anna to take on a task resembling a career outside her connubial duties, to cast off the restrictions of women's lowliness mentioned in the first act. Writing her play signifies her rewriting her own identity. *The King and I* underscores the significance of Stowe's and later Tuptim's being a woman writer when, upon hearing Tuptim ask Mrs. Anna for a copy of Stowe's novel, the King asks, "A woman has written a book?" (23). But ultimately the stylized dance-drama, with all its fascinating slippage between races and genders, fails to bring about freedom for Tuptim or the other wives.

HOUSE AND HOME

The Rodgers and Hammerstein musical explicitly promotes basic rights for women, yet within its 1951 American context, those rights have already been achieved. In mid-century America, there is hardly revolutionary potential in the depiction of an effective female schoolteacher, or in upholding a young woman's right to choose her own husband, or in the rejection of absolute monarchy as a form of government, or in the firm abolition of slavery as a social system. While the books *The English Governess at the Siamese Court* and *The Romance of the Harem* focus on the intricacies and inequities of harem life, the play conflates the plight of all women in the harem with all slaves and erases their differences; the net result is that audiences feel good about their own level of freedom and/or their own virtue in not owning slaves. While the old king is dying, the young crown prince asks his mother, Lady Thiang, to demonstrate the innovative (and Western) way of bowing that he has just decreed as law, at his father's prompting. This gesture symbolizes the importance of the historical King Chulalongkorn's abolition of slavery in 1905.[22] The orchestra plays "Something Wonderful" (Lady Thiang's earlier song about loving her husband) as Anna and the Kralahome (or prime minister) recognize that the ailing King has at exactly that moment passed away. Unaware, his Queen bows to her son; in this act she demonstrates to the others on stage the new way to show respect without complete prostration, while simultaneously and unwittingly becoming the first subject whose obeisance acknowledges the new sovereign and the first actor to bow to the audience as the curtain falls. The intensity of the swelling music literally underscores the audience's torn emotions, both sadness at the death of Mongkut and pleasure at recognizing the value of progress toward democracy that the King, by encouraging the crown prince to make his first proclamations, has tacitly approved. The conflict between slave owner and slave seems resolved by the new freedom from bowing low.

The links among the successful fight to end American slavery discussed by Anna and the King, the symbolic loosening of restrictions implicit in the crown prince's decree, and the nascent American civil rights movement in 1951 may seem subtle to an audience in the twenty-first century, but they would have been clear in the mid-twentieth. Promoting a more racially just society had been important to Hammerstein for a long time. He wrote the book and lyrics for *Show Boat* (1927), the first musical to integrate black and white performers within a complete storyline. Its plot decries laws against miscegenation, still common at the time. His project just before first partnering with Rodgers on *Oklahoma!* was *Carmen Jones* (although not opening until after *Oklahoma!* in 1943), an innovative updating of Bizet's opera *Carmen*. With new lyrics and book by Hammerstein, *Carmen Jones* is set during World War II with an all-black cast. In 1945 he wrote "The Myth That Threatens America," urging "writers, producers and advertisers to avoid inadvertently perpetuating racism through the use of racial and ethnic stereotypes" (Klein 182). He served as a vice president of the NAACP (Most 172). Moreover, in *South Pacific* (1949), Hammerstein's lyrics for "You've Got to Be Carefully Taught" addresses racism explicitly, even though it was not a main feature of its source text, James Michener's 1946 *Tales of the South Pacific* (Most 154). The young Lt. Cable bitterly recognizes but cannot overcome his own prejudice that prevents him from marrying the Polynesian girl he loves. He sings:

> You've got to be taught to be afraid
> Of people whose eyes are oddly made
> And people whose skin is a different shade
> You've got to be carefully taught.
> . . . .
> You've got to be taught before it's too late,
> Before you are six or seven or eight,
> To hate all the people your relatives hate.

This song stirred such outrage that it caused Georgia state representatives to introduce legislation outlawing entertainments that promoted interracial marriage (Fordin 270).

Hammerstein's personal connection to this issue is close: his brother-in-law Jerry Watanabe was interred during World War II on Ellis Island. Watanabe, a Japanese citizen born in Japan with a Japanese father and a British mother, was married to Dorothy Hammerstein's sister Doodie. For the period of his imprisonment, Doodie and the Watanabes' daughter Jennifer lived with Oscar and Dorothy Hammerstein.[23] The adults moved Jennifer from the first school they had enrolled her in because the school refused to protect her from racial discrimination (Klein 182). Race laws were slowly—too slowly—changing in 1951 America. Truman's desegregation of the armed forces in 1948 functioned as a catalyst for the advances to come. The seeds for integrating schools were sown by the initial filing of *Brown v. Board of Education* in 1951, the same year as *The King and I*. Rodgers and Hammerstein directly participated in these vital changes, successfully insisting on desegregated seating in theaters where their shows were performed.

But in 1951 the condition of women was going through a postwar period of regression as they were forced out of the labor market to accommodate returning GIs. Curiously, despite Hammerstein's liberal worldview and well-deserved recognition for his humanitarian deeds and despite the intricate race performances in "The Small House of Uncle Thomas," the end result of this excellent musical play is not so much to forge connections between the harem women and the play's audiences, but to emphasize their differences. The cultural work of the musical play is partially to express

Western self-complacency: from a feminist perspective, the play is a glorification of the 1950s American status quo.

To an extent, this 1951 vision of Mrs. Anna is Victorian. She inhabits a separate sphere, longs to create a home (that brick residence adjoining the palace), dedicates herself to children, excels in advising and guiding a powerful man, rather like Ruskin's "true wife" in "Of Queens' Gardens" (*Works* 18.122–23). But it is not so much the Victorian world depicted by Leonowens in 1870 as it is the Victorian world depicted by Dickens in virtually every novel he wrote, or at least the Victorian world that we imagine as Dickensian; Kelly Hager argues for the prevalence of "the failed-marriage plot" in Dickens (6). Although *The King and I* is among the two *least* Dickensian musicals covered in this book,[24] Dickens affects how Broadway has imagined Victorian culture even here. Unlike most work described as "Dickensian," this inheritance has nothing to do with a plethora of eccentric characters or with Christmas caroling or even with the street urchins and gritty London street scenes that feature so strongly not only in adaptations from Dickens but also in *Sweeney Todd* and *Jekyll and Hyde*. The element deriving from Dickens in *The King and I* is gender. Dickens's "Angel in the House" heroines—women like Agnes Wickfield, Amy Dorrit, Esther Summerson, and Rose Maylie—guide, teach, and counsel those around them. Self-sacrificing, self-effacing, and pure, they modestly devote themselves to running a happy home efficiently. Although the phrase comes from Coventry Patmore's 1854 poem *The Angel in the House,* the character type is best known from Dickens.[25]

To some extent, Rodgers and Hammerstein's Mrs. Anna is more like these women than like the historical Leonowens. Anna educates, guides, counsels, and remains on the moral high ground most of the time. In contrast to the character that Leonowens creates for herself, Anna—motivated by her love for the children she instructs—ultimately stays in Siam to continue to teach and to advise the new young king rather than go home to the England she misses, where presumably she would write her travel memoirs. In her own books, Anna Leonowens speaks seven languages, negotiates dangerous situations, translates important correspondence for the king, records and interprets Thai history and culture for a wider reading public, and ultimately leaves for new adventures, touting her accomplishments and publishing her correspondence from the king to prove it. The musical's Mrs. Anna, as a paid professional teacher and the advisor to a king, seems feisty and modern to audiences in contrast not to the historical Leonowens but to a notion of the ideal Victorian woman that we have inherited from Modernists' reaction against Victorians. Even though Dickens creates many feisty female characters as well, such as Betsy Trotwood, the angelic stereotype also comes directly from Dickens. There is no question that Mrs. Anna is more authoritative and stubborn than Agnes or Esther. But it is only in distinction from the retiring but steadfast Dickensian heroines that she seems modern. Anna's modernity is made possible by the Dickensian icon of a household angel forming the backdrop against which viewers read her.

In chapter 1, I mention how, as part of the Modernist rebellion against Victorian culture, Virginia Woolf found it necessary to strangle the Victorian figure of the Angel in the House inside herself to become a woman writer, to pen even a small book review critiquing the work of a man. Woolf explains that the moment she began to criticize, she "heard the rustling of her skirts in the room"; the angel "whispered: 'My dear, you are a young woman. You are writing about a book that has been written by a man. Be sympathetic; be tender; flatter; deceive; use all the arts and wiles of our sex. Never let anybody guess that you have a mind of your own. Above all, be pure'" ("Professions" 237). Mrs. Anna accomplishes most of her objectives using precisely the tactics that Woolf ascribes to the Angel in the House. She often influences the King through flattery, sympathy, and tenderness. She deceives him into thinking her own ideas are his so that he will want to do them, deriving humor out of these feminine wiles and her somewhat clumsy but successful management. In this respect, the 1951 musical seems to take a lesson from Virginia Woolf, highlighting the artifice behind Mrs. Anna's skill in handling the King. It is tempting to see in this British schoolteacher merely as a rejection of the modernist-feminist Woolf's rejection of the Victorian mode.

Yet it is also clear that Rodgers and Hammerstein's Anna has a mind of her own. Unlike the Angel, she's no prude, although she would never behave outside chaste behavioral norms for a Victorian widow. She critiques the King when she advises him, often outspokenly. So, she is not Woolf's Angel in the House, after all. In a way, this is because a house is not a home. Both Leonowens and Rodgers and Hammerstein focus on the difference between house and home; that distinction reverberates between the centuries and continents. In the musical, the promise of a small brick residence outside the palace represents to Anna her financial, moral, and legal independence from the King. It signifies that she is neither wife nor concubine in a polygamous marriage. In contrast, residing within the palace places her vulnerably within the King's domestic space, associates her closely with the harem, making it a moral and social imperative, from a Western point of view, that she live outside. The opposition between cultures could not be more starkly drawn than in the Kralahome's surprise at her demand, in his asking what she would want to *do* with unsupervised private freedom, hinting that it is living outside, not inside, the City of Women that makes a woman morally suspect, perhaps a prostitute. As I mentioned earlier, Anna's insistence on a home of her own (promised by the King in his letter of offer, both in historical fact and in the musical) provides the chief point of contention and much of the show's humor. Mrs. Anna retaliates against the King's having gone back on his word by teaching his children English songs and sayings about the value of home: "East, West, / Home is Best" and "Be it ever so humble / There's no place like home." His own children unknowingly but continually plead her case. Whereas Leonowens's books describe her moving into her home and living happily in it for years, in the musical, the audience never sees her attain this goal. Only in the final scene, when the King is dying, does he issue a decree that she shall have her brick residence outside the palace. In this capitulation—a masterly feat of negotiation on his part in finally granting only what he had planned to concede all along—he achieves *his* goal of getting her to stay in Siam to continue teaching.

The concern about where Anna is domiciled and what space she calls home speaks directly to how Leonowens depicts herself as a European traveler to the East in *An English Governess at the Siamese Court*. She describes how she finally acquires her own house in a chapter entitled "Our Home in Bangkok"; there she can "queen it" in her "own palace," a home that comprises a combination of English and Thai comforts:

> Bright, fresh, fragrant matting; a table neither too low to be pretty nor too high to be useful; a couple of armchairs, hospitably embracing; a pair of silver candlesticks, quaint and homely; a goodly company of pleasant books, a piano, just escaping from its travelling-cage, with all its pent-up music in its bosom; a cosey little cot clinging to its ampler mother; a stream of generous sunlight from the window gilding and gladdening all,—behold our home in Siam! (75)

The scent, matting, sunlight, cots, and perhaps the candlesticks are Thai; the armchairs, books, piano, and sheet music are English. Susan Brown points out that locating home away from England means that Leonowens's book differs from other colonialist travel narratives that structurally position England as the center or home (603). Leonowens makes a home in Bangkok both historically and narratively. Despite the title's beginning "*An English Governess,*" the woman from Bombay never had a home in England.

This distinction between house and home—which fits neatly into Doreen Massey's thinking of house and home in terms of both gender and "the geography of social relations," as changing according to social structure and relationship to identity categories (Massey 172)—likewise connects to *Uncle Tom's Cabin*, which at first symbolically situates happiness and a kind of limited (but brutally proven illusory) autonomy within the seemingly private, uninvaded domestic space of Tom's slave quarters, until it is destroyed by slavers. That cabin becomes a "small house" in *The King and I*, echoing Anna's small brick residence, the home Mrs. Anna will never have until the King is dead, like King Simon of Legree drowning in the silken waves of the O-hi-o. Leonowens expresses her joy in having a home in which she can "queen it," indicating that real freedom inheres in a domicile over which one is sovereign. In this respect, again, Leonowens is no angel in the house of King Mongkut, but queen of her own castle.

Although *The King and I* flattens Leonowens's more nuanced gender roles, it does not steamroll them completely. The musical recasts the Victorian governess Mrs. Anna as Virginia Woolf's heir in gently satirizing (if not strangling) the Angel in the House. But more than evening out the complexities in Leonowens's depiction of women, the musical recognizes and Americanizes Leonowens's drive toward self-determination, shifting the concern with gender onto a negotiation of race performance that comments subtly on American concerns. Rodgers and Hammerstein reshape slavery, freedom, and racial identity in mid-century American rather than nineteenth-century Thai or British terms. The focus on women's rights, so important in Leonowens, has disappeared by the final curtain, as Lady Thiang bows to her son, the new king. Perhaps in part the applause for the performance is the audience's applause for itself, for having already achieved everything needed by eliminating polygamy and ending slavery. But they also applaud the possibility of changes to come.

3

Performing Jewishness in *Oliver!*

The first time many people encounter the story of *Oliver Twist* (1837–39) is through the movie musical *Oliver!* (1968). Joe Litvak remarks that the scene in which Oliver says, "Please sir, I want some more" is the novel's most famous, even more famous than Sikes's murder of Nancy; he attributes the scene's ubiquity "to Lionel Bart's musical version of the novel" (33). This scene appears frequently in popular culture: a prime example of its pervasiveness is the *Family Guy* cartoon episode in which Stewie asks for more before pulling out a laser bazooka and blasting away at Bumble and the Widow Corney. The costuming and camera angles drawn in the cartoon come directly from Bart's musical film, based on the 1960 stage musical. That an adaptation should be better known than its sources is not odd—it is certainly true, as we have seen, of *One Touch of Venus* and *The King and I,* whose sources are now somewhat obscure—but the surprise here is that the novel *Oliver Twist* is a widely read and taught classic by an author arguably superseded in the British literary imagination only by William Shakespeare. This instance bears out Julie Sanders's assessment that "adaptation becomes a veritable marker of canonical status, prolonging the life of the source" (9); it may be that the pop culture *Oliver!*'s impact enhances the literary *Oliver Twist*'s, not only by introducing new audiences to the novel but also by preparing them to read it with a more sympathetic eye. Nevertheless, Bart recognized that his appropriation of the novel makes significant and perhaps long-lasting revisions when he appeared onstage for the twenty-third curtain call on opening night, remarking, "May the good Dickens forgive us" (Ellis).

As with any adaptation (Hutcheon 39), the musical *Oliver!* affects how people view its source, in particular the character Fagin. Students in my classes are often shocked because they had no idea that he represents such an anti-Semitic stereotype. They routinely express surprise at how nasty the novel's Fagin turns out to be—corrupting children, inciting murder, frequently inviting comparison to the devil—because of their previous familiarity with the musical or other popular cultural artifacts influenced by the musical. A connection to Fagin may be heightened by the frequency with which *Oliver!* is performed by schools and community theaters, cultivating a shared sense of participation in the many who have watched a friend or relative perform, or who even have performed in it themselves. I know the affection I have for the musical's Fagin helps me to locate and to recognize the ambiguity in Dickens's text and to see moments of tenderness, attractiveness, and comedy in what is otherwise a repulsive, racist caricature. Inevitably bound up in the musical's impact is the role of Fagin as a star vehicle. Theatrical producers cast popular comedians to hype ticket sales; theatergoers expect (and usually get) a little extra shtick, adding to their altered interpretation of the character.[1]

While chapter 1 positions *One Touch of Venus* as a jumping-off point for Broadway musicals that rework Victorian books in the wake of Modernism, and chapter 2 examines how *The King and I* negotiates its nineteenth-century sources' treatment of race and gender for mid-twentieth-century America, this chapter examines how the musical *Oliver!* serves as a vehicle for refashioning the role of Fagin in part in order to make *Oliver Twist*'s powerful commentary on class legible in a modern, post–World War II, post-Holocaust era. Bart's recuperation of Fagin affects representation of race and gender as well as class, and of nationality as well as Jewish identity. How to perform Jewishness is a tricky question in a time and place where anti-Semitism is generally rejected, and actors tackling the role of Fagin have handled it a variety of ways. Lionel Bart, the show's creator, intervened in a long line of negative Fagins to create something new, not only resulting in a version of the character as a playful, curmudgeonly, ultimately good-hearted scallywag, but also yielding a brand-new kind of British musical. Bart made history in British musical theater by seizing the American idiom of the integrated Broadway musical and reshaping it into an English triumph. But first, in order to set up Bart's achievement in reimagining Fagin for the musical stage, I lay out the genealogy of adaptations that made *Oliver!* possible.

BEFORE *OLIVER!*

Oliver Twist is in a sense itself already a kind of adaptation, emerging from previous works and literary forms, including melodrama, a precursor genre of the Broadway or West End musical.[2] Initially published serially, every installment of *Oliver Twist* was conceived by Dickens as a separate mini-narrative at once enjoyable on its own and fully based on the earlier numbers as they grew into the completed story. Rachel Malik contends that the multiform approach to publication that Dickens employed (first serial, then volume, etc.) along with his initial audience of "sophisticated genre switchers" sets the stage for his novels' adaptability to new vehicles (483, 479). Each issue surrounded the novel's text with whatever poems and articles that Dickens, as editor, selected for the pages of *Bentley's Miscellany*. He worked closely with his illustrator, George Cruikshank, whose influence on our understanding of the characters and situations cannot be overestimated and whose hook-nosed Fagin reflected, exaggerated, and perpetuated an ugly visual stereotype. Also, in creating Fagin, Dickens followed his good friend William Harrison Ainsworth in writing a Newgate novel, the genre that focuses on criminals of the kind that would be hanged at Newgate Prison (Patten).[3] Dickens revised *Oliver Twist* heavily for publication in volume form and personally adapted his novel for his own performances. His celebrated readings of Nancy's murder, rewritten in 1868 as a complete stand-alone narrative especially for performance, were so passionate and powerful that women fainted; his blood pressure would soar to the point that it may have accelerated his death from a stroke at the age of fifty-eight (J. Hillis Miller, *Victorian Subjects* 47).

Although Dickens wrote and performed his own adaptation of the murder scene "Nancy and Sikes," he was not the first to dramatize the novel. His novels debuted on stage instantly upon publication. Indeed, unauthorized dramatizations appeared before he had even penned the last installments. Because copyright did not extend to theatrical adaptation of novels, playhouses pirated good stories with an insatiable and gargantuan appetite. The concluding number of *Oliver Twist* came out in *Bentley's Miscellany* in April 1839; *Oliver Twist: A Serio-Comic Burletta* by George Almar opened at the Surrey in November of 1838; before the novel's final installment appeared, probably at least two other adaptations were staged (Bolton 104). Attending a performance of Almar's play, Dickens was so humiliated that he lay prostrate in his box during the first scene and did not get up again until the final curtain (Cox 121). Yet it played on for months, becoming the most frequently produced adaptation of *Oliver Twist* throughout the rest of the century, even after it had been revised to account for narrative developments in Dickens's plot that appeared after the play's premiere (Zemka 29). Such early pirating of the unfinished novel helped establish which episodes would become favorites in later adaptations. For example, the novel's descriptive paragraph with no dialogue detailing how Fagin and his boys teach Oliver to pick pockets, acting out all the roles and making him laugh, becomes in Almar a fully voiced and choreographed scene, complete with dialogue and stage business (Almar 11–12). It recurs as a crucial scene in all important subsequent adaptations, including Frank Lloyd's 1922 silent picture, David Lean's classic 1948 film, and *Oliver!*, which gloriously transforms the moment into Fagin's triumphant "You've Got to Pick a Pocket or Two."

Even before Almar's influential adaptation, on May 21, 1838, Charles Zachary Barnett's melodrama *Oliver Twist, or, The Parish Boy's Progress* hit the Royal Pavilion, so early in the novel's run that Nancy had not yet even been murdered. Later published by Duncombe's, this adaptation is particularly interesting because of Barnett's treatment of Fagin. A highly successful East End dramatist and one of the first self-identifying Jewish playwrights in England (Rubens 153), Barnett slightly softens Dickens's anti-Semitic caricature for performance at the Royal Pavilion in Whitechapel, a theater with a large Jewish clientele. For example, while most subsequent adaptations (including *Oliver!*) closely follow the novel's first presentation of Fagin in a devilish pose, standing by the cooking fire with toasting fork in hand as he greets Oliver, Barnett's Fagin simply opens the door to let in the Artful Dodger and Oliver to his den (Barnett 18). Unlike the novel, in which Fagin is generally called "the Jew" (identifying his villainy with his Jewishness), the play's dialogue only once mentions Fagin's Jewish identity. The character never incites Sikes to violence (Barnett 25); since the play premiered in May, seven months before the installment in which Sikes murders Nancy, Barnett had no foreknowledge of Sikes's heinous act. Yet Fagin's diminished ferocity anticipates the far greater rehabilitation of Fagin by Lionel Bart, also Jewish; indeed, both Barnett and Bart highlight an earlier scene in which Fagin calls for "civil words" between Sikes and Nancy (Barnett 30).

Cinematic versions of *Oliver Twist* stand among the earliest ever films. Now lost, "The Death of Nancy Sykes" appeared in 1897; made under two years after the Lumière brothers debuted moving pictures, it was the first movie adapted from any of Dickens's works (Zemka 30). The stage-to-screen industry helped sustain Dickens's relevance while bestowing the great man's credibility to the new medium.[4] Not just story lines, but even "actresses would step back and forth between the two media. Playwrights became screenwriters. Plays became films" (Bolton 106). For example, in 1912 Marie Doro played Oliver at the New Amsterdam Theater in the Broadway revival of J. Comyns Carr's popular melodrama *Oliver Twist* (1905) (fig. 2). She

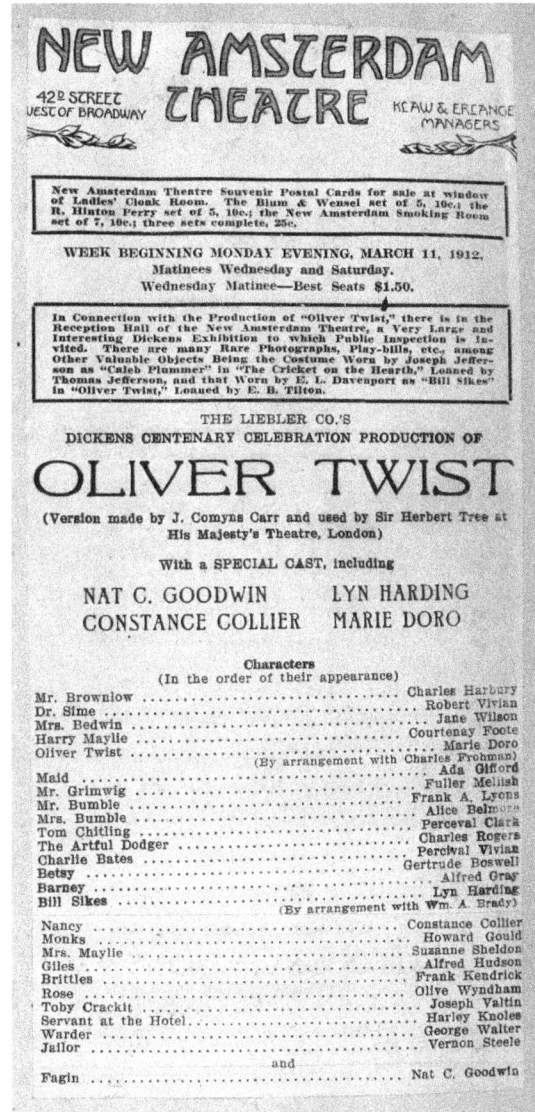

Figure 2. Playbill listing Marie Doro as Oliver in *Oliver Twist* at the New Amsterdam Theatre in New York, 1912. (Image courtesy of Hill Memorial Library, Louisiana State University, Baton Rouge; Hayden [Estelle] Theatre Scrapbooks, vol. 4, Louisiana and Lower Mississippi Valley Collections, Louisiana State University Libraries, Baton Rouge)

Figure 3. Character portrait of Nellie Bowman as Oliver in *Oliver Twist* at His Majesty's Theatre in London, 1905. (Image courtesy of Hill Memorial Library, Louisiana State University, Baton Rouge; Anonymous Program Collection, MSS 1106, Louisiana and Lower Mississippi Valley Collections, Louisiana State University Libraries, Baton Rouge)

recreated the role in Paramount's *Oliver Twist* directed by James Young in 1916. Casting a woman to play a boy was typical in Victorian theater, particularly in pantomime and melodrama; a Miss Carson, for instance, played Oliver in C. Z. Barnett's 1838 adaptation, and Nellie Bowman played him in Carr's *Oliver Twist* at His Majesty's Theatre in London with Herbert Beerbohm Tree as Fagin for the 1904–5 season (fig. 3). The convention survives to this day with *Peter Pan,* whose title character is almost always played by women, such as Mary Martin (1954 on Broadway, plus multiple live NBC television broadcasts), Sandy Duncan (1979 revival), Cathy Rigby (1990 and 1998 revivals), and Allison Williams (2014 NBC television broadcast). But Oliver also continued to be portrayed onstage by women until at least until 1933, when Betty Bligh performed the role at the Lyceum (Bolton 106). Though the custom carried seamlessly into early film,[5] it subsided during the 1920s. Nevertheless, in the 1968 film *Oliver!*, the title character's songs are voiced not by the child actor Marc Lester, but instead by the singer Kathe Green.

In Lloyd's 1922 *Oliver Twist*, boy-star Jackie Coogan played Oliver, and Lon Chaney played Fagin. Here Fagin continues the Victorian stage business of the pickpocket scene; such entertainment, with the stage and screen boys laughing and the audiences in both playhouses and movie houses laughing, creates out of Fagin a villain who is at once abhorrent and attractive. Though Lloyd's movie is called a "silent film," this was never a silent medium, because musicians (at the very least a pianist) would accompany virtually all early film, just as they had accompanied stage melodrama, creating a soundscape to manipulate these complex emotions of repulsion and attraction. With the advent of synchronized sound, so-called silent films based on Victorian plays were again remediated as talkies.[6] David Lean's critically acclaimed but controversial 1948 film is most important in leading up to Bart's *Oliver!* Like Lloyd's film, David Lean's relies on both earlier Victorian dramatizations and their *realizations* of George Cruikshank's illustrations of the novel. In a realization, actors create precise living facsimiles of familiar images, creating a pleasurable shock of recognition (Meisel 247–65); this technique still occurs in such Broadway shows as Stephen Sondheim's *Sunday in the Park with George* (1984), in which performers end the first act by assembling themselves in a replication of Georges Seurat's painting *A Sunday Afternoon on the Island of La Grande Jatte* (1884–86). The Victorians were so familiar with Cruikshank's etchings for *Oliver Twist* that political cartoonists ridiculed early Jewish politicians in England such as Benjamin Disraeli or Lionel de Rothschild by depicting them as a version of Cruikshank's iconic Fagin. For example, "Fagin's Political School" (*Punch*, November 9, 1867) depicts Disraeli (then Chancellor of the Exchequer) corrupting the "young" Parliamentarians as he shows them how to pick a pocket (fig. 4). More than a century later, David Lean's film again realizes Cruikshank's illustrations of Fagin with remarkable accuracy. Alec Guinness's enormous prosthetic nose brought denunciations of anti-Semitism

Figure 4. "Fagin's Political School." Cartoon by John Tenniel. *Punch* 52 (November 9, 1867): 189. (Image courtesy of Hill Memorial Library, Special Collections, Louisiana State University, Baton Rouge)

and provoked demonstrations by Holocaust survivors in Berlin. Guinness's artificial physiognomy looked appallingly like Nazi propaganda; particularly in 1948, this proved too much. The film could not be released in the United States in its original form; it appeared only after twelve minutes were cut, mostly of Guinness's profile (Marsh 218–19).

The instant and incessant adaption of Dickens's *Oliver Twist* differs markedly from the treatment of the source texts that ultimately produced *The King and I* and *One Touch of Venus*. The first appropriations of Anna Leonowens's Thai travel narratives from the 1870s to a new medium did not occur till the twentieth century. In contrast, F. Anstey's fantasies from the 1880s received solid attention from nineteenth-century adapters (including by the author himself) in his own lifetime and even a little afterward.

But Dickens operated on an entirely different scale even from Anstey. *Oliver Twist* was Dickens's most adapted book before 1900, with at least two hundred versions performed in England or America by the century's end (Bolton 104–5). Most early adaptations depicted Fagin as heinous, drawing on Dickens's text and on Cruikshank's illustrations. Twentieth-century stage and screen adaptations followed suit, often directly remaking earlier versions and retaining the anti-Semitic stereotype. Even when picking up on aspects of these earlier dramatizations, *Oliver!*—which built upon an accretion of prior adaptations and appropriations—was a marked departure not only in shifting to the genre of musical theater but also in its treatment of Fagin.

CIRCUMSTANCES ATTENDING *OLIVER!*'S BIRTH AND PROGRESS

When *Oliver!* opened in 1960 at the New Theatre in London, it was an immediate hit. It got 23 curtain calls and ran for 2,618 performances. It was the longest-running musical in London until superseded by Andrew Lloyd Webber's *Jesus Christ Superstar,* which opened in London in 1972 (Stanley Green 201).[7] Lloyd Webber acknowledges his debt to *Oliver!*'s creator, Lionel Bart, by describing him as "the father of the modern British musical" (qtd. Pace) and considers *Oliver!* to be "one of the greatest musicals of all time" ("*Oliver!* Creator Dies"). London's commercial musical theater was so dominated by American shows that when David Merrick brought it to New York in 1963, it was the first British musical on Broadway that American theater critics and theatergoing audiences took seriously (Morrden, *Open a New Window* 165). With 744 performances, it ran longer than any other British musical up to that point (Hischak 127), a record held until Andrew Lloyd Webber's *Evita* arrived in 1979 (Stanley Green 201).[8] Indeed, theater historian Mark Steyn considers *Oliver!* to have been the most popular British musical in the United States until *Cats* (171). Bart won the Tony for best music and lyrics; he also wrote the book. This multiple accomplishment attests to Bart's extraordinary talent. Shows typically require separate composers, lyricists, and book writers, as we have seen with *One Touch of Venus;* Hammerstein often tackled two of these tasks, serving as both lyricist and book writer for *The King and I,* but not all three. All this Broadway success meant that this was the first musical play recognized by the British as rivaling the Americans in their own genre, a Rodgers and Hammerstein–style integrated musical. With multiple tours and at least six major successful revivals in London or New York between

1977 and 2009 and an expensive Broadway flop starring Patti LuPone in 1984, *Oliver!* seems always to be in production somewhere and is a perennial favorite for school performances (Steyn 172). It was so popular when it premiered in 1960 that critics worried it would inspire a whole rash of musicals based on nineteenth-century classics and especially Dickens. The *Evening Standard* theater critic Milton Shulman "imagined being called upon to review 'The Pickwick Capers' or 'Miss Havisham Misses a Wedding'" while Kenneth Tynan of the *Observer* predicted *David!*, *Great!*, and *Bleak!* (Ellis).

Although we have had no more exclamatory Dickens musical adaptations,[9] there is no doubt that *Oliver!*'s staging a specifically Dickensian musical theater is part of its initial success, its longevity, and its broad impact. It has heavily influenced subsequent representations of Victorian culture in American and other musical theater. Bart identified the famous revolving set of *Les Misérables* as due directly to Sean Kenny's influence (Steyn 173). Kenney won the Tony for best scenic design for *Oliver!*: he devised ingenious wheeled steel-and-wooden scaffolding, stairs, and bridges that continually and rapidly reconfigured as the workhouse or Fagin's den, leading to other bare-bones Victorian scenic design, such as the similarly constructed modules in the 1979 production of Stephen Sondheim's *Sweeney Todd*. But the set is not *Oliver!*'s only influence on *Sweeney Todd*. The high-pitched, large-bodied, singing beadle Bumble found a home in Sondheim's musical as the even crueler Beadle Bamford. Likewise, the lusty, fast-talking, middle-aged Mrs. Lovett from *Sweeney Todd* owes almost as much to *Oliver!*'s Mrs. Bumble as to the beautiful but diabolical young widow in *Sweeney Todd*'s source text, *The String of Pearls* (1846–47). The 2007 Tim Burton film *Sweeney Todd* carries the debt to *Oliver!* even further, casting a much younger boy in the role of the barber's apprentice than does the stage play; it even interpolates the beadle's having brought the little waif from the workhouse. There is a sense in which—particularly for a twentieth- or twenty-first-century American audience—Victorian simply means Dickensian, and Dickensian means *Oliver!*[10]

The musical has also had an impact on other adaptations of *Oliver Twist*. Most obvious is the Disney animated *Oliver & Company* (1988), in which Oliver is a little kitten who gets mixed up with a gang of thieving dogs. Although billed as inspired by *Oliver Twist*, it owes several debts to Bart's *Oliver!* Not least is Dom DeLuise's portrayal of Fagin as victimized by Sikes (both figured as animated humans); there is no indication that Fagin is Jewish. Another is the cartoon's Nancy, now a shapely Afghan hound (renamed Rita) with red fur, much like the curvy redhead Shani Wallis who played Nancy in the movie-musical *Oliver!*[11] Although in the final version of the film, Rita survives to the happy ending, in early plans for the cartoon, vicious Dobermans chasing Oliver murder her as she protects Oliver (Fleming 192–93). Even the film's title *Oliver & Company* is an homage to Bart's play; in the score of *Oliver!*, several musical numbers are designated in the play's score as to be performed by "Oliver and Company." It also seems significant that Disney chose *this* story to make as a musical, their first foray back into the animated musical format after nearly a decade hiatus (during which Disney Animation Studios released nonmusicals: *The Rescuers* in 1977, *The Fox and the Hound* in 1981, *The Black Cauldron* in 1985, and *The Great Mouse Detective* in 1986). *Oliver & Company* ushered in the renaissance of high-quality animated Disney movie musicals such as *Little Mermaid* (1989), *Beauty and the Beast* (1991), and *Aladdin* (1992), begun by the composer/lyricist team of Howard Ashman and Alan Menken, who also worked on *Oliver & Company*.[12] Later Menken would go on to compose the music for the annual Madison Square Garden *A Christmas Carol*. Far beyond adaptations of *Oliver Twist*, *Oliver!* is a phenomenon of influence.

ABOUT BART

Neither the musical *Oliver!* nor its creator has received the critical attention each deserves. Every year important scholarly work appears on Stephen Sondheim or on Rodgers and Hammerstein. But despite the historical importance and artistic achievement of *Oliver!* and despite Bart's other musical theater contributions and his many hits as a popular song writer, Bart and his work still remain underexamined. Some exceptions indicating that the situation may be changing are Marc Napolitano's show-biography *Oliver! A Dickensian Musical* (2014) and Millie Taylor's comprehensive overview in *The Oxford Handbook of the British Musical* (2016), where she argues persuasively that "Bart's musical and lyrical language altered the way British musical theatre spoke to a local audience" (483). But most of what appears on Bart remains the occasional biographical profile in the press outlining Bart's wild days and an exclamatory celebrity tell-all called *Bart!*[13] It is not hard to see why Bart's astonishing life story would interest people. His beginnings were poor. Of his parents' eleven children, only seven survived to adulthood. Bart was the youngest child of Jewish immigrants who fled from a pogrom in Galicia, a region between Poland and Ukraine. His father was a tailor, a trade taken up by all Bart's surviving siblings. Bart received virtually no formal training in music, which he could not read. He composed by singing tunes into a tape recorder, apparently keeping one in every room in the house in case inspiration struck. His first musical theater hit was *Fings Ain't Wot They Used T'Be* (1960), a Cockney musical for which he wrote the lyrics; it was still running when *Oliver!* premiered.

After *Oliver!* Bart created several other award-winning shows, such as *Blitz!* (also with an exclamation point) in 1962 about children being evacuated from London to escape the bombing during World War II, based on Bart's own experience. Soon followed *Maggie May* (1964) about a Liverpool prostitute and her dockworker lover, another critical and financial success. He wrote numerous hit pop songs, some topping the charts for as long as six weeks, for Cliff Richards, Tommy Steele, Anthony Newley, and Matt Monro, including the 1963 James Bond movie theme song "To Russia with Love." He was good friends with Judy Garland, who recorded his music. In fact, the press linked them romantically, even though he was gay. He hung out with Noël Coward, Princess Margaret, and Liberace. He entertained so extravagantly that he apparently kept two bowls for guests in his lavish Chelsea home to take what they liked, filled not with candy, but one with cash, the other with cocaine. Even more notorious was his toilet, perhaps throne-shaped and flushing to the tune of Handel's "Water Music." Some estimate that he was as rich as the Beatles, earning sixteen British pounds a minute just from *Oliver!* (Vallance).

Then in 1965 came a colossal flop about Robin Hood called *Twang!!* As one theater historian puts it, here Bart went "an exclamation point too far" (Steyn 171). Unfortunately, he put his entire fortune into producing his own show; and when it was clearly failing, he sold his rights to *Oliver!* and spent all the rest of his money trying to rescue *Twang!!,* to no avail. The last straw came in 1969; his *La Strada* opened and closed on Broadway in one night. He declared bankruptcy in 1972, losing his swanky London house, his Malibu getaway, and his castle in Tangier. He developed diabetes. He tried to go on the wagon and, in the early 1990s, finally came out of the closet. In 1994 producer Cameron Macintosh sought Bart out, invited him to help with a revival of *Oliver!,* and signed a percentage over to him. Bart's health remained precarious, and he died in 1999 from liver cancer. Perhaps this larger-than-life history—this meteoric rise to the very top of the pop music and musical theater worlds at the age of just thirty, followed by such a total, catastrophic collapse—distracts potential scholars from thinking hard about Bart's work. As of this writing, there is as yet no authoritative biography or full-length study that systematically analyzes his creative contributions.

LA-DEE-DA AND UPPITY

There are some obvious reasons why Bart would have been attracted to adapting *Oliver Twist*. His childhood privation, his belonging as a boy to what he describes as a street gang, his strong identification with the underclass (he briefly joined the Communist Party and worked with the leftist Unity Theatre)—these all speak to the experience of the novel's children both in the workhouse and in Fagin's den (Napolitano, *Oliver!* 34). All his musical theater work deals with class; even the Robin Hood disaster *Twang!!* focuses, like *Oliver!,* on a gang of thieves and the redistribution of wealth. Although the genre of Broadway or West End musical theater is both middle-class and middlebrow, both the novel and this musical are associated with melodrama, a working-class genre. Dickens himself likened *Oliver Twist* to melodrama in the novel's famous passage describing alternating comic and tragic bits as being like the stripes of meat and fat in "streaky, well cured bacon" (117). The magazine *Tatler* described *Oliver!*'s 1960 premiere as "a roaring transpontine melodrama" (qtd. Ellis). The musical hall, another tradition influencing Bart, is working-class amusement also. Both the novel and the show's vivid evocation of the underclass makes them—like melodrama and music hall—sites of contestation as well as class containment.[14]

Also importantly bound up in the issue of class solidarity is national identity. Bart speaks of identifying with Jewish American composers and lyricists, such as Rodgers and Hammerstein, with what he describes as a shared sense of minority outsider-ship (Roper 8). But, although many important Jewish American musical theater composers and lyricists grew up in straitened circumstances, such as Irving Berlin and George and Ira Gershwin, neither Richard Rodgers nor Oscar Hammerstein (nor Stephen Sondheim, born the same year as Bart, nor Alan Jay Lerner, Frank Loesser, or Frederick Loewe) shared either Bart's working-class background or his childhood experiences with poverty. Besides class, another difference between Bart, Berlin, and the Gershwins on the one hand and Rodgers, Hammerstein,

Sondheim, etc. on the other is German versus Eastern European (Galician, Russian, or Lithuanian) parentage (Gottlieb 158). German Jewish identity was long an additional marker of elite—or at least more assimilated—status in an American context. But none of them grew up in Stepney, the heart of London's Jewish East End, as Bart did. In fact, not only Bart but also Ron Moody (who originated the role of Fagin in the London production of *Oliver!* as well as on film) and Georgia Brown (who originated Nancy in London and on Broadway) were Jewish East Enders, from various sorts of working-class backgrounds. Their birth names were Lionel Begleiter, Ronald Moodnik, and Lillian Klot.

Lerner and Loewe's *My Fair Lady*, which had opened on Broadway in 1956, arrived in London in 1958 to great success and critical acclaim. In 1958, Bart began working on *Oliver!* (Napolitano, "Reviewing" 140). One could imagine Bart's thinking that if the Jewish American duo of Lerner and Loewe, both educated men from privileged backgrounds, could take George Bernard Shaw's *Pygmalion* (1913), about the transformation of a crass flower-seller into an aristocratic lady, craft it into a musical theater masterpiece full of singing and dancing Cockneys, and re-import it to England, why shouldn't a real British Jewish Cockney composer/lyricist turn *Oliver Twist* into a musical, and send it back again? With the exception of *La Strada,* all of Bart's musicals are based on British raw materials, set in London or Liverpool or Nottingham. Yet, of all of these musicals, several of which were quite successful in the UK, only one conquered the US market. If one is to write the first British musical that will take on the American dominance of musical theater,[15] what better vehicle than the quintessentially British, universally revered, and class-conscious Dickens?

ANTI-SEMITISM

But while *Oliver Twist* might have attracted Bart because of class and national identity, there remains the problem of Fagin. There is some appeal to the idea of revising a book that offers so much, but how to do it in a way that makes it bearable to those who find its unrelenting anti-Semitism frankly painful? One might think that a Jewish composer/lyricist/playwright would want to avoid the novel for this reason, but Bart resolves the difficulty by re-creating Fagin, a virulent anti-Semitic stereotype, in a way that makes the character likable while still utterly recognizable.[16] Bart would not be the first Jewish reader to wish that Dickens represented Fagin differently—that is, less anti-Semitically. The *Jewish Chronicle* asked in 1854, "Why should Jews alone be excluded from 'the sympathizing heart' of this great author and powerful friend of the oppressed?" (qtd. Baumgarten 50). Mrs. Eliza Davis's now-famous letter to Dickens in 1863 prompted him to write back that in creating Fagin he did not mean anything insulting to Judaism as a religion (he makes clear that such anti-religious animus would be vile) or to Jewish people in general; he meant only to indicate Fagin's race, as he would "a Chinaman" (Dickens 378), as though this would make it better. But the point that, for Dickens, Fagin's Jewishness was a matter of *race* and not religion or culture is important.

As many critics have noted, Dickens's Fagin is not religious: he does not keep kosher, as is obvious from the sausages he eats (65); he derisively sends away the "venerable men of his own persuasion" who try to comfort him in his cell at the end of his life (353). Nor, as Harry Stone and others point out, is he particularly Jewish in any cultural way, other than his stereotypical profession of old-clothes dealer: he uses no identifiably Jewish mannerisms (233). What makes him a Jew is simply that Dickens repeatedly says so. In contrast, Bart's vision of the story includes no overt indication of Fagin's Jewish identity, racial or otherwise. Bart never identifies Fagin as a Jew in dialogue, lyrics, or the dramatis personae. The actor playing *Oliver!*'s Fagin is often wigged and costumed according to Dickens's description of fiery red hair, a "long gabardine coat and broad-brimmed hat," which is based on the tradition of the "stage Jew" as a stock character going back at least to Renaissance drama, to Shylock from *The Merchant of Venice* (1605) and Barabas from *The Jew of Malta* (1592) (Stone 233). But for late-twentieth- and twenty-first-century audiences, that redheaded, red-bearded ragged type has virtually disappeared as a recognizable icon. More importantly, Bart moderates Fagin's villainy so fully that "the *Guardian*'s Philip Hope-Wallace was disappointed; he thought Bart had softened the role to 'a queer old auntie'" (Ellis).[17] But Bart is not aiming for fidelity to the novel; he indicates both on the theatrical program and on the film's opening credits that the play is "freely adapted" from *Oliver Twist* (Dianne Brooks 117).

As stage adaptations of long novels must (and as do all the musicals discussed based on novels covered in this book), *Oliver!* compresses and streamlines the story to fit into approximately a two-and-a-half-hour running time, drops and combines characters, and uses song and dance to showcase emotion or advance the plot. Like British director David Lean's 1948 film *Oliver Twist*, *Oliver!* cuts out Rose Maylie. Dropping Rose reduces the dual female protagonists to one and puts the prostitute center stage through much of the musical. When the musical goes from stage to screen, the debt to earlier adaptations, such as Lean's film, is even more obvious. John Romano points out that the movie director Carol Reed "stole shot for shot Lean's version for the narrative portions of the musical. The story boards are the same" (Joseph 18). But perhaps an even more important influence on Bart is the reaction against the 1948 Fagin, which appeared when Bart was eighteen, arousing public outrage against the anti-Semitism in Alec Guinness's portrayal. Bart rewrites Fagin into a singing, dancing, joking, kindly scamp unlikely to be interpreted in the same way. Several of Bart's structural changes also contribute significantly to this softening effect. He goes even further than Lean in simplifying the story by omitting Oliver's evil half-brother Monks completely. Far more than serving the need for story compression, eliminating Monks removes Fagin's motivation to corrupt Oliver, since Monks had hired Fagin specifically to do so. Fagin no longer spies or connives destructively. He leaves no eerily missing footprints, so disturbing in the novel (232). He loses any ulterior motive for introducing the orphan to the gang's mode of employment; stealing becomes simply an effective method of keeping everyone fed, because in the oppressive Victorian economic system, "you've got to pick a pocket or two" just to survive. Petty theft born of poverty is much more the sort of crime an audience will accept and forgive.

In addition to structural changes that alter the portrayal of Fagin, the generic shift from a novel with an omniscient narrator to a play presenting the action as though mimetically, using the traditional fourth wall, means that the musical offers nothing like the novel's moving and horrific peek into Bill Sikes's psychological state after he murders Nancy. Sikes becomes unambiguously brutal. In contrast, Fagin seems hardly a villain at all. Gone is the effect of—in Juliet John's terms—Sikes and Fagin as hot and cold sides of the same villain (9). Beyond structural changes, simple judicious cutting of dialogue contributes to Fagin's recuperation. For example, the novel's Fagin may be seen as egging Sikes on to kill Nancy with the somewhat ambiguous lines that start out "You won't be—too—violent, Bill? . . . I mean . . . not too violent for safety" (315), in which (no matter how sure a reader may be of Fagin's villainy) the dialogue does not explicitly state either that Sikes should murder or that he should not, nor whose safety Fagin wants to protect. Even following it with "Be crafty" apparently is too subtle for Sikes, whose bludgeoning of Nancy could not possibly be considered crafty or anything other than "too violent." In the musical Bart tweaks these lines into the unambiguously nonviolent admonition, "Careful, Bill, please. No violence!" Without the addition of comic songs and dances, Bart has reformed Fagin significantly and avoided most charges of anti-Semitism just by cutting and adjusting with care.

What happens when you take an anti-Semitic stereotype that was based on a received caricature of a villainous Stage Jew, rewrite him as a lovable rogue, and then put him back on the stage, where the original had done so much damage for so many centuries? Juliet John points out that the reader's response to the novel's Fagin depends upon the reader's "recognition of, and openness to, well-worn theatrical, literary (and racist) conventions" (*Villains* 129). The converse is also true of the musical. Because—unlike many previous dramatizations of *Oliver Twist*—Fagin is never referred to as a Jew in the musical, viewers unfamiliar with the novel might not know the character is Jewish. While David Lean's film also eschews the label of "Jew" for Fagin, Alec Guinness's performance loads the character with many stereotypical features fully recognizable to the 1948 audience as well as to more recent ones, including the notorious nose, a strong Yiddish accent, and a nasal twang. Less recognizable now but held over from the Victorians is the lisp. The novel is even more explicit, labeling Fagin "the Jew," and sometime "the villainous old Jew," literally hundreds of times,[18] driving home repeatedly the anti-Semitic point that Fagin's identity as villain and Jew are one. Yet Fagin never performs his Jewishness in the novel. Unlike Barney, he has no nasal twang; and he certainly observes no Jewish rituals or religious commandments, which is what makes Timothy Spall's performance in the 2007 BBC adaptation so bizarre: his Fagin wears a yarmulke, says Hebrew blessings over his food, and won't eat the sausages he cooks for the children. Nevertheless, even if every identification of him as "Jew" were removed from the text (and certainly Dickens removed many of them after Mrs. Davis complained), Victorian readers would still recognize the common stereotype.

The musical makes no verbal or visual reference to the character's Jewishness whatsoever. One effect of removing the label is to ameliorate somewhat the worry about the play's replicating the novel's anti-Semitic qualities (although they can be reintroduced in production). Removing the particularity of any overt verbal reference to Fagin's Jewishness, Bart channels the character's ethnicity into the rhythms and melodies of songs, where they work powerfully for the many people who recognize them, but only as subliminal information for everyone else. These are essentially a set of musical cues, particularly in Fagin's song "Reviewing the Situation," which has a klezmer beat and uses either a violin, as in the original production, or clarinet, as in the 1994 London revival (both are traditional Jewish klezmer instruments), going from free tempo to a slow boom-chick that accelerates in typical klezmer fashion. Klezmer is a genre of traditional Jewish dance music, originating in Eastern Europe where itinerant bands of musicians would play for weddings that would last for days. Klezmer forms the basis of many popular Yiddish songs, incorporating influences from both the Russian and Ottoman empires. Often playing by ear, instrumentalists improvise, performing musical tricks that sound, for example, like the human voice laughing or sobbing. In addition to the klezmer elements in the instrumentals, the actor playing Fagin often goes into a seemingly improvised cantorial riff either in "Reviewing the Situation" or in "Pick a Pocket or Two"; both are in minor key, as is typical of Jewish liturgical and secular music. Bart even described his music for Fagin as "like a Jewish mother hen clucking away" (Steyn 173). As a result, Bart leaves the task of indicating that Fagin *is* a Jew up to the actor, musicians, and dancers rather than the play-text, making Fagin's Jewish identity solely a matter of performance.

Although it is fairly safe to say that a clearly anti-Semitic musical would be unlikely to succeed on post-Holocaust Broadway (but isn't that what *The Producers* is all about?), there have been complaints that the musical is exactly that, from the moment it premiered on both sides of the Atlantic in the 1960s until now (Steven Marcus 478; Napolitano, "Reviewing" 187–89). One production that received little such reaction was the 1994 London revival with Jonathan Pryce playing Fagin. He deliberately emptied the role of any identifiably Jewish gestures, mannerisms, or hint of Yiddish accent, commenting, "Yes, I played a Jewish character, but what do you need to see to know that he's Jewish?" Ironically, some complained about this strategy as well; as Pryce explains it, "I was being criticized for not being a Jewish stereotype" (Nathan). And while Ron Moody used plenty of Yiddish sounds and expressions and cantorial effects in the original 1960 London production, that interpretation of the role raised red flags for the American producer David Merrick; Clive Revill intentionally toned down Fagin's Jewishness for the 1963 Broadway run, for fear it would offend the New

York audience. Ron Moody did likewise when he modified his role for the 1968 film adaptation of the musical.

Yet Rowan Atkinson chose consciously to reject Jonathan Pryce's approach to Fagin. He explains,

> Many have sought . . . though it certainly wouldn't be my view . . . to drain the Jewish identity away as much as possible and it was something I was very unkeen on because it seemed to me that's so much part of . . . his exoticness if you like, of what makes him so interesting. I know it just manifests itself in terms of musical rhythms and turns of phrase, speech. But, it seemed to me to be an important part of the depth of him. Because you take that away and suddenly you're left with something rather sort of shallow and indeterminate. (Atkinson interview with author, July 10, 2009)

For Atkinson, part of the appeal of performing Fagin lies in performing "his exoticness," so that Fagin's Jewishness and his exoticness or Otherness are one. Atkinson used just a few identifiably Jewish expressions—an occasional "ai-yai-yai," for example. Atkinson indicated his character's Jewishness by switching the instrument associated with Fagin in the orchestration from clarinet, which had been used in the 1994 Cameron Macintosh production, back to the violin, used in the original London premiere with Ron Moody (Atkinson interview with author). Switching instruments in order to signify more effectively that the character is Jewish is a prime example of how performing Jewishness depends on cultural context, because Atkinson was mistaken about the clarinet not being a Jewish sound.[19] Perhaps that just goes to show how influential another important 1960s musical, *Fiddler on the Roof* (1964), has been in developing a legible vocabulary of Jewish cultural identity.

Any doubt that many people think of Fagin as the real protagonist in this musical play named *Oliver!* is obviated by the iconography of the musical's advertising posters and logo over time. The 1960 and 1963 productions feature images of a waif-like Oliver; these productions were the first in England and America, so Bart's Fagin was as yet unknown. But the 1994 Cameron Macintosh production at the London Palladium introduces a new image, depicting Fagin, also used for his 2009 production. The title word "Oliver" forms Fagin's face, with the addition of a hat and beard. Most strikingly, it elongates the L in "Oliver" to serve as Fagin's nose. Given the furor over Alec Guinness's infamous prosthetic nose in Lean's film, this might

Figure 5. Cover of playbill for *Oliver!*, Baton Rouge Little Theater, July 1998. (Author's private collection; used by permission)

seem a curious approach. In fact, some fierce annoyance was expressed in the *Guardian* about it (Pascal), although one could alternatively read it as a comic and subversive appropriation of the nasal symbol. It became the logo for this production, appearing on programs from Drury Lane in London to the Cabrillo Stage in Aptos, California—everywhere the show was licensed, such as Baton Rouge Little Theatre, in Baton Rouge, Louisiana (fig. 5). The design graphically represents the recognition over the decades that even though Fagin is not the title character, he is the star.

Another possible contender for the musical's starring role is Nancy. Changing Nancy changes Fagin, allowing him to take on the task of making a rough but entertaining and tolerably happy home for his gang. When the novel first introduces her, she is a stout and painted streetwalker who yells, drinks gin, and dresses none too properly (70). Her first appearance in the role of Angel in the House in the novel is entirely meta-theatrical: winking at Fagin and Sikes, Nancy gleefully disguises herself as a mock proto-Esther Summerson—with household key, clean apron, and respectable cap to hide her curl papers—when she goes to discover Oliver's whereabouts (93). Soon repenting of her part in bringing Oliver back to the den of thieves, the novel's Nancy grows into a figure evoking Alexander Welsh's notion of angel of the hearth (Welsh 6–8). She first defends Oliver from being hit by Fagin with a club, seizing it and throwing it into the fire (115). Sikes later beats Nancy to death with a similar club; he, too, thrusts it, covered with her blood and hair, into the fire, to destroy the evidence (317). Often Nancy gazes into the fire (136), "mends the fire," or sits "perfectly motionless, before it" (145). Nancy nurtures with food and drink, bringing brandy to the table for Sikes and Fagin (133) and "a pot of porter and a dish of sheepsheads" to Sikes and Oliver the night before the housebreaking (144). She makes them breakfast and clothes them with handkerchief and cape (145). As the novel progresses, she chides Sikes with "something like sweetness of tone" for mistreating her when she has nursed him "with a touch of woman's tenderness" (258). When visiting Rose, she even more fully displays "something of the woman's original nature" (266); this "womanly feeling" overcomes the mixture of pride and degradation that had been masking Nancy's inner angel, fully fledged by the moment of her sacrificial death (166).[20] Nancy's connection to domesticity culminates in her own murder in the home she makes for Sikes. He drags her from their bed before killing her in front of the home fires she had kept burning for him.

In the novel, it is this very link to home that kills her. Diana Archibald points out that while most critics see Nancy as sacrificing herself to save Oliver, in fact, in the novel she dies not because she reveals the crucial information that saves the boy but because she goes home afterwards. In choosing to return to her batterer rather than to save herself by accepting Rose Maylie's offer of help, Nancy follows the path that leads to her death. Archibald argues that this demonstrates neither her altruism, nor her sexual attraction to

Sikes, nor her voluntary sacrifice to save Oliver (all of which are true of her as well—at least in other moments); instead, she explains, Nancy goes home to Sikes because she "can't break away from her co-dependent behavioral patterns and thus she returns to her abuser" (57). Archibald points out that "Nancy fits the profile of a battered woman," pointing out that the Victorians also recognized the syndrome, calling it "the Magdalen problem" (57). And while Thackeray famously disparaged Nancy as unrealistic, Archibald regards Dickens's understanding of the battered woman's psychology as accurate when in his 1841 preface to *Oliver Twist* he defended the portrayal of Nancy by saying, "It is useless to discuss whether the conduct and character of the girl seems natural or unnatural, probable or improbable, right or wrong. IT IS TRUE. Every man who has watched these melancholy shades of life, must know it to be so" (6). This domestic space—tragic though it is—is one that the musical's Nancy never occupies.

While the novel allows Nancy to grow in tenderness and womanly feeling, she never gains the capacity to bring simple happiness to others, which is reserved for her angelic double, Rose. Since the musical evicts Rose, leaving Nancy as the only leading female character, it would have made sense for Nancy to inherit Rose's capacity to bring happiness to everyone around her. Yet Bart's Nancy is associated with happiness only when she sings counterfactually, ironically. She addresses the issue of happiness directly in "It's a Fine Life." Basically a drinking song (like "Oom-Pah-Pah" later on), precipitated by *Nancy* asking *Fagin* for a drink (which is not how it works in the novel), this rollicking number ranks gin among the "small pleasures" the underclass can claim fully, for "who would deny us these / Gin toddies— large measures." Suggesting that her life choices are merely a rejection of bourgeois convention, the song continues, "Let the prudes look down on us, / Let the wide world frown at us, / It's a fine, fine life." Lines expressing class solidarity recall Dodger's earlier singing to Oliver in "Consider Yourself," "Nobody tries to be lah-di-dah and uppity / there's a cup a tea / for all." Nancy and Bet make fun of middle-class fashion with its flounces, feathers, and frills. Rounding out the introductory verse, Nancy exclaims of her life, "I rough it, I love it."

The film version of *Oliver!* alters this scene. Now Nancy is gainfully employed as a bar maid, and she sings "It's a Fine Life" in the pub while she serves drinks. This modification allows the much broader family audience of the movie house freedom from thinking that Nancy might be a prostitute. To make perfectly clear that she is neither prostitute nor thief in the film, this Nancy sympathetically sings the lines that fancy people with "fine airs and fine graces / don't have to sin to eat" to other women at the pub whose identity as prostitutes is signified by their garish clothes and their exceedingly close proximity to male customers; Nancy shows them a kindness while she continues to serve drinks to more customers in her honest labor as bar maid. But in the stage musical, the song takes place in Fagin's den, and it is Fagin who serves the gin, not Nancy.

All this about a "fine life" might seem upbeat, and many live productions of the musical take the fun at face value. But these cheerful protestations of satisfaction sound more and more ironic and dangerous as the song continues. Starting innocently enough, as though their wretched deprivations were merely careful frugality, Nancy sings, "If you don't mind having to go without things," it is a fine life. No matter how bad things are, even though "diseased rats threaten to bring the plague in," you still just "take it as it turns out" because, "if you don't mind having to like or lump it," it's a fine life. Soon she admits not only to scrimping and to vermin-infested living quarters, but also to "the occasional black eye." But somehow that's okay because "you can always cover one / 'Til he blacks the other one." It's still a "fine, fine life." By the time Nancy arrives at the song's concluding verse, the lines "Not for me, the happy home / Happy husband, happy wife" no longer seem a scornful rejection of the sneering "straightlaces" in conventional bourgeois marriage. The increasingly abusive circumstances described in the song jar disturbingly with the upbeat melody and the game she plays in singing with Bet, Fagin, and the boys. The reiterated line of the chorus, "It's a fine life," may lead the audience to understand that the rousing jollity of this drinking song is emphatically and even painfully ironic.[21]

While the novel's Nancy displays hearthside skill and shows her domestic capacity in caring for and serving Bill Sikes, the stage musical Nancy is never shown at home and hearth. Even her murder is removed from the domestic space of her bedroom at home to the public space of London Bridge at night. We have already seen the musical's Nancy *being* served rather than *serving* drinks in the Thieves' Kitchen, as Bart labels Fagin's den. At the pub known as the Three Cripples, she performs; this is something she clearly does often, regaling her friends and customers with another merry, cynical drinking song, "Oom-Pah-Pah," the opener for act 2. Again in the stage musical she does not serve drinks or food, or tend the hearth, or behave domestically in any way. "Oom-Pah-Pah" tells the story of "pretty Sally" "from the country" who walks through the alley showing off her "garters / But not for free and gratis"; now in the city, she's no longer "the same blushing rose." Still, she's "glad to bring a coin in" and "join in this song." In other words, "Oom-Pah-Pah" is a raucous but sympathetic take on William Hogarth's 1732 *A Harlot's Progress*, a series of six paintings and etchings satirically depicting the seduction, degradation, and death of a country girl come to London. The song serves to remind us that *Oliver Twist*'s subtitle "A Parish Boy's Progress" may be as much derived from Hogarth as from Paul Bunyan's happy Christian allegory *A Pilgrim's Progress* (1678), suggesting strongly that Nancy and Sally have a lot in common; this is an important metaphorical connection since the play does not explicitly present Nancy as a prostitute, although unlike the movie musical (where she is unequivocally an honest bar maid at the Three Cripples), she possesses no other visible means of support. Nancy gives a rowdy performance, whipping up the tavern crowd to ever greater heights of hilarity as they drink and carouse, but she hardly brings them a homey contentment or domestic bliss. Even her earlier song "I'd Do Anything" with Artful Dodger and the rest of Fagin's crew is ripe for a dark interpretation, with its reiterated question and answer "'Anything?' 'Anything'" hinting at violence and other extremes kept at bay only by the playfulness and seeming security of Fagin's Kitchen. The only other time she mentions "home" is again counterfactually, when in order to abduct Oliver, she pretends that he has run away from his grieving parents; here the stage Nancy, like the novel Nancy, creates an entirely fictional domestic space and a fictional family in which she styles herself as his sister, just to steal the boy.

With Rose gone from the story, and without Nancy's tragic connection to home and hearth, Fagin becomes the domestic center of the musical. Other than "Oom-Pah-Pah" and subsequent dialogue at the Three Cripples, every one of Fagin's scenes is in his own Thieves' Kitchen. As in the novel, our first acquaintance with him involves his cooking hot sausages. In *Oliver!*, he also makes coffee in a saucepan. He cooks and cleans for the children, cares for them, feeds them, houses them, sings to them, plays with them, teaches them, entertains them, expresses affection for them, disciplines them, rewards them, and puts them to bed. Many critics have pointed out Fagin's feminized position in the novel and its association with queerness, Jewishness, and pedophilia (Hirsch 321, Wolff 603, Dellamora 30–47). But the musical does not show his domesticity in a negative light. In creating this lovable rogue of Fagin, Bart softens or perhaps eradicates Fagin's villainy in part simply by retaining every scrap of fun and tenderness the novel provides and highlighting what Jonathan Grossman has called his "odd, but cozy domesticity" (38). Obviously, the boys in the novel would probably die of starvation were it not for Fagin's care and training, but also (as many critics have shown) Fagin amuses the children and occasionally even shows some gentleness when taking care of Oliver, as when the sleepy boy "feels himself gently lifted onto one of the sacks" at bedtime (66).[22] But in the novel these moments serve ultimately to make an otherwise vile and repulsive Fagin even more insidious as a villain because, through his humor and his caretaking, he is able to corrupt his young charges. Yet those moments in the novel provide just enough ambiguity to make the musical's good-hearted Fagin believable as an adaptation.

The musical puts Fagin at the center of a family—albeit a kind of crime family—based as much on class as on criminal behavior, emphasizing clannish class loyalty within Fagin's gang in a way that goes far beyond what Dickens provides. For example, in the musical, when inviting Oliver back to the thieves' den, Dodger first asks Oliver two questions not in Dickens—if he's got any mother? father?—before reverting to dialogue directly from the novel: he can take Oliver to a "respectable old gentleman . . . wot'll give you lodgings for nothink, and never ask for the change." This play's introduction of the idea that the respectable old gentleman might serve as both mother and father is reinforced in Dodger's song of welcome, "Consider Yourself"; Oliver should consider himself "one of the family," consider himself "at home." The musical further cements the connection to class solidarity by having Dodger and Oliver joined by bustling workers at Paddington Green. The stage direction calls for "costers, porters, children, street vendors, and tumblers" who all sing the second chorus, extending the "family" from Fagin's boys to London's workers and uniting them in a familial relationship based on class consciousness as well as criminality.

Fagin's family and the home he makes for them in the musical are also based on affection. When Fagin sends the boys off to pick pockets, in "Be Back Soon," he urges them "to come home / safe and sound." He continues, "I dunno, somehow I'll miss you / I love you that's why I / Say cheerio . . . not goodbye." The audience believes Fagin and believes that the boys need this affection. Proving the genuineness of his feeling, in the soliloquy song "Reviewing the Situation," Fagin sings, "A man's got a heart, hasn't he / Joking apart, hasn't he?" Despite the fact that the home he supplies the boys is based on stolen goods, despite the humor and irony in lines such as "Shut up and drink your gin" (perhaps recalling Eliza Doolittle's comment in *My*

Fair Lady and *Pygmalion* that "Gin was mother's milk to her"), the happy home and parental care Fagin provides are materially and emotionally superior to the workhouse or the undertaker's, Oliver's earlier places of habitation. The boys are reasonably happy with him. There are many examples of the boys' affection for Fagin. For example, in "Be Back Soon," they sing without apparent irony (other than the obvious situational irony), "How could we forget / How could we let / Our dear old Fagin worry / We love him so / We'll come back home / In, oh, such a great big hurry."

Even Oliver is happy during his first stay at the Thieves' Kitchen. He is unhappy there only later, when abducted by Bill Sikes and Nancy, and forcibly returned. In the musical, the haven that Fagin offers Oliver is surpassed solely by Mr. Brownlow's home. Yet Mr. Brownlow's world includes no leading role in this play, not even Mr. Brownlow himself, now Oliver's grandfather. In fact, Oliver's care is primarily in the hands of the kindly—but paid—housekeeper, Mrs. Bedwin, no more a blood relation than Fagin. The set indicates Mr. Brownlow's home primarily by putting Oliver's bed onstage. This comfortable bed—complete with mattress, pillows, sheets, comforter—indicates the upper-middle-class environment of his new circumstances, in great contrast to his meager sleeping arrangements in the Thieves' Kitchen and the miserable quarters at the undertaker's, where he slept under the counter or among the coffins. At Mr. Brownlow's, the bed he wins stands in for Mrs. Bedwin, as plump as clean and nearly as featureless as the bedding, the only mother figure the musical gives Oliver in the end. Mr. Brownlow and Mrs. Bedwin have no complete songs of their own, a sure sign in a musical that they are minor characters, merely a plot device to provide a suitable resolution to the story. Neither is as fun as Fagin.

There is also a sense in which Fagin's appeal in the musical is that his playfulness is akin to childishness. This is certainly the view of the actor Rowan Atkinson:

> I was very keen that there should be genuine warmth between Fagin and his . . . gang, that connection because my interpretation—and it's only mine—of the character of Fagin is that he is, essentially, a child; . . . I mean . . . he feels happiest is with his guys, and it helps that they're very useful to him. And, one mustn't forget that he's a highly criminal and an avaricious individual. . . . , and yet he has a very happy subterranean existence, with his little people scuttling around at his behest. So, it's that connection with the children that I've been very keen to nur-

ture and to present, and a lot of people who have seen it have said that there is a—more, I would say, maybe even than Ron Moody was, who was still a very user-friendly character, but I never sensed any great connection between him and the children. They were just useful to him. But he didn't really need them on any social or emotive level. Whereas I think that is quite an interesting thing, because I think that Fagin does and I've tried to convey that. (Atkinson interview with author, July 10, 2009)

As Atkinson points out, the childlike playfulness available for performance in the musical's Fagin explains how Bart can retell much of the story of *Oliver Twist* without reinscribing the anti-Semitism so fully ingrained in the novel. The scheming villain of the novel is never childlike, not when he entertains children and certainly not when he obsesses with miserly and murderous glee over his treasure box.

Like Dickens, Bart had a gift for depicting the plight of children. There may be biographical reasons for this. We have seen that Bart came from a large family in which only seven of eleven children lived to adulthood. He experienced the blitz as a child in London and was among those evacuated. It is also possible to interpret *Oliver!* quite plausibly as dealing with the loneliness of the closeted homosexual. "Where Is Love?" and "As Long as He Needs Me" have special resonance along those lines, in terms of Bart's biography, since he only came out as gay in the 1990s. But the real force of the pain and the palpable experience in the musical is the hunger and poverty combined with the nevertheless childlike playfulness of the kids. Atkinson points out that Fagin is the biggest kid, in a way. He plays with his treasures in a manner more childlike than miserly; he's afraid of the bully Sikes; he has no romantic interest in anyone.

The difference in endings between the novel and stage musical highlights how the musical changes Fagin through performance. In its penultimate chapter, the novel depicts Fagin's last night in the jail cell before his hanging, notable for its sympathy in expressing the horror of a man in Fagin's position, which suggests that Dickens sees Fagin as a human being rather than the devil his earlier imagery invokes. It is also the moment in which the novel makes clear that some Jews are moral; when pious Jews come to Fagin to pray with him and offer consolation, he just "beats them off" with curses (353). Nevertheless, as is fitting for a novel named *Oliver Twist,* the final chapter focuses not on Fagin but on Oliver, in his pastoral life with Brownlow and the Maylies, closing with an image of the memorial plaque to Oliver's mother, weak and erring. In the stage play, however, the final scene of dramatic action is a reprise of Fagin singing "Reviewing the Situation." He knows the game is up and the authorities are on their way. He has just lost his beloved treasure box,[23] and, singing that change is possible, determines to turn over a new leaf. He goes off alone into the sunrise, silhouetted with his back to the audience, wearing his broad-brimmed hat and gabardine coat, as a figure strongly reminiscent of the Wandering Jew. In the 2009 London revival, he even plays a fiddle as he goes off, slamming us with the iconography of *Fiddler on the Roof*. Focusing the end of the dramatic action solely on Fagin reemphasizes him as the musical's lead character. This is equally emphatic in the movie musical: Fagin starts off down the dank alleyway, but the Artful Dodger joins him, carrying a stolen wallet, which he displays to his mentor with pride. It is clear that the two scamps will continue their lives of petty crime in happy harmony. By concluding the stage and screen versions of *Oliver!* with Fagin unharmed, a Wandering Jew instead of cringing in his cell on "The Jew's Last Night Alive," as Dickens first entitled the chapter in *Oliver Twist*, Bart invokes another medieval and often anti-Semitic image. But this one that had been used more sympathetically in later popular Victorian melodrama than the Fagin-like stage Jew, which still abounded throughout the nineteenth and into the mid-twentieth century. But *The Bells* (1871) and *The Wandering Jew* (1873) by Leopold Lewis portray peripatetic Jews in a restrained but noticeable amelioration of the stage Jew caricature that Bart appropriates and remakes for his rascally but redeemable Fagin.

Although the story ends there, the show does not. The play's finale brings everyone back onstage to perform three reprises: "Food, Glorious Food," "Pick a Pocket or Two," and "Consider Yourself" with Oliver and Company. All the performers, including Fagin, return to the stage to sing and dance together. The London 2009 revival production goes even farther from the novel's leaving Fagin to hang at Newgate, presenting choreography that Judaizes the entire cast, with folk-dance steps in the reprised "Pick a Pocket or Two" again redolent of *Fiddler on the Roof*.

Collapsing Rose and Nancy, the musical *Oliver!* funnels both women's fidelity and self-sacrifice into the morally ambiguous Nancy, who—in both novel and musical play—betrays Oliver before she saves him. Nancy's subsequent heroic response to the child Oliver's need, combined with stalwart loyalty to her man, glorifies the Dickensian feminine ideal of woman's "original nature" (266). Yet the musical does not relocate Rose's capacity to bring domestic happiness to others in Nancy or even retain Nancy's own growing capacity to nurture, as depicted in the novel. In an ironic turn, that task belongs to the musical's Fagin, who becomes a scamp instead of a villain, but one whose genuine affection for his charges corresponds to his ability to provide hearth, housing, and nourishment in the only home established by a lead character. Ultimately it is Fagin, not Nancy, who twists the notion of an Angel in the House; in a sense, he is the original fallen angel, the "merry old gentleman" himself.

The musical, although named *Oliver!,* ends with Fagin, either alone, wandering safely into the sunrise, or leading the entire cast in song and dance. Still Jewish but no longer "the Jew," he throws off the anti-Semitic caricature and integrates more fully into his class; audiences who have seen and heard Bart's Fagin read Dickens's Fagin with new eyes. Often the most entertaining performer in any good production, even more than Nancy (who should always be a showstopper), Fagin gets the last word, the last laugh, and always the last bow. Frequently played by a marquee-named comedian, the anti-angel Fagin fills the theater with happiness, the producers' pockets with cash, and usually brings down the house.

4

Dickens, Cultural Anxiety, and Victorianness in *Sweeney Todd*

In this chapter, I take up Stephen Sondheim's musical *Sweeney Todd: The Demon Barber of Fleet Street*.[1] This award-winning show evolved from the now virtually forgotten serial tale of terror *The String of Pearls* (1846–47), published anonymously on eighteen Sundays in the penny weekly *The People's Periodical and Family Library*. The story filled narrow columns alongside light anecdotes, thrilling travel sketches, and recipes for rat poison. It is a Newgate novel—that is, a novel based on the career of a criminal likely to go to Newgate Prison and be executed—like William Harrison Ainsworth's *Jack Sheppard* (1839) or Dickens's *Oliver Twist*. In fact, *The String of Pearls* includes many characters and plot elements imitating Dickens. Unlike Dickens's novels, neither its comedy nor its depiction of villainy offers significant social criticism. Yet Sondheim's masterpiece does.

Partly by way of the musical's book by Hugh Wheeler and its hefty debt to Christopher Bond's melodrama *Sweeney Todd: The Demon Barber of Fleet Street* (1973), a nonmusical re-dramatization of the story that Sondheim saw and admired in London, Sondheim's musical adaptation reinserts the kind of critique that viewers associate with Dickens. In all versions before Bond's, Todd is pure villain, a mercenary brute. By inserting a tragic motive for revenge, Bond added a large measure of social protest into a story that had none. Because of this sympathy, Sweeney Todd's rise and fall—even after he has become a mass murderer—takes on the grandeur of tragedy, allowing Sondheim's extraordinary music to enter opera repertoire.[2] The musical also reinstates specific aspects of the novel that stem from Dickens but dropped out of earlier adaptations. In bringing the Victorian tale to current audiences, Sondheim and Wheeler make it seem more Victorian for us by making it seem more Dickensian.

Theater critics reviewing *Sweeney Todd* typically refer to it as "Dickensian" without describing what that word means. Examples from reviews of twenty-first-century British and American productions include *Sweeney Todd*'s "Dickensian-laden revolving stage" (Dunnett) and the "perverse Dickensian cartoons" (McNulty).[3] Newspapers identified Dickensian qualities even more vehemently with the original Broadway opening: the *New York Times* remembers the "Dickensian social framework" from Harold Prince's 1979 production that it does not observe in Richard Doyle's 2005 revival (Brantley); likewise *Newsday* recalls the "vast Dickensian epic" from 1979 (Winer, "Smaller Bite"). Reviews of the Burton film also recognize Dickens in *Sweeney Todd*. According to the *Minneapolis Star-Tribune,* Timothy Spall, who plays Beadle Bamford, comes "straight out of a Dickens illustration" (Covert). The *New York Times* likens Burton's London to the set in the movie musical *Oliver!* (A. O. Scott).

While all these reviews agree that there is *something* Dickensian about *Sweeney Todd,* none explains precisely what characteristics they mean to invoke by that term.[4] I argue that it is from Dickens—and adaptations of Dickens—that Sondheim inherits the characteristics that audiences read as Victorian. When I asked Sondheim what he pictures or hears when he thinks of Victorian literature and culture; he answered "Dickens": both his books and the movies made from them (personal interview). The musical *Sweeney Todd* incorporates several elements from Dickens rather than from more obvious sources that also influence the show, such as Kurt Weill and Bertolt Brecht's *The Threepenny Opera* or even from the actual Victorian pulp novel from which *Sweeney Todd* sprang.[5] In fact, Sondheim and Wheeler (and Bond before them) magnify the Victorianness of the musical based on a Victorian work *not* by faithfully following the original—which was set in eighteenth-century London—but instead by inserting details, characters, themes, and a setting drawn largely from Dickens's *Oliver Twist* or, perhaps more significantly, from the musical adaptation *Oliver!*

In the four sections that make up this chapter, I trace three parallel sets of relationships among the novel *The String of Pearls,* the works of Dickens, and Sondheim's *Sweeney Todd* as well as the musical's cultural work on stage and screen. First, I demonstrate the debt of *The String of Pearls* to Dickens's novels; second, what *Sweeney Todd* owes to Dickens directly or through adaptations, such as *Oliver!*, even though *The String of Pearls* (already an imitation of Dickens) leaves them out. Third, I consider how Sondheim's musical confronts the exposure of our consumer vulnerability in two situations involving market networks: as customers submitting voluntarily to the barber's blade and as customers of ready-made food. In both cases we must trust strangers, and we have no control over what they may do to us. A fourth section addresses the Doyle stage productions in London (2004) and New York (2005) and Burton's 2007 film to explore what twenty-first-century conditions resonate with the success of a major *Sweeney Todd* stage revival on both sides of the Atlantic and the movie musical's playing in cinemas around the world.

DICKENS IN *THE STRING OF PEARLS*

While Sondheim's *Sweeney Todd* boasts many fervent fans and a considerable body of study by musical theater scholars,[6] very few people have read or even know of the novel that is the musical's earliest source, *The String of Pearls*, despite Oxford University Press publishing a 2007 paperback edition with Johnny Depp's photo on the cover. This obscurity is partly because Bond's 1973 melodrama, not an earlier version, moved Sondheim to write the musical. Hugh Wheeler's book follows Bond's play very closely, and at times Sondheim musicalizes Bond's dialogue verbatim.[7] Nevertheless, the story originated long before Bond, Wheeler, or Sondheim got involved. The author of *The String of Pearls* is often misidentified as George Dibdin Pitt,[8] who did in fact first adapt it for the melodrama stage in 1847, just before the concluding installment of the novel appeared in print (as commonly occurred with many Victorian novels, including, as we have seen, *Oliver Twist*). The reason for this misattribution is likely because in 1883, when Dibdin Pitt's melodrama *Sweeney Todd* was finally published as no. 499 in Dick's Standard Plays, the incorrect year of 1842 (instead of 1847) was printed for its first performance. The novel was probably written in part by Thomas Peckett Prest. The alcoholic Prest often wrote for Edward Lloyd, a successful publishing entrepreneur who created inexpensive Salisbury Square periodicals for the working class, not only the *People's Periodical and Family Library* but also the *Penny Sunday Times and People's Police Gazette* and *Lloyd's Weekly Newspaper* (Law 21).[9] Additional contenders for the novel's debated authorship are other Lloyd authors: James Malcolm Rymer (recent scholarship renders him the most likely suspect for the majority of the tale), George Macfarren, Lloyd himself, or a combination, with one of them beginning it and others continuing or expanding.[10] Because Prest has been traditionally (mis)identified as the sole author and because no critical consensus yet exists regarding how much of the novel was written by whom, I have for convenience in this chapter attributed *The String of Pearls* to Prest, whenever syntax makes avoiding the name of an author awkward.

The prolific Prest spent much of his career copying Dickens, who by 1846 had already written *Pickwick Papers* (1836–37), *Oliver Twist* (1837–39), and *Nicholas Nickleby* (1838–39), writing under the pen name "Boz." Prest imitated Dickens so blatantly that he published under the name of "Bos." Novels attributed to Prest include *The Penny Pickwick* (1837), *Oliver Twiss* (1838), and *Nickelas Nicklebery* (1839). Although *The String of Pearls* does not pirate Dickens outright, it imitates some identifiable characteristics of Dickens's writing—such as outrageous characters, Pickwickian humor, and most obviously, a sensational Newgate plot. The novelist I am calling "Prest" deftly regurgitated Dickensian characters, plots, and titles, but crucially left out Dickens's powerful social critique. In contrast, Sondheim's musical emphasizes Dickensian concern for reform. Sharp class and cultural criticism in Sondheim's musical rendering of *The String of Pearls* results in a kind of re-Dickensing of it. In other words, Sondheim provides a version of Sweeney Todd that is more Boz than Bos.

No matter what its provenance or literary merit, *The String of Pearls* spawned over a century and a half of wildly popular adaptation and, even for this reason alone, merits investigation.[11] It has been made into at least four films, two TV movies, radio plays, and a ballet. The British actor Tod Slaughter (a serendipitous name) was able to perform the role of Todd in a version of Pitt's stage melodrama over 4,000 times by the time he died in 1956.[12] Also in 1956, the comedian Stanley Holloway (perhaps best known for the role of Eliza Doolittle's father in *My Fair Lady,* both on Broadway and film) recorded the comic music-hall favorite "Sweeney Todd: The Barber."[13] The main character is so famous that Sweeney Todd hair salons flourish in cities across the world.[14] The myth of Sweeney Todd is so powerful that many people claim in print that the story was based on a factual case of murder and cannibalism, despite the fact that there is no evidence of this—at least, not on Fleet Street, not in London.[15] While the playbill for Dibdin Pitt's stage melodrama claims the drama is "based in truth," the novel is subtitled "A Romance," underscoring its status as fiction. Sondheim renews the emphasis on fictionality by subtitling his show "A Musical Thriller."[16]

The novel *The String of Pearls* is so little known as to warrant three paragraphs of summary. Readers who are well acquainted with Sondheim's musical will see the points of similarity and difference. This summary smooths over the novel's nonessential comic subplot, randomly interposed stories, dropped plot lines, and rushed ending, but it gives a sense of the book's solidly entertaining (if wildly sensational) narrative. In the novel's opening chapter, the barber Sweeney Todd murders a customer, the sailor Mr. Thornhill, for a valuable string of pearls. Thornhill had stopped for a shave on his way to deliver the necklace to the beautiful Johanna Oakley. They were a gift from her beloved, Mark Ingestrie, presumed drowned at sea. Thornhill's friend Colonel Jeffrey decides to visit Johanna instead, not only to break the bad news about Mark's probable briny death but also to mention Thornhill's worrisome disappearance with her valuable gift. Tobias Ragg, Todd's apprentice, notices that Mr. Thornhill is suddenly missing from his master's barber chair. Tobias suspects foul play.

Meanwhile, a handsome and desperately poor young man takes a job baking meat pies for the lovely widow Mrs. Lovett, whose delicious pastries are famous throughout London and whose shop is around the corner from Todd's. The peculiar job requires the young baker to stay locked in the cellars below the bakeshop and never to ask where the meat comes from. Back at the barber's, Todd recognizes that his apprentice has become suspicious and claps him into Dr. Fogg's cruel insane asylum. Colonel Jeffrey goes to the magistrate and tells him of his friend Mr. Thornhill's having vanished, last seen at Todd's barbershop. A terrible stench wafts up from the cellars of St. Dunstan's church, which stands near Todd's and Mrs. Lovett's shops, causing an official inquiry, including a visit from the magistrate whom Colonel Jeffrey had consulted earlier. In the meantime, the distraught but resourceful Johanna disguises herself as a boy and fills the now vacant position of Todd's apprentice to spy on the barber.

Mrs. Lovett's recently hired bake house chef grows restive in his incarceration, so Mrs. Lovett tells Todd that it's time to kill the inquisitive young man. Unknown to Mrs. Lovett, the good-looking fellow has already discovered an unspeakable secret about her meat locker. Back at Sweeney Todd's shop, the magistrate impersonates a customer as part of his investigation. Because Sweeney Todd tries to kill him instead of shave him, the magistrate knows the truth. His hidden officers seize Todd, relieving readers who are at this point worrying about Johanna's safety while she is dressed as an apprentice under Todd's control. At the same time, the brave young baker puts himself on the dumbwaiter used to carry pies from the basement bake house to the pie shop. When the next load of pies is supposed to come up, he jumps out of the dumbwaiter, crying to the hungry pie-lovers, "Mrs. Lovett's pies are made of *human flesh!*"[17] In the middle of being arrested by the magistrate, Mrs. Lovett dies of the poison Todd has secretly put in her brandy so that he won't have to split the proceeds from selling the string of pearls he stole from the sailor Thornfield. Johanna has come to the pie shop, too, brought there by the magistrate, the colonel, and the apprentice Toby—who had previously escaped the madhouse and told his story to the Law—so that she might be reunited with her long-lost love. Indeed, the attractive pastry cook is none other than Mark Ingestrie, thought drowned at sea. They embrace. Todd is executed at Newgate Prison.

The parallels between Prest's Todd and Dickens's Fagin, who both hang at Newgate, are among the most significant examples of Bos copying Boz in *The String of Pearls*. In *Oliver Twist*, Fagin has no family to avenge. We've seen in the previous chapter how the manipulative scoundrel Fagin of the novel modulates into the lovable rogue of the musical *Oliver!*, prompting us to recognize in the original those moments of tenderness and humanity that Lionel Bart has retained. But Dickens's Fagin is nevertheless a villain, and if Bart stresses hints of gentleness amidst the villainy, then Prest presses on the most villainous. One scene in which *The String of Pearls* imitates the Inimitable is the scene in which Todd imagines that his apprentice, Toby, has seen him kill a victim. The passage shows notable similarity to Fagin's discovering that Oliver has observed Fagin's treasure box. In *Oliver Twist*, Fagin,

> . . . laying his hand on a bread knife which was on the table, started furiously up. He trembled very much though; for, even in his terror, Oliver could see that the knife quivered in the air.
>
> "What's that?" said the Jew. "What do you watch me for? Why are you awake? What have you seen? Speak out, boy! Quick—quick! for your life!'
>
> "I wasn't able to sleep any longer, sir," replied Oliver, meekly. "I am very sorry if I have disturbed you, sir."
>
> "You were not awake an hour ago?" said the Jew, scowling fiercely on the boy.
>
> "No—no, indeed," replied Oliver.
>
> "Are you sure?" cried the Jew: with a still fiercer look than before: and a threatening attitude.

"Upon my word I was not, sir," replied Oliver, earnestly. "I was not, indeed, sir."

"Tush, tush, my dear!" said the Jew, abruptly resuming his old manner, and playing with the knife a little, before he laid it down; as if to induce the belief that he had caught it up, in mere sport. "Of course I know that, my dear. I only tried to frighten you. You're a brave boy. Ha! ha! you're a brave boy, Oliver!" The Jew rubbed his hands with a chuckle, but glanced uneasily at the box, notwithstanding. (67–68)

Prest borrows several elements from Dickens, intensifying the violence with physical contact between Todd and Toby:

In two strides Todd reached him, and clutching him by the arm he dragged him into the farthest corner of the shop, and then he stood opposite to him glaring in his face with such a demoniac expression that the boy was frightfully terrified.

"Speak!" cried Todd, "speak! And speak the truth, or your last hour is come! How long were you peeping through the door before you came in?"

"Peeping, sir?"

"Yes, peeping; don't repeat my words, but answer me at once, you will find it better for you in the end."

"I wasn't peeping, sir, at all."

Sweeney Todd drew a long breath as he then said, is a strange, shrieking sort of manner, which he intended, no doubt, should be jocose,—

"Well, well, very well; if you did peep, what then? It's no matter; I only wanted to know, that's all; it was quite a joke, wasn't it—quite funny, though rather odd, eh? Why don't you laugh, you dog? Come, now, there is no harm done. Tell me what you thought about it at once, and we will be merry over it—very merry." (7)

The String of Pearls imitates Dickens's characters and their relationships, dramatic situations, and dialogue. Even the name "Tobias Ragg" echoes "Oliver Twist" in syllable count. Todd's "demoniac expressions" recall the abundant devil imagery associated with Fagin, who is at once the "merry old gentleman" and a gliding, creeping, crawling "loathsome reptile" (66, 132). In both cases the criminal/protectors worry that the boys have observed evidence that could convict them. Both enjoin the boys to say what they have seen or risk losing their lives. Both then joke to control the damage of having revealed the intensity of their concern. Neither adult finally is sure he is safe from the boy's prying.

The fun in the novel's Todd springs not only from his being an excessively bad guy, but also from the borrowed quirkiness that we associate with Dickens's creations. Fagin's "villainous-looking and repulsive face" is "obscured by a quantity of matted red hair" (65), but Todd sports an even more outlandish coiffure. The narrator first describes the barber's "terrific head of hair" in one of the most memorable images from the novel: it had "the appearance of a thick-set hedge, in which a quantity of small wire had got entangled.... Sweeney kept all his combs in it—some people said his scissors likewise" (2). The irony of a barber with hair so wild, thick, and unkempt that he can store all his combs and scissors in it is funny enough, but the mad villain effect is heightened by Todd's evil laugh. In the first scene in which a customer is about to be—in what becomes Todd's favorite expression—"polished off,"[18] the unfortunate says,

> "What the devil noise was that?"
> "It was only me," said Sweeney Todd: "I laughed."
> "Laughed! Do you call that a laugh? I suppose you caught it off somebody who died of it." (5)

In addition to Todd's fearsome headdress and his hideous laugh, he has huge hands, mouth, feet, and even a squint. His physical grotesqueness may remind some readers of Quilp, the villain from Dickens's *The Old Curiosity Shop* (1840–41); in a classic ableist trope of bodily otherness figuring criminality, his disproportionate physique and alarming merriment magnify the effect of his villainy.

The novel restricts its lampooning to evangelical hypocrisy, schoolgirl sentimentality, and foolish fashion, rather than Dickens's reformist agenda exposing abuse of power or exploitation of poverty. It takes aim against feminine mawkishness when the heroine Johanna Oakley's friend Arabella Wilmot (whose excessively romantic name recalls Arabella Allen in *Pickwick*) bases all her actions and advice on silly novels. Johanna herself is almost equally sappy and extravagant in her romantic diction. For example, when she realizes that she will soon hear news of her lover, Mark, she says, "Joy, joy! He lives, he lives! Mark Ingestrie lives! Perchance, too, successful in his object, he returns to tell me that he can make me his, and that no obstacle can now interfere to frustrate our union. Time, time, float onwards on your fleetest pinions!" (34). Johanna's dialogue sounds ripe for the melodrama stage, begging for appropriately grand gestures. One may hear echoes of the actress Mrs. Crummles from *Nicholas Nickleby*, whose theatrical manner of speech in everyday discourse ("What mean you? ... Whence comes this altered tone?") spoofs the diction of melodrama just as her "tragic recoil" spoofs melodrama's gesture (596).

Like Dickens, *The String of Pearls* includes a subplot that pokes fun at women snookered by religious frauds. The Reverend Mr. Lupin wolfishly fascinates Johanna's mother, Mrs. Oakley. These characters prompt Robert Mack to conclude that the Oakleys are based on the Varden family in *Barnaby Rudge* (1841), a historical novel, set like *The String of Pearls* with action beginning around 1775. The parallels include a sneaky apprentice in both books, named Sim in Dickens and Sam in Prest. But *The String of Pearls* also reaches further back in Dickens's oeuvre. The mooching minister and his comic comeuppance in *The String of Pearls* seem blatantly borrowed from Sam Weller's father's revenge against the pineapple-rum-and-water-swilling "shepherd" in *The Pickwick Papers*.[19] Mr. Weller tackles the punch-loving preacher who had long been poaching off Sam's wife and her friends. In *The String of Pearls*, Big Ben (Mr. Oakley's bulky Beefeater cousin) physically chastises the hypocritical sponge and lassoes the gullible, fanatical Mrs. Oakley, dangling her unharmed but furious from a hook on the wall, to quell her attempts to protect the freeloader. Yet such imitation seems less to interrogate evangelical hypocrisy than to comically condone a misogynist rule by the paterfamilias.

Even the cannibal pie-maker of *The String of Pearls* has antecedents in Dickens, as Mack points out (Introduction xvii). Dickens writes of food made of human flesh, both in *The Pickwick Papers* (1837) and in *Martin Chuzzlewit* (1844). In Dickens, the problem simultaneously plays on the readers' anxiety about the dangers of urban society (where impersonal machines beyond our control grind one's meat) and on our readers' sense of superiority to the foolishness of country rubes who believe that they will be either poisoned or eaten in the city. In *Pickwick*, Sam Weller describes the sausage maker who is ground up by his own "patent-never-leavin'-off sassage steam-ingin" and discovered to have been eaten by his customers only by the bits of brass button "seasonin'" (407–8). In *Martin Chuzzlewit*, the kindly Tom Pinch expresses his concern that his friend John Westlock will worry he's "been made meat pies of, or some such horrible thing" because he has taken so long to return; the novel subsequently reassures the reader that Tom does not fall "into the dens of any of those preparers of cannibalistic pastry, who are represented in many standard country legends as doing a lively retail business in the Metropolis" (544). *The String of Pearls* comes hard on the heels of both these novels, but, other than a general sense that Mrs. Lovett's pies are just too delicious to be true, her pastries provide neither a warning against the brutality of the industrial revolution nor a razzing of a rural population for imagining cannibals in the metropolis.[20]

While Sally Ledger points out that Dickens's use of the aesthetics of melodrama serves the aesthetics of class protest in *Pickwick* and *Oliver Twist* (101), that process does not extend to *The String of Pearls*. No matter how many of Dickens's characters or plot elements *The String of Pearls* imitates, the social satire has no institutional or systemic object: no Workhouse like *Oliver Twist*, no Yorkshire schools like *Nicholas Nickleby*, no Chancery court like *Bleak House* (1852–53), and no Debtor's Prison like *Little Dorrit* (1855–57). Although we associate social criticism more strongly with Dickens's later novels, these critiques appear as early as *Pickwick*, which already includes scathing (if hilarious) indictments of the Marshalsea Prison and the legal system. The only candidate in *The String of Pearls* for a serious critique of social evil is Dr. Fogg (from whose madhouse the apprentice Toby escapes), who incarcerates and kills patients for a fee from their families. But this Gothic asylum seems less a protest than a plot device.

In *The String of Pearls*, most of Todd's victims, like himself, are small tradesmen, shopkeepers, farmers, and service providers. There is no immoral judge or deceitful beadle, as in the musical. Law and justice coincide: the criminal barber is caught by the brave and clever magistrate Sir Richard and his plucky officers, who serve the public faithfully and at personal risk. The heroine Johanna, her sailor boyfriend Mark, Toby the apprentice, and their friend the colonel help. Public health is ensured by Mrs. Lovett's exposure; order is restored by Todd's lawful arrest, trial, and punishment. This is not a radical aesthetic. Deriving from a novel that copied Dickens's fiction while cutting his efforts to strike a "sledge-hammer" blow for the poor (qtd. Schlicke 102), the musical reinstates explicit cultural commentary. There is some irony, however, in the fact that this costly middle-class, middlebrow amusement—a Broadway musical—criticizes class hierarchy and the mistreatment of the working man, while the original working-class entertainment of this "penny dreadful" novel does not.

MEET THE BEADLES: DICKENS AND *SWEENEY TODD*

"Times is hard. Times is hard," sings Mrs. Lovett to Todd, in a direct echo of the title of Dickens's novel *Hard Times* (1854), suggesting that, while Mrs.

Lovett arrives in some respects unchanged from novel to musical, in others, she is more Dickensian than Prestian (37).[21] Her name and occupation as cannibal pie-maker remain intact. But the comical character that Angela Lansbury originated on Broadway is a cheery, maternal, fast-talking, opportunistic, and lusty woman in her forties or fifties.[22] She convinces us that using the free meat from Todd's tonsorial parlor is merely practical business sense: "Waste not, want not," she says. In contrast, the novel's Mrs. Lovett is nubile, beautiful, aloof, and diabolic. The villainess from *The String of Pearls* imprisons and enslaves handsome young workmen, planning to have them murdered as soon as they figure out the business. Rather than seizing a fortuitous opportunity, she operates with icy premeditation. The novel describes her as "buxom, young, and good-looking," traits she uses to ensnare her hapless helpers (26). Still, if the unfortunate young men were more alert or less hungry (she entices them as much with the promise of all the pies they can eat as with her personal charms), the unlucky cooks would have noticed that "her smile was cold and uncomfortable, . . . the set smile of a ballet-dancer" (27).

While the novel's chilly femme fatale serves primarily as a monstrous vehicle for the story's cannibal horror, Sondheim's more complicated Mrs. Lovett pushes the murderous plot along through bourgeois aspirations for lace and a slightly singed harmonium. In her down-to-earth motherly manner, Mrs. Lovett even takes the orphaned Toby under her wing; she pities, feeds, and employs him to serve her customers in the pie shop, taking care that he continues without knowledge or access to the nefarious nature of the business. He is emphatically not Todd's apprentice, though he had previously worked for the barber Mr. Pirelli. Todd, Mrs. Lovett, and Toby live together, parodying the bourgeois family and cut-throat aspirations of upward mobility. Through their unorthodox entrepreneurship, Todd and Lovett provide new clothes and a comfortable living for all three. The used harmonium that appears in their parlor in act 2 stands as a particularly prominent reward for their successful entry to a state of financial security through a seemingly respectable business.[23] Mrs. Lovett as a middle-aged, middle-class anti-mother recalls the Widow Corney (later Mrs. Bumble) from both *Oliver Twist* and *Oliver!* more than Prest's cold dominatrix. The musical Mrs. Lovett shares with her Dickensian predecessor a coy courtship (in *Oliver!* this takes place during the song "I Shall Scream"), considerable spousal manipulation, a relationship based on a combination of lust and avarice, and hypocritical misuse of their maternal roles vis-à-vis the boys

Tobias Ragg and Oliver Twist, surely the ur-orphan here. I stress the debt of Sondheim's musical to Lionel Bart's musical *Oliver!* over the debt to Dickens's novel because, for the 1979 Broadway audience, Mrs. Bumble already exists as a stage type—middle-aged, disingenuously maternal, very materialistic, somewhat plump, and vocalizing—so that her appearance in *Sweeney Todd* seems more Victorian to a theatergoing audience than would the fiendish, tantalizing ice queen of *The String of Pearls*.

But the mock happy bourgeois family that Todd, Lovett, and Toby compose goes sour by the end of the Sondheim play in a way that is neither Prestian nor Dickensian. Toby wants to protect his "mother" from his "father," whom he perceives as a violent danger to the complacent Mrs. Lovett, whom he wants for himself. All this is managed in the song "Not While I'm Around," at first a tender sort of declaration by Toby that he will always protect his adoptive mother. Once it becomes clear that he means to protect her from Todd, the tender way in which the simple-minded adolescent has been resting his head on Mrs. Lovett's bosom seems inflected not only with the reasonable suspicions that the plot provides, but also with some obvious Oedipal desires to replace the father, whose relations with the mother, according to Freud, appear to a witnessing child as violence. In this case, however, Todd will indeed kill Mrs. Lovett, once he realizes that she has deceived him about the fate of his wife, Lucy. Mrs. Lovett's silence about Lucy's identity inadvertently helps to cause the madwoman's death, since Todd kills the anonymous mad beggar woman—who turns out to be his wife—just to rid himself of an inconvenience hindering his opportunity finally to wreak vengeance on Judge Turpin. And Toby will fulfill the Oedipal fantasy by killing Todd in a deranged but belated effort to keep his beloved "mother" safe.

An antecedent hovering in cultural memory here is Bill Sikes's horrific murder of Nancy in both *Oliver Twist* and in the musical *Oliver!* As we have seen, the adaptation *Oliver!* eliminates *Oliver Twist*'s angelic Rose Maylie from the plot altogether, making Nancy the closest thing Oliver gets to a viable substitute mother (other than the feminized and domesticated scallywag Fagin). Magnifying this view of a maternal Nancy in *Oliver!* is the boy's singing "Where Is Love?" The context of this song (a lonely orphaned child forced to sleep among coffins) makes clear that Oliver really asks, "Where is my mother?" In "I'd Do Anything," Oliver expresses his devotion to Nancy. She genially teases Oliver and the Artful Dodger by singing a list of questions that test the limits of what they are willing to do for her, culminating with, "Even fight my Bill?" While the Artful Dodger artfully dodges the question with one of his own, "What, fisticuffs?," Oliver implies his readiness to defend her with childlike alacrity by singing that he'd do anything just for her smile.[24] However, unlike the adolescent Toby (generally played on professional stages by an adult), Oliver is only a nine-year-old in both the novel and the musical. He can't do anything at all to protect Nancy, and—properly repressing any Oedipal urge—certainly can't kill Sikes.

Another strong example of how the show *Sweeney Todd* inserts or alters familiar characters from Dickens to establish itself as a Victorian tale of class struggle in Dickensian terms is Beadle Bamford, who is imported straight out of *Oliver Twist*, or maybe just *Oliver!* The beadle barely exists in the novel *The String of Pearls*. A very minor unnamed character, he is a self-important functionary attached to St. Dunstan's church who enters the story during the investigation into the stink wafting up from the ecclesiastical cellars, which happen to be adjacent to Mrs. Lovett's basement. *Oliver Twist*'s beadle, Mr. Bumble, is a much more important character. Recurring through most of the novel, he reports Oliver to the parish board for requesting "more" and then dispatches the lad to Mr. Sowerby, the undertaker. He marries the Widow Corney for her "six teaspoons, a pair of sugar-tongs, and a milk-pot" (240). Later, when his misdeeds and those of Mrs. Bumble are discovered, before he is sent to his own poorhouse, he utters the novel's famous assessment of the British legal system, "The law is a ass" (347). His presence emphasizes a vision of a Victorian world in which petty officials keep other people in their places and puff their own minimal importance. He carries out the edicts of an unjust system, and he does so cherishing his perks and his authority over the powerless.

Likewise, Sondheim's sycophantic beadle enjoys lording it over the poor. But the evil of Sondheim's beadle far exceeds that of Dickens's or Lionel Bart's. Sondheim's beadle salaciously enjoys advising and abetting the corrupt and perverse Judge Turpin. He physically threatens Johanna's beau and wrings her pet bird's neck. He directly assists the judge in raping Lucy. From *Oliver!* to *Sweeney Todd,* the beadle's shift from bumbling to brutal intensifies Sondheim's bitter indictment of law, no longer merely the "ass" we have seen in Dickens but the catalyst for unspeakable carnage. The show *Oliver!* gives the beadle a solo and a duet, making it a proportionally larger role than *Sweeney Todd*'s beadle, who has a duet and a trio. But the fact that *Sweeney Todd* includes a beadle at all—let alone as a prominent character when the original story had none of significance—is remarkable.

Again, our sense of Victorian culture is so influenced by Dickens, and by adaptations of Dickens, that a musical version of a Victorian novel requires a large singing beadle.

Sondheim's characters of the appropriately named optimistic young hero, Anthony Hope (the Mark Ingestrie figure in the novel), and heroine, Johanna, owe more to the tradition of stage melodrama than to either Dickens or the novel *The String of Pearls*. The Victorian stock theater companies needed roles for both a young and a middle-aged couple to keep their actors employed. In the novel, Mark does little but mope anonymously in Mrs. Lovett's basement and provide a love interest for Johanna. In the musical, he moves the plot along, sings gorgeously, and provides the rivalry that spurs the judge first to plan his marriage to Johanna and then to execute her imprisonment in Dr. Fogg's insane asylum. But ultimately, he is a passive hero, much like Scott's Edward Waverly. He even cannot go through with shooting the dastardly Dr. Fogg to effect his beloved's escape. That task falls to Johanna, who catches Anthony's pistol and, by shooting the wicked doctor, saves them both. This plot twist suggests two things. First, Sondheim's Johanna is not merely the caged bird locked in her room that her frantic song in act 1, "Green Finch and Linnet Bird," highlights, making the same comparison between woman and caged bird that Victorian literature and art often made.[25] Johanna also reveals herself to be a feisty heroine whose forceful action feminizes the hero. Second, like father, like daughter: whereas the noble Anthony is incapable of killing, Todd's daughter has no problem blowing away her captor.[26]

MEAT OF THE MATTER

On March 1, 1979, when Sondheim's *Sweeney Todd* opened at the Uris Theater, Broadway audiences were faced with many reasons to distrust the nation's major social institutions. The war in Vietnam was a recent memory, kept fresh in everyone's mind as turmoil in that region continued throughout the decade. Still current was the 1970 shooting of unarmed American college students by the Ohio National Guard at Kent State, with a wrongful death suit in 1975, protests in 1977, a second trial in 1978, and a controversial out-of-court settlement on January 9, 1979. The 1973 and 1979 oil crises raised prices dramatically, causing hardship and lasting changes in the US economy. The Watergate scandal, which broke in 1972, did more perhaps than any other event to undermine Americans' trust in their government, leading to President Nixon's unprecedented resignation on August 9, 1974. *Sweeney Todd*'s social critique resonated with a population still angry and cynical, with yet more worries in 1979 to propel a sense of despair and outrage against the nation's leadership: on March 28, the Three Mile Island nuclear power plant released radiation; on January 16, 1979, the shady US-backed Shah left Iran in a shambles, with the Ayatollah Khomeini assuming control a few weeks later and American hostages taken at the US embassy in Tehran on November 4. Such a cultural context seems a ripe milieu for a musical play about lashing out against the authority of a crooked, cruel, and morally bankrupt system of power. In addition to the loose parallels between the fictive world of Todd's oppression and the real worries confronting a 1979 American musical theater buff, the story chimes with two other current or remembered vulnerabilities—prepared food and a barber's shave—in which for convenience we voluntarily relinquish control over own health and safety.

By 1979, when the musical *Sweeney Todd* arrived, men no longer got professional shaves with any frequency. Part of the show's appeal both then and now is nostalgia for the thrill imagined in a public shave and haircut. In using a Victorian setting, when shaves were a commonplace service for every class in London and New York, the late twentieth-century musical allows us to relive the fear that surely must have crossed some audience members' minds, perhaps especially men, as they imagine or remember the routine of shaving or being shaved with a straight razor.[27] Now most men who shave close risk only a nick from a disposable blade or the tiny metal surfaces encased in a molded plastic razor, introduced by Bic in 1975 to immediate success (McKibben 98). In the musical *Sweeney Todd*, we see man after man exposing his throat trustingly to the barber who is about to slit it; but we know that few men now incur (or in 1979 incurred) any such imagined peril to enjoy the luxury of a barber's shave. Surely this wistful longing for a real barber, perhaps never personally experienced, makes watching Sondheim's *Sweeney Todd* different for audiences since 1979 than for the audience watching George Dibdin Pitt's melodrama in 1847, when getting shaved by a barber was an ordinary occurrence. The same is true for an 1885 reader of *The Tinted Venus*, in which (as we have seen) the goddess thinks the barber Tweddle threatens men's "bared throats with the gleaming knife" (89).

In the 1870s, decades after Dibdin Pitt's play premiered, a Sheffield steel manufacturer invented the safe hoe-shaped razor. The safety razor became popular in the US because King Gillette, who won his safety razor patent in 1904, got a contract with the American army in World War I, so that thereafter every American soldier was supplied with a razor. Beards interfere with gas masks, motivating the mass supply for GIs. In other words, the notion of the individual taking care of himself rather than depending on another to shave him becomes integral to his own and his nation's safety. Not only can no one else cut his throat, but also he can be ready to don his gas mask at a moment's notice. The arrival of American soldiers in Europe further disseminated the safety razor. During the sixty years that elapsed between World War I and the opening of *Sweeney Todd,* three generations had grown up with the safety razor. When the electric razor, patented by Jacob Schick in 1928, became a hit in the 1930s, it further reduced the barber's business so that by 1939, only about 10 percent of a typical New York barber's revenue would come from shaving, whereas it had been approximately 50 percent in 1898 (McKibben 18). While Tod Slaughter's audiences of the famous George King–directed film in 1936 would still have found the idea of a barber's shave ordinary, they were already living in a world in which a clean-shaven man had other options.

By 1976 Bic was able to count on the nostalgia for the straight-edge razor to encourage success of its television commercials pitting their new disposable shaver against Gillette's Track II safety razor. In the well-known ads, blindfolded customers enjoyed professional shaves using either the Bic or the Gillette product (as though a real barber would have used a plastic disposable razor!). The result of the shaving contest, Bic claimed, was that most customers could not tell the difference. Outraged, Gillette demanded that the ads be yanked unless Bic could prove its claims. In the musical *Sweeney Todd,* Todd regains his position on Fleet Street as a master barber by winning a public shaving contest against the mountebank barber Mr. Pirelli; the scene depends—like Bic's ads—on the mystique of perfection in a close shave by a barber who is "a proper artist with a knife" (37).

Another context helpful in understanding Sweeney Todd's significance in 1979 is the 1973 American beef boycott. A beef shortage occurred because a consortium of ranchers held cattle back from market to raise prices. Consumers revolted. In April of that year, housewives across the United States refused to buy meat because of its suddenly high cost; prices increased 8 percent from February 20 to March 20. Monroe Friedman describes the protests, widely covered in the press: "Women from Los Angeles to New York took to the streets with picket signs during the first week of April, leafleting supermarkets with meatless menus and urging shoppers to join the boycott. In Washington, D.C., consumer groups rallied at the White House where they delivered a 'Precious commodity'—a steak, which was brought to the rally in an armored truck" (78). Although instigated by economics, the beef boycott reinforced news about the unhealthiness of red meat. The seemingly ever-increasing popularity of books by Adele Davis (originally published in earlier decades, but revised and enlarged in the 1970s) and others promoted nutritious foods and decried the disastrous health effects of American beef, part of what Davis described as the "slow murder" that "begins in the kitchen" (Howard 68).[28] Health food stores then opened even in shopping malls, and farmers markets proliferated in American cities. The International Federation of Organic Agriculture Movements formed in 1972. Ralph Nader awakened consumer rights advocacy, in the purview of housewives, who were America's expert domestic purchasers. The beef boycott also resulted from the convergence of a new consumer consciousness with the women's liberation movement. An important aspect of second-wave feminism involved encouraging women who worked inside the home to develop the idea of collective action (Friedman 78–79).

Anger over the high price of meat resonates in *Sweeney Todd*'s lyrics. Mrs. Lovett's lines in "The Worst Pies in London" describe her "nothing but crusting" pies before she and Mr. Todd begin their gruesome collaboration: "And no wonder with the price of meat / What it is . . . / When you get it . . . / Never" (35–36). When Mrs. Lovett thinks up the scheme of disposing of Todd's first victim, she reiterates that language in a reprise: "Seems an awful waste / . . . I mean, / With the price of meat what it is, / When you get it, / If you get it" (104). Todd's appreciative response is full of double-entendres regarding beef, even punning on USDA official grades such as "choice" and "prime," terms that go back at least to 1902 and were codified by federal law in 1939, and states of doneness, such as "well done" and "rare" (Harris): "How delectable! / Also undetectable. / How choice! / How rare!" (105). The annoyingly high price of beef would have been a recent memory (high food prices remained a popular focus of magazine articles throughout the 1970s), bringing a topical piquancy to the lines quoted above (Hansen 192–93).

Another ironic connection to the importance of meat can be traced beyond the 1970s to the success of the 1984 Wendy's commercial striking out against the corporate behemoth McDonalds, coded as Big Bun Burgers. In this famous ad, octogenarian actress Clara Peller reacts to a minuscule burger on an enormous bun with the instant pop culture classic line,

"Where's the beef?" That commercial relies not only on a demand for high-quality meat but also on a demand for truth and sincerity, on a rejection of hypocrisy, fakery, and filler. The humor and the power of Peller's question arose partly from the contrast between her tiny stature and her rough, old-woman voice, and partly from the idea that a frail, elderly lady—rather than perhaps a strapping young male athlete—would insist on more or better meat. But underneath all this is the notion that it's our old women who have the common sense and the guts to stop foolishness, to demand what's fair, to expose hypocrisy, to show us the truth.

Sweeney Todd includes an old lady figure in the crazy Old Beggar Woman. Todd's beautiful young wife, Lucy, took poison to kill herself after Judge Turpin raped her, the same judge who sent Todd to Australia to get him out of the way.[29] In the intervening years before Todd's return to London, Lucy did not die as Todd thinks, but went mad (and aged quickly from life on the streets). Her matted, grizzled hair, her cackling voice, her hunched posture, and her bad hygiene—not to mention her madness—all make her look older than she is and unrecognizable to her husband. She disgusts the men to whom she continually offers herself, lifting her skirts and singing obscene ditties about her muff, which she inventively also calls her "squiff," "bush," "parsley," and "crumpet." But she is the voice of truth, nonetheless, fulfilling the role of the wise fool. Early in the show in the song "The Barber and His Wife," Mrs. Lovett foreshadows Lucy's taking on this function by explicitly calling her a "poor fool" (38). As the mad beggar woman, Lucy tells the world that Mrs. Lovett is up to no good, singing out when she suspects Mrs. Lovett is burning bones that there's a "city on fire," and labeling Mrs. Lovett a witch (156); that is proven metaphorically when, in the final scene, Sweeney Todd dances Mrs. Lovett into the hot oven and slams the door, à la Hansel and Gretel, to revenge himself for Mrs. Lovett's part in Lucy's misery and ultimate death by his own hand. Even though chronologically she must be only middle-aged, like Todd, Lucy is the truth-telling old lady, exposing evil and hypocrisy.[30]

The themes of *Sweeney Todd*, which premiered five years earlier than the Wendy's commercial and ran for a year a half on Broadway before touring, fit neatly with the commercial, although I am not suggesting any influence. My point is a confluence of concerns: Mrs. Lovett's meatless pies are dreadful, and her rival's feline-filled pies are not much better. Yet anyone would prefer even the loathsome pussy pastries sold by Mrs. Lovett's neighboring tart-maker to the delicious pies Mrs. Lovett serves up by the second act, once they know what's in them. The anxiety this aspect of the plot creates in the audience stands in for knowledge that the powerful in the musical play—Judge Turpin, Dr. Fogg, the ruling class—deceive as well as devour their fellow citizens: in other words, just as we worry about the quality of meat we trustingly receive and are convinced to want through advertising, so ought we to be worrying about the quality of truth in government and other institutions made fun of in Todd and Lovett's song "A Little Priest." This song is the musical's most explicit statement that Sweeney Todd's actions further class warfare; he turns the tables so that although "The history of the world . . . / Is those below serving those up above," now "those above will serve those down below" (108). The idea that consumer advocacy can resonate with class conflict—the little guy against the corporate giant—is clear in that Wendy's, a very large company, successfully trades on the perception that they are dominated by the megacorporation McDonald's.

DOYLE, DEPP, AND DEBASEMENT

Although it won eight Tony awards, including best musical, *Sweeney Todd* ended its first Broadway run of 577 performances in the red. Despite that initial financial disappointment on the Great White Way, the show has been often performed by theaters nationally and internationally and by opera companies (first the Houston Grand Opera/New York City Opera production in 1984) and saw a four-month Broadway revival at Circle in the Square in 1989. A string of highly touted concert versions, beginning in 2000 at Lincoln Center in New York as a celebration for Sondheim's seventieth birthday, ran in major cities in America and in London. The successes of these concerts paved the way for Doyle's innovative productions. More revivals have followed, including the 2017 off-Broadway hit in which the theater was set up as a pie shop, with audiences eating real (and reputedly delicious) meat pies during the show.[31]

The most obvious difference between the Doyle production and the original is that the actors are also the orchestra. For example, in both New York and London, the actress playing the ingénue Johanna simultaneously sang, acted, and played the cello. The audience reacts with fascination to the astonishingly varied capabilities of the performers. The effect emphasizes the Brechtian aspects of the play over the Dickensian by alienating the audience from the melodramatic action as they marvel at the performer's virtuosity and at the sheer talent of the multiply gifted cast. Rarely do the actor-instrumentalists face one another in this production, not even in moments of dramatic intensity. One reason is simply logistical: they need to see the conductor to play their instruments together. As a result, they seldom appear to interact onstage, abandoning fourth wall realism. Although the production is fully staged, it undermines theatrical expectations that characters generally look at one another when conversing. When actors focus their attention on each other, they create a dramatic connection that the audience recognizes. In contrast, Johanna sits and plays her cello concert-style (which has nothing to do with the storyline) while singing her heart out about plot developments. This concentrates audience attention on the performances *as* performances rather than as a seemingly transparent window into the story.

Other changes further de-emphasize the Dickensian/Victorian aspects of the drama, resulting in further dissociation from the action. They include the abandonment of Victorian costumes and set. In 1979, Harold Prince used the massive scaffolding from "actual nineteenth-century foundries shipped from Rhode Island" to emphasize "the soullessness of the industrial age" (Kantor 361–64), but Doyle shifts to a conceptual set composed primarily of a few chairs, a ladder/cupboard, and a coffin that doubles as the judge's bench. Gone are the slightly singed harmonium and any trappings of upward mobility. The steam whistle still blows when Sweeney kills someone, but reference to the factory as corollary murderer is gone.[32] None of the cast is costumed as a worker and there is no chorus: both changes subdue the play's overt depiction of class conflict. The effect is that even though the Doyle production follows Bertolt Brecht in alienating the audience from the story by focusing attention on the performers *qua* performers (since for Brecht, an audience should be moved to social action, not merely lulled into enjoyment by a bourgeois narrative experience), it results in less rather than more of a revolutionary response. The diluted representation of class issues coupled with the distraction from the emotional impact of the story means that viewers do not care as much about the injustice done to Todd as they do about the ability of the performers to act and sing while playing a difficult instrument.

Another difference between the 1979 and 2004/2005 productions is one that has direct relevance to the 2007 Tim Burton film, and that is an increased attention to the play's debt to the Grand Guignol tradition of bloody horror.[33] Doyle emphasizes this connection by representing the murder of each victim by a large bucket of blood being poured center stage into another bucket, as each new dead person puts on a bloody white lab coat and continues to sing and act. This production also invokes a kind of vampirism that the original production did not, with Todd's first appearing out of a coffin. The coffin remains onstage throughout; Toby kills Todd on top of it; Todd lies down in the coffin as he dies. The finale replicates the opening exactly, suggesting an eternal round of living death, topping off the vampire symbolism. The superabundance of blood anticipates Burton's cinematic effects to make the movie even bloodier, with streams of it flowing, spurting, gushing, smearing, spattering; it courses down gutters and splays across the screen.

Such adaptation to the medium of film is part of its aesthetic success, although not for the faint-hearted. The up-close visceral visuals of meat we know to be human churning out of a grinder can only be suggested onstage, just as the cockroaches onstage in Mrs. Lovett's unsanitary pie shop are mimed with a solid stomp rather than featured larger than life scuttling across the retina. Although this blood-drenched grotesquery comes from the French tradition of Grand Guignol, which began at the very end of the nineteenth century and flourished in the first half of the twentieth, it has both Victorian and Dickensian antecedents. Viewers have no trouble assimilating the Grand Guignol style to a Victorian milieu. Melodrama has roots in reaction to the guillotine of the French Revolution; likewise, an innocent victim's imminent danger of a grisly, sensational death—trapped in a burning building in Mrs. Henry Young's *Jessy Ashton; or, The Adventures of a Barmaid* (1862), tied to a railroad track in Augustin Daly's *Under the Gaslight* (1867), strapped to a log in a sawmill in Joseph Arthur's *Blue Jeans* (1890)—was stock-in-trade for Victorian melodramas and remains firmly associated with it (Daly 47–56). The horror of serial murderers can easily read as Victorian to audiences familiar with graphic accounts of Jack the Ripper and the fictions of *The Strange Case of Dr. Jekyll and Mr. Hyde*, *The Picture of Dorian Gray* (1890), and *Dracula* (1897). Certainly, Dickens has bloody moments, such as Sikes's gruesome murder of Nancy, with so much blood that the dog's paws track it around the room (317). Likewise, he provides scenes of horror: again, Sikes swinging above the angry crowd, having inadvertently hanged himself, "with the open knife clenched in his stiffening hand" while young Oliver, "thrusting aside the dangling body," calls for help (340).[34]

Although the successful crossover of Sondheim's *Sweeney Todd* from musical theater to opera might seem surprising for a gruesome show with such lowbrow origins,[35] the shift to the 2007 horror movie might seem even more so. Do slasher film fans overlap significantly with Broadway musical buffs? Previous musical horror films, such as *Rocky Horror Picture Show* (1975) and *Little Shop of Horrors* (1986), are campy send-ups that rely on ridiculing horror movie conventions.[36] But Burton's *Sweeney Todd* takes both its horror and its music very seriously, with the humor coming primarily from Sondheim's wit rather than campiness. While Sondheim's musical thriller has long appealed to both middlebrow musical theater and highbrow opera audiences, for the first time it also attracted much larger popular culture viewership through Burton's film. Because of Depp, fans of the *Pirates of the Caribbean* trilogy and his many other flicks flocked to it. In a sense, the movie musical returns to *The String of Pearls*'s original function as working-class entertainment, whether for the readership of Lloyd's *People's Periodical and Family Library* or for the East End audiences at the Britannia Theatre, Hoxton, where Dibdin Pitt's dramatization first played in 1847 (Richards 147). In addition, a Burton film starring Depp raises expectations about a certain kind of Gothic effect, macabre humor, and sex appeal, as well as excellent film-making. These expectations draw considerably younger crowds than would ever attend an opera, a concert at Lincoln Center, or a Broadway show, appealing to the same age demographics that read comic books and see Depp in *From Hell* (2001).[37]

Like the stage musical, the film also borrows Dickensian features to intensify its Victorianness. For example, Toby is a child, like Oliver, rather than the stage musical's adolescent. Dialogue added to the film indicates that Toby is from the Workhouse, an innovation for filmgoers who apparently expect that all Victorian orphans come from workhouses—like Oliver. In this respect, Burton's film recalls King's 1936 film, which goes so far as to interpolate a scene directly from *Oliver Twist* in which the beadle first brings parish boy Tobias as apprentice to Todd's shop.[38] One effect of Burton's Toby being a little boy is that when the angelic-looking child and the fetching Mrs. Lovett sing "Not While I'm Around," the Oedipal significance is largely muted, perhaps because an adolescent apprentice's singing with his head on Bonham-Carter's breast instead of Angela Lansbury's might look less like Freudian family dynamics and more like a potential ménage-à-trois. While Bonham-Carter's Mrs. Lovett recalls the attractive original from the novel *The String of Pearls* more than Mrs. Bumble, the film's Tobias Ragg resembles Oliver Twist more than ever.

If *Sweeney Todd* offered American audiences a vehicle to query issues facing them in the late 1970s and early 1980s, then what cultural work did

Burton's film and Doyle's revivals (which toured till 2008) do in the mid- to late 2000s? Anxiousness over tainted food supply remained strong, particularly regarding ground meat (so graphically depicted in Burton's film), as the March 2012 national outrage over "pink slime" demonstrates. News continually springs up about recalls of ground beef due to *E. coli* and—even more disconcertingly—about discoveries of mad cow disease. The United Kingdom suffered the most in terms of sick cattle (over a thousand) and humans affected, with up to 167 dead since the mid-1990s, according to the *Telegraph* (Devlin). But even the few cases of mad cow disease found in cattle in the United States caused widespread reaction and significant economic impact; for example, Japan, formerly the largest importer of US beef, twice banned American beef imports during the decade for fear of insufficient safeguards in the inspection system, first in 2003 and again in 2006. Films such as *Supersize Me* (2004) and *Fast Food Nation* (2006) expose, feed off, and foster these fears; *Sweeney Todd* speaks to such concerns as well. Even the Wendy's commercial resurfaced in the 2008 presidential primaries, with Hillary Clinton criticizing Barak Obama's slimmer record of public service by asking of his experience, "Where's the beef?,"[39] and it remains a perennial favorite for newspaper headlines and GIFs. Likewise, for American and British audiences, the theme of disillusionment in government had renewed meaning post 9/11, in a complex situation where people dread real dangers and yet distrust leaders who expose us to extended and far-flung armed conflict, often under false pretenses.

Resonating with this anxiety, the 2007 film ends even more bleakly than the 1979 play, focusing on the grisly demise of Todd as his blood streams over his dead wife, Lucy; the ending offers no glimpse of the fate of Johanna and her lover.[40] Although, like the stage play, the musical film punishes evil and hypocrisy in high places (and, like the novel, it punishes Todd's and Mrs. Lovett's serial murder), the film goes even further than the stage musical in eliminating melodrama's generic feature of restoring order. Although evil is punished, in no way does good appear to triumph. In the stage musical, the teenage Toby's surprise murder of Todd seems tragically appropriate—not only is justice served, and not only does he save his own life, but he avenges Mrs. Lovett (in whom he still believes) and becomes a man, albeit a demented one. But in the movie, depressingly and disturbing, we see the child Toby/Oliver fill this role, as though the incorruptible Oliver had finally yielded to the depraved influence of Fagin and Sikes. We have gone from *The String of Pearls,* in which the law properly upholds justice; to the stage musical, in which Todd wreaks his own terrible vengeance on the law and everyone else, with the ultimate result that the new generation will inherit a world rid of both the corrupt institutions and the vitiated avenger, Todd; to the film, in which, as a result of too-extravagant retribution, the young lovers become irrelevant and even the child is debased.

Without any direct allusion to specifics, Sondheim's depiction of Sweeney Todd taps into thrilling nostalgia for a barber's close shave and worry about an urban food supply. These concerns reflect the 1970s disgust with and distrust of the government generated by Vietnam and Watergate pervasive at the time of the musical's debut. Similar disillusionment may be a contributing factor in audience reception of the show's major revivals in 2004 and 2005 and Burton's film in 2007, when American audiences felt (and likely feel again) betrayed by governments that are inadequate or dishonest. The stock characters of Victorian melodrama join with a plot that indicts social institutions guilty of wantonly victimizing a helpless population. In addition, just as the musical's chorus of laborers responds mechanically to the shriek of a steam whistle that calls them to work as it simultaneously masks the cries of Todd's victims, so the reiterated murders become analogous to the alienating repetition of factory jobs. Finally, the lyrics of the "A Little Priest" suggest that Mrs. Lovett's scheme of meat pies only realizes and reverses the figurative cannibalism rampant in the capitalist social structure's mode of allowing the rich to feed off the poor. At the same time, in a modern urban industrial society with a division of labor, we are necessarily dependent on others for processing the food we eat. We subsist in a complex and fragile network tied both to exploitation and expediency, in which fast food burgers and disposable razors set the scene for imagining an even more dangerous Victorian world in which a slow, luxurious shave could cost you your life and in which meat pies are filled with something much worse than pink slime.

5
The Meta-*Mystery of Edwin Drood*

While Sondheim's *Sweeney Todd* comes by its Dickensian qualities both directly from the source's own imitations of Dickens and more obliquely from Broadway's Dickensian vision of Victorian culture, the 1985 Tony Award–winning Broadway musical *The Mystery of Edwin Drood* by Rupert Holmes is—like *Oliver!*—an adaptation of a novel by Dickens himself. The show is famous for its do-it-yourself denouement, in which the action stops and the audience votes for who has committed the murder of the title character, Edwin Drood, before the story resumes to play out the audience's will.[1] Though not everyone loves its self-reflexive campiness or central gimmick, it has succeeded both popularly and critically both in 1985 and in subsequent revivals and productions worldwide. Holmes wrote it at the encouragement of the New York Public Theater's legendary producer, Joseph Papp, a purveyor of high theatrical and intellectual standards. In addition to the music and lyrics, Holmes—like Lionel Bart, creator of *Oliver!*—wrote *Drood*'s book. As we have established earlier, authoring all three creative elements—music, lyrics, and book—is a striking accomplishment in the musical theater world because each requires a specialized skill and is most generally handled by different individuals. But Holmes, formally trained in musical composition at the Manhattan School of Music, did Bart one better by writing his own orchestrations as well, an even more uncommon and time-consuming feat. Not even Richard Rodgers did that; Robert Russell Bennett orchestrated *The King and I* and many of Rodgers's theatrical scores. Before *Drood*, Holmes already had a distinguished résumé. He had written and conducted for Barbra Streisand and had seen a half dozen of his songs make it to Billboard's pop charts. Nevertheless, he is still best known for his 1979 number one hit "Escape," aka "the Piña Colada song."

Like *Oliver Twist,* Holmes's source text, the unfinished novel *The Mystery of Edwin Drood* (1870), was written by Dickens; but whereas Bart had an entire novel to work with, Holmes dealt with a novel only half written when its author died in 1870 of a stroke. Adapters have been trying to finish *The Mystery of Edwin Drood* ever since. Thus, rather than using Bart's strategy of seeking to cut extraneous storylines, the challenge for Holmes was how to solve the mystery Dickens left hanging and finish the tale. In *Drood,* as the musical is often called informally, Holmes places Dickens's Edwin Drood plot as a performance inside a fictional Victorian music hall, the Music Hall Royale, complete with a jolly Master of Ceremonies who introduces performers and their play called *The Mystery of Edwin Drood.* The theater—even the front of house, meaning the auditorium and lobby—is decorated as though it were the Music Hall Royale. That means that the Broadway (or wherever) audience is in a sense performing a role as Victorian music hall audience; their stage set is the entire interior of the theater. Holmes's innovative solution to the mystery of how the novel might end is to let the Broadway audience (in their guise as fictional Victorian audience) decide by a vote conducted by the "music hall performers," who then resume their roles in the Edwin Drood story to finish the drama in the manner that the audience has dictated.

Dickens's novel is already musical-theatrical in that it employs music and gesture when language becomes insufficient for characters to converse. Musical theater is ideal for representing precisely such multiple modes of communication because it is a commonplace of the genre that when emotion becomes too strong for speech, you sing; when it becomes too strong for song, you dance.[2] As in Broadway musicals, so in the novel: music, movement, and spectacle reveal character and structure plot. They are integral to Dickens's storytelling. To illustrate how Holmes responds to and uncovers these elements in Dickens, I analyze two important moments in the novel and consider their rendering in the musical. The first is the episode in which John Jasper, the villain, plays the piano while Rosa Bud, the ingénue heroine, sings before a parlor audience. It is not only an inherently musical-theatrical incident, but also key to understanding the relationships among characters as they struggle for control of the music, themselves, and one another. The same moment occurs in an 1871 melodrama entitled *Lost,* adapted from *The*

Mystery of Edwin Drood by Walter Stephens, and in the corresponding scene in *Drood*. The second incident in the novel involves Jasper's famous opium dream in the novel's opening paragraph, which describes a visual and sonic experience more like the spectacle of a Victorian pantomime than like anything directly out of *Arabian Nights* (37), to which is it often compared.³ In the musical, the novel's first lines combine with Jasper's other opium dreams to become an opium dream ballet entitled "Jasper's Vision."

The musical's unique construction capitalizes not only on the novel's musicality but also on the narrative's unfinished state, interrogating conventions of the mystery genre and driving home how much the sense of an ending matters, particularly when the novel "ends" in the narrative middle. At once teaching about Dickens, the mystery genre, the Victorian theater, and literary-critical speculation about what Dickens might have written had he lived to finish the book, Holmes makes not only performers but also playwrights of the audience as they collaborate in creating a solution to the mystery. The novel's incompleteness permits the musical a self-reflexive negotiation for authority among the principals, in which Dickens, Holmes, the performers, and the audience as well as the characters all seem to participate, recalling the struggle between character in the crucial scene of Jasper and Rosa's performance. I conclude with *Drood*'s representations of Victorianness and the fluctuating power dynamic between author, adapter, actor, and audience.

A NOTE ON HISTORICAL CONTEXT

The 1970s and 1980s were a time of continued change and innovation in musical theater; "concept musicals" proliferated, building on and responding to what is often called the Golden Age of Broadway and its insistence on integration of dance and song into the plot. A concept musical is generally nonlinear, propelled less by plot and more by expressing a vision or concept. It is most often associated with Sondheim's shows, particularly *Company* (1970), in which the unmarried lead character Bobby turns thirty-five and his friends respond as they consider the nature of marriage and relationships; *Follies* (1971), about aging showgirls at a reunion as they remember their past performances in a revue; and *Assassins* (1990), analyzing the psyche of four men who assassinated US presidents. Although sometimes *Sweeney Todd* is also seen as a concept musical because of its thoughtful revamping of the seemingly old-fashioned form of melodrama, that very revivification of a form that is always plot-heavy to begin with complicates its classification as primarily conceptual. *A Chorus Line* (1975), also produced by Papp, is perhaps the best-known example of a concept musical, even employing the phrase "conceived by Michael Bennett" after its title; it explores the aspirations and fears of each finalist auditioning for a Broadway chorus line. Another is Andrew Lloyd Webber's *Cats* (1981 London, 1982 Broadway), based on the poems by T. S. Eliot from *Old Possum's Book of Practical Cats* (1939); here an ensemble of individuals, now felines, sing and dance as they decide which one gets to go to "the Heaviside Layer," or cat heaven. Holmes's *The Mystery of Edwin Drood* fits temporally and generically into the concept musical paradigm because of its innovative structure that meta-theatrically acknowledges the specific challenge of adapting an unfinished novel.

The 1980s was not only a period of innovation in musical theater but also a banner decade in adaptations of Dickens to stage and screen. The Royal Shakespeare Company's eight-and-a-half-hour production of *Nicholas Nickleby* in 1980 transferred to Broadway in 1981 to ecstatic reviews, preparing the way for further Dickensian novelties. Another successful experiment in Dickensian storytelling came soon after *Drood*: Christine Edzard's two-part epic film *Little Dorrit* (1987) comprises two three-hour movies, one following the main male protagonist, Arthur Clenham, the other following the eponymous Amy Dorrit, each offering overlapping perspectives on the multi-plot story. In addition to these cutting-edge theatrical and cinematic events, the decade showed a tremendous appetite for traditional television adaptations, creating a noticeable spike in the history of Dickens adaptations. CBS produced *A Tale of Two Cities* for TV in 1980. George C. Scott starred in two made-for-TV movies, *Oliver Twist* in 1982 and *A Christmas Carol* in 1984, both directed by Clive Donner. BBC aired a record number of serial TV adaptations of Dickens in that ten-year span, some with as many as twelve episodes, including *A Tale of Two Cities* (1980), *Great Expectations* (1981), *Dombey and Son* (1983), *Oliver Twist* (1985), *Bleak House* (1985), *Pickwick Papers* (1985), and *David Copperfield* (1986). Disney also created *Great Expectations* (1989) in six parts. ("EVERY").[4]

What drew so many adapters to Dickens in the 1980s, in such different forms? Neil Sinyard suggests that the Royal Shakespeare *Nicholas Nickleby* and Edzard's *Little Dorrit* reveal Dickens as "the most relevant and trenchant of social commentators in a Thatcher (and Reagan) era that openly espoused the virtues of self-interest and so-called 'Victorian values'"

(Sinyard). Dickens's interest in social and economic justice, which surely engaged Bart decades earlier in his creation of *Oliver!*, makes his novels enduringly pertinent; the Thatcher-Reagan era provided ample cause to respond to politicians who sentimentalized Victorian culture with the pointed use of the great Victorian novelist's social critique. But in direct contrast to Sinyard's view, Robert Hewison assesses the heritage industry in film and television as an expression of a Thatcherite impulse. Dianne Sadoff agrees, arguing that the 1980s and 1990s vogue for nineteenth-century costume drama on television and film is neoconservative, delivering the spectacle of aristocratic privilege to bourgeois audiences who respond by "applauding private ownership of stately mansions" as recompense for their own dearth of riches (Sadoff xvii). Such conservative romanticization of the Victorians continued throughout the 1990s with Newt Gingrich's infamously and repeatedly recommending Victorian-style orphanages as a solution to illegitimacy and the welfare state (Hadley, "Past" 8). Julie Sanders addresses this kind of binary conflict when she points out that all adaptations are simultaneously "inherently conservative" and "oppositional, even subversive" in that they preserve the source text's prestige while intimating its deficiency for the present climate (9), recalling what Eve Kosofsky Sedgwick would identify as "kinda subversive, kinda hegemonic" about 1980s critical theories of gender and performativity ("Queer" 15).[5]

But if there were ever a show that seems designed as purely escapist entertainment rather than social commentary, a frothy confection of campiness and silliness and fun, Holmes's *Drood* is surely that show. Its message, if it has any, would seem at first glance, to be about show making and novel writing; its play-within-a-play structure, its toying with an only partially written novel as source text, its performance of an unfinished show that requires the audience's participation before it can conclude, all this meta-theatricality and meta-textuality make it a musical about the musical format more than about current events outside the theater. And yet, as we shall see, Dickensian social issues relevant to the 1980s make their mark as the musical treats addiction, gender, race, identity, and colonialism.

TOUCHING THE KEY NOTE

It should not surprise us that a novel filled with melody has been made into a successful musical. The entire town of Cloisterham seems to sing continuously and to comment on music frequently, as just a few examples will show. The titular character Edwin Drood (Ned through most of the novel) tosses off a few lines of the song "Begone, Dull Care" in his very first scene, a conversation with his uncle Jack Jasper (45). Jasper is the town's talented choirmaster; his beautiful voice and skillful accompaniment directly impact the plot and reveal character. He is a "sweet singer" (268), as the opium den proprietress Princess Puffer describes him. Critics also focus on Jasper's musicality: as Martin Dubois observes, Jasper is "the central figure in the musical life of Cloisterham" (351); Phyllis Weliver goes so far as to say that in this novel "music *is* Jasper" (her emphasis, *Women Musicians* 129). Meanwhile, the young minister of Cloisterham, the "musical" Mr. Crisparkle, "melodiously ... delivers himself" of the glee "Tell Me, Shepherds" in bidding goodnight to the morose Jasper (42, 43), who must get mightily sick of people singing to him all the time. The boy called "Deputy" continually chants "Widdy widdy wen!" while stoning the stonemason Durdles home, a task that Durdles himself has hired the lad to do since only being pelted by stones will get the man to leave off drinking and go to bed (72). Virtually everyone in Cloisterham dances or makes music, and not only on the "Alternate Musical Wednesdays" (43) at the church.[6] And Rosa sings in one of the novel's most vital dramatic scenes. Likewise, Jasper's famous opium dream in the novel's opening paragraph resembles a Victorian pantomime spectacular (37). Although quite a bit of important work has been done on this passage, particularly from a postcolonial perspective, its resonance with musical theater needs further attention, as does the way the entire novel pulses with music. Even when the novel is dramatized as a straight play, film, or telecast, these adaptations incorporate song, as in both the 1935 Universal Studios movie and the 2012 BBC production. The novel itself seems to beg for musicalization. Rupert Holmes's show prompts us to think about it in terms of not only theatrical but also musical performance.

Contemplating the novel with regard to musical theater may open room for additional discussion of something critics have puzzled over for a long time: what precisely Dickens had in mind when he wrote "Touch the Key note" as an item in his memoranda planning the book. They often point to the next entry on his list, the words "When the Wicked Man," speculating that they refer to Jasper as much as the opening prayer of the Vespers service.[7] *Keynote* is a term we've seen Dickens use before, most notably in *Hard Times* as the title of the chapter that so famously describes the industrial cityscape of Coketown. Extrapolating from *that* keynote, we might assume that this keynote also refers to social critique, to some large societal problem that Dickens would attack. One hypothesis raised by some of Dickens's contemporaries, as Edmund Wilson points out, was that Dickens meant the opium trade and its collateral ills (100–101). Certainly some nineteenth-century readers interpreted the novel this way: in May 1882 the *Nassau Literary Magazine* identified opium as the story's main social target, pointing out that every book Dickens "wrote was a mortal thrust at a giant evil of his day, and in Edwin Drood the very first chapter paints in lurid tints an opium eater's den, which forms the gloomy frame-work of many ghastly, vivid scenes, at which many a rich opium merchant in England must have started" (2).[8] Or the keynote could simply be Cloisterham as a kind of throughline, as Dickens's plan twice underlines the phrase "Cathedral town running throughout" (Cardwell 230).

Considering the keynote musically and theatrically offers another vantage point from which to consider this question. Musically, the keynote is simply a form of organization that keeps the musical composition and all the performers centered on it; but it is an ever-changing center as the music moves through time, creating tension and excitement. As the keynote changes, it draws everything else in the composition along with it. It is easy to see how the keynote could become a metaphor for the shifting center of power, and that is partly how I will put it to use in this chapter in relation to the novel and its musicalization.[9] However, in *The Mystery of Edwin Drood* itself, Dickens employs the word *keynote* only once, when Jasper accompanies Rosa as she sings, as he touches the keynote on the Crisparkle piano. This is a musical-theatrical moment in the novel in which passion, power, and intrigue are communicated through music and movement rather than through language.

In discussing performativity in Victorian novels, critics often focus on how a fictional character constructs an identity by performing it; likewise, interest in a novel's theatricality often revolves around how a novel's scene takes place in a theater or is in some way like a play, perhaps incorporating spectators into the action, a common technique in Dickens that we see in this scene. What I am interested in exploring in *The Mystery of Edwin Drood* is something different, more like what David Kurnick lays out in his book *Empty Houses:* that in some novels, theater becomes not only a metaphor but also "a condition of the text" (102). In *The Mystery of Edwin Drood*, the scene in which Rosa Bud sings is such a key moment. Rosa must sing for

Jasper to follow her lips in his accompaniment. He must play to communicate his terrifying attraction to her. Neville Landless must hear her sing to fall in love with her. His sister Helena Landless must witness the complex interaction between teacher/accompanist and pupil/soloist to understand and to protect her new friend and to demonstrate her own characteristic fearlessness. Only in a narrative of musical performance can this crucial scene accomplish so much.

Here is the passage:

> Mr. Jasper was seated at the piano as they came into his drawing-room, and was accompanying Miss Rosebud while she sang. It was a consequence of his playing the accompaniment without notes, and of her being a heedless little creature, very apt to go wrong, that he followed her lips most attentively, with his eyes as well as hands; carefully and softly hinting the key-note from time to time. (92)

The novel begins the paragraph from the point of view of the rest of the company who enter the room with the song already in full swing. It is a theatrical moment, with the effect of curtains rising on the duo, as though the stage directions were to say they are "discovered" in their places, mid-song.

Dickens describes Jasper as "playing the accompaniment without notes," that is to say, without sheet music. Samuel Luke Fildes faithfully depicts that comment in his illustration, which shows the sheet music closed on the piano as Jasper plays (fig. 6).[10] As with any skillful accompanist, Jasper's hands touch the keyboard to support her vocal line; the narrator insists that the music master follows her lips "with his eyes as well as his hands," insinuating that he focuses an excessive intensity of concentration on Rosa. Yet this is precisely what an accomplished accompanist does at least from time to time; his accompanying her gives him license to focus as intently on her face as an artist painting a live model. This scenario raises several questions about the performance: How does Jasper both follow Rosa and direct her? What does it mean to *hint* a note? To play it in a chord? To play related notes of the same tonic chord? To play it in another octave, say in the bass line? To play it softly? What musical information is actually expressed here?

The teacher-pupil power relationship is in direct opposition to that of accompanist and soloist. The teacher-pianist—or Music Master, in this case (194)—directs the student-singer from the piano by supplying the

Figure 6. "At the Piano." Illustration by Luke Fildes. In *The Mystery of Edwin Drood*, by Charles Dickens (London: Chapman and Hall, 1870), 44. (Image courtesy of Hill Memorial Library, Special Collections, Louisiana State University, Baton Rouge)

notes, tempo, and dynamics, which the student obediently follows; certainly, a teacher might play individual notes to help a singer—especially a beginner—stay on pitch. In contrast, the piano accompanist supports the soloist by following the singer's lead, providing complementary piano music to create a richer musical fabric for the audience. The soloist has artistic license to hold a note longer than the written music requires, for example, and a skilled accompanist accommodates. Jasper's playing the keynote occasionally, "from time to time," means that he does not play the melody line, something a weak or inexperienced student would need. A minimal accompaniment suggests that Rosa holds her own musically, perhaps not so "apt to go wrong" after all, with Jasper supplying the musical undercurrent that enriches the sound. Yet he attempts to control her vocal line by emphasizing the keynote while rejecting the musical text that Fildes depicts as right in front of him. The intensity of the musical power struggle and the tension between who leads and who follows becomes the story.

The passage next places the characters as though they were onstage, just as Fildes's illustration of the scene looks like a play set. Rosa performs. Neville and Jasper watch her. Helena watches Jasper. Crisparkle watches

Helena. Miss Twinkleton watches everyone. Mrs. Crisparkle sleeps, and Ned twiddles a fan:

> The song went on. It was a sorrowful strain of parting, and the fresh young voice was very plaintive and tender. As Jasper watched the pretty lips, and ever and again hinted the one note, as though it were a low whisper from himself, the voice became less steady, until all at once the singer broke into a burst of tears, and shrieked out, with her hands over her eyes: "I can't bear this! I am frightened! Take me away!" (92)

Communication in this passage is largely musical and gestural rather than verbal. "Ever and again hint[ing] the one note," John Jasper (or "Johnny One Note," as Rodgers and Hart might call him) [11] uses both his hands and his eyes to convey meaning without saying a word. Rosa sings, cries, and makes the grand melodramatic gesture of distress by placing her hands over her eyes, before shrieking. Helena effectively stops Rosa from further speech by placing her hand "on the little rosy mouth," exactly where we suspect Jasper wanted his hand to be, instead of on the keyboard; Helena uses her other hand to signal to the rest of the company that which she also conveys in words, "Don't speak to her for a moment" (92–93), forbidding verbal communication. Music and gesture trump words. The novel here suggests that it is impossible to articulate in or through language what this scene communicates. The scene only fully makes sense when we understand it as underwritten by the conventions of musical theater.

So important is it dramatically to stage a song, "a sorrowful strain of parting" (92), at this juncture, it is no wonder that every major adaptation, even nonmusical plays and films, presents Rosa singing a love ballad in this scene.[12] It is usually a preexisting traditional Victorian parlor song that audience members would already find familiar and had perhaps sung themselves around their home pianos, perhaps one like the 20-guinea pianoforte advertised on the inside cover of all six numbers of *The Mystery of Edwin Drood*. Using a familiar song establishes a sympathetic relationship between the singing audience and the singing heroine. The 1871 melodrama *Lost* incorporates a setting of "When the Stars Are in the Quiet Skies." The 1935 film incorporates Caroline Norton's poem "Would I Were with Thee!"[13] The 2012 BBC miniseries uses yet a different popular nineteenth-century song for this scene, Thomas Moore's "Believe Me, If All Those Endearing Young Charms," a traditional Irish melody, perhaps best known as the tune of "Fair Harvard," the Ivy League school's alma mater. These are all simple, pretty, hymnlike parlor songs within the vocal reach of musical amateurs, published as sheet music in four-part glee harmony for home consumption. In all three cases, Jasper puts the words he wants to hear into Rosa's mouth by assigning these popular love songs for his music pupil to sing to him. The musical *Drood* stages the moment with an original song, like the rest of Holmes's score. The similarities and differences among the songs that Rosa performs in the melodrama, the film, the TV show, and the 1985 Broadway musical illustrate how powerfully music works in staging the scene for actual performance.

The earliest British adaptation of *The Mystery of Edwin Drood,* Walter Stephens's *Lost: A Drama in Four Parts,* was first performed on November 4, 1871, at the Surrey in London, where it ran for twenty-two performances.[14] The title recalls the novel's monthly wrapper illustration (the cover for each installment); on the left side of the image, a young woman examines a flier with the word "Lost" posted on a door, simultaneously evoking a missing person notice and a theatrical poster (fig. 7). So long as Stephens can use Dickens's plot and dialogue, the play works well. But once Stephens must embark on his own, he runs into trouble. Jasper drugs and kidnaps Rosa and then carries her to the cathedral, where she must either accept his love or die. The play becomes almost a parody of Victorian melodrama in its use of canned characterization, abandoning the distinct and wonderfully hilarious personalities Dickens creates. For example, the novel's Rosa frequently refers to herself as just "a little mite of a thing," typically stuffing her mouth with a finger or Turkish delight, making her an annoying heroine, but an original and memorable one. At her most indignant, the worst the novel's Rosa can call Jasper is "a bad, bad man" (228). In contrast, Stephens's Rosa responds to the dastardly Jasper in the elevated diction befitting a stock melodramatic damsel in distress, with lines utterly *un*characteristic of Dickens's Rosebud. On the brink of death, Stephens's Rosa exclaims, "Begone! Dare not to threaten me! Thou craven, mean-spirited wretch, whom to call a man would for ever defile the appellation" (48).

Lost reveals the mysterious Dick Datchery (clearly someone in disguise, though Dickens died before he revealed Datchery's identity) to be Neville Landless, who doffs his camouflaging wig in time to foil Jasper and save Rosa. Stephens then offers a choice between two endings: to conclude either with the exposure of Jasper (who laughs madly before dashing off to his death in the depths of the crypt) or with an additional silent scene entitled "A Dream of the Future," which shows a tableau of a double wedding:

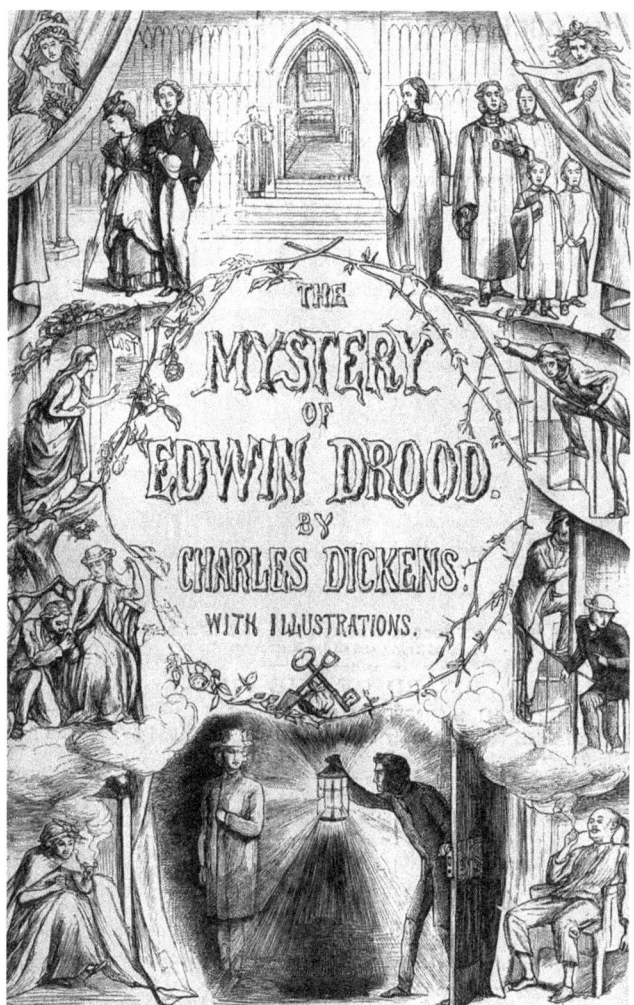

Figure 7. Wrapper by Charles Collins and Luke Fildes for *The Mystery of Edwin Drood,* by Charles Dickens, no. 2 (London: Chapman and Hall, May 1870). (Image courtesy of the Irvin Department of Rare Books and Special Collections, University of South Carolina, Columbia)

Helena Landless to Reverend Crisparkle and Rosa to Neville (51). The first ending emphasizes the villain's comeuppance and leaves the marital conclusion likely but not certain. The second intensifies the happy ending with weddings, while simultaneously making a statement about race and empire. It explicitly joins the orphaned and homeless Landless twins from Ceylon, described by Dickens as "very dark, and very rich in colour" (84–85), in marriage with the whitest and most English of characters, Rosa Bud and the Anglican minister Septimus Crisparkle. Their light complexion and their Englishness in the novel could not be more evident. Dickens repeatedly tells us that the crisply sparkling Anglican clergyman is "rosy" (124) or "fair and rosy" (42). In Dickens, the heroine Rosa Bud's eponymous rosiness is reiterated often, quintupled even, as in a single sentence in which Rosa rolls up "her little pink gloves, like rose-leaves" and puts "her pink fingers to her rosy lips" to clean her teeth of candy (58). She is obviously a sweet "English rose," suggesting a complexion most often thought of in Shakespearean terms, damasked red and white (sonnet 130, lines 5–6), or, more recently, in terms of Elton John's "Candle in the Wind," his song eulogizing Princess Diana, with the line "Goodbye, England's rose."[15] While casting, makeup, and lighting would determine the appearance of these (or any) characters onstage, Stephens includes language indicating racial difference. Flexibility in concluding the drama with or without the double wedding encourages those mounting the play to decide how to end it themselves, underscoring the mercurial quality of the Victorian theater and, perhaps, recognition that acceptance of racial intermarriage might vary among audiences. Stephens's option of two conclusions shifts the significance of the whole work. It also marks Holmes's innovative musical as an extension of already dynamic and inventive Victorian theatrical practice.

As in the novel, the scene in *Lost* in which Rosa sings to Jasper's accompaniment takes place in Mr. Crisparkle's drawing room, following Dickens closely, although there are a few significant differences. In the play, Miss Twinkleton suggests music, and Helena leads Rosa to the piano. Jasper *"runs over the keys with skill and dexterity"* (6), a virtuoso show that contrasts with the restraint of Jasper's playing in Dickens's passage. The stage directions instruct the actors to "group as the picture of 'Edwin Drood'" (6), a straightforward example of the stage practice of realization. Rosa begins to sing lyrics provided in the play text; the popular Victorian song "When the Stars Are in the Quiet Skies" is a setting of Edward Bulwer-Lytton's poem "Night and Love" from his 1837 novel *Ernest Maltravers* (117). In 1859 the *New York Times* reported that this "sweet and simple little song ... is found on almost every piano-forte in America."[16] The Victorian music anthologist Helen Johnson agrees that "no moonlit ride is complete without it" (Johnson vi). Writing in 1869, James Wood Davidson refers to it as a song that *"tout le monde* knew and sang" in its day; it was one "like any one of the multitude" that are popular and are later "considered trite and old fashioned" (556), indicating that by the time the song was performed onstage at the Surrey in 1871, it evoked an earlier era.[17] Rosa's song is one that many in the theater had themselves likely sung around their own pianos or had joined in singing at a more public venue, adding to their identification with Rosa and to their sense of ownership of the song itself.

> When the stars are in the quiet skies,
>   Then most I pine for thee;
> Bend on me, then, thy tender eyes,
>   As stars look on the sea!
>
> For thoughts, like waves that glide by night,
>   Are stillest where they shine;
> Mine earthly love lies hush'd in light
>   Beneath the heaven of thine.
>
> There is an hour when angels keep
>   Familiar watch on men,
> When coarser souls are wrapp'd in sleep—
>   Sweet spirit, meet me then.

Despite its decorum, this love song hints at the erotic. At night, when everyone is in bed, the speaker pines for her beloved. She invokes images of rhythmic waves and earthly love. She asks him to meet her at night. But the erotic is camouflaged in a wash of sentimental otherworldliness: angels keep watch as celestial chaperones, and the lovers' tryst will happen only in the spirit realm. Nevertheless, the stage directions call for Jasper to watch her intently. The climax comes in the last line: halfway through the familiar song, when suggesting that the lover meet her, Rosa "*shudders,*" "*places her hands over her face,*" in a classic melodramatic gesture, and "*almost shrieking*" is overcome (7). The sexual subtext of the popular song coupled with the proprietary interest the audience already feels cultivates a kind of amicable power struggle between the performers and theatergoers; this tension provides energy for the depiction of the more diabolical power struggle onstage, so that Jasper's effort to control Rosa resonates throughout the house. It is a dynamic that we see Holmes profitably exploit in his version of the scene in the musical *Drood*.

In the musical, Holmes imagines what has happened just prior to this moment to justify Rosa's intense reaction. Jasper has written and composed a new song himself that as music master he assigns to Rosa to learn, emphasizing that aspect of their relationship in performance. Entitled "Moonfall," its language works explicitly not only to avow Jasper's love but also to put into Rosa's mouth *precisely* the words he designs to place there, words that force her to express desire for him. Far more demanding musically than the songs included in earlier adaptations, "Moonfall" is an art song, often performed as a solo soprano recital or audition piece. Unlike the song used in *Lost,* which stays in one key throughout, "Moonfall" modulates frequently from key to key, becoming almost dissonant with the use of augmented fourths and never returning to the tonic in the vocal line but only in the very last note the orchestra plays.

When asked to sing "Moonfall," Rosa balks at first, saying it would not be proper (1). Rosa recognizes right away the overt sexuality in the imagery she sings. Lying on "a steely sheet of light" conjures the thought of prosaic white bed sheets. Words such as "fingers" and "lingers" and lines wishing "betwixt our hearts, let nothing intervene" connote fleshly as much as emotional connection. She registers the impropriety of the line promising that in the moonlight; "I'll give myself to you," which has straightforward corporeal as well as sentimental implications (17). Even the title "Moonfall" suggests that the virgin goddess of the moon will become a fallen woman. Holmes's innuendo-filled lyrics and the technical difficulty of the music with its lush orchestral accompaniment run counter to Dickens's description of minimalist piano accompaniment but effectively expose the sexual tension and power dynamic implicit in the novel's scene. With Jasper's piano no longer even audible behind the swelling strings, the musical muscle is all Rosa's as she dominates the stage; but we know the power struggle remains in part because of the dissonance and partly because of her tonal quality: the stage directions specify "*tremendous tension, almost fear in her voice, as she watches Jasper watching her*" (17). A duet reprise of "Moonfall" concludes the first act in the scene depicting Jasper's open declaration of his feelings for Rosa and his plans to further manipulate her; Rosa's revulsion and the tension between them mount to the point that Rosa will become ready to murder him in the second act.

Holmes handles the questions of the Landless twins' race and the show's approach to British colonialism by addressing them head-on in characteristically satirical fashion. Throughout the novel, Dickens presents a mash-up of the Eastern world and British colonial holdings. He uses Arabian Nights to represent an Opium den where the customers—identified as sailors from the Indian subcontinent or from China (37)—speak "gibberish" because they are deep in their Opium dreams, but also in a classic colonialist trope dismissing languages of the colonized as unintelligible. Rosa Bud consumes Turkish Delight, mirroring British mercantile consumption of global goods. Despite Dickens's care in this novel to present the Landless twins sympathetically and to overcome British prejudice against these clearly racialized characters, he is nevertheless a product of his moment, demonstrated by the hodge-podge of Orientalist images. Holmes tackles all this directly through intensification of the tropes. As Hyungji Park points out (534), the musical *Drood* parodies Edwin's colonialist project of "waking up Egypt," making Edwin Drood say that Ceylon and Egypt are "much the same" (drawing Neville's scorn) and that he plans to build a highway from Cairo to Alexandria using stones from the Great Pyramid (provoking Neville's outrage). Neville continually alludes to his own hot-bloodedness (sometimes with lines directly from the novel, although always exaggerated). And Helena articulates the point explicitly when she states, "I only wish I could express my gratitude without this strange, somewhat geographically indecipherable accent!" (66). Thus the musical pokes fun at the novel's ambient imperialism, always evident despite Dickens's clear concern with inclusiveness, his effort to avoid xenophobia and to protest mistreatment of the Landless twins on the basis of race.

It's instructive to compare Holmes's treatment of the Landless twins not only with *Lost* but also with the 1935 film, the first sound picture adapted from *The Mystery of Edwin Drood*, directed by Stephen Walker.[18] Much of the dialogue comes directly from the novel, which the film follows closely for as long as possible. The film concludes with Neville Landless (disguised as Dick Datchery) and Durdles proving that Jasper is the murderer by uncovering Rosa's mother's ring in the crypt. Cornered in the cathedral, Jasper climbs the bell tower, plunging to his death. Neville and Rosa Bud marry in the final frames. Because Neville Landless here is played by Douglass Montgomery and his sister Helena Landless is played by Valerie Hobson, described in her IMDb biography as "quintessentially English," the film appears not to make an outright statement about race in marrying a Landless to Rosa.[19] Nevertheless, Neville has a hot temper and drinks too much, intimating a lax foreignness that he must overcome during the film to earn Rosa's hand. Moreover, his makeup and hair coloring are a tad darker than his sister's, hinting at the possibility of a mixed-race heritage. Whereas the 1871 play recognizes race as part of the equation with a choice on whether to stage a future dream of interracial marriage, the 1935 film eliminates such a possibility other than a metaphorical hint. In 1985 Holmes undercuts the stereotypes of racial difference and the geographical reach of empire through camp, with a knowing wink in collaboration with the audience.[20]

OPIUM DREAM BALLET

The musical Jasper's erotic and murderous opium dream not only critiques Dickens's Orientalism but also exposes musical-theatrical moments in the novel. It is a conflation of several passages, including the novel's famous opening paragraph detailing Jasper's dream-thoughts as he awakens in Princess Puffer's opium den:

> An ancient English Cathedral Tower? How can the ancient English Cathedral tower be here! . . . What IS the spike that intervenes, and who has set it up? Maybe, it is set up by the Sultan's orders for the impaling of a horde of Turkish robbers, one by one. It is so, for cymbals clash, and the Sultan goes by to his palace in long procession. Ten thousand scimitars flash in the sunlight, and thrice ten thousand dancing-girls strew flowers. Then, follow white elephants caparisoned in countless gorgeous colours, and infinite in number and attendants. Still, the Cathedral Tower rises in the background, where it cannot be, and still no writhing figure is on the grim spike. Stay! Is the spike so low a thing as the rusty spike on the top of a post of an old bedstead that has tumbled all awry? (37)

Critics have been very interested in Jasper's dream both for its Freudian elements (the phallic spike of the bed post and the equally phallic tower of Cloisterham's cathedral) and for its Orientalist appropriation of *Arabian Nights* (associating opium with Turkey rather than China) and other Orientalist aspects, such as Jasper's identifying his fellow customers once he fully awakens as a "Chinaman" and "a Lascar" (37). But these important readings overlook the sheer theatricality of the spectacle Jasper envisions, so reminiscent of Victorian pantomime, a genre so important to Dickens that its conventions underpin all of his novels (Eigner x). In other words, although the narrator invokes imagery and stylistic features from the *Arabian Nights* (for example, the reiterated use of "thousand" to mean "many"), it is not the prose tales but the performed *Arabian Nights* that most forcefully inhabits Jasper's dream here.

A thousand men on caparisoned elephants trot through the story of Sinbad, and a sultan occasionally appears in grand procession in other tales; but none rivals the visual and choreographic excess of Jasper's opium dream. With such an abundance of scimitar-flashing soldiers, flower-tossing dancing girls, and richly dressed elephants, Dickens evokes here something his readers in 1870 would find very familiar: the Victorian penchant for hundreds of stage supernumeraries dazzling their audience in fairy-tale extravaganzas. Perhaps as a little tease, Dickens brings pantomime directly into *The Mystery of Edwin Drood:* on that "fateful night" of Christmas Eve, the last when Edwin Drood is seen alive, "a new grand comic Christmas pantomime is to be produced at the Theatre" close to the Cloisterham cathedral (171). In addition to the opium dream's significance in critique of Empire and its saturation with Orientalism, it is also grounded in the most English (via *Commedia dell'arte*) of all theatrical institutions, the pantomime.

One way in which the musical *Drood* alerts us to this scene's explicit concern with theatrical tradition is by turning it into a dream ballet, a convention of American musical theater in classic Broadway shows such as *On the Town* (1944). These dances often portray the protagonist dreaming of possible outcomes that will matter decisively to the plot, as in the dream ballet "Laurey Makes Up Her Mind" in *Oklahoma!* and in *One Touch of Venus*, when Venus imagines living in the suburban community Ozone Heights and, horrified, rejects life as a human. *Drood* plays with that convention by turning Jasper's opium dream into an opium dream ballet. In the 1985 original Broadway production of *Drood,* Graciella Danielle choreographed an innovative modern dance. In a surreally fluid emergence of seemingly naked women, "succubae pour from the bed" that Jasper lies upon in Princess Puffer's lair (30). Wearing nude body stockings, the women dancers stack their own bodies quadruple as they lie prone facing the audience, creating a many-headed hallucinatory contortion that mimics an orgy. The moment culminates in an act of simulated fellatio, not with Jasper but with the god Pan (whose presence is a bit mysterious but suggestive of orgiastic rites); all perform above, around, and on Jasper's bedstead in a highly sexualized reinterpretation of Dickens's pantomime Orientalism. This scenario may have been too risky for the 2012 revival at Roundabout in a limited run scheduled for the Christmas season. Warren Carlyle's choreography is far less sexual, less surprising, more gymnastic, and more current. The women in Carlyle's dreamscape perform lateral walkovers with splits over Jasper's sleeping body, incorporating contemporary hip-hop moves, wearing not nude bodysuits but much less revealing white bandeaux tops. There is no Pan and no fellatio.

In both Danielle's and Carlyle's opium dream ballets, Jasper lusts for Rosa and murders Edwin, the same dreamwork he accomplishes in the novel's later passage describing his experiences in Princess Puffer's opium den (268–72). In addition to dramatizing the sexuality and violence implicit in Jasper's dreams, the musical's dream ballet embodies for twentieth- and twenty-first-century audiences the music and dance inherent in the passages' pantomime roots. The opium dream ballet also assists our zeroing in on the unintelligibility of speech and the substitution of other modes of communication that preoccupies Dickens's narrative fragment, abruptly cut off before the author could finish what he wanted to say. Three times in the novel's opening chapter in the opium den, Jasper exclaims "unintelligible" as he listens to the other opium eaters mumbling in their narcotic stupor. He hears "chattering and clattering enough between them, but to no purpose. When any distinct word has been flung into the air, it has had no sense or sequence" (39). Jasper depends precisely on this unintelligibility to mask his own murderous thoughts while under the influence of the drug. But by the end of the incomplete novel, Princess Puffer understands him, and the dream-mutterings are not so unintelligible after all.

Is there a connection between the unintelligibility of speech, particularly as stressed by Jasper's scoffing at other men still engulfed in their opium dreams, and the hyper-intelligibility of music, so expressive of emotion even without words? Words without "sense or sequence," without semantics or syntax, resemble individual notes that have no musical meaning without the structure of rhythm, melody, and key. Jasper, Rosa, Puffer, Neville—many characters in *The Mystery of Edwin Drood* vie for control of events and relationships during the course of the novel, with actions and words alike unintelligible as the mystery remains unsolved and the composition ends without resolution. In a way, what happens with the novel unfinished is that the composition loses its keynote; the suspended chord can never resolve, and readers can never hear the tonic. The Broadway show, like every other satisfying adaptation of this incomplete novel, supplies an ending, in this case voted on by the audience. Holmes doesn't resolve the unfinished story with a single solution, but he controls the continually shifting keynote—limiting the range of improvisation available to the actors and of outcomes available to the audience. He also helps us to see how scenes in the novel such as the opium dream and Jasper's playing while Rosa sings are already musical-theatrical, already a condition of the text.

META-THEATRICALITY

Drood is an unusual, multilayered show that plays structurally on the tension between who leads and who follows, except now the author, adapter, actors, and audience members participate in negotiating the outcome. Those who have seen it—or even its advertisements—are aware of *Drood*'s principal gambit. Despite approximately a century and a half of scholarly investigations and speculations, we cannot know for sure how Dickens planned to solve the mystery of who killed Edwin Drood (or even whether Ned is dead). Unlike the 1935 film, the musical does not invent a single solution. Instead, *Drood* offers an elaborate system of alternative endings among which, as the advertising posters and television spots have proclaimed to potential patrons, "YOU decide." Midway through the second act, the dramatic action moving Dickens's mystery plot forward stops. One actor steps forward and lays out the voting process. Actors descend from the stage to poll the theatergoers on their choices among several possible solutions. Then members of the staff rapidly tabulate the ballots backstage, and the players resume, performing the denouement dictated by the audience's response. Because the audience is given the task of voting not only on the identity of the murderer but also of the enigmatic Dick Datchery, as well as on the selection of which two characters will be joined in wedded bliss, the play has 400 possible outcomes.

Pulling off this variability demands an impressive level of dexterity from the performers, but the mechanics are planned to make the potential plot changes smooth and the workload manageable. For example, the orchestra and the actors do not have to learn a lot of different music for the multiple outcomes because most of the suspects sing their confessions to the same melody, with altered lyrics inserted to cover their particular motives and modi operandi. The biggest complication for the orchestra is inserting the correct reprise from earlier in the show, either the leitmotif associated with the individual character selected or a dramatic reuse of someone else's song. For example, Rosa-as-murderer substitutes new lyrics about her homicidal mental state to the melody of Jasper's earlier song expressing his dual personality, "A Man Could Go Quite Mad." In contrast, Princess Puffer's confession reprises her *own* earlier solo, again urging the audience to join her in the jolly chorus, "There ain't no profit in the Wages of Sin." A single song reveals Dick Datchery's identity, "Out on a Limerick," no matter which character is unmasked in singing it. In an homage to Gilbert and Sullivan, the revelation is always in the form of a limerick, so that each character unveiled as Datchery sings the same chorus but recites an individual limerick tailored to his or her particular motivation for donning the disguise wig and greatcoat.

Although this level of complexity is not beyond professional performers, it's not easy, either; some theaters elect not to do this show precisely because of the challenges posed by the multiple endings (Hoskins). The actors playing Rosa, Helena, and Princess Puffer never know at the beginning of a show which one of them will be called upon by the end to act the lover, or which of seven potential actors will play opposite her. They have only a few minutes' notice which of their prepared lines they will perform to explain their matrimonial decision; for instance, Rosa falls in love with Neville for entirely different reasons from those causing her to pair up with the unlikely Durdles. Part of the fun is Holmes's ingenuity in coming up with somewhat plausible reasons for such unsuitable nuptials as between Helena and Mr. Sapsea or between Princess Puffer and . . . well . . . anyone. The action subsequent to the revelations includes several additional amusing plot twists; these remain the same regardless of whom the audience has denominated as the murderer, the lovers, and Datchery. And here I offer a spoiler alert: it turns out the confessed murderer only thinks he or she has killed Drood, whose merely unconscious body is stashed in the cathedral crypt, with no mention of the quick lime so prominent in the novel that perhaps foreshadows the destruction of Drood's body. At the end of the musical, Edwin Drood bursts out of the tomb and into song, leading the cast in the final chorus.

The exuberantly experimental landmark 1980 Royal Shakespeare Company production of *Nicholas Nickleby* (Broadway, 1981) is always in the background of subsequent Dickens adaptations, particularly this one, since both had ties to prestigious Shakespeare companies. Like *Drood* after it, the play *Nickleby* also included a surprise happy ending in a tomb by incorporating a play-within-a-play production of *Romeo and Juliet* (enacted by the theatrical Crummles family with whom Nicholas had once performed); in this faux Victorian adaptation of Shakespeare, the two young lovers survive and marriages proliferate.[21] John Glavin has pointed out resemblances between the novel *The Mystery of Edwin Drood* and Charles

Kean's 1856 production of Shakespeare's *The Winter's Tale* at the Princesses Theatre. In *The Winter's Tale,* Hermione comes back to life in a spectacular conclusion rather like Holmes's Edwin Drood—and perhaps, as Glavin and others have suggested—as Dickens himself would have written his own Drood to have done (197–202). No matter the genealogy of Drood's reappearance from the crypt, the practical effect of this coup de théâtre in Holmes's *Drood* is that the grand finale is unchanged no matter what the audience has voted for earlier.

The stunt of letting the audience choose solutions to plot puzzles left unfinished at Dickens's death recalls the popular *Choose Your Own Adventure* children's book series in the 1980s and 1990s. Also contemporaneous with the show's premiere is the inception of computer games with multiple narrative paths depending on users' decisions, which began to appear on the market in 1983 and progressively became more sophisticated.[22] Edmund Miller points out other examples of audience or reader involvement, such as the April 10, 1982, episode of *Saturday Night Live* in which 500,000 people participated when Eddie Murphy asked the television audience to call in to decide the fate of Larry the Lobster (49). This episode inaugurated the now ubiquitous audience decisions in such reality shows as *American Idol* that go back at least as far as the life-and-death decisions made with a "turned thumb" by the crowds inside the Roman Coliseum. The movie *Clue* (1985), based on the popular board game, was released with three different possible endings playing in different theaters, only eleven days after the Broadway premiere of *Drood.*[23]

But while *Drood* clearly fits the zeitgeist that buoyed multiple, often interactive, endings that were all the rage in the mid-1980s, the musical has a direct antecedent besides the double ending of the 1871 play *Lost.* During the first three decades of the twentieth century, there was a fashion for staging mock *Mystery of Edwin Drood* trials; Philip Bolton records four between 1900 and 1930 (445–46). The best known was sponsored by the Dickens Fellowship at Covent Garden in January 1914 with a number of literary luminaries taking part, including George Bernard Shaw as the jury foreman. In this case, the accused was John Jasper, and he was convicted of manslaughter. Some participating felt that the proceedings were not taken seriously enough, and G. K. Chesterton, playing the judge, declared everyone in contempt of court. A similar mock trial was mounted by the Philadelphia Dickens Fellowship in April 1914 at the Academy of Music in which Jasper was acquitted, eleven to one (Russo 103). Thus Holmes's musical builds not only on the spirit of the age, with choose-your-own-adventure books and multipath computer games taking off in the 1980s, but also on a long line of adaptations of *The Mystery of Edwin Drood* that anticipate the fertile ground 1985 offered.

But from a theatrical standpoint, halting the action to poll the audience and tally the results in real time should interrupt the narrative momentum and disrupt the suspension of disbelief for so long that the audience would be unlikely to sustain interest in the action, were the musical play a straightforward narrative dramatization of Dickens's novel. But *Drood* is not straightforward. Because Holmes sets the drama of *The Mystery of Edwin Drood* as a play within a play, the lively frame performance never stops. The premise, again, is that the audience has entered a fictional 1895 London music hall named the Music Hall Royale.[24] Victorian music halls began as gathering places for communal singing and drinking, developing over time into popular venues for often raucous variety shows that never lost their emphasis on audience participation. The boisterously appreciative Victorian audience might demand that a favorite actress or singer perform cartwheels in the middle of her solo; if interruptions got out of hand, the master of ceremonies known as the Chairman would restore calm with a few strong taps of his gavel (Bratton, "Music Hall" 171).[25] Despite issues with theatrical licensing that controlled which houses of entertainment could legally perform what theatrical genres, music halls did indeed sometimes perform dramas (Bratton, "Music Hall" 166), such as the one the Music Hall Royale manifests.

As one would suppose in any attempt at a somewhat historically accurate re-creation of a Victorian music hall, *Drood* includes the role of Chairman. He makes jokes, explains to the audience what to expect, serves as the executive epicenter throughout the antics, and announces the frame characters—the music hall actors—as they stroll down the theater's aisles, mugging for applause. While the Chairman welcomes spectators to the Music Hall Royale, he teaches the twentieth- or twenty-first-century audience how to read Victorian theater. He explains that the character of Principal Boy—in this case, Edwin Drood—is being played by Miss Nutting, a cross-dressed actress, as was typical of Victorian pantomime, which is not a silently mimed entertainment but rather a spectacular comic song-and-dance extravaganza. Women also routinely played adolescent boys in melodrama, as in the Victorian productions of *Oliver Twist* and *Sweeney Todd;* in fact, in the 1872 *Mystery of Edwin Drood* at the Britannia, Julia Summers played the character Deputy (Fitz-Gerald 5). Male impersonators such as Vesta Tilly (1864–1952) dominated the music hall stages, performing in drag such enormously popular songs as "Burlington Bertie." In *Drood,* the Chairman mentions that Miss Nutting normally performs as a male impersonator "in top hat and tails" (10). Though he introduces the audience to the frame character Miss Nutting as the lead playing Edwin Drood, obviously through her the character of Drood is indeed being played by a real cross-dressed actress, Betty Buckley in the 1985 Broadway production. *Drood*'s Chairman employs many music hall conventions. He tosses out bawdy double entendres and needles the audience into reacting and participating, all while constructing those sitting in Broadway theater seats as an 1895 audience at London's fictional Music Hall Royale. For example, he invites the crowd to get comfortable, to "kick off your shoes, let out your belts and corsets" (6), eliciting a laugh as the twentieth- or twenty-first-century audience settles into its role. The sets in both the Broadway productions of 1985 and 2012 also model with some accuracy Victorian stagecraft, with painted flats (at which the performers sometimes glance as though to be sure which scene they are about to play) and working footlights that throw visible shadows onto the flats behind the performers. The musical turns the paying customers into fellow actors as they play the part of the Victorian audience watching a music hall performance that includes a rendition of *The Mystery of Edwin Drood.*

 The Chairman also teaches the audience about the detective genre, so that the play is meta-mystery as well as meta-theater. By this I mean that the play overtly addresses how the genre of murder mystery works and exposes its conventions while setting up the fundamental scaffolding for the audience to decide: before calling for votes on the identity of Datchery, the Chairman lectures the audience how to read the play and the novel as a mystery, saying, "This much I do know for certain: Datchery is not John Jasper, the Princess Puffer, Durdles, Deputy, or even Mayor Sapsea . . . for in our play and in Mr. Dickens' novel, they all appear in scenes with him. . . . They are observed to be in his company" (91). Even more to the point, the Chairman explains how each of eight characters could be the murderer— where, how, and why it could be done, including direct quotations from earlier action—in a move that mimics the convention of twentieth-century murder mysteries often set in English country houses, in which a detective such as Agatha Christie's Hercule Poirot in *Murder on the Orient Express* gathers all the suspects and expounds on how each one could have done the deed, just before the final excitement leading to the revelation scene. As Edmund Miller observes, audiences "bring with them to the theater their experience of multiple solutions in complex modern detective fiction" (56).

Despite the Chairman's direct address to the audience, there is no deconstruction of the theatrical fiction, because the Broadway audience plays the part of the Music Hall Royale's audience. The result is not a Brechtian alienation that jars theatergoers out of bourgeois complacency. Rather than breaking the fourth wall, the musical draws the audience inside it. Critics speak of the play as improvisatory, but—other than some joking around while remaining in character during the voting process—there is no actual improvisation (as there would be in a performance of, say, Second City), only the illusion of improvisation. The power of the audience to decide is also in a sense illusory: no one is performing unexpected cartwheels upon an eager patron's demand as they would in a Victorian music hall. Each possible variation of who is the murderer and who are the lovers is rehearsed for polished performance as though it were a surprise.

A prime example of the musical's meta-theatricality that simultaneously comments on the novel's interrupted composition comes in the song "Don't Quit While You're Ahead." On top of its meta-critical contributions, it also satisfies musical theater's generic convention of including one inspiring anthem that advises the characters and the audience "to climb every mountain," "to dream the impossible dream," or to "seize the day."[26] Princess Puffer and Dick Datchery, just come to Cloisterham to investigate, lead the company in its rousing chorus. The song seems to suggest that the two sleuths are hot on the track of the murderer and should keep up the good work. All the characters gradually join in, each individually singing poignantly of what life still has in store for them. Setting up an irony that only becomes apparent after the performers break off mid-tune, they sing, "There's more in store" and "I know there must be love that's yet to be" (84); together they belt out a rousing finale-like chorus when *their voices and the music abruptly cease.* The characters *"look around anxiously"* (86), clearly not knowing what to do next, as though Dickens had written the song and dance as well as the plot and characterization and had stopped composing the music as well as the novel mid-tune. The stage directions require even the orchestra musicians to *"frantically [thumb] through their music looking for the next page of the score"* (86). In response to the confusion, the Chairman tells us, "It was at this point that Mr. Charles Dickens laid down his pen forever" (87). The moment creates a sensory theatrical demonstration of how fully the novel is in mid-swing when it cuts off, re-creating the disappointment contemporary serial readers must have felt, realizing they would never know what was to have come next in a narrative in which they were already so invested. It curiously hints at how disconcerting it would be for fictional characters to abruptly lack a narrative trajectory, could they feel their own vulnerability, indeterminacy, and insubstantiality. One ironic reverberation of the lyrics in the silent aftereffect is the characters' urging themselves—in a kind of self-help exhortation—to keep going, despite the lack of an author. Most poignantly, once the Chairman announces that Dickens has died, the refrain "Don't quit while you're ahead" and lyrics such as "Don't resign!" or "Don't say, 'I'm off to bed, Farewell'" (85), ostensibly sung as advice to fellow characters, become in retrospect a plea from the characters to Dickens himself not to stop, not to be dead. Here *Drood* teaches us, in Caroline Levine's terms, "to take the experience of the uncertain middle seriously" (17).

Drood functions as a kind of criticism itself. It interrogates the mystery genre and focuses attention on the aberration of *The Mystery of Edwin Drood* as an unfinished novel. By writing (in typical twentieth-century mystery convention) semi-plausible motives for eight potential murderers, Holmes not only extends the narrative trajectory but also extrapolates multiple implications for the characters of any continuation of the story. The dynamic structure of a performance that depends on the audience's readings of the plot and dramatis personae up to the point of voting brings home to us how flexible performance is; it amplifies the private reading experience, in which we may all individually imagine the novel's extension and ending, into a collective and ever-changing series of possible pathways. Even Durdles, who in his star turn in the alternative ending that makes him the murderer, was so drunk that he killed Drood thinking the lad was a ghost, justifies his actions in terms consistent with his character, although his confession song includes a meta-theatrical comment that he has to explain his motive only because "I'm the candidate you rowdy lot have chose."[27]

I began this chapter by pointing out that critics have speculated about the meaning of Dickens's phrase "Touch the Key note" in his plans for *The Mystery of Edwin Drood*. But what would it mean to ask the same of the musical *Drood*? Obviously, as one would expect, the individual songs are all in different keys, befitting their varying dramatic or characterological purposes. There is no one musical keynote. We could try to answer the question thematically, finding keynotes in the musical's treatment of colonialism, xenophobia, hypocrisy, the dual personality of Jasper, or drug abuse and the evils of the opium trade. But that would only help us with the Droodian plot of the play-within-a play. Critics such as Wilson and Weliver suggest that in the novel, Jasper may be controlling Rosa through the vibrations of the keynote, which he uses to create a mesmeric resonance between them (Wilson 91; Weliver, *Women Musicians* 132),[28] but no matter how much audiences feel the magic of musical theater, I am not suggesting that they are hypnotized by it. Instead, it is worth considering that the musical has a sort of structural keynote—although maybe I should shift the metaphor to key*stone* if I'm talking about an overarching structure—that also helps us to understand the novel better. In Western tonal music, the key controls what notes work. The pull that the tonic note exerts is very strong. It is so difficult *not* to write in a key that Modernist composers trying to write atonally have often deployed elaborate external systems to resist the dominance of key signatures in choosing the notes they use in their compositions—think of Arnold Schoenberg's twelve-tone technique, for example.[29] Other composers have embraced inventive procedures to insure randomness in their compositions, such as John Cage's famous composition *4'33"* (1952), in which the performer remains silent for four minutes and thirty-three seconds, so that the composition is built from the chance noises made by the audience and environment during that time frame. While the musical *Drood* offers the illusion of randomness, it is in fact entirely rehearsed. Each of the 400 possible outcomes is accounted for and the intricate routes that lead to the show's finale are the result of a carefully plotted and choreographed preexisting design. The insistence that "You Decide," a motif that runs throughout the play, may *appear* to be the keynote, but, in fact, the dramatic pull is always back to the predetermined pathways that Holmes—ventriloquizing Dickens—has invented, rather like Jasper pulling Rosa back to the written text of her song through the accompaniment he plays or Dickens keeping readers on track as he touches his own keynotes throughout all his novels. At a performance of *Drood*, the audience's pleasurable power to change the plot is always for naught in that the show inevitably concludes with an equally pleasurable return of control to the musical's author.

As we have seen in earlier chapters, adaptations indelibly affect our understanding of Victorian literature and culture, even when mediated through previously adapted dramas and films. Holmes literalizes their pedagogical function by creating the character of the Chairman, who takes on the professorial task of educating the audience on how to read Dickens as well as the Victorian music hall. But what Dickens specifically? Is it the Dickens who wrote this unfinished novel, *The Mystery of Edwin Drood*? Or is it the rewritten Dickens of earlier adaptations? Or is it the Dickens he found when, as he explains, he "spent many a long afternoon and evening at the Fifth Avenue Public Library poring over countless old Dickensian biographies, critiques, . . . memoirs . . . , [and] comparisons of *Edwin Drood* to *The Moonstone*" (Sod 5)? Of course it's all of the above, plus at least one more: the ubiquitous Dickens of *A Christmas Carol*. Even when promoting an adaptation of Dickens's final novel, the producers of the 2012 Roundabout *Drood* invoked *A Christmas Carol* to bring in the crowd to a production that opened November 13, 2012 (a Christmas offering), and ran through March 10, 2013. The music video "Bustle Fluffah," a promotional Broadway.com production, was written and performed by members of the Roundabout *Drood* cast, rapping and wiggling their bustles to attract new audiences to the show. In addition to rap and a reference to Kim Kardashian's derrière, this meta-Dickensian YouTube artifact carries the agenda of Victorian relevancy forward to the twenty-first century via Scrooge and Tiny Tim's Christmas turkey dinner, served up on a giant bustle.[30]

The musical's final song belongs to Ned, "risen from the grave" (139). He sings, "I've read the writing on the wall." Although in the Book of Daniel the handwriting on the wall spells our doom, in the musical it drives home Ned's resurrection, Jasper's redemption (since he's not a murderer after all), and a glorification of the written word of Dickens, now transformed into song and dance. Performers often talk about how alive they feel onstage, how they live to perform and to experience the audience's reaction in the present moment, and indeed Dickens loved the connection he felt with audiences at his own readings. But this song also celebrates how alive the audience feels witnessing a live performance, because Ned tells us, "If you hear my voice, then you're alive" (140). The song's words urge us to hold on to life, to "try to live forever" (140). This is the kind of immortality that Shakespeare and Shelley tell us only literature or art can provide.[31] In this musical, Edwin Drood doesn't die, but Dickens does. We already witnessed the consternation of the players and an expression of grief from the Chairman, who claims that the novelist's dying mid-plot was the "one ungenerous deed of his noble career" (6). But one point of the finale's lyrics, a powerful moment no matter how sentimental and schlocky this may sound, is that neither the novel *The Mystery of Edwin Drood* nor *Drood* the musical will die as long as people are reading or audiences are watching. Either way, Dickens lives forever.

Marc Napolitano points out that the simulated music hall of *Drood*, with its elements of audience participation, approximates what the music hall scholar Peter Bailey refers to as "knowingness," the bond between "patron and performer" in which the spectators felt a sense of inclusion as the performers pull them into a kind of intimacy with their craft (132). There are differences, though: a Victorian music hall audience was a group of regulars, largely repeat customers with whom performers built up a relationship, whereas the Broadway audience at a production of Holmes's play experiences only a simulacrum of that connection. Furthermore, it is the not-knowing that is the rub here, because we can never really know what Dickens would have written to conclude his novel. Though it may seem obvious, it bears saying that this is why a musical in which the audience chooses the ending would not work as well if the novel were a completed one, like *The Moonstone* (1868), a mystery by Dickens's friend and collaborator Wilkie Collins that Dickens published in his journal *All the Year Round*. Although counterfactual histories and alternative fictions made for magnificent works of art, like *Wide Sargasso Sea* (1966), which imagines the early life of Bertha from *Jane Eyre*, they do not function in the same register as an adaptation that supplies an ending to a novel that abruptly cuts off with all the suspense left suspended. Like the legend of Mozart's father awakening his boy genius by playing an incomplete scale, impelling the child to leap out of bed to resolve the unbearable musical tension by hitting the tonic or keynote, Holmes makes Mozarts of us all. He does not resolve the untold story with a single solution but lets us conclude it ourselves. But he sets up the scale—that is, he controls the continually shifting keynote—limiting the range of improvisation available to the actors and of solutions to the audience.

6

Goblin Market, Performance, and Sexuality

Drood was not the only show of 1985 to adapt a Victorian text to New York City's musical stage. In the same year, the Obie Award–winning composer Polly Pen joined Peggy Harmon to adapt their musical *Goblin Market* from Christina Rossetti's 1859 poem of that name. Though a 562-line poem might seem an unlikely source for a full-length musical, the play opened off Broadway at the Vineyard Theater on October 17, 1985, to such a positive reaction that six months later it moved to Manhattan's larger Circle in the Square, where it enjoyed a successful run.[1] A chamber opera requiring only two singer-actresses and a four-piece orchestra, it has seen continued performance in regional theaters, such as Princeton Repertory, Nautilus Music-Theater at the Old Arizona Studio in Minneapolis, the Grove Theater Center in Burbank, California, and the Sound Theatre Company in Seattle as well as college performances, such as Louisiana State University and University of West Florida. A Christian allegory, a fairy tale, a children's story, a metaphor for sexual desire (either heterosexual or lesbian, or both), a story of addiction, an exploration of anorexia, a portrayal of incest, a depiction of the brutal market economy of prostitution, a psychological investigation of the divided self, a feminist statement of sisterhood, an investigation of animal or ecological environments, a human and particular tale of sisterly affection—such varied interpretations have made Rossetti's powerful *Goblin Market* controversial.[2]

One of the most striking changes that constitute the adaptation's rendering is that the play simultaneously rejects and reinstates the poem's lesbian implications. Besides substituting nonsexual staging for potentially sexual actions, *Goblin Market* excises important lines commonly used to support a homosexual reading of the poem and adds lyrics that instead emphasize a conventional sibling rivalry. Yet the very changes employed to deflect the poem's homoeroticism reinscribe the lesbian content in new form. In a sort of theatrical return of the repressed, the homosexual meaning ultimately reenters the play through Pen and Harmon's use of cross-gender performativity; by having each sister play the very sexual male goblins in turn, Pen and Harmon metaphorically accentuate the lesbian content their other changes elide.

When I interviewed Pen in 2014, she mentioned that the poem reflected two issues from the 1980s that stand out. One is the National Endowment for the Arts crisis about what counts as art—that is, what gets publicly funded as art. The other is the AIDS disaster. The sexually explicit 1989 exhibit of Robert Mapplethorpe photographs (including one of himself, dying of AIDS, with a bullwhip in his anus) that brought the issue of federal funding for controversial art into national headlines came well after the premiere of *Goblin Market*. But these concerns were already brewing in the mid-1980s, concurrently with the AIDS epidemic. And so, as Pen explains about the play's two protagonists, Lizzie and Laura, "These two girls, they are asking about how far do we go" (personal interview); the musical metaphorically explores both the peril and the necessity of an artist's going too far—too far for safety, too far for funding or professional reputation—in making a fundamental statement for professional artists of all kinds. But she also sees the play as asking "how you know how much can we consume? How you know how dangerous a position can we put ourselves in, and when should we stop?" She suggests that the musical addresses the terror of a disease that kills people for, essentially, loving one another, for giving into sexual temptation, that most basic of desires. The poem as well as the play pitches Lizzie against a terrible and incurable wasting illness that is killing her sister. Ultimately it offers the hope of a magical antidote procured through Lizzie's bravery, cleverness, and devotion, much like the treatment for AIDS so many fervently dreamed of in 1985, still ten years before the life-saving cocktail (highly active antiretroviral therapy, or HAART) appeared.

In addition to its evocation of AIDS and its implication in concerns over arts funding, and in addition to its insights into Rossetti's poem both as a literary text and as a future musical artifact, this show helps to theorize adaptation. Its source is Rossetti's narrative poem rather than a novel, once again subverting the typical novel-to-film model that undergirds most efforts to understand the processes and effects of reworking a text into a new medium. Because poetry derives from lyrical traditions of oral transmission, it might seem generally more suitable for musicalization than prose. Yet only a few modern musicals are based on poems. The clearest immediate antecedent in this regard is *Cats* (1980 in London, 1981 in New York), composed by Andrew Lloyd Webber, based on T. S. Eliot's children's poetry volume *Old Possum's Book of Practical Cats* (1939), but Lloyd Webber's unusual choice has not often been successfully imitated.[3] Pen saw her work making musical theater out of serious poetry as new, as experimental; though Rossetti's poem is "not written for music, . . . that's what I knew I loved about it. . . . I'm always looking for a musical work that extends our idea of what could be done in musical theater . . . because verse poems have gone very much out of our consciousness, a great deal out of the theater, where they lived so beautifully for so long" (personal interview). Even though it has a forceful plot, being a musical based on a poem helps to place *Goblin Market*, like Holmes's *Drood*, among the more conceptual musicals of its decade; in fact, this is what Pen had in mind, explaining, "that, to me, was very . . . exciting: to have a piece in the New York theater that was in verse. I mean, it's just extremely rare, . . . aside from Shakespeare" (personal interview).

Part of the show's experimental force as an adaptation comes from its commitment to the language and medium of its source. Pen explains,

> I was surprised at how easily it sang itself. . . . I didn't have to force it into a structure. You know the voice is an extraordinary thing, and it can do so much. But when you are setting text, there are certain vowels that are great for singing, and there are vowels that are killers. . . . Rossetti— I don't know whether she sang—but it is completely singable. . . . Just her sheer . . . sound sense of the piece is extraordinary. I mean when the goblins . . . have the rhythm—it's all there. She gives it to you. So that was a joy to discover, that . . . wasn't something I was going to have to labor over making her words work. They just did. (personal interview)

Pen's process as composer and book writer reveals the musicality and musical-theatricality already implicit in Rossetti's poem. She articulates explicitly what we have seen the other adapters do with their source texts. The singability that Pen mentions matters enormously in a composer's choice to create a musical, whether from poetry or prose. This is surely part of what Sondheim considers with *Sweeney Todd*, in some cases musicalizing long passages of

Christopher Bond's dialogue almost verbatim. Coincidently, *Sweeney Todd* is Pen's favorite musical (personal interview). But Lerner and Loewe do the same in *My Fair Lady,* taking lines directly from the George Bernard Shaw play, as in Henry Higgins's "I've Grown Accustomed to Her Face."[4]

The pleasurable surprise we feel in hearing familiar text in song differs from the pleasure of recognition we experience in hearing the lines spoken in a nonmusical adaptation in a straight play or in a film or television show in part because of the skills required to make the lines work as lyrics set to music. But there's more to it. Pen notes that the narrative of the poem "can be understood within musical time" (personal interview), suggesting that the vivid economy of image in narrative poetry translates into music differently from how prose narrative can be presented on stage or film. Ultimately, the medium of music provides a vehicle to express the emotion carried by the intensity of poetic language. Ironically, it is the intensity of poetic expression that makes its adaptation to the stage a daunting prospect.

Another way in which Pen parallels Holmes's *Drood* is in the use of cross-gender performance. But while in *Drood,* Betty Buckley's performing Miss Nutting's performance of Edwin Drood is all irony, in *Goblin Market,* the actresses' playing Lizzie and Laura's portrayal of the goblins is in deadly earnest. Judith Butler argues that gender does not exist except as it is performed. The implications of this theory for theater are enormously important, because whenever gender is enacted onstage, it reveals the performative quality of gender offstage as well. In Butler's own words, "Gender is in no way a stable identity or locus of agency from which various acts proceed; rather it is an identity tenuously constituted in time—an identity of a stylized repetition of acts" ("Performing Acts" 270).[5] In other words, since there is no a priori validity for the existence of gender and since it has no material basis, it exists only through presentation. We make gender by acting it:

> If gender attributes ... are not expressive but performative, then these attributes effectively constitute the identity they are said to express or reveal. ... If gender attributes and acts, the various ways in which a body shows or produces its cultural signification, are performative, then there is no preexisting identity by which an act or attribute might be measured; there would be no true or false, real or distorted acts of gender, and the postulation of a true gender identity would be revealed as a regulatory fiction. (279)

If gender is constituted by performance, if performance constructs rather than reveals a preexisting gender, then the fact that the two sisters from *Goblin Market* also perform the roles of the sexually symbolic male goblins establishes the characters as (goblin) men. The musical itself, while it sublimates the lesbian sexuality of the poem, offers a far more extreme sexual transgression onstage by exploding gender itself, exposing in Butler's terms that the idea of a "true" gender identity is a "regulatory fiction."[6]

What follows is an extended close reading of the musical's reading of the poem, emphasizing its simultaneous repression and reinstatement of the verse's lesbian content. This includes theorizing performance and concludes with more observations about the show's implicit commentary on art and AIDS.

READING *GOBLIN MARKET*

To explain more fully the significance of how Rossetti's poem transforms into a contemporary musical theater, I first offer a synopsis. Although very well known to Victorian scholars, the poem is less familiar to general readers. The musical too is the least well known of all I discuss, despite its success. The poem and the show's language require detailed attention, as minute changes from page to stage make an enormous difference in meaning.

Goblin Market narrates the tale of two young sisters, Lizzie and Laura, who hear the daily cry of goblin merchant men, hawking their miraculous fruit, which is first introduced with "a list of fruits" that the composer, Pen, found so "beautifully musical," so "clean and crisp and clear" that, she said, "it just sang to me" (personal interview).

> Come buy, come buy: . . .
> Plump unpecked cherries, . . .
> Bloom-down-cheeked peaches, . . .
> Wild free-born cranberries . . .
> All ripe together
> In summer weather, . . .
> Sweet to tongue and sound to eye;
> Come buy; come buy. (4–31)[7]

While proper Lizzie covers her ears and runs away, adventurous Laura stays in the twilight to purchase her fill of the forbidden fruit with a golden curl of her hair. In a frenzy of oral abandon, she eats and eats "until her lips [are] sore" (136), then goes home joyously to Lizzie, who recognizes Laura's mistake and fears that her sister will suffer terribly for having tasted the goblin's illicit wares. The next day Laura insatiably craves more, but she can no longer hear the goblins, who now call to only Lizzie every evening.

As Laura wastes away for want of the only thing that can satisfy her hunger, Lizzie bravely determines to go to the goblins and purchase some fruit for her sister. The "little men" first try to entice and then to force her to swallow their food herself. When she resists, they violently attack her, hold her, "Kicked and knocked her, / Mauled and mocked her" (428–29), and push the fruit against her closed mouth, resulting in its juices smearing all over her body in a scene often read as attempted rape: "Held her hands and squeezed their fruits / Against her mouth to make her eat" (406–7). Lizzie successfully resists the goblins, refusing to "open lip from lip / Lest they should cram a mouthful in" (430–31); their fruit juices have merely coated her uncovered skin and lodged in its crevices. "Like a royal virgin town" (418) or "Like a lily in the flood" (409), Lizzie triumphantly repels her attackers. She returns home covered with the goblins' fruit juices, which provide the antidote for Laura's illness when Laura "kissed and kissed and kissed" them off her sister's face and body (486). After a night of pain and agonized rejuvenation, Laura awakens healthy and restored. In the final verse paragraph, the narrator tells how, years later, when the girls grow up, they have daughters of their own and that Laura tells all their children of "how her sister stood / In deadly peril to do her good" (557–58). The poem closes in a celebration of sororal harmony, in which Laura gathers the children,

> Then joining hands to little hands
> Would bid them cling together,
> "For there is no friend like a sister
> In calm or stormy weather;
> To cheer one on the tedious way,
> To fetch one if one goes astray,
> To lift one if one totters down,
> To strengthen whilst one stands." (560–67)

THE RETURN OF THE REPRESSED

Even a straightforward reading aloud of the poem entails interpretive choices on the issue of sexuality. For example, we have seen that in the poem Lizzie gleefully returns from her trip to the *Goblin Market* where, without having been tricked into eating, she has endured the torment of the goblins, who unwittingly fill her body's nooks and crannies with the syrupy cure for Laura. She comes before her sister and says, "Hug me, kiss me, suck my juices / Squeezed from goblin fruits for you" (468–69). Here the poem's line break allows a visual pause after "juices," emphasizing its sexual significance. In a silent apprehension of the line, the solitary reader can have it both ways, enjoying the line's ambivalence. In performance, however, one can either linger at the line break to make the visual pause an aural one, or one can read through the line's turn, emphasizing not "suck my juices" but instead their origin in the goblin fruits. The latter emphasis may be equally sexual, but metaphorically rather than literally, because in the syntax of the complete sentence we are talking about fruit juice, not human juice, for Laura to suck. The second reading reduces the shock value of the lines in two other ways. First, because the sexual connection—even if it takes place between the girls—is only at second hand, by proxy; the seminal juices travel from the goblins through Lizzie to Laura.[8] Second, for an audience constructed as heterosexual, it seems less transgressive to imagine metaphorical sexuality between Laura and the goblin men, instead of between the sisters.

In performance, this tiny inflection (pausing or not after "juices") affects the audience's interpretation irrevocably, since the lines cannot be read aloud both ways simultaneously. If one pauses, one implies a lesbian meaning; if one reads through the turn, one does not. In the 1989 Princeton Rep production—the first regional production, approved by Pen on her trip from New York to see it (Liberatori, personal interview)—the actress playing Lizzie spoke the lines without the slightest hesitation at the crucial moment.[9] The actress playing Laura, rather than sucking at Lizzie's dimples onstage, took her sister's face in her hands, drew her hands away to see that the goblin juice now clung to them, and voraciously licked her own palms, avoiding any perceptible sexual gesture between the sisters.

This example comes from a line in the musical unchanged from the poem, spoken rather than sung (and thus without the added significance of musical intonation), embedded within the same lines which surround it in the original, as uncomplicated by the theatrical context as one can get in the whole adaptation. And yet here the interpretive power of performance makes all the difference. But everything is complicated by theatrical context: the experience of seeing an adult flesh-and-blood actress licking and sucking another on live stage differs dramatically from imagining, in the reading mind's eye, a Victorian child in a fable kissing her sister to receive the magic antidote to her illness. This difference operates even when the solitary reader fully recognizes the sexual possibilities that the poem permits.

Not even the late twentieth-century Broadway of *La Cage aux Folles* (1983) or *Falsettos* (1992)—where sophisticated audiences accept a plot that poignantly climaxes with gay men singing in bed together, but never voraciously licking each other—can transgress social boundaries as safely as a nineteenth-century children's poem, as *Goblin Market* is sometimes designated.[10] As one theater critic points out, the line "hug me, kiss me, suck my juices" from this Victorian "children's classic" is unprintable in the context of a modern newspaper review (Bob Campbell 46). Even the Pulitzer- and Tony-winning *Angels in America: A Gay Fantasia on National Themes* (1991 premiere in San Francisco/1993 on Broadway), a heart-wrenching examination of AIDS and homosexuality in the 1980s, defuses its sex scene in some productions by placing the two actors on opposite ends of the stage, facing the audience rather than each other.[11] In *Forbidden Journeys* Nina Auerbach and U. C. Knopflmacher theorize that the genre of children's fantasy literature provided Victorian women writers (Rossetti among them), in their pre-Freudian age of childhood innocence, with a venue for political and sexual subversion that was denied them in their own work for adult audiences. However, the level of transgression in Rossetti's poem is still too great today for presentation to commercial audiences, even when—unlike *Goblin Market* but like *Angels in America*—they are exclusively aimed at adults.

The most noticeable difference between the texts of poem and musical is that, unlike the poem's straightforward, linear narrative structure, the show operates through a flashback. This major structural change focuses attention on the adults present at the beginning and end of the musical. The poem has no frame, beginning directly with the goblin cry. The adaptation relegates the main action to the realm of memory or even of remembered, shared fantasy. By placing all the action retrospectively in the women's return to their girlhood nursery and by introducing it with a word game (based on the goblin's call to "come buy" their fruit), the show suggests that the whole goblin experience is also a game. The effect is necessarily one of reduction, making the fantasy less powerful by denying it the reality that the poem claims for it unabashedly. Framing—and containing—the powerful fantasy constrains its subversive feminist force by wrapping it tightly into a realistic, representative setting.

Several feminist performance theorists, such as Sue-Ellen Case, Jill Dolan, and Elin Diamond, argue that realism is inherently anti-feminist in its mimetic effort to reproduce a masculinist society (Dolan, *Presence and Desire* 138–39; Diamond, "Violence of 'We'" 407). Case contends (with Baudrillard) that "realism . . . impoverishes the suggestiveness of the scene by its excess of means" ("Butch-Femme Aesthetic" 297). Certainly this musical's realistic devices repress its own fantasy elements by suggesting a realistic setting beyond itself. The Victorian mourning clothes that the adult Lizzie and Laura wear imply a funeral; the staircase the women use to enter their childhood nursery suggests a downstairs parlor and so on to the rest of the house; in general, the show conjures a larger realistic universe beyond the action onstage. These added trappings throw the ensuing drama of temptation and redemption—confined as we shall see to nursery and underwear—into a realm of fantasy and myth defined in opposition to the real world of the frame.

The play begins in a spare, stylized version of a Victorian nursery with all the furniture draped. Two women enter slowly one after the other, dressed in black crinoline, shawls, and bonnets. They are the adult Lizzie and Laura. Looking around the room nostalgically, they appear to recall their childhoods, unveiling the furniture and handling objects fondly. Lizzie opens a music box, and it plays a tune. The women pick up the song's refrain, which turns out to be "All Ripe Together," based on the opening "Come buy" cry of the goblins. Pen's composition makes the song lyrical, lilting, harmonic, and very pretty; an audience unfamiliar with the poem does not yet know that this is the goblin men's chant. The song may remind some of the opening bars of "Who Will Buy?" from *Oliver!* because both present the call to purchase mercantile offerings as luscious, pleasant, and harmonious. But there is no musical echo and the words come straight from the poem.

After a memory game based on the sensuous catalogue of fruits that opens the poem, Lizzie asks Laura if she remembers the haunted glen (using lines from the poem's conclusion). Laura is shocked, Lizzie worried. For audiences who know the story, this surprise may seem odd, since the "All Ripe Together" refrain and all the fruits mentioned in the word game are borrowed from the goblins' own discourse. But to a fresh audience, these have seemed only pleasant pastimes; their relationship to the memories that follow only become apparent as the play unfolds. Lizzie's concern may be that she has overstepped the bounds of sisterly courtesy. After all, according to conventional Victorian morality, the adventure is all to Lizzie's credit and Laura's shame.[12] Indeed, in the poem, it is Laura who in loving gratitude tells the next generation the tale of how Lizzie saved her; surely it would be both immodest and indelicate (if not cruel) of Lizzie ever to bring up Laura's past transgression. In performance, before the audience can know the story, Lizzie's indelicacy and Laura's shock builds suspense and fosters an aura of the forbidden. After an uncomfortable moment, Laura releases the tension created by Lizzie's explicit evocation of the haunted glen by recalling the goblins herself.

At this point the lights dim and during a quiet musical interlude the women help each other strip down to pantaloons and a camisole for Laura and a nightgown for Lizzie. They transform the set into a haunted glen by rearranging the artifacts already on stage. Disrobing onstage and using nursery materials again implies that the ensuing action is a childhood game, a fantasy, quite different from the "real" experience of the girls as depicted in the poem. In the play, the women look much younger in their pure white sleepwear than in their mourning attire; a childish appearance is perhaps more appropriate to the poem, where Lizzie and Laura are unequivocally grown up only at the very end of the story, though their age is never stated. This staging paradoxically diffuses the poem's sexual overtones. The women take off each other's gowns soon after they arrive in the nursery in preparation for reliving childhood romps in their white, virginal, Victorian undergarments. They appear to return to their adolescence as they undress, peeling off the veneer of adulthood with their clothes. This process of undressing each other (in one production I saw, Lizzie helpfully unbuttons Laura's dress down the back; in turn Laura unbuttons Lizzie's down the front) establishes the kind of close personal contact sisters who share a bedroom and a bed maintain, without any romantic element in the relationship. The chaste undressing, which certainly could be played to such sexual significance, sets up this nonsexual intimacy from the start, allowing later lines, so charged in the poem, to arrive in the play without erotic force.

In Rossetti's time of state censorship, public stage disrobing would have been risqué, if not unthinkable (in a respectable theater), while sisters' hugging and kissing onstage would not.[13] The Victorian audience for the theater, like the audience for the poem, experienced their literary and dramatic productions through a different set of taboos, resulting in a differently enjoyed erotic experience. Likewise, various sexualities in the contemporary audience affect individual reactions to women's stripping onstage; an informal survey following the Princeton production revealed predictably that those members of the audience sexually attracted to women found the cooperative removal of clothing seductive, those not so attracted considered the actions devoid of erotic significance (Liberatori, personal interview).[14] Regardless of the audience's sexual orientation, playing the rest of the action in even the most demure state of dishabille suggests the vulnerability of private dress and hints at how unprotected the girls are when they encounter the goblins. And finally, despite the effects of sisterly closeness or exposed innocence, one cannot escape the coded sexuality both of undressing onstage and of wearing Victorian underwear in the age of Victoria's Secret.

After establishing the transition from realistic frame to nursery fantasy, the plot proceeds identically to the poem. Each girl speaks her own lines drawn from Rossetti, while the other narrates or plays the goblins, again using Rossetti's language. Since Laura goes to the goblin men first, virtuous Lizzie from the poem becomes a goblin in the play long before Laura transgresses by eating forbidden fruits. Jill Dolan urges cross-gender casting to force audiences to recognize the arbitrariness of sexual difference (*Presence and Desire* 138). Similarly, Sue-Ellen Case notes the feminist utility of "impersonating" the opposite sex in drama (*Feminism and Theatre* 80), and Lizzie's stage directions, which say she "gives voice to the goblins" (16), require her to embody the male role. In essence, the play *Goblin Market* does what Dolan and Case suggest by having the girls play the male goblins. In an almost anti-realistic move, the play forces the audience to read the seductive goblins as male, even while the female actresses in frilly underwear portray them. Nevertheless, the fact of the actresses' sex—their female embodiment—remains part of the semiotic code of the goblins' presentation. Simultaneously girl and goblin, Lizzie seduces Laura with the forbidden fruit; the interaction's lesbian impact cannot be unseen by anyone interested in apprehending it.[15]

In addition to providing the initial instance of gender-crossing in the play, this scene provides the musical's first fully comedic moments. Lizzie gets the fruits, which are obviously toys—in the production I saw, toys of operatic proportions—from the dollhouse, coyly displaying them to tempt Laura while speaking the goblin's poetry. She is all boyish nonchalance. Casually polishing an apple to offer Laura, Lizzie mimics goblin voices while narrating (16). Throughout Laura's earnest answer to the goblin men, Lizzie comically whistles like a bird—or a boy—just as she had a moment earlier voiced the goblins' whistling and animal sounds. Producing toy fruit from the dollhouse once again underscores the fantastical, placing the gender-crossing itself into the world of the sisters' shared desire, emphasizing rather than deflating the poem's homoerotic pressure.

SISTERS

After Laura returns from the goblin den, the girls proceed to sing a song whose lyrics are not from Rossetti's poem at all. However, the song is clearly inspired by this passage from the poem noted for its lesbian suggestiveness:[16]

> Golden head by golden head,
> Like two pigeons in one nest
> Folded in each other's wings,
> They lay down in their curtained bed. (184–87)

The verse paragraph concludes with an image of the girls lying "Cheek to cheek and breast to breast / Locked together in one nest" (196–98). Helena Michie points out how easy it is to see these lines as an invocation of erotic sameness between the sisters. Yet, as Michie explains, this passage occurs after Laura's fall so that, for all their physical similarities, the girls are now in different worlds: Lizzie represents sameness and undifferentiation, Laura (along with the goblins) difference (414–17). This tension in part enables the power of the lines' eroticism.

By cutting this passage, Pen and Harmon obviate the need to deal with the homoerotic nuances of the girls' sleeping "Locked together in one nest." Instead, they heighten images of sameness and insert an element of sibling rivalry that negates further the sense of a lesbian connection between the girls by interpolating "The Sisters," a song with sprightly music and lyrics borrowed from "Die Schwestern" by Rossetti's nearly exact contemporary Johannes Brahms (1833–1897). The duet at first picks up some of the spirit of the missing section, which establishes the girls' sameness. They sing that they are "like as like can be, / As eggs are like each other, / . . . Or one star like another, / You can't tell her from me"; these lines echo in more mundane terms Rossetti's litany of similes "Like two blossoms on one stem, / Like two flakes of new-fall'n snow, / Like two wands of ivory" (188–90). Their hair is just the same, and they are "together all the day," spinning a single thread, sewing a single sampler, and sleeping in a double bed—again the same idea without the poetic force that adds to the erotic potential of Rossetti's poetry.[17] Pen and Harmon's lyrics follow the Brahms closely for four verses. But whereas Brahms's song ends with a twist when the sisters fall in love with the same man, the final verse of the musical's "The Sisters" concludes with a different comic surprise that also highlights sibling rivalry, with both girls singing:

> O sisters we, so lovely, so lovely,
> Now who is the loveliest one?
> I am, I am, I am, I am, I am!
> You see we're quite alike,
> We're both so very contrary,
> Quite alike. (21–22)

For the first three verses the girls sing sweetly, usually in pleasing thirds, with Lizzie taking the soprano part. The Brahms tune—very different in style from Pen's compositions—suggests that we are to hear this as a song made for performance within the Victorian world of the play, an art song that might be sung in a parlor by accomplished young women. In the last verse, a shift from G minor to major signals a change in tone; as the girls sing, their voices become increasingly discordant, so that the rivalry expressed in the final verse is sung brashly. During the string of five "I am"s, Laura takes the higher note three times, resulting in an effect of competition for the upper hand, so to speak. The final "I" is sung by the two women only one note apart, the greatest musical discord in the song. These discordant notes are the longest, held for an entire measure. They are part of a suspended chord—often used in Western music to reflect tension—that is never resolved by the voices (although the piano eventually does offer the resolving note, something we have just seen in *Drood*'s "Moonfall"). "Am" restores the voices to their previous harmony, but with Laura singing the top note, a third above Lizzie. The rivalry expressed in the music and lyrics here does not appear in the poem. It is rather part of a modern view of sisters' relationship that twentieth-century film and Broadway reflect more generally and the musical repeatedly employs both for humor and for increased relevance as well as to dissolve any lingering questions about the possibility of an incestuous lesbian relationship between the girls. Pen vehemently disagrees with an incestuous reading of her own play, no matter what interpretations the poem might permit, recalling, "They tried to sell the show at some point by commenting on, you know, possible incest or something. And I went, 'Oh my God, no, that's actually not what this is" (personal interview).

Pen's "The Sisters" is in some ways very like Irving Berlin's "Sisters" (which echoes Brahms in the spirit of the concluding lyrics), an earlier musical comedy song from the 1954 movie *White Christmas*. In *Goblin Market*'s "The Sisters," Lizzie and Laura's seemingly harmonious unanimity grates on the girls as each successive verse makes them seem to chafe at their lockstep lack of individuality, undermining the erotic force their sameness may carry in the poem. In *White Christmas,* the Haynes sisters—a professional sister-act within the movie (played by Rosemary Clooney and Vera-Ellen) who perform the number diegetically as a paying gig—express their devotion and annoyance with always "caring, sharing / every little thing that [they] are wearing," of always having to think and act "as one." This tension between affection and competition (not necessarily present in the first four verses of Brahms's "Die Schwestern") is highlighted later in the film by the song's reprise, performed (again diagetically in a professional performance) in cross-dress by the sisters' talented beaus, played by Bing Crosby and Danny Kaye. Their drag rendition plays up the rivalry implicit in the number for additional (and arguably misogynist) comic effect. In both the Haynes' and their boyfriends' drag versions of Berlin's "Sisters," the humor and the vitriolic sibling rivalry culminate in the lines "Many men have tried to split us up, / But no one can / Lord help the mister / Who comes between me and my sister / Lord help the sister, / Who comes between me and my man." These lines privilege the heterosexual over the sororal by making the relationship between "me and my man" the last word on the subject. Because Bing Crosby and Danny Kaye sing the reprise, the movie *White Christmas* even gives the last words of the song by and about sisters to men.[18] Pen and Harmon's *Goblin Market* inherits and reworks a legacy of prior texts in Brahms and Berlin's sister songs. Though they retain both songs' sibling rivalry, they omit the focus of that rivalry on an outside male figure. The only men in the musical *Goblin Market* remain the goblins as played or imagined by Lizzie and Laura.

GENDER CODING

Just as in *White Christmas,* in *Goblin Market* cross-gender performance matters. When Lizzie enters the goblin glen to get Laura's antidote, Laura portrays the goblins. The actress playing Laura requires considerable athleticism as she embodies the goblin men. She violently contorts her form into goblinesque shapes. In highly choreographed movements, she buffets Lizzie. The disorienting visual effects, the women chanting eerily in an uncomfortable syncopated counterpoint, and the harsh repetition of the word "bite," sung in lyrics mixed up from both the poem's figurative rape scene and the earlier litany of fruits, fuse to create a frightening theatrical experience. Laura takes the masculine role here, the part of the metaphorical rapist-goblins forcing their fruits on Lizzie. But the layers of cross-gender impersonation have a meaning of their own. As the threatening goblin, Laura remains not only the female actress we see onstage, but also the adult woman character Laura reenacting the original experience, which may well have been a game the girls played together, without any real male goblins to begin with. In other words, through the performance, women become men, and men are embodied only as women. What the play illustrates through this complexity is not that notions of gender evaporate; rather, the woman simultaneously playing Laura and the goblins remains coded as a woman onstage: she still displays a female shape through her knee-length lacy underwear, still sports long hair, and still sings in a female voice. No matter how taken in the audience is by her performance of the goblin attack on Lizzie (completely convincing, in the Princeton Rep production), we know that both the actress and the character Laura are still there onstage embodying the goblins. We always see the goblins with double or triple vision. We know that not only the goblins but also Laura assaults Lizzie, trying to force her to open lip from lip; we know that earlier it is not just the goblins but also Lizzie who seduces Laura, so that the same-sex eroticism of the poem is displaced in the play onto Lizzie's seduction of Laura and Laura's attempted rape of Lizzie.

Laura's aggressive posture signals a more stereotypically masculine goblin in contrast to Lizzie's earlier rendition, whose performance in the production might seem more impish than satanic. The costumes contribute to this interpretation. Compared to Lizzie's nightgown, Laura's pantaloons can be read as pants.[19] In putting Laura in a pants-like costume, Pen and Harmon's musical echoes nineteenth-century operatic pants roles, which provided female singers with an opportunity to play men onstage, and provided respectable audiences with the opportunity to see the somewhat racy spectacle of a woman's legs displayed in breaches or even a doublet and hose.[20] But unlike the pants roles contemporaneous with Rossetti herself, the goblins are not costumed more "realistically" as men—or even as goblins—during the enchanted scenes while the actresses playing Lizzie and Laura are impersonating the opposite sex. They merely hint at a more masculine costume for the more transgressive, more desiring, more virile, more butch sister.

In this scene, Laura's physical prowess in contrast to Lizzie's delicacy also functions as gender coding or as a butch-femme enactment. Sue-Ellen Case explains in her discussion of the lesbian troupe Split Britches' *Beauty and the Beast* (1983), "The butch, who represents by her clothing the desire for other women, becomes the beast—the marked taboo against lesbianism dressed up in the clothes of that desire. . . . *Beauty and the Beast* also returns to a childhood tale of taboo and liberates the sexual preference and role-playing it is designed to repress, in this case, specifically the butch-femme promise. As some lesbians prescribed in the early movement: identify with the monsters!" ("Butch-Femme Aesthetic" 294–95). It is not hard to make the leap from beast to goblin; *Goblin Market* is another childhood tale of taboo for which the play's role-playing may reveal what is repressed. By adding the goblin impersonations and distinguishing Laura in her dress, the play subtly evokes the concept of butch-femme role-playing. Each girl enacts and thus manifestly identifies with the monsters at least temporarily, as actors do while playing a part. When Pen states of the poem, "I saw something that was innately theatrical . . . because theater is about contrast to me" (personal interview), she points to a way that the musical helps us to read the poem through this similarity in contrast: Lizzie so identifies with the Eve-like, monstrous Laura that she braves the goblin glen; Laura so identifies with Lizzie's choice that loving gratitude is figured as desire.

Pen and Harmon choose women to play male roles, casting across gender lines rather than bringing in additional male actors to portray the goblins. In their notes, they explain their choice not to use "real goblins" (one may assume that means real actors, male or female) as part of the process of adaptation, leading them to think "less and less literally about the poem" to discover "instead a world that was based more and more in the imaginations and remembrances of the two sisters" (5). Here they explicitly place the goblin world in the imagination. If there are no real goblins, then Lizzie and Laura really are the goblins they "play"; their reenactment is of their own relationship and not an external adventure with tangible men, goblin or otherwise. If the story is one of their own fantasy, then it is Lizzie who seduces Laura and Laura who nearly rapes Lizzie, at least in their minds.

RELIGION

To end the goblin attack, Lizzie sings "Like a Lily," set as a solemn and uplifting hymn, while she successfully withstands the violent onslaught of the goblins:

> Like a royal virgin town
> Topped with gilded dome and spire
> Close beleaguered by a fleet
> Mad to tug her standard down.
>
> Like a lily in a flood
> Like a fruit-crowned orange tree,
> Like a beacon left alone,
> Like a royal virgin town. (31)

Even more than the corresponding lines in the poem, this song establishes Lizzie as the unapproachable, unrapeable virgin. "Like a Lily" starts calmly, very slow and very low. It requires Lizzie to sing in more than a two-octave range: it mounts higher and higher, faster and faster with ever quicker modulations as she achieves confidence both to withstand the temptation of the goblins' fruit and to resist the goblins' brutality. The highest and longest notes of all come on the final "virgin," the climax of Lizzie's purity and the exultant apex of the hymn.[21] While the poem also renders the image of the virgin town last in the series presented, a full four lines complete the conceit; in contrast, the play wraps the song up very quickly in only one more note on "town," ending the song on the virginal image still reverberating. Moreover, the line is offered twice in the song (it begins and ends the series of similes) and only once in the poem. Since interpretations of the poem often present Lizzie as a female Christ (sacrificing herself for her sister, enduring a beating for her, and resisting the temptations of a feast),[22] the rendition of her triumph through a hymn seems particularly apt. This is the closest that the musical *Goblin Market* comes to the Broadway tradition of an anthem, such as *Drood*'s "Don't Quit While You're Ahead." But unlike most anthems, it does not urge characters on to future action but narrates a plot incident. The only advice one might glean from it would be pro-abstinence, or at least anti-penetration.

The well-known Christian readings of the poem, either as an allegory for biblical fall and redemption or as feminist revision depicting Lizzie as a female Christ, are based not only on the plot of Laura's eating the "fruit forbidden" (479) and Lizzie's self-sacrifice and successful resistance of temptation, but also on a line famous for its sexual meaning: "Eat me, drink me, love me" (471). This is a clear allusion to the Eucharist—Holy Communion as the embodiment of Jesus's telling his apostles to eat his body and drink his blood at the Last Supper—that the musical retains. The Christian and sexual interpretations of the poem are often seen by students and critics as mutually exclusive, despite the rich evidence for both, often stemming from precisely the same tropes, as we see here.[23] Pen and Harmon's adaptation permits viewers to privilege a religious interpretation. In both the Princeton Rep and LSU productions, Lizzie held her hands out in a crucifixion pose when she reached the top of the ladder and the height of her song. But the effort to repress sexuality or to deflect it onto religion through the emphasis on Lizzie as both Virgin and Christ serves further to highlight gender and to concentrate our attention on the flip side of Lizzie's renunciation of sexuality: Laura's luxuriating in it and the goblins' exploitation of it, and thus both Laura and Lizzie's reveling in sexual desire and even sexual aggression as goblin-men impersonators.

When Lizzie has ascended the ladder to escape the goblins, glorying in her ascetic victory, Laura turns to the audience and slyly comments (straight from the Rossetti): "One may lead a horse to water / Twenty cannot make him drink" (31). Not only does this aside break the tension and bring a hearty laugh, it qualifies the meaning of Lizzie's resistance, presenting her as a bit faulty in her inability to err and frigid in her self-righteousness. Without changing a word, the dramatic presentation radically reverses the literal meaning of the poem, which seems unreservedly to applaud Lizzie's triumph, insinuating that like Lizzie anyone with enough faith or perseverance can just say "No" to rape.

RESOLUTION

To guarantee that no one imagines that Laura must "kiss and kiss" her sister "with a hungry mouth" as she does in the poem, the stage directions (normally describing the play's premiere performance) have Lizzie bringing Laura a piece of fruit (33). This change contradicts the poem, whose lines "eat me, drink me, suck my juices / squeezed from goblin fruits for you" (468–69) are predicated on the fact that Lizzie cannot bring back the fruit itself, which clearly Laura pines for. But it also violates the play, where Lizzie still invites her sister to suck her juices in these lines taken verbatim from the poem, without pausing at the line break (as I detailed earlier). The plot of both poem and play depends upon the fruit's non-transportability: it exists only in the moment of its offering, only in the presence of the goblins. Real money can't buy it, only a golden curl; it is not exchangeable for tender, not translatable into a normal market economy, and certainly not a movable feast—at least not by humans.[24] Despite all of this, the stage directions require Laura to eat the fruit Lizzie brings (33), in direct but not ironized contrast to Lizzie's lines. So inappropriate is this physical fruit that the Princeton Rep director could not make sensible use of it, despite its presence onstage. Yet the impetus to erase any visual sexual contact between the women as women is so great that the play makes nonsense of its own parameters—and perhaps of the inexplicability of mores prohibiting the forbidden fruit.

As in the poem, Laura recovers fully. The girls reprise "The Sisters" without the previous sense of rivalry, which is resolved musically: Laura sings the top vocal line throughout, and the slower pace (4/4 rather than 2/4 time) is sung tenderly. Afterward they help each other dress in their opening costumes, returning to the realistic frame. The show concludes with "Two Doves," another song based on the sisters' identity with each other, lines once again inspired by (but quite different from) those suppressed earlier (184–98) that have so contributed to a lesbian interpretation of the poem: "Two doves upon the selfsame branch, / Two lilies on a single stem, / Two butterflies upon one flower." The song continues with new lyrics, "O happy they who look on them / . . . hand in hand / And never give a thought to night" (37). As the sisters exit arm in arm, the stage directions call for them to pause "at the sound of the goblin cry" (37), a magical sort of noise consistently produced during goblin singing. Lizzie and Laura "register recognition independently, and continue out" (37). Although the musical has worked hard to frame the action realistically and relegate the goblin (and the cross-gender) experience to the world of fantasy, memory, and childhood games, it ultimately leaves the question of the goblins' reality unsettled. The goblin cry ironically undercuts the final words of the final song: clearly both women do "give a thought to night." Lizzie and Laura's independent recognition of the sound suggests that neither is willing to admit to the other the truth of their shared goblin (and perhaps sexual) experience; they are still haunted and perhaps isolated by the remembered encounter even after reenacting it together. In the 1989 Princeton Rep production, a funny gesture at the end of the play further tipped the scale toward admitting the goblin men's genuine existence: after the women have left the stage for the last time, little goblin lights—used throughout the play to signify the goblins' presence—pop back on when the goblin cry sounds, but now seen only by the audience, whose fourth-wall point of view confers a sense of surprise legitimacy to what is observed. These playful hints emphasize the drama's ambiguity as compared to the poem, where the goblin experience is narrated as real.

In their notes at the beginning of the published libretto and score, Pen and Harmon recognize that the poem *Goblin Market* has many interpretations, among them "an examination of Victorian sexuality and eroticism." But they see the poem "at its emotional core" as "the story of a very real and intimate relationship between two sisters" (5). The musical fully succeeds as that story. Yet its stringently downplaying the poem's homoeroticism paradoxically reinstitutes it by metamorphosing Lizzie and Laura into male goblins who seduce one sister and try to rape the other. The musical play makes no effort to hide the symbolism of the forbidden fruit they offer. All the hypnotic sexual imagery of the poetry regarding the goblins and their wares remains. Addressing a general middlebrow audience constructed as majority heterosexual, the musical covertly presents the poem's lesbian content embodying the goblins across gender lines, relegating it to the realm of fantasy, but imbuing it with the great power of sexuality repressed.

For Pen, the poem is "a way of looking at the world, a way of thinking about repression of freedom" (personal interview), both in terms of sexual desire and of free expression in art. She sees, and wants her audiences to see, the connections her musical makes to current issues. "My hope with *Goblin Market* or any show that I write," she says, "is that it unexpectedly takes us to where we live now, and it does it more strongly by being more remote. And that's why I . . . I like, things that are in another time" (personal interview). Pen returned to the mid-Victorian period in writing the music, lyrics, and book for *The Night Governess* (2000), commissioned by the McCarter Theater at Princeton and based on "Behind the Mask" (1866), a sensational novella by Louisa May Alcott about a governess who manipulates her employers. The show includes a song entitled "Odd Women," a nod to Gissing's novel of that name about the difficulties faced by the New Woman of the 1890s in a period of shifting expectations with increased rights and opportunities that brought corresponding backlash, making the link to both Victorian and millennial feminism even clearer. Her *Goblin Market* likewise uses its Victorian setting to comment obliquely not only on the struggle for feminist and lesbian rights but also on the rights of artists to free expression.

Premiering in 1985, *Goblin Market* speaks out at a time of increasing awareness of the AIDS crisis, smack in the middle of Larry Kramer's acceleration toward his 1987 founding of ACT UP and its vital interventions. In fact, Kramer's own autobiographical play about AIDS had just been produced; *The Normal Heart* opened at Joseph Papp's Public Theater on April 21, 1985, depicting the lack of progress in curing AIDS; Kramer's (or, rather, the main character's) increasingly militant reaction to sluggish response from the US government; and the tireless work of a female doctor, based on the real-life Linda Laubenstein, to treat the epidemic. Her name suggestively resounds with aural links through alliteration and assonance to both Lizzie and Laura. Given this context, Lizzie's actions to stop Laura's wasting disease stands in clear relation to the efforts by gay and lesbian activists—with ACT UP's motto of "Silence=Death"—to raise political awareness and federal funds to fight the scourge. If Lizzie did or said nothing, Laura would certainly die. It would be disingenuous to claim that this play is replete with social critique. Underlying the play's lyricism there is not so much critique of how our government and our society fail a portion of the population in their lack of response to a terrible social ill as there is an exhortation to help and a symbolic model of how to act (up) like a sister.

7

"Bring on the Men" and Women

Melodrama and Gender Performance in *Jekyll and Hyde*

By the 1990s, megamusicals such as *Miss Saigon* (1989) dominated Broadway. Megamusicals dazzle with overwhelming spectacle, epic plots, enormous casts, complicated sets, a deluge of advertising, "everything big, not small,"[1] so big that these shows deserve the label *mega*, including astronomical production costs (Sternfeld, *Megamusical* 2–3). The singers brandish huge vocal talent, but unlike opera stars, they generally employ a heavily produced pop sound that relies on microphones and elaborate electronic sound systems instead of the naked voice. The term *megamusical* was coined and gained currency in the 1980s by theater critics to describe (often derisively) European shows that were sweeping Broadway via Britain (Sternfeld, "Pitiful" 795), particularly *Les Misérables* and *Phantom of the Opera*. *Phantom*'s crashing chandelier provides a symbol for the megamusical's dependence on sensational, spectacular effects.[2] These two examples were typical also in being based on nineteenth-century or early twentieth-century stories, amplifying a parallel phenomenon in fiction of reviving a self-reflexive Victorian aesthetic through what is known as Neo-Victorian writing. This literary movement, while already brewing since at least the 1960s, took off in the 1990s, coinciding with the megamusical's rise.[3]

Adapted from Robert Louis Stevenson's *The Strange Case of Dr. Jekyll and Mr. Hyde* (1886), the megamusical *Jekyll and Hyde: The Musical* (1997) ran for 1,543 performances at the Plymouth Theater. It was the longest-running show in the theater's history, despite mixed reviews.[4] It began nearly a decade earlier, as a concept album with music by Frank Wildhorn and lyrics by Leslie Bricusse; releasing a concept album introduced the songs and created a young fan base. *Concept albums,* also sometimes called *album musicals,* are designed as complete entertainments in themselves, though famous examples—such as *Jesus Christ Superstar* (1969)—became Broadway musicals soon after (1971). A 1990 Alley Theatre production in Houston kicked off *Jekyll and Hyde*'s long and meandering trek of regional productions in a pre-Broadway tour, starting in 1995. A group of traveling fans called "Jekkies" started attending multiple performances even before the play opened in New York, and the audiences there averaged ten to fifteen years younger than Broadway's usual attendees (Wildhorn, personal interview). The show's biggest hit, "This Is the Moment," became a standard at weddings, on *American Idol,* and at "such anthem-friendly contexts as the Miss America pageant, the Olympics and the 1996 Democratic Convention" (Sternfeld, *Megamusical* 313).[5]

A large part of the megamusical genre's success is its dependence on melodrama. As Jessica Sternfeld points out, the megamusical often has a "dramatic or tragic plot full of noble, pitiable victims of political circumstance" ("Pitiful" 795), in which main characters die and audiences leave weeping. These plots are not only sourced in nineteenth-century tales but also rooted fully in what is commonly understood as the melodramatic mode, employing stock characters, heightened emotion, an emphasis on feeling over thought, a view that "behind reality, hidden by it yet indicated within it, there is a realm where large moral forces" operate for good and evil (Peter Brooks 22).[6] In other words, whereas *Sweeney Todd,* also a melodrama, both engrosses its audience in its melodramatic story and—in a Brechtian sense—alienates them from it, *Jekyll and Hyde* is unabashedly and unironically melodramatic in the popular sense. This is a defining feature of the megamusical, as Howard Kissell points out in his *New York Daily News* review of *Jekyll and Hyde*'s Broadway premiere:

> What such successful British musicals as "Phantom" and "Les Miz" have done is to restore 19th-century melodrama to a theater that imagined it had outgrown such things. The audience, though, never outgrew them. It never cottoned to the cerebralization of the American musical that occurred before the British onslaught. There are, in fact, fascinating undercurrents to a story that examines Victorian sexual repression, that pre-figures Freud's idea of the id. . . . "Jekyll" is, of course, pure melodrama. (40)

Kissell condescends to the genre but recognizes melodrama's force. He does not use "melodrama" as a pejorative term in the way some critics have wielded it to attack the megamusical: examples are Francis King in the *Daily Telegraph* in 1985 reviewing *Les Misérables* as "a lurid Victorian melodrama" or Anthony Lane of the *New Yorker* in 2006 panning the musical film adaptation of *Phantom of the Opera* as "impressively free of anything that does not smell of unpasteurized melodrama."

Both melodrama and the megamusical receive critique as privileging sentiment and spectacle over intellect, yielding escapist entertainment instead of inspiration to political action, as Brecht decried (Taylor 89–90). This is a charge largely sidestepped by musicals that have engaged in the "cerebralization" that Kissell mentions at work on Broadway prior to the megamusical, perhaps thinking of anything by Sondheim, who always fully engages the mind along with the senses. But Victorian stage melodrama also offers cultural critique, mixed with escapism, going back to its roots in the French Revolution and the French *melo-drame* imported from France to England to the United States (McWilliam 56). So, too, perhaps with some megamusicals: it is clear, for example, that *Les Miz* (along with Victor Hugo) sides with the poor just as nineteenth-century "melodrama tends to favour the cause of the dispossessed rather than of those in power" in part because "the graphic depiction of social misery is itself incendiary" (Gerould, "Melodrama and Revolution" 185, 188). Though it is harder to make that claim with *Jekyll and Hyde*, it pays attention to class stratification and addresses some serious social issues. It calls out hypocrisy among the elite claiming to help the underclass. And the fact that "This Is the Moment" showed up at the Democratic National Convention in 1996 suggests that *Jekyll and Hyde* may foster more political influence than appears likely at first glance.

Although primarily an adaptation of *The Strange Case of Dr. Jekyll and Mr. Hyde*, the musical play weaves together materials from far beyond Stevenson's fiction. Tracing the lines of inheritance—from the novel, though a variety of other sources, to the musical adaptation—seems particularly appropriate, given that the story hinges on the legacy outlined in Jekyll's last will and testament stipulating that, in the event of his own disappearance, all his money should go to Hyde. The musical borrows much of its dramatic structure from prior film adaptations, just as we have seen Lionel Bart rework David Lean's *Oliver Twist*, which in turn was influenced by earlier films, dramatizations, and illustrations. The chief difference in plot between the 1997 musical and the 1886 novella is the introduction of female lead characters to provide romantic interest. Indeed, the almost complete lack of women in Stevenson's novella has been a subject of critical discussion.[7] It prompted the novel *Mary Reilly* (1990) and its film adaptation starring Julia Roberts and John Malkovich (1996), imagining the entire tale from the point of view of one of the novel's very few female characters, an unnamed servant in Dr. Jekyll's home whose chief task is to faint. Virtually every dramatization of the novel since its publication, going back to the very first melodrama *Dr. Jekyll and Mr. Hyde* (1887) by Thomas Russell Sullivan, inserts a leading role for an actress. Stevenson's wife, Fanny, saw its New York production in September of 1887, prompting Stevenson himself to approve it as the only version authorized for the stage. Sullivan explained his choice to include women by stating that they are vital theatrically. Similarly, a century later, Frank Wildhorn explains that he and Bricusse chose to include women because "the book is kind of dry—no women. You need women musically" for a full range of sound and musical texture (personal interview).

Like Sullivan's play, the Broadway musical makes explicit the book's implicit conjunction of illicit sexual behavior and physical brutality. Hyde's crimes in prose fiction deal with nonsexual violence (trampling a little girl, murdering an old man without provocation); the narrative hints at sexual misbehavior primarily by mentioning Hyde's pleasure-seeking and by placing Hyde's residence in Soho, a disreputable part of London in the late nineteenth century. But an entirely chance series of events added a new element of sexual violence to the resonance of Sullivan's melodrama. Its London production the season immediately following its New York opening happened to coincide precisely with the horrific series of murders of women in Whitechapel, forever after associating Jekyll and Hyde with Jack the Ripper, as almost all subsequent films and the Wildhorn-Bricusse musical make clear. The 2013 Broadway revival made this graphically evident in the logo displayed on the opening night Playbill cover and in print advertisements: the final letter "l" in "Jekyll" tapers into a bloody knife point, a weapon never used by Stevenson's Hyde, but very much associated with Jack the Ripper (fig. 8).

The doubled women characters in *Jekyll and Hyde* and much of the musical's depiction of Victorian class and gender relations owe a debt to the novels of Dickens: again, for Broadway, "Victorian" means "Dickensian." In addition, the history of adaptation I excavate in this chapter provides a surprising detour into Oscar Wilde's *The Picture of Dorian Gray* via the 1920 Famous Players-Lasky film *Dr. Jekyll and Mr. Hyde,* directed by John

Figure 8. Playbill for *Jekyll & Hyde: The Musical*, Marquis Theatre, New York, April 2013. (Author's private collection; used by permission; all rights reserved, Playbill, Inc.)

S. Robertson and starring John Barrymore and Nita Naldi; Robertson's film assimilates plot, characters, and dialogue from Wilde's novel, contributing a little Wilde DNA to later Hollywood adaptations of Stevenson's story and ultimately to the Broadway megamusical. The pages that follow delineate this complex genealogy of Stevenson's novel, Sullivan's play, Jack the Ripper, *The Picture of Dorian Gray*, Dickens, adaptations of Dickens, and several film adaptations of *Dr. Jekyll and Mr. Hyde* to analyze the cultural work that the musical *Jekyll and Hyde* accomplishes. It negotiates—primarily by taming—the horrors of serial violence dominating the news and popular representations of serial killers in the 1990s. It illustrates the social and psychological damage of living a lie (particularly lies about sexual desire and behavior) and presenting a façade to the world. It presents the hypocrisy of Victorian sexual double standards, implying that we know better now; yet the unrelenting series of sex scandals in high places throughout the 1990s belies this assumption.[8] It revels unabashedly in the melodramatic and Neo-Victorian. It points out the psychological and cultural cost of trying to split off parts of oneself that the dominant culture reviles as evil, a message that fits easily into accelerating mainstream acceptance of the gay community in the final decade of the twentieth century. *Jekyll and Hyde* addresses the myriad issues of identity performance percolating in this period, highlighting that identity is always performed and that performance proves identity. *Jekyll and Hyde* reveals the megamusical theatricality implicit in Stevenson's prose.

MELODRAMA, MURDER, AND SENSATION: SULLIVAN'S 1887 ADAPTATION

Soon after reading Stevenson's novella in 1886, the American actor Richard Mansfield commissioned playwright Sullivan (a friend) to write an adaptation in accordance with Mansfield's own ideas of how to dramatize the story, one that would showcase his considerable thespian talents. The resulting melodrama, *Dr. Jekyll and Mr. Hyde,* premiered on May 9, 1887, in Boston, receiving good notices. It moved to New York on September 12 (after revision, as is typical) to play at the Madison Square Garden Theater, where it proved to be the biggest opening night the theater had ever seen (Danahay and Chisolm 104).[9] Mansfield took the production to London, premiering on August 4, 1888, at the Lyceum Theatre under the auspices of Henry Irving.[10] Besides dropping the words "The Strange Case" from the title, the script's most obvious alteration is that Sullivan's plot provides a "love element," in the *Boston Globe*'s words, "thought so essential to the success of any stage production" ("Mansfield's Triumph" 111). Sullivan creates a daughter for Sir Danvers Carew, Agnes, a young woman as angelic and supportive as her namesake, Dickens's Agnes Wickfield from *David Copperfield*. Her father is the novella's "aged beautiful gentleman with white hair," the MP whose "innocent and old-world kindness" shone in the moonlight before Hyde suddenly and without provocation bludgeons him to death with a heavy cane (46). The play makes Jekyll younger, creating a more appropriate marriage partner for the blooming Agnes; even among the Victorians, for whom significant age differences were not objectionable, a younger suitor would be more, well, suitable. A younger Jekyll would, moreover, better fit Mansfield, in his early thirties.[11] Furthermore, the new circumstances make Hyde's crime even more odious. As the May 10, 1887, *Boston Post* points out, when Sullivan alters the novel's Jekyll—"a large, well-made, smooth-faced man of fifty, with a slyish cast perhaps" (44)—into a young man engaged to marry the newly invented Agnes Carew, his murder of her father "becomes particularly revolting" ("Dr. Jekyll and Mr. Hyde" 109).

But the addition of Agnes does much more than heighten the horror for an audience seeing the brutal destruction of her father; it changes the suspenseful case study into a drama with elements of tragedy or, at least, of pathos. As Mansfield explained to the *Pall Mall Gazette* just before his play opened in London, his "Dr. Jekyll is in love with Agnes Carew, and what makes the story the more tragic is that when he is himself, he, a good man then, feels what a base scoundrel and inhuman villain he is while he's Hyde, and his grief becomes accentuated, for he is for ever thinking 'I'm not worthy of her—I'm not worthy of my darling'" ("Real" 103). Partly to intensify the contrast between the characters of Jekyll and Hyde in his performance, Mansfield simplifies Jekyll by making him less worldly, less smooth, less hypocritical, less a mixture of good, bad, and other traits. The actor complains that Stevenson "made a mistake . . . in making Dr. Jekyll a jovial, happy, amiable dinner party giving, jolly-good-fellow" ("Real" 103). Although the *New York Herald* grumbled that Mansfield's Jekyll was "melancholy from the beginning, not the fine, portly doctor of the original story, but a morose, pale, long, blackhaired youthful misanthrope" ("Dr. Jekyll and Mr. Hyde" 116), Mansfield asserts, "That is where I believe I've improved on Mr. Stevenson's conception" ("Real" 103).

Improvement or not, Sullivan amends the story to focus on the domestic, locating it largely in the Carews' house and peopling it with an innocent ingénue and a comic older companion in her aunt, Mrs. Lanyon—both staple characters of melodrama. The assembled mixed company drinks tea, plays chess, and humors old General Sir Danvers Carew in his reminiscences of long-past Indian campaigns, a touch that suggests the American adapter is at once romanticizing and diminishing British imperialism.

A colonial officer, this Carew is not a democratically elected Member of Parliament; the change removes him from the structures of representative government and intensifies his Britishness for an American audience, for whom elections are symbolic of their own republic. The alteration in setting from a doctor's laboratory to a cozy middle-class drawing room as well as the switch from eerie mystery to a thwarted marriage plot constitutes a part of the generic shift from Gothic tale to melodrama. As Brian Rose points out, the play offers "a close examination of how Jekyll's work disrupts his relationships" with his bride and her family as well as with his friends; "when carried too far, [it] evokes personal catastrophe, the effects of which are displayed as being centered in the home" (38). Rose further explains, "The perceived casualties of Jekyll's actions are the patterns of relationships (including marital and parental) and their connections to the collective social body" (38). Connecting domestic and societal catastrophe is another convention of melodrama, which, as David Mayer tells us, responds "to immediate social circumstances and concerns" (146). No parental or marital devastation can occur in Stevenson's novel, where the bonds between main characters are those of friendship, fellowship, or profession rather than family or romantic love. The only exception is the unnatural splitting of Jekyll into his constituent parts, construed as a familial relationship: "Jekyll had more than a father's interest; Hyde had more than a son's indifference" (84).

Domesticating Stevenson's Gothic by adding women to the dramatis personae not only recasts the tale more fully in a melodramatic mode but also radically changes the homosocial milieu of the narrative as well as the complex gender dynamics between Jekyll and Hyde. In the novella, when Jekyll turns into Hyde, he becomes in some ways more feminine (in traditional Victorian terms): financially dependent on Jekyll, he is smaller, lighter on his feet, less disciplined, less intellectual. The butler Poole once heard Hyde "weeping like a woman" (65) and Hyde, in another context, is described with the comment, "he wasn't like a man" (33). Jekyll himself attributes Hyde's smaller stature and more youthful appearance to the fact that his own evil nature had been less exercised than other parts of himself; being less developed, the incarnation of his soul's evil as Hyde consequently appeared younger and less mature (79). Yet in other ways, Stevenson describes Hyde as more physically masculine (in traditional Victorian terms) than Jekyll: a man of "great muscular activity" (72), he has "lean, corded, knuckly" hands that are "thickly shaded with a swart growth of hair" (82), has a husky voice (41), and indulges in restless movement, unrelenting anger, and unbridled lust for sins unspecified.

Mansfield selects the gender dynamic of a masculine Hyde and a feminine Jekyll from the myriad possibilities in Stevenson's book, explaining his choice to the *Pall Mall Gazette:* "I have a theory that all that is good in a man's character—his affection for others, his love of truth and mercy, his self-sacrifice, patience, and other virtues—all come to him from his mother; and so I make Jekyll somewhat effeminate, that is to say, gentle in his manner and passionate and self-sacrificing in his love" ("Real"103). Mansfield uses gender dichotomy to distinguish between the characters of Jekyll and Hyde, facilitating his enactment of them as utterly distinct. This would be impossible if Jekyll were, as the 1887 *Pall Mall Gazette* interprets Stevenson's conception, "a clever scientific gentleman with the very devil inside him" instead of what Mansfield portrays, "a mixture of a smug young shopwalker and an aesthetic curate, who wishes to be well with the ladies" ("Nightmare" 126). The notion of Jekyll as Hyde's opposite—what Mansfield calls purely "the *good*" in direct contrast to Hyde, "the impersonation of all that was *bad*"—enters the popular imagination here, through Mansfield's need to create a greater contrast between the characters for a maximum dramatic effect in performance ("Real" 103).[12]

Despite the widespread critical disappointment in his interpretation of Jekyll, the press in Boston, New York, and London unanimously lauded Mansfield's performance of Hyde, which they found entirely convincing; a "*tour de force*," said both the *Daily Telegraph* and the *Pall Mall Gazette* ("Lyceum" 123, "Nightmare" 127). So fierce was his Hyde and so shocking was the transformation from his Jekyll that both women and men fainted and people couldn't sleep after seeing the show ("Real" 103). All reviews enthusiastically marveled at Mansfield's virtuoso transitions, which were executed in plain view of the audience, without prosthetics or extraordinary stagecraft. Mansfield managed it solely through excellent acting and clever lighting, plus a few tricks as simple as disheveling his hair while writhing in the agony of metamorphosis into Hyde, as the actor proudly explained and others corroborated on multiple occasions (Danahay and Chisolm 100–132). The startling transition was just as much a sensation scene as those more traditionally associated with melodrama, as in Augustin Daly's *Under the Gaslight* (1867), which initiated the spectacular fad of a victim tied to the railroad tracks to be saved at the last moment from the approach of a speeding train; or the much-copied buzz saw nearly slicing the hero as his unconscious form approaches the rotating blade in Joseph Arthur's *Blue Jeans* (1890). The technique Sullivan used reappears in the Wildhorn-Bricusse *Jekyll and Hyde*. Matthew Sweet explicitly links the Victorian melodrama's sensation scene to the megamusical, describing it as the "Victorian equivalent of today's 'helicopter moment'" (5), citing the principal spectacle of *Miss Saigon* (1989), in which an apparently real helicopter lands onstage, on the roof of the American Embassy, to evacuate the male protagonist during the fall of Saigon.

JACK THE RIPPER, INDETERMINACY, AND THEORIZING IDENTITY PERFORMANCE

Dr. Jekyll and Mr. Hyde opened at the Lyceum on August 4, 1888; on August 7, Martha Tabram's remains were found after she had been stabbed to death in the East End, followed over the next three months by the mutilated bodies of Mary Ann Nichols, Annie Chapman, Elizabeth Stride, Catherine Eddowes, and Mary Jane Kelly. Along with Stevenson's novella, the play quickly provided a metaphor for contemporary coverage of the killings, contributing to the notion that the killer must have been a medical man and a gentleman (Walkowitz 206). The play was linked to Jack the Ripper repeatedly in the press; Martin Danahay and Alex Chisolm give examples from the *St. Stephen's Review*, the *Pall Mall Gazette*, *Punch*, and the *Philadelphia Inquirer* (38–39). On September 29, the *St. Stephen's Review* connected the play and the crime spree explicitly, telling the story of a young man becoming overwrought "between the Whitechapel murders and the weird performance of *Dr. Jekyll and Mr. Hyde*," alluding specifically to Mansfield's acting. On September 8, 1888, the *Pall Mall Gazette* called Jack the Ripper "Mr. Hyde at large in Whitechapel." Even on the other side of the Atlantic, on October 10, 1888, the *Philadelphia Inquirer* claimed, "The police have started the theory that the Whitechapel murders are the result of a case in real life of 'Dr. Jekyll and Mr. Hyde.'"[13] One audience member even wrote to the City of London Police to accuse Mansfield himself of actually being the perpetrator of the Whitechapel murders. The only evidence? Good acting. The letter denouncing Mansfield explains, "*I do not think there is A man Living* So well able to disguise Himself in A moment as he does in front of the Public. *Who So well able to Baffel the Police*, or Public he Could be A *dark man. Fair man. Short man. Or Tall* in A five Seconds if he carried A fine Faulse Wiskers &c in A Bag" (Danahay 180).

The novel's repeated insistence on Hyde's horrifying effect on everyone who sees him relies on the individual reader's imagination supplying what is unspeakably monstrous about the spectacle of Hyde. But the drama or film must show the indescribable to the collective audience. And an actor must play it. While most movies rely on special effects to create Hyde's horror, stage and screen actors from Richard Mansfield to Spencer Tracy to David Hasselhoff often take pride in creating the conversion from respectable Jekyll to monstrous Hyde and back again without the use of elaborate tricks, relying on acting and lighting to carry the illusion. Jekyll becomes Hyde because he acts Hyde, emphasizing the notion that identity is performed, a notion that many people—and the Victorians in particular, perhaps—have found uncomfortable. One reason Hyde's appearance can't be described is that the difference between Jekyll and Hyde is not concrete and permanent but ephemeral as any performance.

Adapting prose narrative to the stage lays bare the challenges inherent in making exterior and corporeal a story that hinges on a metaphor for interior psychological duality. In other words, *Jekyll and Hyde* offers a test case in the differing demands and opportunities in the genres of fiction and drama. The letter writer quoted above focuses on the actor's ability to appear short, tall, dark, or fair, echoing the novel's Enfield in his sense that he cannot pin down what Hyde really looks like: "He is not easy to describe.... He's an extraordinary looking man, and yet I really can name nothing out of the way. No, sir... I can't describe him. And it's not want of memory; for I declare I can see him at this moment" (35–36). Hyde "had never been photographed; and the few who could describe him differed widely, as common observers will. Only on one point were they agreed; and that was the haunting sense of unexpressed deformity with which the fugitive impressed his beholders" (49). If the horror of the novel's Hyde as a malleable blank stems from the sense that readers can form their own private sense of monstrosity, then also in a sense his horror is so profound because it is so limitlessly performable. Without description or preconceived notions of appearance, an actor can make him into anything. The impossibility of expressing precisely what Hyde looks like (and what makes him appear to be so evil) is an aspect of the novel that has received significant critical attention.[14] Part of the interest here is Stevenson's use of the discourse of visibility and embodiment for something that exceeds visibility and is embodied only through the unnatural intervention of Jekyll's experiments. The actor's exciting challenge, then, is to embody onstage in full view of his spectators and reviewers that which the novel states cannot be embodied except in the imagination of the speaker, author, and reader.

That one person can effectively play two (or more) distinct characters on the same stage in the same production unsettles a unitary notion of self or subjectivity.[15] The actor's talent for inhabiting multiple physically different personae embodies Jekyll's prediction in the novella that because of his research people will not merely be proven to have a dual nature but that "man will ultimately be known for a mere polity of multifarious, incongruous and independent denizens" (79). The notion, as Stevenson suggests, that there are many individuals within each of us undergirds any actor's ambition to incarnate a wide array of characters. And the actor's talent to do so attracts audiences.[16] But most fans are well satisfied with the great talent of convincingly bringing to life a throng of different characters one at a time, each in a completely different drama. Dorian Gray represents such admiration in his attraction to Sibyl Vane while she brilliantly acts all of Shakespeare's heroines, playing "Rosalind one night and Portia the other" (84), as well as in his cruelly losing interest in her when she integrates her personalities into one, "a third-rate actress with a pretty face" (85).

There is an ultimate paradox expressed in the letter writer's belief that the man who can perform murder onstage could perform it on the street. His unease goes beyond fearing that identity is malleable, that Mansfield can become Jekyll or Hyde or Jack the Ripper, or that we are a "multifarious, incongruous and independent denizens." In addition to indicating that performance constitutes identity and revealing that all our identities are unstable and without a genuine core, the letter writer's disquiet is built upon the completely contradictory point that acting reveals one's inner nature. On the one hand, Mansfield could be anyone he performs (as could we all, which makes it scarier and more exciting). On the other, Mansfield is really Jack the Ripper. His acting the double persona of Jekyll and Hyde, who seem so much like Jack the Ripper, proves *that* is who he truly is. The bottom line, literally, for a theatrical production is that such uneasiness about identity translates into effective live theater, enhancing viewers' enthrallment with the sensational experience of watching a performer manifest multiple characters in the flesh.

Mansfield's performance succeeds as profitable theater precisely because it *is* visible and legible. The idea that the man who can perform murder onstage could well perform it on the street emphasizes the importance of performance not only for identity but also for legality. It is worth remembering that, as

Diana Taylor explains, "performance has evidentiary power" (public lecture, LSU, March 6, 2013), and, as Philip Auslander explains, performance is "central to the legal process itself" (182). Stevenson's narrative carefully builds the strange legal and medical case not solely through the accretion of documents, anecdotes, incidents, and wills examined by lawyers and doctors but also and most importantly through eyewitness testimony. In the novel, Jekyll's transformation into Hyde *never* occurs in front of the narrator or the reader as an unmediated occurrence. Lanyon is the only character who sees that horrific spectacle. Only through Lanyon's recounting of that moment in which one man visibly becomes another, embodying a different person, does the reader accept the novel's outcome. Jekyll's own account at the end of the narrative tying up the tale's loose ends is credible *only* because Lanyon corroborates it. Without Lanyon's eyewitness account, Jekyll's tale would be dismissed as ravings from a madhouse cell, a different Victorian genre altogether.[17]

Stevenson explicitly sets up the theatricality of this scene. In the letter to Lanyon asking him to retrieve certain drugs, Hyde writes, "Then you will have played your part" (70). But Lanyon quickly turns from player to spectator, audience, witness—important parts in building an evidentiary case—when, after Hyde arrives at Lanyon's office, he commands, like a performing magician,

> "Behold!"
>
> He put the glass to his lips and drank at one gulp. A cry followed; he reeled, staggered, clutched at the table, and held on, staring with injected eyes, gasping with open mouth; and as I looked there came, I thought, a change—he seemed to swell—his face became suddenly black and the features seems to melt and alter—and the next moment, I had sprung to my feet and leaped back against the wall, my arms raised to shield me from that prodigy, my mind submerged in terror.
>
> "O God!" I screamed, and "O God!" again and again; for there before my eyes—pale and shaken, and half fainting, and groping before him with his hands, like a man restored from death—there stood Henry Jekyll!
>
> What he told me in the next hour, I cannot bring my mind to set on paper. I saw what I saw, I heard what I heard, and my soul sickened at it. (71–72)

Lanyon correctly predicts that the shock of having seen and heard this transformation—in other words, of having been spectator and audience to this performance—will kill him. The unspeakable and fatal sight is precisely what all dramatizations of *Jekyll and Hyde* stage and all audiences see.

HYDING DORIAN GRAY

While at first the comparison of Jekyll and Hyde to Jack the Ripper arose from the coincidence of the actor credibly portraying a ruthless killer at the moment that the homicides were taking place, later adaptations exploit this connection by grafting the brutal murder of prostitutes onto Hyde's mysterious list of atrocities.[18] Such a plot point is indicated neither in Stevenson's prose nor in Sullivan's melodrama, which contains no scarlet woman. In other words, the influence went both ways. Just as the assumption that Jack the Ripper was a doctor gained traction from the Dr. Jekyll and Mr. Hyde story, so the assumption that Hyde murders sex workers during his increasingly cruel rampages comes to the adaptations from historical events.

But it took a while before the serial murder of working "Girls of the Night" becomes integral to the Jekyll and Hyde culture text.[19] Danahay and Chisolm's variorum edition demonstrates that Sullivan's play never has a prostitute love interest for Hyde, despite scholars making this claim.[20] The closest any character comes to being a fallen woman during the first few decades of adaptation is Lady Carew from Joseph William Comyns Carr's play *Dr. Jekyll and Mr. Hyde,* produced by Henry Irving in 1910 at the Queen's Theatre in London, with Irving in the leading roles. The villainess Lady Carew, Sir Danvers's wife, enters the play having carried on an affair with Dr. Jekyll before he wed the good and faithful Laura, now blind from accidental explosion resulting from her husband's experiments. But although Lady Carew is an adulteress, and although she proposes to Jekyll that he murder her husband to prevent his being informed of their former affair by a blackmailer, and although she is presented as Laura's opposite— called by Jekyll a "devil" in contrast to Laura, an "angel"—she is no prostitute (198). She is, moreover, of high social class and most importantly, she is not murdered by Hyde and indeed has very little interaction with him. Since even as late as 1910 no murdered prostitutes appear, when and how do they enter the Jekyll-and-Hyde imaginary?

The prostitutes come not from the Jack the Ripper phenomenon directly but in part from aspects of *The Picture of Dorian Gray,* which itself owed a debt to Stevenson's book. Several elements copied from *Dorian Gray* appear in an early movie melodrama of Stevenson's story. In the 1920

Robertson-directed film *Dr. Jekyll and Mr. Hyde*, Hyde indulges his passion with an unprotected dance hall artist named Gina (played by Naldi), "who faced her world alone," according to the intertitle that introduces her. The beautiful dancer tries to entice the handsome young Dr. Jekyll, who is brought by a Lord Henry Wotton–like Sir George Carew (played by Brandon Hurst) to an unsavory dance hall where men and women cavort raucously. Sir George wants to tempt the priggish, idealistic young doctor, who selflessly cures the indigent at his own expense and denies himself all pleasures of the flesh. He resists Gina, being in love with Sir George's daughter (named Millicent in this adaptation, played by Martha Mansfield). So closely does Sir George resemble Lord Wotten that he tells his soon-to-be future son-in-law, "The only way to get rid of a temptation is to yield to it," a line taken directly from Lord Wotten's advice to Dorian Gray, even delivered with the same "graceful wave of the hand that was always so characteristic of him" (Wilde 29). Inflamed with desire, Jekyll turns himself into Hyde and installs Gina as his mistress, until he uses her up and kicks her out to die on the streets. We next see her—now diseased and disheveled—in an opium den, where Hyde again roughly rejects her. David Skal points out that scenario writer Clara Berenger "consciously or unconsciously borrowed Wilde's subplot" of seduction and abandonment (Skal 139), making Gina a lower-class version of the Shakespearean actress Sibyl Vane, whom Dorian similarly seduces and destroys.

There is significantly more evidence of Berenger's borrowing. The opium den in the film harbors an addict frantically swatting at himself. Hyde observes a woman jeering, and the intertitle indicates that she says, "He thinks he's covered with red ants!" Then she laughs at him some more. Again, this scene comes straight out of Wilde's novel; there Dorian visits an opium den and observes two women "mocking an old man who was brushing the sleeves of his coat with an expression of disgust. 'He thinks he's got red ants on him,' laughed one of them" (142). With the caveat that a silent film's scenario writer and intertitle writer were not necessarily the same person, the borrowing of verbatim lines seems too close to be "unconscious." Berenger's screenplay is a straightforward blending of the two novels in a kind of double adaptation.[21] Certainly if we ever needed any more proof of Thomas Leitch's point that it is a fallacy to claim that adaptations adapt only one text at a time (164), we need look no further. The result of Berenger's appropriation is that, although Sullivan included no second female leading character from the demimonde as Hyde's mistress in his stage adaptation, from this 1920 film onward, Jekyll and Hyde each has a love interest of his own.²²

HYDING DICKENS, 1920–97

It is a Dickensian rather than a Wildean trait to provide doubled female characters, one angelic and one fallen: Rose and Nancy from *Oliver Twist* and Agnes and Li'l E'mly from *David Copperfield* are examples. Even the inclusion of the opium den recalls *The Mystery of Edwin Drood* or Dickens's investigative reporting in *All the Year Round,* which influenced popular culture's characterization of the opium den for decades to come, including Oscar Wilde's. And we have seen that Jasper's double life in *The Mystery of Edwin Drood* is repeatedly read as a precursor to Stevenson's conception of Jekyll and Hyde (Milligan 111). Dickensian overdetermination saturates our Victorian inheritance. Perhaps the clearest Dickensian feature in Robertson's film is the vivid depiction of many indigent patients whom Dr. Jekyll tenderly treats in his clinic, free of charge, alluded to only in a brief comment in Sullivan's play, when Mrs. Lanyon speculates that Dr. Jekyll is delayed by one of his "horrid patients" (Danahay and Chisolm 48).The film also shows the seediest side of London, not only Hyde's Soho apartment (now decrepit instead of well appointed, as in the novella)²³ but also the opium den, music halls, and back alleys, with plenty of extras to play policemen, laborers, housewives, dancers, bar maids, prostitutes, drunkards, and drug addicts in Dickensian abundance. Although Stevenson makes a class distinction between Jekyll and Hyde (one that has been much written about, particularly regarding the racialization of class), the class distance between the alter egos is not so extreme in the novella or in Sullivan's play as in Robertson's movie.²⁴ Neither Stevenson nor Sullivan brings in a large cast of secondary characters, headed up by the sympathetic fallen woman, as does the Robertson film, drawing on Dickens as well as Wilde, to populate the story with numerous emotionally powerful representatives of class stratification.²⁵

The dancer's death through seduction and abandonment in the 1920 adaptation becomes the outright rape and murder of a kept woman by the 1931 Rouben Mamoulian film *Dr. Jekyll and Mr. Hyde.* Fredric March won an Oscar for the role of Jekyll/Hyde; Miriam Hopkins played Ivy, the dance hall performer who adds "an unprecedentedly explicit sexual element to the horror" (Skal 144).The overtly sexual content begins early in this movie melodrama with a kind of lighthearted private striptease just for Jekyll, who enjoys it, as no doubt did audiences before the full enforcement of the Motion Picture Production Code. Later, Hyde isolates Ivy, coerces her into living in his love nest (decorated with nude sculptures and paintings), beats her repeatedly, and finally murders her in the bedroom.[26] The link all the way back to Dickens is clear: before Gina the dancer is tossed out onto the streets, before Sibyl Vane dies brokenhearted, and long before Jack the Ripper terrorized London, the brave and good-hearted prostitute Nancy is brutally murdered by Bill Sikes in their bedroom. Despite the explicit violence, *Variety* considers the film to be particularly appealing to women; in a review called "The Woman's Angle," the entertainment journal says, "Classic shocker loses much of its stark horror and consequent unpleasantness for women, by growing logical with psychoanalytic motivation and daringly presented sex appeal. Latest version made enticing instead of repellent to the girls" (19). Echoing Mansfield's opinion, *Variety* clearly does not interpret the violence as a deterrent to women viewers who like connecting with women characters. The 1931 adaptation also includes a fiancée for Jekyll, now named Muriel Carew, played by Rose Hobart. Most of Jekyll's problems seem to derive from their prolonged engagement; both the young people want the wedding to occur sooner than her father, Danvers Carew, will permit, suggesting that sexual deprivation turns men into monsters.

Wildhorn identifies the 1941 Victor Fleming remake *Dr. Jekyll and Mr. Hyde* as an inspiration for his megamusical (personal interview). Emphasizing a Freudian interpretation of the story, Spencer Tracy stars as Jekyll/Hyde in a performance that Tracy worried was so bad it would end his career. It prompted the oft-quoted quip attributed to Somerset Maugham, who "visited the *Jekyll and Hyde* set to watch Tracy in action. 'Which one is he playing now?', Maugham supposedly inquired" (Mank 27). Underlying Maugham's jibe was Tracy's creation of the dual persona without elaborate makeup or physical contortions, depending on lighting, camera angles, and acting to distinguish Jekyll from Hyde. Lana Turner plays Jekyll's kittenish fiancée (again renamed, now Beatrix Emery, daughter of Sir Charles Emery), and Ingrid Bergman plays Ivy, the barmaid—clearly identified as such, to avoid the presumption that she is a prostitute, which by 1941 (well into the Motion Picture Production Code era) would be too salacious, prefiguring Nancy's shift from Dickens's prostitute to barmaid in the 1968 movie musical *Oliver!* Like Hopkins's Ivy in 1931, she suffers bitterly under Hyde's increasingly vicious sadism until he kills her, again in the bedroom of his erotically decorated hideaway. In both influential films, Ivy seeks medical attention from the kind Dr. Jekyll for wounds inflicted by cruel Mr. Hyde.

Predating Wildhorn and Bricusse's show, a hallucinogenic made-for-TV musical *Dr. Jekyll and Mr. Hyde* appeared in 1973, with music and lyrics by none other than Lionel Bart—the composer, lyricist, and book writer of *Oliver!*—and screenplay by Sherman Yellen. Bart's version boasted an all-star cast: Kirk Douglas as Jekyll and Hyde, Susan George as the dance hall singer Annie (perhaps named with the Ripper victim Annie Chapman in mind), Susan Hampshire as Jekyll's fiancée (now named Isobel), Stanley Holloway as Poole, and Michael Redgrave as Danvers. The plot basically follows previous films. But as we might expect from Bart, a mocking class critique features prominently in the lyrics. In an early song, Jekyll is in his bourgeois buggy, a symbol of both class status and mobility. A chorus sings about every person content in his or her immutable spot in the social hierarchy, "his perfectly proper place," including a baker ("this is the way it's always been"), a chimneysweep (and "how t'will always be"). All praise the status quo in cheerful satire of the class system: gentleman and shoeshine boy, nannies and bobbies, iron grinders and patients in the insane asylum where Dr. Jekyll works. In a later scene, Annie is provided with a little match girl protégée, Tupenny, just as Bet is Nancy's young sidekick in *Oliver Twist* and *Oliver!* Together Annie and Tupenny sing ironically of how they are "two fine ladies" in a song reminiscent of "It's a Fine Life." Just as Nancy saves Oliver from Sikes, Annie saves Tupenny from the clutches of the sadistic Hyde, who has sexual designs on the child. In retaliation, Hyde shows Annie a gravestone with her own name and death date, like a perverted Ghost of Christmas Future. But it is to torture her, not to reform her. Hyde's revision of *A Christmas Carol* drives her mad.

The 1997 Wildhorn-Bricusse musical retains the same dual female roles we have seen in its musical precursor and every other major Jekyll and Hyde film since 1920. Lucy, now clearly a prostitute as well as a dance-hall entertainer,[27] is killed by her abusive lover, Hyde, in her bedroom, like Nancy. Lisa Carew, as she is named in the pre-Broadway tour, is Jekyll's angelically pure fiancée. The similarity in the names Lucy and Lisa signifies that, like Jekyll and Hyde, they are symbolic doubles. In fact, in the earliest versions of the show, Linda Eder played both roles, intensifying the idea of the women's doubling in parallel to the men's, since Jekyll and Hyde are always played by the same actor (Wildhorn, personal interview).[28] The Broadway version renamed Lisa. Wildhorn suggests that Bricusse may have chosen the new name, Emma, because it sounds more British (Wildhorn, personal interview), reminding us that an inflated Britishness intensifies Broadway's representation of Victorianness. American adaptations adjust British texts to fit American notions of what seems British, just as in 1887 Sullivan made Stevenson's MP Danvers Carew into General Sir Danvers Carew. Making a play more Victorian means making it more Dickensian, and the name Emma is indeed more Dickensian than Lisa, as there are two Emmas but no Lisa in Dickens's fiction.[29] Whether Lisa or Emma, the musical's character is also more Dickensian than earlier iterations of Jekyll's fiancée in another way: unlike the 1941 film's physically demonstrative Lana Turner or romantically impatient Rose Hobart in 1931, in the musical Lisa/Emma behaves with utmost restraint, as circumspect a Victorian stereotypical Angel in the House as any descended (and exaggerated) from Dickens's feminine ideal.

The doubled heroines of prostitute Lucy and fiancée Emma act as sympathetic foils, reflecting the dichotomy in the title doppelgänger. So much are the women two sides of the same coin that they sing "In His Eyes" in parallel: the original Broadway production had them starting at opposite ends of the stage in their own spaces but converging symbolically in the middle by the duet's end.[30] The virginal Emma wore a long white Victorian nightgown buttoned up to the hollow of her neck; Lucy sported dingy, bedraggled, and revealing garb. Lucy descends from Nancy in other ways. Her job is not primarily prostitution. Just as *Oliver!*'s Nancy sings and dances "Oom-Pah-Pah" to entertain audiences at the Three Cripples, so Lucy performs at the Red Rat, the nightclub attached to the brothel where she lives. The scene may also recall *Drood*'s Music Hall, with plenty of corseted dancers prefiguring Lucy's Red Rat attire in many productions.

The Dickensian elements in the musical here go back through the long genealogy of adaptations to Stevenson's novel, Sullivan's play, and Mansfield's performance. Contemporary reviewers saw Dickens's mark on Mansfield's performance, with the *Sunday Times* applauding his "Quilp-like Hyde" ("Lyceum" 122) and the *Pall Mall Gazette* marveling at the character as a "compound of Quilp and Caliban" ("Nightmare" 126), both favorite characters on the Victorian stage. By creating a Gothic melodrama centered on domestic relationships, Sullivan intensified Dickensian features *already* present in Stevenson's story. As Robert Mighall has pointed out, Dickens "made the Gothic ordinary and therefore arguably more disturbing" (94), constructing the entire metropolis of London as a Gothic setting, with "swirling fogs, cobblestoned labyrinthine streets, with menace or mystery" everywhere. For Mighall, Dickens has imprinted Stevenson because "*Oliver Twist* and *Bleak House* mapped out the cityscape through which Stevenson's Mr. Hyde, and his avatar Jack the Ripper, would permanently stalk our imaginations" (94). It is Dickens—and prior performances of Dickens—that determines Broadway's depiction of what is seen as authentically Victorian, including the portrayal of contrasting heroines for the doubled protagonist.

CHOREOGRAPHING GENDER/IDENTITY

Like so many previous adaptations, the musical *Jekyll and Hyde* ignores the same-gender dynamics of Stevenson's Jekyll and Hyde, but it reinscribes the effect of gender trouble in other ways. These reverberate with how acceptance of different sexualities was becoming—through fits and starts—more mainstream in 1990s stage and screen production, with *Falsettos* premiering in 1992 and winning two Tony awards (best book and best score); Tony Kushner's *Angels in America* winning not only the Tony for best drama but also the Pulitzer Prize in 1993; Tom Hanks winning an Oscar for his role in *Philadelphia* (1993); Ellen DeGeneres coming out on *Oprah* in 1997; and *Will and Grace* first airing in 1998, shortly after *Jekyll and Hyde*'s Broadway opening in 1997.

The musical's most interesting moment of gender doubling and inversion occurs during the "Bring on the Men," Lucy's big production number at the Red Rat in the pre-Broadway tour, choreographed by Larry Fuller.[31] When Jekyll first decides to examine the seedy side of life, he enters Lucy's workplace. There he finds a chorus of dancers providing a mélange of ethnic titillation: a French can-can, a flamenco dancer, a Native American woman with lots of feathers, two harem dancers in Turkish pants and veil. A heteronormative Victorian couple of a man and woman in evening dress also dances; when they turn, the costumes reverse—each partner is half-man, half-woman. Throughout the performance, they present the heterosexual costuming for the audience, but now the former "man" is obviously the "woman" and vice versa, creating a picture of the Victorian sexologist's notion of the invert (Ellis 1) and prefiguring twenty-first-century notions of gender fluidity.[32] At this point Lucy is carried onstage by two male dancers in top hats and tuxedos. At a climactic moment in her song, her male escorts remove their tuxes and reveal themselves as women. Likewise, for the finale, the harem dancers rip off their veils and reveal they are men. Throughout the song, men dance with men, women dance with women, while other men and women frolic raunchily. The gender reversals and the use of non-white, non-English ethnic Others makes the whorehouse represent Hyde's distance from Jekyll, just as it signifies this twentieth-century adaptation's distance from Stevenson's depiction of Hyde's actions. Yet, as we have seen in discussion of *Drood,* spectacular drag performances are as Victorian as one can get, at least in music halls and the song-and-dance extravaganzas of pantomime, which always feature a woman playing the Principal Boy and a man playing the Dame.

"Bring on the Men" from the pre-Broadway tour was replaced in the original Broadway production by another song, "Good 'N' Evil," that more blatantly emphasizes the theme of moral duality. In the 1997 Broadway production, Utterson brings the overworked Jekyll to this place of amusement to relax, not to tempt him the way the Lord Wotton–cum–Sir George does in the 1920 film. The choreography for "Good 'N' Evil," while full of sexual innuendo, involves no gender surprises, except for men dressed in sequined Victorian bathing suits that mildly resemble women's teddies. "Good 'N' Evil" conforms to virtually every previous adaptation's simpler emphasis on Jekyll's discovery of our being "not truly one, but truly two" (76), while the multiplicity of possibilities celebrated in "Bring on the Men" resembles the "polity of multifarious, incongruous and independent denizens" that Stevenson's Jekyll further postulates may yet be found in us (76). Such multiplicity is echoed in the peculiar genre of Wildhorn and Bricusse's musical. Wildhorn explains that he and Bricusse wrote a whopping eighty songs for the show. In 2000, during the original Broadway run, he stated that there were nine international productions, plus the road show, plus Broadway, all playing concurrently, all different. Some touring productions were still including "Bring on the Men" (personal interview). Normally, official touring productions are as "cookie cutter" as possible, providing the public with a known brand, such as the Disney *Beauty and the Beast* or *The Lion King,* or the carefully monitored Rodgers and Hammerstein shows. Thus, the musical *Jekyll and Hyde'*s mercurial makeup is in this sense unique. Such an entrepreneurial operation makes what might seem the ultimately commercial megamusical entertainment of *Jekyll and Hyde* (a straightforward pop sound, sentimental plot, shameless exploitation of sex yoked with violence, simplified morality, glitzy special effects) into a complex, modular, multiple, maybe even postmodern experiment: in its ever-changing permutations, the text of *Jekyll and Hyde: The Musical*—already over-determined—was never unitary to begin with and still never resolves into a single theatrical artifact. Its commercial megamusicality contributes (perhaps counterintuitively) to its own flexible identity created by ever-changing constituent parts.

The 2013 revival made several significant modifications. In this version, it is now Jekyll who suggests to Utterson that they enter the Spider's Web, as the nightclub is now called, reverting to the name used in the original Alley Theatre production, back in 1990. Instigating the visit makes this Jekyll more like the randy Spencer Tracy's or Kirk Douglas's—who clearly goes to Annie's dance hall for sex—than the priggish Barrymore's good doctor; it is now Utterson instead of Jekyll who objects. "Bring on the Men" also returns from the pre-Broadway tour to feature in the revival as Lucy's big production number in which Jekyll first sees her, replacing "Good 'N' Evil." But the director-choreographer Jeff Calhoun includes none of the gender-bending that made Fuller's choreographic vision of "Bring on the Men" so interesting pre-Broadway, in 1995. Instead, the female dancers manipulate long cords—reminding us of the club's eponymous web—to indicate bondage, whipping the customers (who are all male), reminiscent of Ingrid Bergman's Ivy shown intercut with horses being whipped as part of Hyde's psychopathic enactment of sexual fantasy in Spencer Tracy's performance of 1941. In the musical's choreography, the women tie the cords around their own wrists and wrap ropes around their waists. There are no male nightclub dancers. There is no cross-dressing. There are no transgender surprises. Instead, it is, as the *Entertainment Weekly* review puts it, "an S&M-inspired, quasi-Cabaret, rope-swirling maypole-esque mess" (Bernardo). It is possible that Calhoun found no shock value in depicting gender-shifting dancers in 2013, the age of the musical-theater television hit series *Glee* (depicting multiple gay, lesbian, bi, and trans characters in a high school glee club) and the musical reality show *RuPaul's Drag Race,* which both debuted in 2009. Featuring explorations not only in LGBT sexuality but also in gender identity, *Glee* was still going strong when *Jekyll and Hyde* was revived, and *RuPaul* has kept going for years afterward.

Ever since Mansfield created the dual role of Jekyll and Hyde on stage, the virtuoso transformation from one to the other and back again has fascinated audiences. Even when the advent of cinema allowed one face to dissolve into another in early film, critics such as Edward Weitzel of the *Moving Picture World* praised Barrymore's acting as the greatest performance of Jekyll and Hyde since Mansfield's, still a matter of living memory: no cinematic effect could carry the experience; "the art of the actor sufficed"

(63). The Wildhorn-Bricusse musical raises the stakes for actors performing the dual role in creating the showstopper called "The Confrontation," in which Jekyll and Hyde battle to regain control of the actor's body onstage, fighting in song over whose identity will dominate.

From the Alley Theatre production in 1990 onward, the lead actor in the musical (like Mansfield) managed the shift from Jekyll to Hyde and back again primarily by altering his posture, gait, expression, and voice, and by disheveling his hair and adding or removing his glasses, a technique we are all familiar with from Superman and Clark Kent.[33] Whenever the actor's neat ponytail reveals a sober, spectacled, kindly visage, he is Jekyll; but when wild locks hang recklessly across sneering, snarling, lascivious facial gyrations, he is Hyde. In the musical's earlier scenes, the actor's thrashing on the ground during the excruciating throes of change allows ample time to undo the ponytail; as silly as this may sound, it all works well as a traditional "quick-change artist" technique, in which an actor turns away from the audience, distracting viewers momentarily, revealing a new character taking center stage when they next focus on the face.

In "The Confrontation," the musical's star engages in rapid-fire dialogue with himself, with no time for manipulation of his long tresses; to prepare, he has already surreptitiously fixed his hair so that when the audience sees one side of his profile, the ponytail is visible; when he turns his head to the other profile, the hair dangles in greasy disarray (a technique that resembles Fuller's choreography in "Bring on the Men," but in much quicker succession).[34] A huge mirror behind the actor upstage allows for both characters to appear to the audience simultaneously. This stagecraft permits the performer to play the heated dialogue between Jekyll and Hyde by flipping his face from profile to profile, along with some help from lighting and some extra reverberation added to the sound when Hyde sings. It is a coup de théâtre that many singer-actors consider an ideal opportunity to display their skill. Some succeed more than others. David Hasselhoff's stilted performance on the commercially released DVD has resulted in years of YouTube ridicule, with the video sped up to augment its vocal and visual hilarity, à la chipmunk.[35] But when performed by a strong singer-actor like Robert Cuccioli, who won several awards for the double role that he originated on Broadway, it is a compelling theatrical experience. It is *Jekyll and Hyde*'s sensation scene.

In the short-lived 2013 Broadway revival, Jekyll transforms into Hyde and back again in early scenes as in previous productions. But in "The

Confrontation," when Jekyll and Hyde argue, instead of the star Constantine Maroulis's performing both roles alternately in rapid succession, changing his voice and expression, flipping from ponytail to hanging hair, Maroulis stayed in character as Jekyll and argued with a pre-recorded video of himself as Hyde, who appears as a silhouette superimposed on the enormous portrait that has been hanging prominently over his living room throughout the play. This modification brings us back to *The Picture of Dorian Gray*, still haunting adaptations of Stevenson's novel, with the portrait exposing the evil side of Jekyll. This choice of staging means that Maroulis did not have to enact the differentiation between his two-sided character in this scene. Some critics saw this directorial choice as reveling in the gimmickry of digital projections over bravura acting; Elizabeth Vincentelli of the *New York Post* went so far as to suggest that "maybe Jeff Calhoun, the usually capable director/choreographer ("Newsies," "Bonnie & Clyde"), lacked confidence in his star" (Vincentelli), though Maroulis won praise from the *New York Times* and the *New York Daily News* for his performance (Isherwood; Dziemianowicz).

Vincentelli's reference to the Broadway musical *Newsies*, about the 1899 newsboys' strike in New York, is telling. One of the most successful elements in Calhoun's production of *Jekyll and Hyde* is the use of digital projection of newspaper headlines during the song "Murder, Murder." The song's title is the call of the newsboys hawking papers about Hyde's nocturnal killing sprees. It opens with a boy singing "Read about the 'ideous murder." Panels behind the action display projected images of Victorianesque newspapers, including the red-ink headlines associated with turn-of-the-century American yellow journalism. The effect of disjointed panels works as a visual pun: the audience can see that these are serial murders—very Jack the Ripperish—but also reportage in the periodical press means that the unfolding narrative of the murders is reported in serial format. Indeed, the link between the serial press and the serial murderer is particularly clear in the history of Jack the Ripper, which is, as Marlene Tromp explains, "the moniker for an unidentified perpetrator who was linked to real and brutal murders, but had an identity that was largely crafted by mass media narratives" ("Victorian Murder"). In other words, the serial press essentially created the fictional serial killer persona we know as Jack the Ripper, whose historical identity is still a mystery.

The indelible association of Jack the Ripper with Stevenson's story means that the musical *Jekyll and Hyde* continues to do the work of processing such reiterated horror. The 1990s provided ample opportunities for public dismay over serial murder. The musical taps public awareness, reinterpreting the serial killer's psyche. A few high-profile examples stood out during the period of *Jekyll and Hyde*'s development, pre-Broadway tour, and Broadway debut. The most notorious is the murderer and cannibal Jeffrey Dahmer, who dominated the news cycle during his 1992 trial and conviction for fifteen ghastly murders. He was beaten to death in prison in 1994, again a grisly media phenomenon. Merging with the horror generated by gruesome serial murder was terror regarding the murderers' ability to blend seamlessly into respectable society, fooling victims and everyone else. John Wayne Gacy, whose 1994 execution after fourteen years on death row was itself a vivid news event, had become something of a poster boy for revolting hypocrisy. He was known as the "Killer Clown" because of his assuming the role of a clown at charitable events and children's parties, posing as an upright citizen. Serial killers were not particularly more active in the 1990s than before, but these and similar cases are among those that captured popular imagination. The film *Silence of the Lambs* (1991), starring Jodie Foster and Anthony Hopkins, haunted the entire decade. *Jekyll and Hyde* necessarily helps to negotiate the horror of real serial killers by corralling them into megamusical, Neo-Victorian entertainment. In other words, like Neo-Victorian fiction, this show extrapolates from the Victorian setting the opportunity to make explicit various issues and situations implicit in period fiction that aesthetic and moral conventions of the time would never permit. Conversely, pop music and flashy effects distance the spectator from the action by displacing the events safely into the nineteenth century.

Jekyll and Hyde mimics the previous Victorian serial killer musical, *Sweeney Todd,* in several ways beyond the murderous protagonists and Victorian sources. It incorporates a chorus that comments on and interprets the action. Two songs recall the earlier show. One is *Jekyll and Hyde*'s "Murder, Murder," sung by newsboys and others, bearing some similarity thematically to *Sweeney Todd*'s "City on Fire," in which the old Beggar Woman acts the wise fool. She declares the truth no one hears, including the refrain "Mischief! Mischief!" about Mrs. Lovett's meat pie shop, anticipating the reiterated "Murder, murder." Similarly, "The "Ballad of Sweeney Todd," which sets out that musical's indictment of hypocrisy ("Freely flows the blood of those who moralize!"), finds an analogue in *Jekyll and Hyde*'s recurring song "Façade," which drives home the musical's message that Victorian respectability is a sham: every gent or lady we see is not a "pillar of society" but "sinners an' crooks," living a "masquerade." Just as Bond's twentieth-century rewriting of Sweeney Todd gives him a revenge motive, so do most of the twentieth-century Jekylls discussed in this chapter, going all the way back to Robertson's 1920 film (suggesting a bit of reciprocity in the two stories' culture texts). The musical's Dr. Jekyll wants permission from the hospital's elite Board of Governors to perform an experiment that he believes will save his own father from madness. When they self-righteously deny the right to experiment on a human subject but are later proven to be hypocrites (the bishop, for example visits underage prostitutes), Hyde begins murdering them one by one. Giving Jekyll a sympathetic motivation domesticates Hyde and de-fang's the fear of serial murderers, which pose a very minimal statistical threat. *Jekyll and Hyde* reminds us that serial killers are a Victorian phenomenon, whether historical like Jack the Ripper—the first to take hold of global media—or fictional like Sweeney Todd and Dracula.

The unfavorable critical reception of Maroulis's faux duet with himself takes us back to the importance of the audience's *seeing* the transformation, just as the novella's Lanyon sees it. Seeing is believing. Likewise, readers need Lanyon's eyewitness account as evidence that Jekyll becomes Hyde in the flesh and not in Jekyll's mind. Seeing Mansfield's performance is the only evidence the letter writer needs to believe that the actor is Jack the Ripper. It is a critical commonplace that much theater depends on the audience's willing suspension of disbelief, which allows them to enjoy unlikely occurrences on the stage despite their implausibility. It also depends on the audience's sophisticated understanding that what they see enacted onstage is just acting, is fiction. Anti-theatrical prejudice has long aligned acting with duplicity, and the talent for creating alternative characters has made people besides Mansfield's accuser anxious long before the Victorians.[36] It might be tempting to see the letter writer fitting into that tradition, believing actors generally to be liars, whores, vagabonds, and worse. Or one might see him as a rube who imagines an actor can only perform what he actually feels, so that to play a double personality successfully one must be a kind of Jekyll and Hyde already. But the letter doesn't reveal the writer to hold either of those opinions. Twice he explicitly rejects them. First, he says, "I have A great Liking for Acters So that I Should be the Last to think because A man take A dreadful Part he is therefore Bad"; later, "I don't know Whats Put this into My Head I Can assure you it is not because I see him Take Such A dretfull Part for I have had Friends on the Stage Take Bad Parts but did not think they were bad in Consequence" (Danahay and Chisolm 180). He is not accusing Mansfield of really being Jekyll and Hyde, but of really being Jack the Ripper. He is not accusing Mansfield merely of lying or of murdering, but of transforming. He worries that the skills evidenced on the proscenium have practical applicability, that someone who can change his form so effectively onstage might have the skill and talent to do so on the streets of London.

The metamorphosis between Jekyll and Hyde has fascinated theater audiences for over 130 years. One aspect of the novel that its adaptation to the musical stage (with its rapid-fire confrontation between Jekyll and Hyde) helps us to consider is what it *means* that several characters describe the horror of Hyde as an unreadable and indescribable deformity. That indescribability permits readers to project their private sense of deformity onto the character, heightening its power. But it also allows actors to create Hyde's deformity anew on their own malleable bodies. In a way, the horror Hyde generates is so profound *precisely* because it is so performable. In other words, there is a link here between deformity and performability. The indescribable deformity of Hyde is only made visible through his performance for Lanyon, who dies from it. Ever since, actors incarnating the transition to Hyde's deformity have risked an accusation of murder. But actors avoiding that risk, like Maroulis, have gotten worse—a bad review.

While Enfield cannot describe Hyde other than to say that, although the deformity is invisible, he must be deformed *somewhere*, the 1888 letter writer's denouncement of Mansfield suggests that because the actor's transformation is entirely and explicitly visible on the West End stage, it must also be performed *elsewhere* invisibly, secretly, on the streets of London's East End. The *Pall Mall Gazette* expresses the "hope that the 'possum-like leap with which he pounces on his victims, and the claw-like paw with which he strangles them, may not suggest a new method to the garrotter" ("Nightmare at the Lyceum" 127); while not suggesting that Mansfield is a murderer, this certainly suggests he could inspire murder. The reviewer also connects the audience and the press to crime, as well as the actor, marveling at the British population's thirst for tales of blood and murder, recommending that any reader who doubts this claim corroborate it by asking "the men and women and boys who sell newspapers in the street. They will tell you" (Danahay and Chisolm 127). And that performance is played out in the press not only in sensational coverage of the Whitechapel murders but also in the entertainment pages of mainstream periodicals—just as in Stevenson's novella—where a "'Special edition. Shocking murder'" is announced by "newsboys... crying themselves hoarse along the footways" (52).

Contemporary fascination with Victorian violence, particularly when linked with sex or with the interruption of clearly demarcated gender identifications, draws on our popular but erroneous misconception of the Victorian era as a monolithically more prudish age, in which gender roles were clearly delineated and in which violent emotions were repressed. And yet, in part because of never-ending fascination with Jack the Ripper and in part because of Sweeney Todd, Dracula, and so on, the notion of serial murder as specifically Victorian prevails in our cultural imagination. Victorianesque serial killers proliferate because of their intertextuality and their intertheatricality (to use Jacky Bratton's term), "the mesh of connections between all kinds of theatre texts, and between texts and their users" for generations (*New Theatre History* 37). As a case study, the Jekyll and Hyde culture text qualifies as what Tracy Davis calls "repertoire," the "associational, polytextual, intertheatrical, recombinant patterns that sustain intelligibility" (14). *Jekyll and Hyde* works in part because it combines familiarity with innovation but also because by blinding ourselves to the historical reality of quotidian Victorian violence and by focusing on the distance the Victorian period provides from contemporary criminals, we see the hideous depiction of spectacular murder with deeper horror. But it is a safe horror, far removed in time and place. By our mythologizing Victorian stories, it lives only as an aberration, not as a present danger.

8
Broadway's "Jane! Jane! Jane!"

Charlotte Brontë's *Jane Eyre* (1847) has prompted countless sequels, prequels, rewritings, and spin-offs; it has inspired ballets, operas, symphonies, fine art, and graphic novels; it has been made into radio shows and television miniseries; it has become no fewer than seventeen major films. It has been adapted to the stage many times, first in John Courtney's 1848 melodrama *Jane Eyre or the Secrets of Thornfield Manor,* in which Jane is given two faithful servants who follow her wherever she goes. Providing comic relief, they scuffle with Brocklehurst's lackeys while Jane is at Lowood and rescue Rochester from the fire at Thornfield. Brontë never saw this production but—in response to her publisher William Smith Williams's description—assessed it quite accurately as "*strange*" (Stoneman, *Jane Eyre* 31).[1] Given such a rich history of adaptation, it is no surprise that the novel was also made into not one but three musicals, all called at times (perhaps this is also no surprise) *Jane Eyre: The Musical.*[2]

The best known of these plays, the only one produced on Broadway, opened at the Brooks Atkinson Theatre in New York on December 10, 2000. Paul Gordon—a pop songwriter whose work has been recorded by Bette Midler, Amy Grant, Smokey Robinson, Quincy Jones, and Patti LaBelle—created the music and lyrics, with the book and additional lyrics by John Caird. Caird also co-directed with Scott Schwartz. Reviews were mixed: the *New York Times* called it "gloomy and mundane" but praised the "Tony-worthy lighting," the "techno-sleek" set, and the performance of Marla Schaffel as Jane (Weber). John Napier designed the set; previous Broadway credits include design for *Cats, Les Misérables,* and *Miss Saigon.*

Napier collaborated with the lighting designers Jules Fisher and Peggy Eisenhauer to create innovative projected Impressionist scenery, garnering praise for the set. It recalled the exciting Pointillist realizations of Seurat in Stephen Sondheim's *Sunday in the Park with George* (1983) and anticipated the spectacular projected railroad effects in Andrew Lloyd Webber's *Woman in White* (2004). Napier also used not one but two turntables—one in the stage, à la *Les Misérables*—the other above the stage, bringing scrims for the projected scenery into place, along with props such as topiaries, furniture, and chandeliers. Schaffel went on to win the Drama Desk Award for Best Actress in a Musical for her creation of the role. The rich-voiced James Barbour, already a Broadway veteran from *Beauty and the Beast* (1994) and the revival of *Carousel* (1994), played Edward Fairfax Rochester. Having been nominated for several Tonys but winning none, *Jane Eyre: The Musical* had a somewhat respectable run of 209 performances (and 36 previews), grossing over $8 million. But it never played to full capacity, despite developing a loyal following of "returnees who were dubbed 'Eyre Heads'" (Jones). Upon the announcement on May 16, 2001, that the show was about to close, Alanis Morissette bought 150,000 tickets (donated to charity groups) to keep it open at least one extra week so that more Tony voters could view it. The play closed in the red on June 10, 2001 (Suskin 344).

Jane Eyre: The Musical's opening in December 2000 closes twentieth-century American musical theater's appropriation of Victorian literature and serves as the end point of this study. It draws together many of the concerns I have been addressing. Like *One Touch of Venus*, it generates discussion of the middlebrow. In fact, it may be the most self-consciously middlebrow of all the musicals under consideration, with "the rarefied yet convincing air of BBC Masterpiece Theater or a Merchant-Ivory movie" (Barnes). The *New York Times* review comments on its "earnestly literate book," an aspirational quality that is a dead giveaway—in Bourdieu's negative terms—of middlebrow art (Weber). Like *The King and I*, the modern musical version of *Jane Eyre* is less radical than its Victorian precursor in its depiction of gender equality. Like the musical *Goblin Market*, *Jane Eyre* experiments effectively with staging narration through the construction of heroines who are both adults and children. Opening on Broadway only three years after the opening of *Jekyll and Hyde*, it too inherits the pop sound of the megamusical—or what the *New York Times* describes as coming "straight from the Broadway schmaltz kit of Andrew Lloyd Webber and Claude-Michel Schonberg" (Weber). Like every Victorian-sourced musical I discuss, *Jane Eyre* is steeped in melodrama and the Neo-Victorian recuperation of melodramatic tactics. The *New York Post*'s review gladly trumpets its returning Broadway to "romance and melodrama," noting also the score's musical debt to the "Sondheim of 'Sweeney Todd'" (Barnes). The playbill cover—which blurs the two leads into the Pointillist, dreamy, jewel-like projected scenery—emphasizes the emotional intensity of the characters and the fantasy of romantic escapism. Jane's stance and gaze suggest tension in that her body angles largely to the side while her head faces frontally, away from Rochester and toward the audience. Rochester, who stands behind her in the middle distance, faces forward, but his gaze is ambiguous. Does he also look at the audience? Or is he watching Jane? Frankly, it could easily serve as the cover of a middlebrow romance studied by Janice Radway (fig. 9).

The melodrama that the critics note originates in the novel, proving again that the musicals help focus on elements in the source that we may have overlooked or forgotten. Brontë's *Jane Eyre* (like *Oliver Twist, The String of Pearls, The Mystery of Edwin Drood,* and *The Strange Case of Dr. Jekyll and Mr. Hyde*) operates richly in the melodramatic mode of heightened emotion, sensational events, and stark moral contrasts, satisfying Elaine Hadley's description of "graphic depictions of gruesome incidents, scenes of physical danger and inflicted torture, plots premised on criminal behavior, affected verbalizations of overwrought emotion, an aura of atmospheric menace, and narratives of familial and social crisis" (*Melodramatic Tactics* 78). These techniques sometimes elicit rebuke. David Cecil calls the novel *Jane Eyre* a "roaring melodrama" (107) for its dependence, like Dickens, on coincidence. George Henry Lewes complains in his otherwise laudatory *Fraser's* review that Brontë employs "too much of melodrama and improbability, which smack of the circulating library" (692), a barb that sounds a lot like Virginia Woolf's jab at middlebrow tastes. But the novel's elements drawn from melodrama—such as the sensational scene of Thornfield hall ablaze—are among its most symbolic, reminding us again that melodrama is also complex, sophisticated, and powerful.

One crucial aspect of the show is not in the original: as we have seen with *Jekyll and Hyde*'s prostitute and *Sweeney Todd*'s beadle, the musical *Jane Eyre* incorporates Dickensian components not found in the source text. The best example is the complete fabrication of a comic butler. Clive Barnes of the *New York Post* praises him, not seeming to notice that he is sheer

Figure 9. Cover of playbill for *Jane Eyre: The Musical*, Brooks Atkinson Theatre, New York, December 2000. (Author's private collection; used by permission; all rights reserved, Playbill, Inc.)

invention: "And all of the other creatures of the novel, good and bad, are memorably captured, particularly ... the Dickensian dimensions of Bruce Dow as the butler, Robert." The *Wall Street Journal* is even more complimentary, and even clearer on how the portrayal is Dickensian: "Bruce Dow makes a shambolic butler, clapping a disheveled peruke on his head whenever he's required by the lordship"; in fact, the reviewer declares that the entire cast of *Jane Eyre* is Dickensian, with Brocklehurst (played by Don Richard) also singled out: "Like so many of the actors in this fine cast, Mr. Richards brings a Dickensian vividness to the small role of this sneering redeemer with pallid skin and mutton-chop whiskers" (Gamerman). As *Jane Eyre* demonstrates, for Broadway critics and audiences as well as for Broadway creators, a Victorian show is simply not Victorian unless it is also Dickensian.

I focus in this chapter on three significant and related aspects of *Jane Eyre: The Musical*'s adaptation from the novel. All three give clues to the cultural and ideological work that the show performs. First, the play individualizes concepts of freedom and equality, which in turn alters the novel's feminist and class messages. Second, in staging the most musical-theatrical moments in the novel (those involving performance and spectators), it shifts the depictions of the novel's anti-Janes (Bertha and Blanche) by fitting them into received types that resonate with American theatrical traditions. Third, the play consistently interprets the novel's supernaturalism through a religious lens. These changes combine to create a kind of Americanization of Jane, which resonates with the appropriation of all the British nineteenth-century literary texts for the American musical stage discussed in this book, but particularly with *The King and I*. The show's lyrics use familiar tropes of American individualism, foundational Protestantism, and the right to liberty in emphasizing a *personal* journey toward liberation (as opposed to promoting rights for a whole class of people). They de-emphasize Gothic mystery in favor of an unambiguous depiction of Christianity. While we might expect a twentieth-century Broadway musical version of *Jane Eyre* to reinforce social equality (as a reflection of American democratic ideology) in contrast to the 1847 English novel, in fact the opposite is true: the novel's powerful drives toward class and gender parity seem to evaporate, as does the novel's unsettling Gothic ambiguity, replaced by static hierarchies associated with American identity.

SWEET LIBERTY

The play begins with the adult Jane alone onstage, walking out of the mist, toward the audience, smiling. She narrates through song the early part of her life, directly addressing the audience to tell of her past. She moves to the side of the stage to reveal her childhood self as represented in the famous opening of the novel, reading *Bewick's Book of Birds* in the window seat. The play adds a rag doll (plucked from the novel's later scenes) for the young Jane to hold, intensifying the audience's reaction to her as a child. Time moves rapidly here, with songs substituting the lyricized emotions of childhood for the novel's vividly drawn incidents. Throughout the early part of the musical, the adult Jane shadows the child Jane. This generates a curiously maternal effect even though the two actresses portray the same person; at one point the adult Jane even helps her child-self get dressed in her school uniform.

The shadowing also creates onstage a dramatic manifestation of fictional autobiography and what Jean Starobinski identifies as the double "I." In autobiography (and the subtitle of the novel *Jane Eyre* is "An Autobiography"), the present narrator uses "I" to speak both about the current self and retrospectively about the past protagonist whose story is told (Starobinski 79). The narrating "I" knows things the child "I" cannot know. The identity between the two "I"s often seems nearly seamless in Victorian autobiography and fictional autobiography. The show exposes that seam through staging, gesture, and vocal choices. Although at times the child Jane sings on her own, usually the adult sings for her; at times they sing duets, musically blending the child and adult self while simultaneously depending on their being separate entities, since vocal harmony can only occur with at least two voices. The adult Jane takes over vocally for the child Jane as she visits Helen Burns's grave, suggesting that the emotions associated with death are too mature for the younger "I" to express; only the retrospective narrator can make sense of the situation. In this way the musical manifests the novel's slippage between the voices of the adult narrator and the child protagonist.[3] After intermission, the men and women of the chorus at times narrate Jane's story in first person, taking the same position toward the adult Jane that she had taken toward the child Jane. Rather than highlighting the sense of retroactive narration of the double I as the two Janes did, the choral narration makes the adult Jane into a kind of Everyperson, emphasized by a broad morphology of body types and voices. In the musical *Jane Eyre*, the staging of the double I—whether as child-adult Jane or adult-choral Jane—functions as an allegory of the cultural work the Victorians do for us now, providing to current readers and audiences a vision of past selves and cultures that we reconstruct and interpret.

Part of what first the adult Jane and later the choral Jane interpret for the audience is how to understand Jane's longing for liberty—and what the keyword "liberty" actually means in this Broadway play. In the novel, Jane (as narrator) announces, while still teaching at Lowood, that she hungers for liberty. She explains:

> I desired liberty; for liberty I gasped; for liberty I uttered a prayer; it seemed scattered on the wind then faintly blowing. I abandoned it and framed a humbler supplication; for change, stimulus: that petition, too, seemed swept off into vague space: "Then," I cried, half desperate, "grant me at least a new servitude!" (72)

This passage is closely related to another, one of the book's most famous. Once at Thornfield, where Jane has found her "new servitude," she expresses a universal plea for women's greater range of action; she delivers the speech to herself—and to the reader—on the leaded roof of Thornfield Hall:

> It is in vain to say human beings ought to be satisfied with tranquility: they must have action; and they will make it if they cannot find it. . . . Women are supposed to be very calm generally: but women feel just as men feel; they need exercise for their faculties and a field for their efforts as much as their brothers do; they suffer from too rigid a restraint, too absolute a stagnation, precisely as men would suffer. (93)

The novel could not make the point more clearly that Jane's longing for liberty is one she shares with women generally; like them, Jane's scope of opportunity is limited to a mere change of location for service. These paragraphs protest a system of oppression, not just an individual's sense of constraint.

These solitary outbursts in the novel become a public statement in the show as part of Jane's sung lecture to her students at Lowood in the song "Sweet Liberty." In fact, the lesson she sings is doubly public, announced both to Jane's students onstage and to the audience in the theater, who are an extension of Jane's classroom. In the musical play, Jane's song about liberty also becomes the hallmark of her pedagogy because it is the only lesson the audience sees her teach at Lowood. In other words, the musical takes Jane's declaration (often read as a direct statement of Charlotte Brontë's belief)[4] about how women need the same expanse of vision and field of endeavor as their brothers, to be Jane's sole point when she teaches. Such a public statement alters Jane from a subversive feminist force to an outspoken proponent of feminist values. Yet this change paradoxically reduces its feminist impact.

The song "Sweet Liberty" pulls several key terms from the speeches at Thornfield and Lowood. From the Thornfield speech, the musical's Jane emphasizes the insufficiency of "tranquility" to satisfy women and their basic similarity to men in needing a field of action: "But is this all we're meant for / condemned to mere tranquility? / Well, women feel as men do . . . / like our brothers, / let our worth define our roles." And from the Lowood speech comes the recurrence of the words "liberty" regarding what women want: "Breaking custom and convention / Let tradition give way / For we all need our liberty / For sweet liberty we pray." While the children file out at the end of class, Jane continues the song, packing a suitcase; suddenly she is striding across the stage with her bag, traversing the countryside on her way to her new post at Thornfield Hall, all while singing of sweet liberty. This staging fundamentally alters the idea of liberty. In sharp contrast to how "liberty" is invoked in *The King and I,* where it is tied to a group of women coded as slaves, this musical represents freedom as an individual act, achieved in Jane's case by leaving Lowood with all its institutional restrictions and getting a cushier position where, as many in the audience already know, she will meet her future husband. Here liberty equals a better job description, followed by marriage.

In the novel, however, Jane has already left Lowood when she makes this speech. Speaking out alone on the ramparts of Thornfield, having freed herself from the strictures of the repressive school, Jane recognizes how hemmed in she still is because she and all other women are bound within the rigid rules of Victorian patriarchy itself. In addition to individualizing Jane's rebellion, the repeated lyric "sweet liberty" recalls "sweet land of liberty" from "My Country 'Tis of Thee." The effect is to Americanize both Jane and the notion of freedom, as though staking a national or cultural claim on individual sovereignty. This appropriation is further emphasized in later lines in which she explains her hope "to find a better destiny" (perhaps manifest?) that would be "far beyond the troubled sea." Given that there are no seas between Lowood and Thornfield, it almost suggests that Jane—like an Anglican Yentl—is heading to America for a better life. By collapsing Jane's personal journey to liberation into a sense that she has arrived at the sweet land of liberty, the musical seems to celebrate American individualism, while ignoring the novel's focus on women's general subjugation.

Sung by the adult Jane about her adult self, the song "Sweet Liberty" is a kind of reprise of the play's opening number (same tune, same rhythm, same voice), "The Orphan." It ties thematically and verbally as well as musically to this initial musical piece, sung by the adult Jane about her child self (pitiably visible onstage), in which the lyrics describe the young Jane's emotional rebellion, restlessness, and longing for liberty. The verse focuses the audience's attention immediately on the issue of feminism: "her life is not of value"; she is "condemned to be a woman / barely fit to educate." But the chorus reiterates the theme of freedom as a personal goal, reducing it to freedom to travel: "How her restlessness stirs / For she longs for her liberty / When will liberty be hers?" This musical, thematic, and verbal link between the adult Jane's teaching of the students at Lowood and her previously interpreting the child Jane's emotions and gender/class status for the audience (who stands in for the novel's readership) makes the adult Jane—the narrating "I" in Starobinski's terms—into not only the interpreter/narrator but also in a sense the teacher of the child protagonist, as the lecture at Lowood suddenly mimics the child and adult Jane's relationship. Once the child Jane grows into her adult voice, she can act on her restlessness and travel to her newfound land to give her life value by seizing "her liberty." The ensemble backs her up vocally, as does the orchestra, including the suddenly vibrant brass section, unusual in this strings-heavy orchestration. "Sweet liberty at last," Jane blasts, with trumpets literally trumpeting her triumph.[5] Far from merely trading an old for a new servitude, the musical's Jane no longer needs to sing of Victorian women yearning for liberty, because she has already achieved her far less extensive individual goal of geographical freedom.

BLANCHE AND BERTHA

As we have seen in *Oliver!* and *Jekyll and Hyde,* just as Victorian stage adaptations influence early film adaptations of Victorian novels, so intervening film versions also often greatly affect Broadway musicals that adapt the same story. The impact may even be seen in casting, so that visual expectations set up by earlier film versions may feature significantly in staging, even when contrary to the source text's explicit description. The 2000 Broadway production of *Jane Eyre: The Musical* cast Marla Schaffel, who resembles the Jane played by Charlotte Gainsbourg in the 1996 Zeffirelli film: high cheekbones, big eyes, dark brown hair parted in the middle to a small bun in the back, broad-shouldered and flat-chested. Both women portray Jane as very controlled, but passionate, without the vulnerability of Joan Fontaine's interpretation in the 1943 film directed by Robert Stevenson.

In the novel, Jane is small, pale, mousy, and elfin. She contrasts with both Blanche and Bertha, who are big, buxom, and resemble each other in body type. The housekeeper, Mrs. Fairfax, describes the novel's Blanche to Jane:

Tall, fine bust, sloping shoulders; long, graceful neck: olive complexion, dark and clear; noble features; eyes rather like Mr. Rochester's: large and black, and as brilliant as her jewels. And then she had such a fine head of hair; raven-black and so becomingly arranged: a crown of thick plaits behind, and in front the longest, the glossiest curls I ever saw. (135)

In contrast, Broadway Jane originated by Schaffel was taller and more powerfully built than the five-foot-four Elizabeth DeGrazia's Blanche, who is smaller than the powerfully built Jane embodied by Schaffel. DeGrazia is so slight that she doubled as a one of the schoolgirls. Unlike the novel, the musical's Blanche does not use her statuesque form and curvaceous figure to undermine the young governess. Instead of height and curves, this Blanche—in addition to beauty, money, and position—intimidates through her light step and her lilting coloratura.[6] The musical emphasizes the novel Jane's misery as she recognizes how far out of her league she is musically as well as socioeconomically when Rochester and Blanche croon mellifluous parlor duets worthy of Broadway. The novel makes clear that Jane can only play piano "a little," while she draws and paints with great skill. But the musical's staging of the novel's theatricality brings home the significance of performance; the audience enjoys Blanche and Rochester's party songs for themselves while noting (and pitying) their demoralizing effect on Jane.

Blanche sings self-reflexively of her own attractions and attributes in terms that shift her characterization away from the complacent snobbery of the British county aristocrat of the novel to something more doll-like and artificial. The effect is oddly reminiscent of a decorative Southern belle as mythologized in American popular culture, as though this Blanche were as much DuBois (or perhaps Devereaux, of *Golden Girls* fame) as Ingram.[7] Complete with an "I declare" in the lyrics, Blanche—as selfish and vain as Scarlett O'Hara, but more materialistic and better educated about music—warbles in "The Finer Things" that "Mozart and Schumann and Bach / Wrote the finest notes / Every cadenza delights / Every cadence floats." But her point is that a decorative woman is better than decorative music: "When it comes to a woman / Schumann cannot compare." Blanche's voice runs up and down the scale in seemingly effortless arpeggios. Trills ornament the song in a frothy excess of musical enchantment, and only a very strong (and very high) soprano can meet the demands of this virtuoso role. But for Blanche, skill adds up merely to an accomplishment of the kind that raises a woman's value on the marriage market. Her argument throughout the song is that all Rochester's elegant possessions (she even alludes to their current historical period as "the age of elegance")[8] like the furniture ("Chinese Chippendale"), the champagne ("Chateau Lafite '28"), the art ("Rembrandt and Breughel and Bosch"), and the carpet "from Chen Chou / That spent a thousand days on the loom" are meaningless without the most important luxury of all, "a wife." She equates her prodigious musical gifts (her "arpeggios and trills") with mere frivolity ("frolics and frills"). Perfectly comfortable with her role as beautiful object, she sings, "Soon you will see / Of all your things / The very finest thing / Is me!" Blanche's line "not a soul could give you more" has a double meaning here: the contrast between Jane's insisting on her own identity as a person and as a soul in the schoolroom and, as we shall see shortly, in her relationship with Rochester, contrasts markedly with Blanche's willingness to commodify her person and her talent in order to acquire Rochester and his fortune.

Such a petite and decorative Blanche works against the novel's identification of Blanche with Bertha, unless the casting of both roles were to keep the physical similarity in mind. In the novel Bertha is specifically stated to have been in her youth the same type of beauty as Blanche: dark hair, statuesque form, and well-endowed figure. The fact of their similarity gives credence to the notion that Rochester is genuinely attracted to Blanche as he had been in his youth attracted to Bertha. By the time Jane sees Bertha in the novel, she is "a big woman, in stature almost equaling her husband, and corpulent besides" (250). Jane encounters a terrifying, brutish, wild figure, her black hair a matted mane, raging and crawling on all fours. The 2000 Broadway production abandoned the novel's vision, which would have required casting the role of Bertha to resemble Blanche. The actress originating the role of Bertha, Marguerite MacIntyre, is taller than average. Her Bertha was thin, fair-haired, and appeared to have wasted away in captivity. In addition to diminishing the chances of an audience reading these two characters in parallel, such changes preclude interpretations based on race. Bertha is whitened and distanced from the once-beautiful Creole woman of the novel, whom one can interpret as racially non-white. Many critics have read *Jane Eyre* within the context of race and colonialism;[9] other appropriations, such as Jean Rhys's novel *Wide Sargasso Sea,* have expanded on the Othering of Bertha. Although directorial choices could certainly reinsert issues of race through casting, neither the libretto nor the music addresses the novel's implicit commentary on Victorian racial or colonial ideologies.

GOD/GOTHIC

In addition to muting the novel's feminism by individualizing (and Americanizing) Jane's quest for liberty and to shifting its representation and conflation of racial difference and disability onto a critique of individual selfishness and materialism, the Broadway musical is also more overtly religious than the novel. The generic shift from a triple-decker novel to a performance with a two-and-a-half-hour running time necessitates enormous compression.[10] But rather than the consolidation of events, it is the musical's more emphatic invocation of God that flattens the complexity and nuance of the novel's exploration of faith, even while using lines verbatim from Brontë.

Jane sings a kind of prayer when Rochester seems tormented by a secret, which an audience already familiar with the novel knows is Bertha: "God save him if he can be saved / Free him if his soul's enslaved / . . . / Let his spirit be reborn / Help him gather sight where he is blind." While it might be a stretch to suggest that the line "Let his spirit be reborn" hints at a "born again" theology, it invokes a fundamentalism that seems out of sync with Brontë. The word "reborn" never appears in the novel.[11] Brontë uses the word "saved" eight times in *Jane Eyre,* but not once in a spiritual sense—the novel's Jane speaks of furniture, trouble, money, and even lives that can be saved, but never souls. And while the novel depicts both Jane and Rochester praying at a few monumental turning points in the plot, the use of the word "God" is usually spoken by characters other than Jane, sometimes with utmost sincerity (Helen Burns and St. John) and sometimes hypocritically (Mr. Brocklehurst and Mrs. Reed), and sometimes simply as a figure of speech (Mr. Rochester, who repeatedly tosses comments such as "great God" and "God knows" into conversation). The musical's intensified religious interpretation of Jane's outlook becomes even more apparent in the latter part of the play, when the show makes no bones about Jane's leaving Rochester because it would be immoral to stay with him after she discovers that he has a wife. Although in her lyrics she goes on to ask if it would be possible to break heaven's law by sailing away with Rochester, the swelling music makes clear that the imagery of sailing away from it all is merely escapist fantasy; the tragic sweep of the vocal performance intensifies that for her such a move is not possible. This goes much further than the novel in presenting a clear-cut moral choice, in which—remarkably for a Victorian heroine—Jane appears to consider and vehemently reject living with Rochester as his lover, despite the temptation.

Although part of the novel Jane's journey of growth and development involves maturing away from her rebellious fervor through the tutelage in patience and religion imparted by Helen Burns, Jane's energy in standing up to Rochester despite the inequity in their rank and gender is partly what provoked claims of the book's anti-Christian and pro-Chartist sympathies. Elizabeth Rigby (later Lady Eastlake), in her oft-quoted 1848 review of *Jane Eyre* in the *London Quarterly*, went so far as to characterize Jane's as "a mere heathen mind which is a law unto itself" with "no Christian grace" despite her "great moral strength"; she goes on to call the novel "pre-eminently an anti-Christian composition" (173).

In making this assertion, Rigby accentuates the novel's insistence on class equality between governess and employer, which—again—the musical mutes:

> There is throughout it a murmuring against the comforts of the rich and against the privations of the poor, which, as far as each individual is concerned, is a murmuring against God's appointment—there is a proud and perpetual assertion of the rights of man, for which we find no authority either in God's word or in God's providence—there is that pervading tone of ungodly discontent which is at once the most prominent and the most subtle evil which the law and the pulpit, which all civilized society in fact, has at the present day to contend with. We do not hesitate to say that the tone of mind and thought which has overthrown authority and violated every code human and divine abroad, and fostered Chartism and rebellion at home, is the same which has also written *Jane Eyre*. (173–74)

Broadway audiences of *Jane Eyre* already enjoy the right to vote that the Chartists fought for and failed to gain. Broadway audiences also typically do not suffer Jane Eyre's poverty. Like *The King and I*'s presenting a feminism that goes no further than urging rights that women already had acquired by 1951, the musical *Jane Eyre* abandons the novel's sense of anti-authoritarian politics, of fomenting a Chartist class rebellion that angered Rigby, and replaces it with Jane's individual fight against a personal sense of oppression.[12] Instead of the personal being political, it's just personal.

Broadway Jane's declaration to Rochester in the garden by the chestnut tree is another scene that uses lines verbatim from the novel (as we have seen in every adaptation), yet the musical removes Jane's avowal of equality and rejection of convention. These changes also prepare the ground for the musical's intensifying religious imagery. Here is the crucial speech in the novel:

> "I have talked, face to face, with what I reverence, with what I delight in,—with an original, a vigorous, an expanded mind. I have known you, Mr. Rochester; and it strikes me with terror and anguish to feel I absolutely must be torn from you for ever. I see the necessity of departure; and it is like looking on the necessity of death. . . . Do you think, because I am poor, obscure, plain, and little, I am soulless and heartless? You think wrong!—I have as much soul as you,—and full as much heart! And if God had gifted me with some beauty and much wealth, I should have made it as hard for you to leave me, as it is now for me to leave you. I am not talking to you now through the medium of custom, conventionalities, nor even of mortal flesh;—it is my spirit that addresses your spirit; just as if both had passed through the grave, and we stood at God's feet, equal,—as we are!" (215–16)

The lyrics from the song called "The Proposal" borrow directly from the novel. In contrast to musical theater convention in which emotion too strong for dialogue triggers song and too strong for song triggers dance, here—in what is largely a through-sung musical—Jane sings until emotion overwhelms the song and she breaks into speech in the middle.

> I know you think because I'm plain
> That I feel nothing inside
> If I were rich, if I were beautiful . . .
>
> . . . then I should think I would make it as hard for you to leave me as it is for me to leave you. I love Thornfield and I grieve to leave it, for here I have talked, face to face, with what I reverence, what I delight in—with an original, a vigorous, an expanded mind—but I see the necessity of departure and it is like looking on the necessity of death.

Rochester resumes with his own lyrics in response. Fans of the novel thrill to hear the familiar lines spoken on stage, as they have done as far back as both Courtney's very first adaptation and John Brougham's *Jane Eyre*, which premiered at New York's Bowery Theatre on March 26, 1849. But there is nothing in this song to suggest the novel Jane's statement of equality with Rochester, no declaration that she has as much heart and soul as he, or that their spirits are equal before God, which both Courtney (50) and Brougham (95–96) emphatically include.

Instead, the subsequent lines of "The Proposal" invoke highly devout Angel in the House imagery to depict Jane and her positive influence on Rochester, providing a more stereotypical vision of Victorian womanhood than that of Brontë's novel—or *The King and I*, or *Oliver!*, or *Sweeney Todd*. And when the statement of egalitarianism does occur in the Broadway musical's staged scene, it is uttered only by Rochester (as indeed in the novel he reiterates Jane's point), so that equality is his gift to her, rather than her right. He also objectifies Jane in the same breath by calling her his "reward": "Are you my savior, are you my saint / Protecting my soul / With communion and light? / Stand as my equal, be my reward." This sacred imagery is reiterated in the title of a later song of Rochester's, sung when Jane leaves after discovering that Rochester is already married to Bertha, called "Farewell, Good Angel." In the novel, the scene concludes with a lightning strike destroying the ancient chestnut tree in a Gothic gesture of supernatural disapproval. The musical emphasizes this moment with a song as a retrospective comment by Rochester after Jane returns to him, for whom the tree symbolizes himself as blind and crippled, rather than God or Nature's immediate wrath at his wrongdoing in planning to commit bigamy: "A blind man, a cripple, / Tell me, Jane, what right do I have to you?" And as in the musical's proposal scene, the lyric highlights Jane as an object for possession, something Rochester could have a right to own. While Rochester uses discourse of ownership in the novel as well, it occurs after his engagement to Jane, and she consistently resists it.

The musical continues to present a worldview more imbued with religiousness than does the novel, or at least religiousness more overtly expressed.[13] For example, in the novel, having received St. John's proposal of a loveless marriage that would allow them to travel together as missionaries, Jane needs to decide what to do, and makes a simple, single, brief statement of prayer: "Show me, show me the path!" (369). In contrast, in the show she sings gushingly to God for guidance: "What can I do now, my precious lord? / .. is this part of your eternal plan? / .. oh God, I pray / .. give me a sign, my lord." The novel's Jane never prays in this way and certainly not at this most important juncture in the plot, when she is about to hear Rochester's disembodied voice calling out to her. She never speaks of an eternal plan or addresses God as "My Lord" or "My precious Lord." The word "Lord" appears fourteen times in the novel, almost always regarding Lord Ingram. The only time the word is used as a religious term is in the novel's final sentence, a biblical quotation uttered not by Jane but by the coldly pious St. John.

As narrator, the novel's Jane refuses to venture an opinion on "whether what followed was the effect of excitement," explicitly leaving it to the reader to judge. She describes the moment in terms of the sublime, an experience so strong that it affects the body:

> The one candle was dying out: the room was full of moonlight. My heart beat fast and thick: I heard its throb. Suddenly it stood still to an inexpressible feeling that thrilled it through, and passed at once to my head and extremities. The feeling was not like an electric shock, but it was quite as sharp, as strange, as startling: it acted on my senses as if their utmost activity hitherto had been but torpor, from which they were now summoned and forced to wake. They rose expectant: eye and ear waited while the flesh quivered on my bones. (357)

Other than rejecting superstition or witchcraft, the narrating voice of Jane does not venture an opinion on what the coming incident indicates; she makes no assumptions of its being the result of divine intervention. Jane hears, "wildly, eerily, urgently," Rochester's supernaturally audible plea for her to return to him: "Jane! Jane! Jane!" (357). Having prayed for God's guidance, Jane receives not God's but Rochester's voice in what Carolyn Williams calls an "extraordinary trope of secularization" ("Closing" 79). Jane shouts back to the air, "Wait for me!" (358) and sets out in search of Rochester. When they are reunited, Rochester tells Jane that he heard a voice like hers in response to his crying her name. But in the novel, she never reveals to him that she also heard his voice. She never admits she called out in reply. She says, "I listened to Mr. Rochester's narrative, but made no disclosure in return. The coincidence struck me as too awful and inexplicable to be communicated or discussed" (381). She allows the Gothic intrusion to speak for itself.

In contrast, the musical again tames the Romantic sublimity of this moment, permitting none of the book's ambiguity. Once they are reunited, both Jane and Rochester attribute the supernatural event to God directly. Their duet, "Brave Enough for Love," uses words and melody heard earlier in Helen Burns's song "Forgiveness." The melodic parallel to the devout Helen emphasizes its religious content. It goes, "It was a miracle of God / And I'll never lose faith / . . . You have restored my trust / . . . I knew it was a sign from God above / One I could not deny." This shift away from an uncanny and unexplained phenomenon whose origin is ambiguous to an unequivocal representation of God's providential intervention mutes the novel's disruptive Gothicism, characterized by Robert Heilman as emphasizing "the depth or mysteriousness or intensity or ambiguity of impulses and feelings" (458). The musical ends with Jane and Rochester singing together in their new home with their new baby about how they are "brave enough for love." As Dino Felluga and Emily Allen have pointed out, the musical here "is determined to undercut its gothic effects with a compensatory promise of a benevolent patriarchy (call it God, call it Love) that looks for all the world like the freedom Jane seeks" (Felluga and Allen). The ensemble joins the strings in churchlike harmonies to back up Jane's and Rochester's assertion that, now together, they "will never lose faith."

In the novel, neither Jane nor Rochester blatantly attributes this supernatural occurrence that brings them together directly to God's divine intervention. It is indeed so inexplicable as to prevent expression. In evicting the Gothic and replacing it with God, the musical again Americanizes Jane. In the musical's final scene, the nuclear family of Jane Eyre is fully Americanized. Having traveled across oceans, Broadway Jane has gained her sweet land of liberty on the great white way, now living in the home of the "brave enough for love," happily married to the born-again Rochester, secure in her wealth, because in God they trust.

Conclusion

In *Victorians on Broadway,* I analyze closely both musical and literary artifacts so that each brings reciprocal insights to the other. I read the source through the adaptation and the adaptation through the source, considering the inherent musical theatricality of Victorian texts, excavating a genealogy of prior adaptations to understand how the meta-text alters over time, examining the musical's negotiation of current issues through the lens of Victorian literature, and finding that for twentieth-century Broadway, "Victorian" means "Dickensian." This method demonstrates that the systemic analysis of musical theater adaptations with their literary sources across time and national boundaries opens a new area of inquiry. Studying musicals in this way shows us that they connect significantly to the literary, cultural, and theatrical past and that they are interwoven fully into the broader fabric of social and intellectual life in their own moment.

Audiences who know the Victorian text anticipate delight in discovering how the creators will transform it to the musical stage. This process is part of what Sanders sees as kind of joy shared by audience and adapters, what she calls "the ongoing experiences of pleasure for the reader or spectator in tracing the intertextual relationship" (25). It is the "inherent sense of play," the "informed sense of similarity and difference," the "interplay of expectation and surprise" in adaptation generally that works with special force when stagecraft, dance, melody, and lyrics—sometimes verbatim from the source—combine in live performance (25). But bound up in the delight in musical theater artistry is also recognition of its relevance, particularly when, as Sondheim explained to me, a story from the past retains its contemporaneity better than a contemporary story does (despite this seeming paradox). This is because a current story's topicality and up-to-date word choices become outdated in the short term (personal interview with author).

Although this study focuses on Victorian-sourced Broadway musicals from the second half of the twentieth century, the musical stage continues to adapt nineteenth-century literature and culture in the twenty-first century. A few examples since 2000 include the off-Broadway *A Man of No Importance* (2002); it incorporates some of Oscar Wilde's writing and biography into a story about a contemporary amateur actor-director putting on a church production of Wilde's *Salome* while coming to terms with his own sexuality.[1] Stephen Schwartz and Winnie Holzman's blockbuster *Wicked* (2003) adapts Gregory Maguire's 1995 *Wicked: The Life and Times of the Wicked Witch of the West* deriving from L. Frank Baum's *The Wizard of Oz* (1900), which does not fit the parameters of this book because the source is American, not British; yet the musical includes clear Dickensian elements (Hirschhorn). In the *Guardian,* Michael Billington quips, "Miriam Margolyes, as a statuesque, magic-dispensing college principal, has a Dickensian exuberance that evokes the world of Boz more than Oz." Webber's *The Woman in White* transferred to Broadway in 2005 for three months, operating unapologetically in the melodramatic mode and sharing with *Jane Eyre: The Musical* both an innovative use of projected scenery and the occasional hint of Mozart. It was revived in London in 2017. *A Tale of Two Cities* (Broadway, 2008), like *Jekyll and Hyde,* first traveled the country for years before its Broadway debut.[2] Major twenty-first-century Broadway revivals include *Sweeney Todd* (2005 and 2017), *The Mystery of Edwin Drood* (2012), and *The King and I* (2015). Victorians are still very much on Broadway.

A famous incident in 2016 will help illuminate why examining musical theater that reinterprets the literature and culture of the past matters beyond aesthetic appreciation. I refer to the exchange between the cast of *Hamilton* and then president-elect of the United States, Donald Trump. This event highlights the political stakes of understanding live musical theatrical performance and public assembly inside a performance venue. On November 18, 2016, one of the stars of *Hamilton,* Brandon Dixon, standing onstage with the entire cast at the end of the show, read aloud a hastily scribbled note to a member of the audience, Mike Pence. Dixon urged him to use his future office as vice president to protect all of America's diverse people.

In addition to its direct appeal to Pence, Dixon's language in this speech explicitly emphasizes the power of the theater more generally ("we hope that this show has inspired you") to move audiences to thought, change of heart, and political action. President-Elect Donald Trump's response in several tweets chastised the cast for their public statement. In his message of November 19, 2016, he defines theater as a "safe and special place," insinuating that its proper role is not political action but purely escapist entertainment, the very charge Brecht lays against conventional, commercial, middlebrow, bourgeois theater. This, unsurprisingly, puts Trump and Brecht in opposite critical camps, so to speak.[3] The spontaneity of the cast's seizing the opportunity to speak directly to Pence and of Trump's barrage of unscripted tweets in reply, coupled with the crowd's booing Pence and cheering Dixon, suggests the applicability here of Judith Butler's notion of the meaningful power of assembly.

In *Notes toward a Performative Theory of Assembly,* Butler argues that demonstrations like Tahir Square and the Occupy movement constitute communal bodily signification. She does not discuss gatherings in a public theater, and of course neither the *Hamilton* actors nor their eager audience on November 19, 2016, assembled in order to protest anything. The company came for a paying job, as usual, eight performances a week; the audience—more than 1,300 customers per show—forked over heaps of cash for an expensive and entertaining night on the town (Weltman, "Melodrama" 305). Yet something else occurred in the newly charged political climate within the theater. Prepped by their collective enjoyment of music and spectacle to feel a special connection with the performers and one another, the audience reacted throughout the show with fresh strength to lyrics proudly claiming Alexander Hamilton, American founding father and first secretary of the treasury, as an immigrant. When the racially diverse cast seized on their collective bow as an occasion to speak out and when the audience of pleasure-seekers erupted in audible support, something more happened.[4] The event took on the discursive power of political assembly that Butler defines, signifying "in excess of what is said" (8). The power of Dixon's message was not just in his words but also in the event bringing actors and audience together with new political valence.

I conclude with this incident because it underscores the importance of the liveness of musical theater: only in a live venue can the cast act spontaneously to address an individual member of the audience, whom they see in the theater's house as much as the audience sees them onstage. Only in a live performance can the audience's reactions to another member of the audience inspire the cast to reply. Through its race-conscious and cross-racial casting of historical figures in a variety of voices as well as its range of musical and choreographic styles, *Hamilton* comments on contemporary American issues of the immigrant experience, racial inequality, and population diversity.

Mikhail Bakhtin's landmark study *The Dialogic Imagination* (1981, English translation) relies on Dickens for the development of his theory of double voicing, with clear application to the diversity of contrapuntal voices in musical theater adaptation of Victorian texts. Although Bakhtin famously rejected theater as an example of the Carnivalesque in his statement that "Carnival does not know footlights" (7), he is useful in drawing our attention to musical theater's interplay of competing discourses. Bakhtin borrows the term *polyphony* from music to apply to the novel, but his theories also effectively illuminate musical theater (and opera), which are constitutionally polyphonic and multivocal. The musical goes even further than nonmusical drama, which—when understood in broader terms than Bakhtin was willing to define it—can be equally dialogic as the novel. Bakhtin helps me here to conclude the argument that the middlebrow musical adapting Victorian classics is not the critically uninteresting form of entertainment it is often maligned as being (aimed at out-of-towners, suitable for families, minimizing artistic risk to attract large audiences) but actually complex and theoretically sophisticated, negotiating multiple elements, incorporating a variety of voices, and employing a powerful diversity of media within a single staging. All the musicals I have examined in *Victorians on Broadway* contain crucial moments of meta-theatricality that highlight how integral to the genre is recognition of its own artifice.

Like many of the Victorian books they adapt, musicals such as *The King and I, Oliver!,* and *Sweeney Todd* are themselves "culture texts"—so ubiquitous that people recognize aspects of them without having actually encountered the prototype (Paul Davis 4). When the cartoon *Family Guy*'s Stewie is suddenly transported into a workhouse à la *Oliver Twist* asking for more, the iconography of the scene comes from the movie musical *Oliver!* in a shot that replicates the stage musical closely. Yet viewers read the scene as though it were directly from Dickens's novel. Sourced in a twenty-first-century biography of an eighteenth-century Founding Father, Lin-Manuel Miranda's *Hamilton* is already a culture text, with homages, critical analyses, and parodies, some written by Miranda himself.[5] But even this musical, it turns out, owes a debt to Dickens. Miranda explained that Chernow's biography inspired him in part because Hamilton's "childhood out-Dickenses Dickens" (Toppman). And so, perhaps, while we learn that "Victorian" equals "Dickensian," we learn also that Dickens is shorthand for tales of all kinds of childhood privation, all kinds of powerful entertainment that effects social change.

NOTES

Introduction

1. For an example of the widespread influence of and debate on this musical, see *Historians on Hamilton*.

2. See McMillin's *The Musical as Drama* for a straightforward explanation of how interpreting musical theater through the lens of dramatic analysis yields important new ways to understand it. McMillin draws from Kerman's classic study *Opera as Drama*, which previously established the legitimacy of approaching opera in this way.

3. Theater historians differ on what period, if any, constitutes the Golden Age of the American Musical. Bordman and Norton say 1924–37 (441); Engel places it from *Pal Joey* in 1940 to *A Little Night Music* in 1973 (80); Naden entitles a reference book *The Golden Age of American Musical Theatre: 1943–1965;* Block ironizes the whole notion by putting the phrase in quotation marks (*Enchanted Evenings*, xix). Wolf points out that "the labeling of 'the golden age musical,' as well as the 'integration' narrative, are ubiquitous in musical theater historiography, even as some scholarship strives to refute these historiographical, formalist assumptions. Still, most scholars see Kern, Hammerstein, or the team of Rodgers and Hammerstein as the key players in the forms development" (*Changed for Good* 348n16).

4. Although *Oklahoma!* is credited with changing the course of musical theater when it premiered in 1943, *Show Boat* (Kern and Hammerstein), also an integrated musical, premiered over fifteen years earlier in December 1927 without the same immediate impact on subsequent musical theater writers. But some melodramas used integrated songs long before *Show Boat,* sometimes diegetically, sometimes thematically, etc. See Weltman, "Melodrama."

5. Swain, *Broadway Musical;* Block, *Enchanted Evenings;* Grant, *Rise and Fall;* Mordden, *Coming Up Roses.*

6. Banfield, *Sondheim's Broadway Musicals;* Bordman, *American Musical Comedy;* Sternfeld, *Megamusical;* Wollman, *Theatre Will Rock* and *Hard Times.*

7. Woll, *Black Musical Theatre;* Miller, *[Place for Us];* Clum, *Something for the Boys;* Jones, *Our Musicals, Ourselves;* Most, *Making Americans;* Wolf, *Changed for Good;* Sandoval-Sanchez, *José Can You See?*

8. Kucich and Sadoff, *Victorian Afterlife;* Clayton, *Dickens in Cyberspace.*

9. Glavin, *After Dickens.*

10. Cult films—often musicals, like *Rocky Horror Picture Show*—that include the live element of lip-syncing on stage in front of the screen before a participating audience of costumed fans, are almost exceptions. But the film keeps rolling and the screen actors are not present. The event is a hybrid of film and live theater. Musical theater also differs from live nonmusical theater in this convention. We do not call out "Encore!" when a tragic actor has just brought us to the point of weeping.

11. For a critique of "fidelity theory," see Hutcheon, *Theory of Adaptation;* Leitch, *Film Adaptation;* and Sanders, *Adaptation and Appropriation.*

12. The chance that New York audiences buying Broadway tickets would mistake *Jekyll and Hyde: The Musical* or *Jane Eyre: The Musical* for anything but a musical, even without the subtitle, is very slight. There is no mistaking a movie ticket for a Broadway musical theater ticket, which would be many times the price. But there is also little opportunity for confusion between musicals and plays because they are marketed differently. Shows are clearly noted as either "musicals" or "plays" on such entities as TKTS, *Playbill,* and Broadway.com. The two genres compete in different categories for Tonys and other awards. Musicals are priced much higher because hiring dancers and musicians costs money.

13. A Google search on March 10, 2019, revealed that Goodreads listed 1,496 books as better than the movie, according to people who posted ("The BOOK was BETTER than the MOVIE"). There was no category "The Book was Better than the Musical" on Goodreads (or anywhere). While a message board thread on Broadwayworld.com from 2005 includes ten posts discussing the relative merits of *Phantom of the Opera* as novel and musical, focusing on the different endings, most allude to the movie, not the live stage show ("Phantom of The Opera, Musical vs. Book").

14. Obviously, this is not a problem in novels: no matter what appears on the printed page, solitary readers do not literally hear ditties or see *pas de deux.*

15. But just as Hammerstein innovated songs and dances that propel the plot of musicals, so Christoph Willibald Gluck and Ranieri de' Calzabigi decided to reform the writing of opera with their *Alceste* (1767), determined to avoid musical ornamentation that distorted the libretto's meaning. Gluck wanted to write music that would allow the audience to understand the words and focus on drama.

16. For critique of the heritage industry as a manifestation of a Thatcherite agenda, see Hewison's *Heritage Industry;* for a succinct history and placement of the debates, see Vidal's *Heritage Film.*

17. These include Miller's *[Place for Us],* Clum's *Something for the Boys,* and Wolf's *A Problem Like Maria.*

18. These include Knapp's *The American Musical and the Performance of Personal Identity* (2006) and Wolf's *Changed for Good.*

19. Level of education and cultural capital that come with financial capital may contribute to Broadway audiences' more inclusive point of view. As Savran explains, "Surveys demonstrate that middle-class Broadway audiences have considerably more economic and educational capital than most Americans," with "the average annual income of Broadway musical theatergoers" being "roughly three times the national average" and "four times as likely to have had some postgraduate education" ("Class

and Culture" 239–40). This holds even though musicals—less highbrow, despite their higher ticket prices—"attract larger and less affluent audiences" than spoken drama (Savran, *Highbrow/Lowdown* 106).

20. *Why Marry?* by Jesse Lynch Williams won "for the original American play, performed in New York during the year, which shall best represent the educational value and power of the stage in raising the standard of good morals, good taste and good manners" (http://www.pulitzer.org/winners/jesse-lynch-williams). A New Woman social satire about upper-middle-class matrimony and modernity, it also specifically addresses brow-level (17).

21. See Weltman, "Adopting and Adapting Dickens."

22. A cinema pioneer, Griffith created the first feature-length film—the racist *Birth of a Nation* (1915), which glorified the Ku Klux Klan. He followed with *Intolerance* (1916), comprising four vignettes exploring the topic (perhaps partly in recompense for provoking such outrage with *Birth of a Nation*), and many other movies, including *Broken Blossoms* (1919), with its famously claustrophobic closet scene.

23. See Eisenstein, "Dickens, Griffith, and Film Today."

24. There is a profusion of books on adaptations of Dickens. See Davis, *The Lives and Times of Ebenezer Scrooge;* Guida, *A Christmas Carol and Its Adaptations;* Hammond, *Charles Dickens's Great Expectations;* and Napolitano, *Oliver! A Dickensian Musical,* which provides a detailed biography of one very influential musical stage adaptation. The larger cultural landscape has been examined by such scholars as Sadoff in *Victorian Vogue,* Clayton in *Dickens in Cyberspace,* and Glavin in *Dickens on Screen.*

25. A third, the musical *A Christmas Carol,* performed every Christmas season at Madison Square Garden from 1994 to 2003, could have garnered its own chapter as well. Based on Dickens's first Christmas book, *A Christmas Carol* (1843), this musical (music by Alan Menken, lyrics by Lynn Ahrens, and book by Mike Ockrent and Lynn Ahrens) targeted the family Christmas audience. It does not figure in its own chapter in this study for several reasons. It did not run continuously from 1994 to 2003 seasons but rather recurred—like *The Nutcracker* or a British Christmas pantomime—every year during the month of December. While not strictly children's theater per se, it is aimed at a young audience, more so than Disney's Broadway productions such as *The Lion King* or even *Beauty and the Beast* (with music by the same composer), which provide substantial entertainment to all ages.

26. This is evident from such titles as Kurnick, *Empty Houses: Theatrical Failure and the Novel;* Voskuil, *Acting Naturally: Victorian Theatricality and Authenticity;* and Litvak, *Caught in the Act: Theatricality in the Nineteenth-Century English Novel.*

27. Felski's "Context Stinks!" is useful here: "A text's sociability—that is, its embedding in numerous networks and its reliance on multiple mediators—is not an attrition, diminution, or co-option of its agency, but the very precondition of it" (589).

28. For opposing views, see Susan Brown's "Alternatives to the Missionary Position" and Zlotnick's "Jane Eyre, Anna Leonowens, and the White Woman's Burden."

29. See Kermode, *Sense of an Ending;* and Levine and Ortiz-Robles, Introduction to *Narrative Middles.*

30. For just a sampling of standard essays from this variety of perspectives, see Arseneau, "Incarnation and Interpretation"; Carpenter, "'Eat Me, Drink Me, Love Me'"; Connor, "'Speaking Likenesses'"; Golub, "Untying Goblin Apron Strings"; Helsinger, "Consumer Power"; Menke, "Political Economy of Fruit."

31. For a magisterial history of this topic, see Kooistra's *Christina Rossetti and Illustration*.

32. For the definitive study on Victorian slumming, see Koven's *Slumming*.

33. Examples are John Williams's 1971 symphonic suite *Jane Eyre* (Audissino, 243) and the Northern Ballet's 2016 production of a ballet *Jane Eyre*, choreographed by Cathy Marston (Ward).

34. Go to https://www.youtube.com/watch?v=-NKXNThJ6io.

35. See Alexander and Smith for numerous examples (356).

36. For theorization of the "double I," see Starobinski.

1. Broadway, Victorian Venus, and the Middlebrow

1. See Weltman, "Melodrama."

2. *The Girl in Pink Tights* was composed by Sigmund Romberg, with lyrics by Leo Robin and book by Jerome Chodorov and Joseph Fields. In musical theater parlance, *book* means everything that is not music and lyrics, such as storyline and dialogue. The term *libretto* denotes everything verbal about the musical play, including dialogue and lyrics.

3. So bad was the 1935–36 season that the only show to make a clear profit was Richard Rodgers and Lorenz Hart's *On Your Toes* (Block, "Melody" 133).

4. The book is by George S. Kaufman and Morrie Ryskind. *Of Thee I Sing* was the first musical to win the Pulitzer Prize for drama (1932).

5. Kurt Weill's first American musical, it was declared by the *Washington Post* to be "a pungent political satire" (qtd. "*Knickerbocker Holiday*").

6. Wikipedia provides an extremely helpful chart displaying the changes in musical numbers in a variety of performances: http://en.wikipedia.org/wiki/Anything_Goes.

7. Another genre-bending show is *Porgy and Bess* (1935), adapted from DuBose Heyward's 1925 novel *Porgy* and its 1927 dramatization by Dorothy Heyward (DuBose's wife).

8. Black and white entertainers already performed in the same revues on Broadway, such as the white Eddie Cantor (in blackface) playing the black Burt Williams's son in comic sketches in *Ziegfeld Follies of 1917* (Forbes 273).

9. Roger Cushing Aikin makes the important point that the farm is Laurey's, not her Aunt Eller's.

10. It's not difficult to project a tragic future for young Laurey and Curly, joyfully married just prior to statehood, but conceivably uprooted and living miserably in Hooverville by the time they are in their forties or fifties.

11. Elia Kazan directed, rounding out a top-notch creative team. Produced by Cheryl Crawford, *One Touch of Venus* opened at the Imperial Theatre on October 7, 1943; it closed on February 10, 1945, after 567 performances. Paula Laurence played

Molly, the sharp secretary who gets some of the best songs. Mary Martin played Venus, her first time starring in a Broadway musical. *One Touch of Venus* was the second of Weill's two big Broadway hits, running even longer than Weill's previous success, *Lady in the Dark* (1941). The costume designer for *Lady in the Dark,* Irene Sharaff (who also designed the costumes for *The King and I*), may have given Weill *The Tinted Venus* to read with an eye to its possible musicalization (Block, *Enchanted Evenings* W98n17) https://global.oup.com/us/companion.websites/fdscontent /uscompanion/us/static/companion.websites/companion.websites.binaries /9780195384000/appendices/pdfs/notes1.pdf.

12. Integrating folk elements quickly became popular, including from the British Isles, but still explicitly seen through American eyes. *Brigadoon* (1947), with lyrics and book by Alan Jay Lerner and music by Frederick Loewe, is set mostly in Scotland. The two male leads are New Yorkers who stumble upon the magical village of Brigadoon while touring the Highlands. It is neither based on a Victorian text nor set in the Victorian period, but in an eighteenth-century town that reappears once every hundred years. *Finian's Rainbow* (1947), composed by Burton Lane with lyrics by E. Y. Harburg and book by Harburg and Fred Saidy, takes place partly in Ireland but mostly in the state of Missitucky, USA. It too is neither adapted from a Victorian source nor set in Victorian times. Like *Brigadoon,* in incorporates magic, including a leprechaun.

13. See Roach for the identification of the author of this interview as M.M.B (98n87).

14. It is also worth noting that Shakespeare is the only dramatist on the elite roster.

15. Some portions of the book had previously come out earlier in the decade in the journal *Scrutiny.*

16. Only George Eliot (1819–1880) is unequivocally, unambiguously Victorian. Jane Austen (1775–1817) is too early. Henry James (1847–1915) wrote his nineteenth-century fiction while still an American, becoming a British subject in 1914. Joseph Conrad (1857–1924), whose British citizenship was granted in 1886, published most of his books after the death of Queen Victoria in 1901, although importantly *Heart of Darkness* (1899) appeared before the century's end.

17. This book has prompted an MLA special forum to analyze its significance (later published in *Nineteenth-Century Studies*) "Jerome Hamilton Buckley's *The Victorian Temper* and the Shaping of Victorian Studies."

18. Other examples of the 1950s explosion of interest in reinterpreting the Victorians abound. *The Reinterpretation of Victorian Literature,* a collection of essays edited by Joseph E. Baker (1950), urges a clearer view of Victorian literature and culture as funnier, smarter, and less hypocritical than stereotypically represented. George Rowell's *The Victorian Theatre: A Survey* (1956) has influenced generations of theater historians. Victorian academic journals founded during the 1950s include the *Victorian Newsletter* (in 1952) and *Victorian Studies* (in 1957); both remain major players in the field. Influential new collections of Victorian poetry and/or prose appeared during the 1950s for academic use, such as *Prose of the Victorian Period* in 1958, edited William Buckler, and *Victorian Poetry and Poetics* in 1959, edited by Walter Edwards Houghton and George Robert Stange.

19. There has been astonishingly little criticism written on Anstey in the past eighty years. As of April 2, 2019, the MLA Bibliography shows only eleven distinct entries on F. Anstey. However, Peter Merchant's 2011 scholarly edition of Vice Versâ for Victorian Secrets Press provides helpful information and may signal (or spark) a revival of interest.

20. *Vice Versâ* tells of a man who trades bodies with his son through supernatural intervention, so that the father experiences the son's life at school—and vice versa—with comic results that yield renewed understanding of each other's lives. Mary Rodgers also wrote the screenplay for the first film adaptation of *Freaky Friday* in 1977, starring Barbara Harris and Jodie Foster. The composer of the Broadway hit *Once upon a Mattress* (1959), Rodgers adapted her novel to the musical stage herself for Theatre Works/USA in 1991. She is the daughter of Richard Rodgers, one of Broadway's most important composers of all time, and the mother of Tony Award–winner Adam Guettel, composer/lyricist of *The Light in the Piazza* (2005). Disney produced a stage musical of *Freaky Friday* with music by Tom Kitt and lyrics by Brian Yorkey (who collaborated previously on the 2008 Pulitzer Prize–winning hit *Next To Normal*). The book is by Bridget Carpenter, based on Rodgers's novel and its movie adaptations. The show opened on October 4, 2016, at Arlington, Virginia's Signature Theatre, hopping to half a dozen other premier regional theaters, such as the La Jolla Playhouse, the Cleveland Playhouse, and the Alley Theatre (all often pre-Broadway venues) throughout 2017. The Disney Channel premiered a television adaptation of the musical on August 10, 2018 (Verne).

21. She then took it on several American tours, including an extensive 1885 circuit of New York, Boston, Philadelphia, etc., and a six-week repertory residence at the Daly's Theater in New York in April and May 1891. See *From Studio to Stage* for a brief description of Grossmith's first performance opposite Rosina Vokes's Venus as Leander Tweedle (*sic*) in Liverpool in 1885 and his subsequent experiences in New York and American touring. (Perhaps "Tweedle" is a name change from "Tweddle": the extra "e" appears in "At the Theaters" in *New York Dramatic Mirror*, 2, and the entry for Weedon Grossmith in *Who's Who in the Theatre*, 297). An American musical adaptation, *Aphrodite, a Farcical Romance in 3 Acts*, with lyrics by Thomas Addison (a Boston journalist) and music by Charles Blake, was copywritten in 1885 (Library of Congress 79). It was performed in such theaters as the Watertown, New York, opera house in 1885 ("Amusements" 5). My thanks to Peter Merchant for noticing this newspaper clipping.

22. His royalties on the performances came to only £50 (Anstey, *Long Retrospect* 202). Anstey himself dramatized it in a play in three acts, as *A Statue at Large* in 1911, with many revisions that he felt made it "more plausible," but no producers were interested then, wanting him to wait until interest in yet another play currently running about an animated statue—of Niobe, this time—had subsided (*Retrospect* 330–31). He also adapted it into a silent screen scenario, co-written with the actor Ernest Holman Clark, in 1915 (BL Millar Bequest. vol. 82, Add. MSS 54308). My deep thanks go to Peter Merchant for alerting me to this archival material. Adaptations continue after *One Touch of Venus*. In 1988 Vanna White starred in the unabashedly dreadful

nonmusical made-for-TV movie *Goddess of Love,* clearly retelling Anstey's tale. Another film that owes a debt to the trope of a ring placed on the wrong (inanimate) finger is Tim Burton's *The Corpse Bride* (2005), a musical.

23. Alma Taylor and George Dewhurst starred. See Merchant, "Madhouse Shuffle" and Stratford, "F. Anstey."

24. The live Matilda Collum is for much of the novel more of a cold, morally inflexible stone column than the marble statue, warm in her desire for the lowly barber. Leander Tweddle's name is likewise significant, suggesting he is a handsome lad from Greek myth and also, perhaps, a bunch of twaddle. Venus approves of his name being Leander, linking him to "a goodly and noble youth who perished for the sake of Hero," a comment setting up Leander's typically lowbrow response, "I'm not a hero myself, I'm a hairdresser" (49).

25. Green is himself an author of fantasies based on myths as well as a scholar and biographer. A member of the Inklings, he was friends with C. S. Lewis and J. R. R. Tolkien. *Vice Versâ* and *The Tinted Venus* are among several works of important speculative fiction written in the 1880s, including Stevenson's *The Strange Case of Dr. Jekyll and Mr. Hyde* in 1886 and H. Rider Haggard's *She* in 1887, both immediately adapted to the stage and later to the screen, demonstrating the rich theatrical context for dramatizations of Anstey. Norman Etherington identifies a dramatization of *She* by Edward Rose, W. Sidney, and C. Graves that opened on May 10, 1888, at the Novelty Theatre; Haggard addressed the audience. Etherington points to a negative review in *Punch* (September 22, 1888: 132) called "She-That-Ought-Not-to-Be-Played" (xlii).

26. Anstey sets his novel in the contemporary London of 1885, replete with specifics of the cityscape: Bloomsbury, Westbourne Grove, theaters such as the Adelphi, streets such as Edgeware Road, Fenchurch Street Station. Though the novel's Rosherwich Gardens appear to be fictional, they strongly resemble real pleasure gardens of Rosherville Gardens in Kent (very popular in the 1880s), with private nooks along secluded pathways with classical statuary and benches, tea, live music, dancing. Other fiction depending on Carnivalesque pleasure gardens that permit aberrant events include Frances Burney's *Cecilia* (1782) and William Makepeace Thackeray's *Vanity Fair* (1848), both with scenes set in London's most famous Vauxhall Gardens.

27. Among them may be Prosper Mérrimée's 1835 short story "La Vénus d'Ille," in which a statue of Venus's coming to life after an engagement ring was placed on her finger has particularly negative effects on the humans around her. My thanks go to Marguerite Murphy for making this connection.

28. Merchant explores specific debts *Vice Versâ* owes to *Dombey and Son* (Introduction 9).

29. My thanks go to Peter Merchant for telling me about this film scenario and sending me this citation.

30. Words were by Henry Pottinger Stephens and W. Webster, music by Wilhelm Meyer Lutz.

31. See Marshall, *Actresses on the Victorian Stage,* for full analysis of this phenomenon. See also Williams's *Gilbert and Sullivan* on the classical extravaganza, an upscale

burlesque parodied in Gilbert and Sullivan's first collaboration, *Thespis, or The Gods Grown Old* (1871), a work commissioned by John Hollingshead, the manager of the Gaiety (33).

32. His second series on the subject, painted in 1875–78, it is displayed at the Birmingham Museums and Art Gallery.

33. The statue is housed at the Walker Art Gallery in Liverpool.

34. See Altick, *Shows of London*.

35. This usage of the word "coloured" as "non-white" was common throughout the nineteenth century and goes back to the seventeenth, according to the *OED* (s.v. "coloured").

36. A related contrast is Hiram Powers's marble statue *Greek Slave* (1844), exhibited in the American section of the Great Exhibition of 1851. One of the most famous and influential American sculptures in the mid-nineteenth century, it inspired Elizabeth Barrett Browning's anti-slavery sonnet "Hiram Powers' 'Greek Slave.'" Unlike Gibson's Venus, Powers's white marble statue was not tinted. Based on the Uffizi's Medici Venus, the nude depicted a young Greek woman in chains, being sold into sexual slavery in a Turkish market. The racial overtones of her marble whiteness is made explicit in the way Barrett Browning brilliantly shifts Powers's indictment of the Turkish empire's recent oppression of the Greeks to an indictment of American slavery and the suppression of black people. Addressing the statue, the speaker says, "Catch up in thy divine face, not alone / East griefs but west, and strike and shame the strong, / By thunders of white silence, overthrown" (lines 12–14). John Bell's 1862 *The American Slave* echoes Powers while representing the darker skin of African Americans with patinated bronze.

37. Venus is like Keats's Lamia in that by being too much of a goddess, Leander is not attracted to her, just as Lyceus is not drawn to Lamia until she makes herself more of a woman. In this case, Tweddle is not attracted to his own handiwork in making Venus more lifelike and womanly, in contrast to the mythical Pygmalion.

38. This fear provides the basis for *Sweeney Todd*'s perennial success as culture text.

39. Readers may be more familiar with the tamer 1948 movie *One Touch of Venus* starring Ava Gardner. It retains only three of Weill's songs and radically changes the plot, including shifting the protagonist's profession from hairdresser to department-store window dresser, augmenting the stage musical's critique of commercialism and de-emphasizing an element that links the stage show to the novel and its Victorian cultural connections.

40. Spewack was at this time a Broadway novice, but she and her husband, Sam, would soon write the book for the Cole Porter hit *Kiss Me Kate* (1948).

41. A useful counterpoint is Keats's "Ode on a Grecian Urn." In that poem, the lovers and their beloveds will never kiss, forever panting, forever young, because they are "marble men and maidens"—a "Cold Pastoral!" (lines 42, 45).

42. Perhaps it was the sort of lyrics found in this song that convinced Marlene Dietrich that the whole show was too risqué for her to participate; she withdrew, opening the opportunity for Mary Martin to play Venus. Dietrich stated that the musical's book is "vulgar and profane" and "too sexy and profane" (Barranger 72)

and that she had to think of her teenage daughter (Ronald Davis 72). The producer Cheryl Crawford considered Kitty Carlisle for the role before settling on Mary Martin. Her subsequent girl-next-door persona makes her seem a surprising choice to play a part that the sex symbol Dietrich—star of *Blue Angel*—deemed too daring. But although we now may think of Martin as Nellie Forbush, Maria von Trapp, and Peter Pan, before all those wholesome roles, she made her Broadway debut singing the breathy "My Heart Belongs to Daddy" (from the 1938 Cole Porter show *Leave It to Me!*) while tossing off layers of clothing. Nevertheless, Martin worried that she was too much a "cornball" for the role and that her slightly less than average height made her too short for a goddess. To help convince her to take the job, her husband took her to the Metropolitan Museum of Art (how appropriate for this musical!) to look at the variety of body types used to depict Venus. Once she saw a statue with a particularly large derrière, she agreed (Ronald Davis 73–74).

43. A surprise ending to this news story: DNA evidence proved in 2011 that the body found in the cellar could not have been Elmore's because it was male ("Was Dr. Crippen").

44. Likewise, Tuptim uses "The Small House of Uncle Thomas" to awaken the King to consciousness of his own tyranny in *The King and I* (see chapter 2), and Mrs. Lovett's retelling of Lucy's rape portrayed in dumb show provokes Todd to reveal emotion and thus his identity in *Sweeney Todd* (see chapter 4).

2. *The King and* Who?

1. See Caren Kaplan (43) and Berlant (292–302) for further historicizing *The King and I*. Bruce McConachie argues that Rodgers and Hammerstein's musicals—despite their palpable effort to combat racism—helped pave the way for US entry into the Vietnam War (386), "justifying the American empire in the East on humanitarian as well as political grounds" (397). Viswanathan's *Masks of Conquests* discusses education as a central tool of colonialism.

2. Leonowens's books about Siam have an ample history of adaptation. Landon's popular 1944 novel *Anna and the King of Siam* wove Tuptim's story from *Romance of the Harem* as a tragic subplot into the autobiographical narrative of *The English Governess at the Siamese Court*. The wives of Rodgers and Hammerstein (both named Dorothy) read Landon and recommended to their husbands that they musicalize the novel, the official source of their musical. But the Oscar-winning Darryl F. Zanuck film, also called *Anna and the King of Siam* (1946), directed by John Cromwell and starring Irene Dunne and Rex Harrison, demonstrated that a sufficiently condensed narrative could work onstage. *The King and I* opened on March 29, 1951, at the St. James Theater, running for 1,246 performances. It won the Tony for best musical in 1951 and for best revival 1996 and again in 2015, prompting major productions all over the world. In 1951 Gertrude Lawrence, for whom the show was written, won the Tony for best actress. Best actor went to Yul Brynner, who played the King of Siam for the rest of his life in revivals and on tour. It also won Tonys for best scenic design (Jo Mielziner) and best costume design (Irene Sharaff), whose lush vision ignited a

craze for sumptuous, vibrant silks in fashion and interior design, helping to raise the public profile of Thai silk, which became the country's "best-known export" (Howe). The 1996 Broadway production was similarly successful: besides best revival, it won best actress (Donna Murphy), best scenic design (Brian Thomson), and best costume design (Roger Kirk). Many songs and some characters were retained for the disappointing 1999 animated feature *The King and I,* which simplifies the plot and adds a dragon. Landon's novel was also recast into *Anna and the King,* a short-lived American television situation comedy in 1972. In 1999 Jodie Foster and Chow Yun-Fat starred in a film that returned to Anna Leonowens's books more directly for inspiration, although the influence of Rodgers and Hammerstein can be seen in the romantic attachment between the leading characters (not historically factual and not hinted at by Leonowens herself).The show's 2015 Lincoln Center revival met with accolades; it was directed by Bartlett Sher and starred Kelli O'Hara as Anna and Ken Watanabe as the King. The production aimed at less Orientalism and more accuracy in depicting nineteenth-century Siam, winning four Tonys and a Drama Desk Award.

3. After leaving Thailand, Leonowens moved to New York, where she taught school, wrote, and lectured. Later she relocated to Canada to join her daughter and lived for many years in Quebec, dying there at the age of eighty-three. For research on the implications of racial passing in an American context, see Dawkins, *Clearly Invisible;* Wald, *Crossing the Line;* and Sollers, *Neither Black nor White.*

4. For a book-length explanation of many elements distressing to Thai viewers, see Chantasingh, "Americanization of *The King and I.*"

5. See Griswold, *King Mongkut of Siam;* Bristowe, *Louis and the King of Siam;* Moffat, *Mongkut, the King of Siam;* Terwiel, *History of Modern Thailand.*

6. Donaldson sees the musical film Leonowens's use of feminist abolitionist discourse as complicit with racism and the uplifting educational project as complicit with imperialism, arguing for a complex view of Anna's "oppressed and oppressive participation in the Anglo-European imperial project" (55). Like Donaldson, Caren Kaplan argues that the memoirist Leonowens's "role as a producer of colonial harem discourse hinges on their construction of a form of international sisterhood that legitimates Western intervention" (37). She argues that "the sisterhood that Leonowens constructs as part of her autobiographical strategy lends credence to whatever statements she makes about the Nang Harm; . . . their 'freedom' is linked to her own" (42).

7. Historians and critics have pointed out that Tuptim and her cruel fate of being burned alive for infidelity to the king is a fabrication, suggesting that this makes Leonowens a liar or a bad historian, despite clear clues that this book is fiction—a "romance" (Morgan, *Bombay Anna* xiii).

8. Other governesses to non-European aristocratic children published memoirs in this vein, such as Emmeline Lott, *The English Governess in Egypt: Harem Life in Egypt and Constantinople* (1865); the title first excluded the word "English," but its addition by 1867 tightens the connection to Leonowens's first book. Like Leonowens, Lott brought out additional books about her harem experience.

9. See Zonana, "Sultan and the Slave"; Reina Lewis, *Gendering Orientalism;* and Yeazell, *Harems of the Mind.*

10. A US territory in the 1870s, Utah became a state in 1896 upon including a ban on polygamy in the state constitution.

11. For the opposite interpretation, see Zlotnick, who argues that Leonowens's depiction constitutes a "feminist dystopia" in "White Woman's Burden."

12. Jane as a child is incensed at being considered by her aunt as even lower than a servant because she does not earn her keep. The adult Jane knows she is appreciated when Rochester, whom she calls Master, insists that she is not a servant.

13. This scene is cut from the film version of the musical.

14. In fact, sometimes they could leave. This is one of the historical inaccuracies critics note. See Susan Brown (613n49).

15. Curiously, the musical does not comment on the unsuitability of wearing stiff Victorian gowns layered over heavy petticoats in the tropical Thai climate.

16. Sometimes American slaves also bought their freedom; a famous example is Elizabeth Keckley.

17. Often Hispanic or Filipino actors have played principal non-British roles (another interesting twist on depicting racial difference), including the 1956 Hollywood film (Puerto Rican actress Rita Moreno as Tuptim and Mexican actor Carlos Rivas as Lun Tha), the 1996 revival (Filipino Americans Lou Diamond Philips as King Mongkut and Jose Llana as Lun Tha), and late 1990s touring companies. Actors of any Asian descent (Korean, Japanese, and Chinese, for example) have also played smaller roles in major productions of *The King and I* throughout American production history, and very prominent roles in the 1996 and 2015 revivals. Obviously, Asian productions usually feature Asian actors in all roles. The most famous portrayal is Yul Brynner's. A Eurasian born in Russia of Swiss and Mongolian descent, Brynner was raised partly in Manchuria before he immigrated to the US at the age of eighteen, speaking very little English. He originated the role of King Mongkut on Broadway (for which he won a Tony) and starred in the film (for which he won an Oscar). After several revivals and tours, he went on to win another special Tony for his total of 4,625 stage performances in the role.

18. The choreography appears with few changes, performed by many of the same dancers, in the 1956 musical film.

19. Thai theater included a tradition of blackface; the historical King Chulalongkorn, who was the historical Leonowens's student as Crown Prince, wrote a blackface drama called *Bot lakho'n Ngo Pa*, "A Negrito Drama," about the Semang, a people of Southern Thailand and the Malay Peninsula (Harrison 610–11).

20. For more on the pre-history of "Uncle Tom" as a slur and the genealogy of theatrical adaptations of this novel, see Spingarn, *Uncle Tom.*

21. Hammerstein's mother was not Jewish.

22. In fact, the historical King Chulalongkorn also rejected the public practice of complete prostration before the king in 1873, at the time of his second coronation when he turned twenty-one. For more information, see "Chulalongkorn" by Anand Panyarachun, former prime minister of Thailand.

23. Jerry Watanabe was born in Japan and educated in England, with a Japanese father and British mother. He was a citizen of Japan (Fordin 183).

24. The other, also based on a work by a Victorian woman writer, is *Goblin Market*.

25. For the standard study on this motif, see Langland's *Nobody's Angels* (80–112).

3. Performing Jewishness in *Oliver!*

1. Atkinson alludes to this, stating that he tried to avoid that in his own portrayal of Fagin (personal interview with author, July 10, 2009).

2. See Weltman, "Melodrama."

3. See Grossman, *Art of Alibi*, and Rosenthal, *Good Form*.

4. See Weltman, "Editorial."

5. See Horak, *Girls Will Be Boys*.

6. The first sound *Oliver Twist* was the 1933 movie directed by William J. Cowan, with Dickie Moore playing Oliver.

7. The cast of British child actor-singers performing at one time or another in that first London run launched several important careers, including Davy Jones (The Monkees), Phil Collins (Genesis), and Tony Robinson (later Baldrick on *The Black Adder* series). Yet *Oliver!*'s success with both British and American theatergoers and moviegoers was defined by its achieving success in an American medium. According to Dianne Brooks, the film *Oliver!* (1968), directed by Carroll Reed, was financed entirely by Columbia Pictures (116) and was more popular with American audiences than with British (114). It won five Academy Awards, including the Oscar for best picture in 1968 (Muir 49).

8. It was preceded by *Stop the World, I Want to Get Off* (London, 1961; New York, 1962), also a smaller-scale success brought over by David Merrick (Mordden, *Open a New Window* 163).

9. Although there have been many successful stage musical adaptations from Dickens's fiction, such as Alan Menken's annual musical *A Christmas Carol*, first performed at Madison Square Garden in 1994, the only other Dickens musical to succeed in a huge way on Broadway since *Oliver!* was *Drood*. Among the less successful attempts to bring Dickens to the Broadway musical stage are *Pickwick* (1965 on Broadway), *Copperfield* (1981) and *A Tale of Two Cities* (2008). For more on Dickens and musical theater, see Weltman, "Dickens and Musical Theatre."

10. For a detailed analysis of *Sweeney Todd*'s debt to *Oliver!* and *Oliver Twist*, see Weltman, "Boz versus Bos."

11. Thanks to Rebecca Gorman O'Neill for pointing out how Rita's chest fur mimics a full-breasted silhouette.

12. For more on *Oliver & Company*, see Marc Napolitano, "Disneyfication" (82–88).

13. By Roper, this biography came out several years before Bart's death.

14. For melodrama as both containment and resistance, see John, *Dickens's Villains* (25).

15. Taylor points out that *Expresso Bongo* (1958) by David Henneker and Monty Norman incorporated "a new sense of realism" generally associated with John

Osborn's *Look Back in Anger* (1956) into a rock-inflected British musical that already began to change British musical theater into a less lighthearted form, even before *Oliver!* (485).

16. Bart is not the only Jewish pop culture author to want to recuperate Fagin; see, for example, Will Eisner's graphic novel *Fagin the Jew* (2003).

17. See Furneaux, Wills, and Wolff for scholarship on "queer" Fagin.

18. I count just over 320 mentions of "Jew" in the Gadshill edition, edited by Andrew Lang and digitized by the University of Virginia.

19. Atkinson explained, "I'm not Jewish myself, so my perspective is uninformed. And, in the end, I'm relying probably on cliché to supply the basic grammar of the character and the way he talks, which is probably not very good. I should have read more about it . . . read more about the nature of Jews in Victorian London" (personal interview with author, July 10, 2009).

20. In the 2007 BBC production of *Oliver Twist*, Nancy is played by Sophie Okonedo, who is black. The overall effect of race-blind casting accurately expands our sense of Victorian London as multicultural and multiracial. Nevertheless, this choice for Nancy evokes a hint of Tragic Mulatta that runs counter to the normalizing impulse behind race-blind casting. Although Okonedo is the first black woman to play Nancy visibly, Sheryl Lee Ralph voiced the Nancy role (Rita) in the animated *Oliver & Company*. Even earlier, the film *Oliver!*'s director Carol Reed asked for Shirley Bassey to play Nancy, but "Columbia vetoed her because it was felt that a black Nancy would alienate filmgoers in the American South" (Moss 251). See Weltman, "Adopting and Adapting Dickens."

21. Jolly as most of them seem, the only one of Nancy's songs not steeped in irony is the dramatic "As Long as He Needs Me," the abused woman's anthem. Jollity is not the same as happiness, and her story is entirely tragic.

22. Dellamora hints that even this small kindness may have sexual undertones (40). See J. Hillis Miller for other examples in the novel of Fagin as sympathetic, indeed as the character most similar to Oliver.

23. Atkinson's Fagin calls out to his "ladies," as he calls the jewels, when they fall. This builds on his comic bit in contemplating his treasure box in act 1 (just before Oliver spies him), in which he playfully introduces a necklace named "Ruby" to another named "Pearl." None of this is in Bart's libretto; it is part of the value added by casting an excellent and well-known comedian in the role of Fagin.

4. Dickens, Cultural Anxiety, and Victorianness in *Sweeney Todd*

1. With music and lyrics by Sondheim and book by Hugh Wheeler, *Sweeney Todd: The Demon Barber of Fleet Street* opened on March 1, 1979, at the Uris Theater and played for 557 performances. Len Cariou played Sweeney Todd and Angela Lansbury originated Mrs. Lovett. Directed by Harold Prince, the show won eight Tonys, including for best musical, best original score, best book, best director, best actor, and best actress. In a fun coincidence, the original melodrama adaptation of the Sweeney Todd story, *The String of Pearls* by George Dibdin Pitt, also opened

on March 1. But that was 132 years earlier, in 1847, at the Britannia in Hoxton, in London's East End.

2. There have been numerous major productions by the word's great opera companies, including the Houston Grand Opera (1984, 2015), New York City Opera (1984, 2004), Chicago Lyric Opera (2002), Royal Opera House at Covent Garden (2002), and Boston Lyric (2014). Smaller opera companies and university opera programs also regularly perform *Sweeney Todd*, such as the University of Notre Dame (2012) and the Eugene Opera (2015). Concert versions also abound, like Sondheim's seventieth birthday celebration at New York's Lincoln Center in 2000 and Sondheim's eighty-fifth birthday in 2015 in London at the English National Opera (starring Emma Thompson as Mrs. Lovett).

3. Dunnett writes for the *Independent* describing the 2004 Derby Playhouse production in England's Midlands. McNulty describes the New York City Opera's production of that year in the *Village Voice*.

4. In contrast, Jones—a scholar—explains what he means by invoking Dickens when he suggests that *Sweeney Todd* reveals "that the United States today is as overindustrialized and depersonalized as Charles Dickens's London" (291).

5. Early critics of Sondheim's *Sweeney Todd* recognized its debt to the Brecht-Weill musical *The Threepenny Opera* (Berlin, 1928), which debuted in an English adaptation by Mark Blitzstein on Broadway in 1954. Certainly, the connection is there: not only the murderous anti-hero, the murky staging, the Victorian backdrop, the low-life cast, the dark humor, but also and more importantly the class struggle, the cultural critique, and the alienating effect of horror mixed with pathos, beautiful music, and humor. See Richard Eder in the *New York Times* (March 2, 1979); Jones points also to *Sweeney Todd*'s turning *The Threepenny Opera*'s "metaphorical cannibalism to actual cannibalism" (293). Among other scholars who explore *Sweeney Todd*'s Brechtian qualities are Scott McMillin, Joanne Gordon, and Thomas Adler.

6. Useful criticism is too plentiful to list here. A few of the best-known books on Sondheim include Banfield, *Sondheim's Broadway Musicals;* Block, *Enchanted Evenings;* Goodhart, *Reading Stephen Sondheim;* Gordon, *Art Isn't Easy* and *Stephen Sondheim*. *The Threepenny Opera* adapts John Gay's *The Beggar's Opera* (1728), changing the setting from the eighteenth century to the Victorian period—as does *Sweeney Todd*.

7. See Gordon for a close analysis comparing these texts (*Art Isn't Easy* 221–23, 227–28).

8. See, for example, Bond's introduction to Sondheim's published libretto (2). See also Louis, *Fiction for the Working Man* (162), and Haining's largely fictional *Sweeney Todd*. Also useful is Anglo, *Penny Dreadfuls*.

9. See Law, *Serializing Fiction*.

10. Helen Smith argues persuasively against Prest and for James Malcolm Rymer as author of *The String of Pearls* in her pamphlet *Sweeney Todd, Thomas Peckett Prest, James Malcolm Rymer and Elizabeth Caroline Grey*. Dick Collins suggests that Prest and Rymer each contributed revisions to a text started by a yet unidentified writer (Introduction vii–viii). Mack also points to George Macfarren and to Lloyd himself

as possible authors (Introduction xxxi). Nesvet's digital analysis of prose style corroborates the stylistic examination done by textual scholars, indicating at least two authors (conference paper).

11. Despite the two-dimensional characters, the disjointed plot, the episodes that lead nowhere, the characters left dangling, and the very abrupt ending, the novel creates a phenomenally popular villain whose longevity exceeds *Dracula*'s and comes within thirty years of *Frankenstein*'s.

12. There have been many versions of this play. See Morley, "Dickens' Contributions," for wholesale passages of *Pickwick* (specifically "The Madman's Manuscript") interpolated into Pitt's play as printed and performed at various times (92–93), as well as for a substantial list of later plays based on Pitt's. See Weltman's "Introduction" for a full accounting of the original Sweeney Todd melodrama—surprisingly, an abolition play—as performed at the Britannia in 1847; a full transcription of the playbill is included.

13. My thanks go to Dick Stein for alerting me to the wonders of Stanley Holloway and sending me this song.

14. A Google search for "Sweeney Todd hair salon" on April 2, 2019, revealed stores in Los Angeles, Minnesota, Connecticut, Ohio, Pennsylvania, New Jersey (multiple locations), and Australia—on just the first two pages.

15. The closest "true story" appeared in "Archives of the Police" by Joseph Fouche, Minister of Police in Paris, 1799 to 1815; he tells of a Parisian barber-murderer in cahoots with a pastry chef neighbor in 1800. The item was republished in 1824 as "A Terrific Story of the Rue de la Harpe, Paris" in the *Tell Tale,* a London magazine. The Newgate Calendar's Scottish cannibal clan leader Sawney Beane lived in a cave and dined for decades off unwary travelers. Other antecedents are the Greek myth of Procne and Shakespeare's *Titus Andronicus*. See Mack's *Wonderful and Surprising History* (135–94).

16. For why Sondheim calls it "A Musical Thriller," see Gerould (7–8).

17. Stanley Greenberg, the screenwriter of *Soylent Green* (1973), echoes Mark's cry when he adapted Harry Harrison's short story and added the cannibal plot and the film's famous last line, "Soylent Green is people!"

18. Mack correctly points out that the catchphrase "I'll polish him off!," so associated with Sweeney Todd, originates in Dibdin Pitt's 1847 stage melodrama adaptation (xxxi). It is also almost in the novel, where Todd tells Colonel Jeffrey that when Thornhill had come for a shave, he had "polished him off" (24). The colonel responds with the question, "What do you mean by polishing him off?" (24), so that the shaving joke already operates, although Dibdin Pitt's pithy phrase had not yet crystalized.

19. In *Everywhere Spoken Against,* Cunningham points out that such scenes are a staple of the period.

20. In *Little Dorrit* (1855–57), Dickens again refers to cannibal pie-making, when Mrs. F's aunt becomes the center of rumors among "credulous infants" that she had sold herself to a pie-maker to be "made up" into pies (853). The Penguin edition's endnote incorrectly suggests that the popularity of Frederick Hazleton's stage adaptation

Sweeney Todd, The Barber of Fleet Street: or, The String of Pearls might be behind this comment (984), but Hazelton's version was first performed later, in July 1865 at the Old Bower Saloon, Stangate Street, Lambeth (Nicoll 412). If a *Sweeney Todd* play influenced Dickens here, it was Dibdin Pitt's.

21. Gordon makes this observation also (*Art Isn't Easy* 220).

22. For a feminist reading of Mrs. Lovett and Johanna, see Lodge (90–94). See Adler for a Brechtian reading, comparing Mrs. Lovett to Mother Courage (42).

23. The Tim Burton film places the harmonium in her parlor from the beginning, so that—while just as funny—it loses its value as a symbol of their upward mobility.

24. In some productions Oliver sings this line to Nancy, some to Bet (who is usually cast as a young teen), some to both; but as Bet is a junior version of Nancy, the audience understands through these lines how Oliver feels about the grown woman.

25. See Danahay, "Nature Red."

26. But this plot development, while not in the novella and certainly not in Dickens, is also not a 1970s invention. It goes back at least as far as Byron's *The Corsair* (1814), in which the hero Conrad is unable to kill the evil Seyd in his sleep to save the girl Gulnare, who dispatches the bad guy herself with a scimitar. Curiously, while the incident does not occur in *The String of Pearls*, the novel does quote from *The Corsair*, canto 1, stanza 3, in describing the ship that brought Mr. Thornhill and the string of pearls to London; it "walk'd the waters like a thing of life" (17).

27. See Jerden's review of *Essays on Craniology* by Richard Winter Hamilton (1826).

28. As an indication of Davis's widespread impact, *Life* magazine did a spread in 1971 that refers to her as the health food's "High Priestess" and quotes her slamming hormone- and chemical-laced beef in particular: "The great American hamburger," she says, "has done tremendous harm to health. . . . Most beef we eat consists of saturated fat, not to mention stilbestrol . . . [which] can induce cancer" (Howard 68).

29. Here again Dickens's influence emerges: there is no mention of Australia in the novel *The String of Pearls*, whereas multiple characters in Dickens emigrate or are transported there, perhaps unfairly, such as Magwitch in *Great Expectations*.

30. Burton's film adaptation changes much of this effect. His Lucy is younger, prettier, and never raunchy. No prostitute, she never mentions her muff. There is no crazed singing of "Don't I know ya, mister?," so unrecognizable in her degradation that the grieving stage Todd has no idea whom he pushes aside in disgust. In the film, Lucy's function is restricted to focusing attention on the pathos of Todd's loss and to heightening the tragedy when he murders her, rather than to act the wise fool, screeching the terrible truth that no one hears.

31. Directed by Bill Buckhurst at the Barrow Street Theater, the Tooting Arts Club production originated in 2014 in London at Harrington's—an actual pie and mash shop.

32. The shriek of the whistle also denotes the end of some scenes, a fitting throwback to the use of a whistle to mark scene changes in Victorian stagecraft.

33. Sondheim "saw some Grand Guignol in Paris in the 1960s," which he cites as an influence on *Sweeney Todd*. It had "lots of blood and outlandishness" (Gerould 4–5).

34. Ironically in the novel *The String of Pearls,* the denouement reveals that Todd cuts no one's throat: his victims die from the twenty-foot fall from his rigged barber's chair into the cellar, landing directly on their heads. This is also true of the stage melodrama by Dibdin Pitt (whose Todd does occasionally use a knife to stab, however) and the 1936 King film. But Todd's razor always features prominently as a fearsome prop.

35. Sondheim has said that his initial instinct was to write it as an opera (Gerould 8).

36. *Sweeney Todd* doesn't fit most horror film formulas. See Clover's *Men, Women and Chain Saws.*

37. In December 2007, I heard another member of the audience whispering to her companion, "I didn't know this was a *musical!* Did you know it was a musical? It's a musical!" For more about the Doyle productions and the Burton film, see Weltman, "Sondheim's *Sweeney Todd*."

38. See Richards, "Tod Slaughter."

39. This approach worked well for Walter Mondale in the 1984 presidential primary season against Gary Hart. See Kornblut, Weisman, and Kane.

40. In the film, our last view of a possibly traumatized Johanna is when Todd unaccountably lets her live, still alone in his tonsorial parlor. We never see the young lovers reunite. In the stage musical, Todd was still intent on killing Johanna (whom he thinks is a boy) before he rushes away in response to screams from the basement. Johanna and Anthony show up below stairs together, clinging to each other, to see what has happened.

5. *The* Meta-*Mystery of Edwin Drood*

1. The play opened in August 1985 for performance at the New York Shakespeare Festival in Central Park to such success that it moved to Broadway's Imperial Theater, premiering December 2, 1985, and running for 608 performances. It won five Tony awards, including for best musical, best book, and best original score. In 2012 New York's Roundabout Theater revived the show in a limited run that garnered enthusiastic reviews and large crowds.

2. This convention exists also in film musicals, both Hollywood and Bollywood. They are particularly useful world over for expressing erotic content through song and dance that dialogue would make too explicit.

3. There is a strong tradition of postcolonial criticism on *The Mystery of Edwin Drood.* Among the most influential are De Wind, Faulkner, Mara, and Park.

4. BBC has redramatized many of the same novels in subsequent years. For the most comprehensive discussion of the Australian Broadcasting Company's *Great Expectations: The Untold Story,* see Jordan (45–52).

5. My thanks go to Carolyn Williams for reminding me of Sedgwick's comment.

6. More examples include Deputy goading Dick Datchery (a mysterious figure who has come to town to solve Edwin Drood's disappearance) with a "demon dance" (219), and it is through song that Cloisterham's mayor Mr. Sapsea is able to judge Jasper as worthy, because the choirmaster sings "'no kichshaw ditties', favorite with

national enemies," but instead gives "him genuine George the Third home brewed" tunes (147). Durdles sings doggerel to Mr. Jasper (159), and the angular lawyer Mr. Grewgious likens himself to a sparrow in comparison to the canary Rosa (237), shortly before he escorts her across the way in a kind of awkward "minuet" (241). Princess Puffer rattles when she whispers (37) and "blows at her pipe" when she inhales smoke from it ((38). Then Crisparkle stays up late to "very softly" touch his piano, "practising his favourite parts in concerted vocal music" (103). The choir performs repeatedly. The church bells chime at least four times. The girls hold a ball. A sea of music overtakes the cathedral service toward the end of chapter 9.

7. From Ezekiel 18:27, this prayer opens the Vespers, the Anglican evening service. In the novel's first chapter, Jasper barely makes it to the cathedral in time to hear it and lead the choir.

8. However, Wilson believes Dickens to have abandoned social critique for a psychological study in this novel (101).

9. The imagery of Jasper's organ playing and his choir's glorious, nearly orgiastic performance in overcoming the dry, uninspiring voice of the preacher suggests a powerful overriding oceanic metaphor: "The organ and the choir burst forth, and drowned it in a sea of music. Then the sea fell, and the dying voice made another feeble effort, and then the sea rose high, and beat its life out, and lashed the roof, and surged among the arches, and pierced the heights of the great tower; and then the sea was dry, and all was still" (117–18). It is tempting to assert that the book is written in the key of Sea. Such a thought also gives the name of the mayor Mr. Sapsea's name new meaning.

10. Dickens worked with several of his illustrators closely. His impact on the illustrations in *The Mystery of Edwin Drood* has interested scholars intensely because of the clues they may hold to the author's plans for the mystery's solution. See Jane Cohen's *Charles Dickens and His Original Illustrators* for detailed analysis of this wrapper. The first illustrator was his son-in-law, Charles Allston Collins (Wilkie Collins's brother), who designed a wrapper for use in all installments, including the first, depicting scenes that would later appear in the novel—indicating that, as usual, the illustrator had some foreknowledge from Dickens of what would come after, but not enough to give away the plot. Collins dropped off the project early on (he was ill), and Fildes took over, also presumably with some guidance or approval from Dickens. Unfortunately, no correspondence survives.

11. "Johnny One Note" is a song from *Babes in Arms* (1939), composed by Richard Rodgers, with lyrics by Lorenz Hart.

12. Within Holmes's musical, Jasper composes a song just for Rosa called "Moonfall," which Rosa sings in this crucial scene that reveals Jasper's lust, Rosa's excruciating awareness of it, Helena's strength and sensitivity, Drood's cluelessness, and Neville's attraction. In addition to Rosa's singing the song as a performance within the Dickensian story of the musical, Rosa and others reprise it at a climactic moment in the second act, making Jasper into a kind of author-composer of the musical *Mystery of Edwin Drood* as well.

13. Written in 1830 and set to music in 1850 by Carlo Bosetti.

14. Henry Neville played John Jasper; E. F. Edgar played Neville Landless; Maria B. Jones played Rosa Budd (*sic*) (Bolton 443).

15. Shakespeare's sonnet 130 pokes fun at other sonnets that blaze the conventional fair beauty, including the lines "I have seen roses damask'd, red and white, / But no such roses see I in her cheeks" (lines 5–6). This imagery carries over into the musical; Holmes's Chairman introduces the frame character-actress playing Rose, Miss Nutting, as "that most delicate of English roses, that blossoming bud that has even yet to be plucked" (15–16).

16. When dining with Bulwer-Lytton, the *New York Times* (April 9, 1859) reporter remarks, "I could not have given the great Novelist any information that would have gratified him more touching the Transatlantic appreciation of his works, than the fact that his sweet and simple little song, 'When the stars are in the quiet skies, / Then most I pine for thee, &c,' is found on almost every piano-fort in America" ("English Celebrities").

17. The poem was anthologized and reprinted repeatedly throughout the nineteenth and early twentieth century. Music is not included in Stephens's play text. But it is possible that the Surrey production used a popular setting published by the editors of the often reprinted and repackaged 1881 American song collection *Our Familiar Songs and Their Authors*. The editor, Helen Johnson, indicates the song's popularity when she comments that "no moonlit ride is complete without it" (Johnson vi). It has been much anthologized and set to music several times, most significantly by Charles Ives in 1891, and also by George Whitefield Chadwick in 1910. For information on its multiple settings, see the song's entry on the LiederNet Archive. The punctuation, etc. that I have supplied here is from Bulwer-Lytton's novel. The play's spelling and punctuation differ slightly; both the Ives and Chadwick settings also vary the punctuation and some word choices as well.

18. It was produced by Carl Laemmle Jr. and Edmund Grainger, with screenplay by Leopold Atlas, John L. Balderston, Bradley King, and Gladys Unger. Charles Dickens also receives a writing credit.

19. See http://www.imdb.com/name/nm0387753/bio?ref_=nm_ov_bio_sm.

20. Holmes does not bring in all aspects of the novel's dependence on British imperialism. One area he ignores rightly is Edmund Wilson's subscription to the Thugee theory to motivate Jasper's murder of Drood, refuted by Wendy S. Jacobson (526), in which Dickens supposedly saw Jasper's actions as a result of his subscribing to a purported religious movement in India of devotees known as Thugs (from which our term for criminal derives), who committed murder for their faith. Wilson considers Jekyll and Hyde aspects of Jasper's personality as prompted by his being under sway of the Thugs; but this notion is completely undercut by Wilson's pointing out that the Thugs were "in their own eyes . . . virtuous persons . . . serving the cult of the goddess" (94). But Jasper does not see himself as virtuous. He recognizes his own hypocrisy, and he hates his life. Wilson concocts his own intriguing (but Orientalist) ending with Helena's hypnotizing Jasper to get him to confess in the cell. While Dickens may well have planned for Helena to be the disguised Datchery (to prove her brother innocent of Drood's murder and to save his reputation), she employs no

hypnotism. Holmes does not include any mention of Thugs in the musical, nor does he depict Helena as another mesmerist. A final point to remember in Holmes's treatment of race and empire is that the musical is an American play making fun of British imperialism. The degree to which this satire transfers to a recognition and critique of American foreign relations is debatable and depends on performance choices.

21. My thanks go to Elsie Michie for bringing this Shakespearean connection to my attention.

22. Perhaps the clearest precursor to audience voting on Broadway is Ayn Rand's play *Night of January 16th*, which opened at New York's Ambassador Theater on September 16, 1935, and ran until April for 283 performances. It takes place entirely in a courtroom. Jurors are selected from the audience at the opening of act 1; they hear testimony during the play and are sent out to deliberate the case afterward. Once they deliver the verdict, the actors perform one of two prepared endings, depending on the outcome of the jury's decision.

23. The projects of the musical *Drood* and the film *Clue* were in production/post-production simultaneously and share the concept of multiple solutions to the mystery; the film was released to theaters December 13, 1985. The film *Clue* (Paramount, directed by Jonathan Lynn) was released theatrically only six months after the New York Shakespeare Festival performances in the park during the summer of 1985. While *Clue*'s movie theater audiences did not have the opportunity to decide on which ending they prefer, nowadays, home audiences streaming or watching the DVD do have that pleasure. The film received poor reviews and did not even recoup its investment in its theatrical release, but it has since become something of a cult classic. Based on the film, the off-Broadway musical *Clue* opened on December 3, 1997, at the Players Theater to devastating reviews. It lasted 29 performances, although it is still mounted regionally, billed as an "interactive musical," owing an obvious debt to *Drood*. The audience uses forms and pencils to keep track of clues (if they wish) and to select the murderer, the murder weapon, and the room where the murder occurred. There are 216 possible endings. The composers are Wayne Barker, Galen Blum, and Vinnie Martucci; Tom Chiodo is the lyricist and Peter DePietro wrote the book. Thanks to Elsie Michie for bringing the film *Clue* to my attention.

24. In the published libretto (prepared before the Broadway premiere) and in New York's Shakespeare Festival original production, the setting is 1873, but Holmes adjusted the year to 1895 for the Broadway production and subsequent tours and revivals.

25. The Chairman is also a stock feature of minstrelsy.

26. These lyrics are also the song titles from *The Sound of Music* (1959), *Man of La Mancha* (1965), and *Newsies* (2011), respectively.

27. He is the sole murderer who breaks frame during his confession, acknowledging that only a vote based on the perverse fun of choosing the least likely suspect could induce an audience to select him. The other seven confessions are motivated emotionally from the character's situations.

28. Wilson argues that Jasper uses "animal magnetism" to mesmerize and terrorize Rosa: "It was supposed in Dickens' time that this influence could be projected through

the agency of mere sound: hence the insistent keynote in the piano scene and the swelling note of the organ that frightens Rosa in the garden. And it was also supposed to penetrate matter: hence Rosa's remark to Helena that she feels as if Jasper can reach her through a wall. It could be made to impregnate objects in such a way as to remain effective after the master of the magnetic fluid was no longer himself on the scene" (91). Much of the sexual imagery here derives from Dickens, but some is Wilson's alone.

29. My thanks go to Jerry Weltman for this point.

30. "Bustle Fluffah" is available to view at https://www.youtube.com/watch?v=TzNcry02Rg4.

31. Shakespeare's sonnet 18 concludes, "Nor shall Death brag thou wander'st in his shade, / When in eternal lines to time thou grow'st; / So long as men can breathe or eyes can see, / So long lives this, and this gives life to thee" (lines 11–14), granting immortality to the beloved long after both poet and subject are dead. Also invoking the power of poetry to outlast the death of the author, Percy Shelley's "Ode to the West Wind" invokes the spirit of nature to "Drive my dead thoughts over the universe / Like wither'd leaves to quicken a new birth! / And, by the incantation of this verse, / Scatter, as from an unextinguish'd hearth / Ashes and sparks, my words among mankind!" (lines 63–67).

6. *Goblin Market,* Performance, and Sexuality

1. In both locations, *Goblin Market* starred Terri Klausner and Ann Morrison, was directed by Andre Ernotte, and was produced by Douglas Aibel, Barbara Zinn Krieger, and Gary Steuer. The Circle in the Square Downtown production opened on April 13, 1986. This venue at 159 Bleeker Street was retained after the main stage moved in 1972 to its current Broadway home on 50th Street.

2. Among critics of Rossetti's *Goblin Market* offering these interpretations are Arseneau, Battiscombe, Campbell, Carpenter, Casey, Connor, Garlick, Gilbert and Gubar, Golub, Helsinger, Holt, Jed Mayer, Menke, Mermin, Helena Michie, Moers, Rappoport, Heidi Scott, Shurbutt, Stern, and Watson.

3. A rock musical called *Hamelin: A Musical Tale from Rats to Riches* (music and lyrics by Richard Jarboe and Harvey Shield and book by Jarboe, Shield, and Matthew Wells) is not based on Robert Browning's *The Pied Piper of Hamelin*. It opened at Circle in the Square on November 10, 1985, just a few weeks after *Goblin Market*'s premiere at the Vineyard. The *New York Times* panned it as utterly derivative of *Cats* ("its feline relative uptown"), so much so that it should have been called *Rats* (Gussow). Browning's poem was, however, the source for the 1989 opera *Koppelberg* with music by Steve Gray and lyrics by Norman Brooke. It is not unusual for poems to be adapted to the opera.

4. The lyric comes from a line in which Higgins first says, "I have grown accustomed to your voice and appearance," followed by "face" in the next line (Shaw, *Pygmalion*, act 5, p. 275).

5. Butler continues, "Further, gender is instituted through the stylization of the body and, hence, must be understood as the mundane way in which bodily gestures,

movements, and enactments of various kind constitute the illusion of an abiding gendered self" ("Performing Acts" 270).

6. Butler is not the first person to suggest that "gender is a performed role"; both Dolan and Case talk about drag and cross-dressing "to foreground the arbitrary construction of gender" (Dolan, "Gender Impersonation" 7).

7. References to the poem *Goblin Market* are to the standard edition, *The Complete Poems of Christina Rossetti,* edited by Rebecca W. Crump. Line numbers are given parenthetically in the text.

8. See Gayle Rubin's "The Traffic in Women" for a model of women exchanged in a patriarchal economy and Sedgwick's *Between Men* for women acting as homosocial conduit between men in patriarchy. The question is how the goblin juice functions to tie the girls together in a society otherwise entirely without men and whether it is an inversion of the patterns Sedgwick and Rubin delineate. See Sharon Marcus's *Between Women.*

9. The Princeton Rep Company mounted this production as part of their summer season. It ran Thursdays to Sundays, August 3–13. Laura was played by Derry Light and Lizzie by Malia Ondrejka.

10. This goes all the way back to the *Spectator*'s praise in its 1862 review for *Goblin Market* as a "true children's poem," going on to say that though "delightful to all" it is even more so to "the mature" than the young (415). Certainly it can be enjoyed by children, almost as a precursor to Disney's 2013 *Frozen.*

11. This is true of the Richard Hamburger–directed production at the Dallas Theatre Center in April 1996.

12. In Rossetti scholarship, there is a tradition of reading Laura's actions as a fortunate fall, either because her succumbing to the goblins gives Lizzie a chance to redeem her and become a female Christ, or because while Lizzie saves her sister from death, Laura saves Lizzie from ignorance. When she braves the goblin den to save Laura, "for the first time in her life / [Lizzie] Began to listen and to look" (327–28). For interpretations of the fortunate fall, see Casey, McGann, and Carpenter. For a reading of the fall as metaphorical prerequisite for Rossetti's own creativity, see Shurbutt, who builds on Mayberry.

13. Skimpy clothes certainly appeared on the mainstream Victorian stage: not only *The Black Crook,* which so distressed Mark Twain, but also Adah Menken's famous performance in a nude body stocking as she lay across the back of a live horse in *Mazeppa* in performances on both sides of the Atlantic throughout the 1860s. But the act of removing clothes carries additional erotic valence.

14. My Rutgers University students' papers corroborated Liberatori's observation. There is an extensive body of work in film criticism that addresses how audience members who identify differently find their own pleasure in what they watch. Elizabeth Ellsworth's "Illicit Pleasures" cites sociological research that audiences' "lived experience" makes possible "oppositional interpretations" in terms of both politics and sexuality (184). In *Star Gazing,* Stacey also argues that female spectators' identities and experiences affect their viewing film, which can be applied usefully to their reactions to live theater.

15. The fruit's sexual significance derives not only from its allusion to *Genesis* and *Paradise Lost,* and not only to the sensuous descriptions of the fruit ("Oh what figs my teeth have met in") or lines describing Laura "waiting for the night" when she expects to get more of the "fruit forbidden," but also the lines of Lizzie reminding Laura of Jeanie who previously bought the fruit and died "for joys brides hope to have."

16. See Mermin, Greer, Cora Kaplan, and Carpenter; plus the notorious *Playboy* illustrations in their 1973 reprint of the poem. For the definitive study on illustrations of *Goblin Market,* see Kooistra's *Christina Rossetti and Illustration.*

17. Brahms's song in the libretto's translation presents the sisters as brunettes, with "nut brown" hair—light brown or *lichtbraune Haar* in the original (Lewin 233). This change is inconsistent not only with Rossetti's poem throughout, but also with the play's use of Laura's golden curl to buy her goblin delights.

18. For one of the few critical analyses of this song, see O'Farrell's "Sister Acts."

19. Butler argues for the political significance of the transvestite, who "challenges... the distinction between appearance and reality that structures a good deal of popular thinking about gender identity. If the 'reality' of gender is constituted by the performance itself, then there is no recourse to an essential and unrealized 'sex' or 'gender' which gender performances ostensibly express. Indeed, the transvestite's gender is as fully real as anyone whose performance complies with social expectations" ("Performing Acts" 278). If Laura's pantaloons represent pants, this element of the play makes her not only a cross-gender performance, but explicitly a transvestite one.

20. Dolan theorizes that such parts differ fundamentally from men's drag performances ("Gender Impersonation" 6–7).

21. While the word "town," following "virgin" gets two and a half bars and the word "virgin" gets only one, "virgin" has an instruction to hold to the conductor's discretion; "town" is to be sung *a tempo.*

22. See Mermin, Battiscombe, Barr, McGann, Arseneau, and Shurbutt.

23. I teach in Louisiana where many undergraduates attended Catholic elementary or secondary schools. Many immediately recognize the sexual imagery, but most first identify religious symbolism. Several express discomfort with the same lines of verse supporting both readings, but a few easily reconcile both through the traditional notion of figuring love of God through sexual union, offering the examples of the Church as the Bride of Christ and nuns' wearing wedding rings. They almost universally love this poem, and approximately 30 percent write their papers on it.

24. Terrence Holt argues convincingly for the patriarchal exclusion of the girls in the poem from the masculine marketplace. In a subtle and dazzlingly documented close reading, he shows how Lizzie and Laura's is a non-alienated labor that requires no legal tender. They produce everything they need in an ideal feminine economy described above in their domestic labors. However, they are in his interpretation excluded from real power and exchange, even finally linguistic exchange, by their femininity and lack of a phallus, for which money stands. However, his reading depends upon what he perceives as an inconsistency in Rossetti's text. Since Laura has no money to pay the goblins, Holt assumes that the girls have no access to the masculine economy and in fact have no money at all. Later when Lizzie seems to

have magically and without explanation acquired a silver penny to pay the goblins, he assumes that the only way she could have gotten it was by selling her body. I see several problems with this, but most important is that Laura never says that she has no money all, just none with her: "I have no copper in my purse" (118) suggests not that she never has coppers, just none with her or available at the moment; after all, while we do not know why or if she may have carried her moneyless purse to the brook, she wouldn't own a purse, whose primary function is to carry money, unless she occasionally did so.

7. "Bring on the Men" and Women

1. This is how Annie Oakley describes her ideal wedding—big, garish, over the top—in the song "An Old Fashioned Wedding" in *Annie Get Your Gun* (1946), not a megamusical.

2. *Les Misérables* opened in Paris in 1980, in London in 1985, and on Broadway in 1987. Composed by Claude-Michel Schönberg, the original lyrics (in French) are by Alain Boublil and Jean-Marc Natel. The English lyrics are by Herbert Kretzmer and James Fenton; the English book by Kretzmer, Trevor Nunn, and John Caird. It is adapted from Victor Hugo's 1862 novel. Composed by Andrew Lloyd Webber, *Phantom*—musical theater folks are fond of nicknames for shows—opened in London in 1986. Lyrics are by Charles Hart and Richard Stilgoe, with book by Webber and Stilgoe. It opened in New York in 1988 and has become the longest-running Broadway musical ever. It is also based on a French novel, *Le Fantôme de l'Opéra* by Gaston Leroux (1910).

3. Jean Rhys's *Wide Sargasso Sea* (1966) and John Fowles's *The French Lieutenant's Woman* (1968) are often named as the first Neo-Victorian novels. But the 1990s brought three of the best-known and most critically acclaimed, signifying a movement that is still gaining momentum: A. S. Byatt's *Possession* (1990), Peter Carey's *Jack Maggs* (1997), and Sarah Waters's *Tipping the Velvet* (1998), quickly followed by Michael Faber's *The Crimson Petal and the White* (2002) and Waters's *Fingersmith* (2002). Neo-Victorian criticism tends to focus on fiction that directly responds to specific Victorian texts or incorporates and reworks Victorian literary techniques, but it also addresses film, television, graphic novels, material culture, and occasionally musical theater based on or responding to Victorian literature. The journal *Neo-Victorian Studies* published several articles quoted in this book on *Sweeney Todd* and *Drood* in the special issue 9.1 (2016) entitled "Performing the Neo-Victorian," guest edited by Beth Palmer and Benjamin Poore.

4. It was revived on Broadway in 2013, opening on April 18 at the Marquis Theater for a limited engagement that was originally slated till June 30 but closed early on May 12, "after 15 previews and 30 regular performances" (Gans). *American Idol* finalist Constantine Maroulis played the dual title roles. Rhythm and blues star Deborah Cox played Lucy, Teal Wicks played Emma Carew, Laird Mackintosh played John Utterson, and Richard White played Sir Danvers Carew. Jeff Calhoun directed and choreographed.

5. Like most Broadway shows, *Jekyll and Hyde* closed in the red, despite the celebrity casting of David Hasselhoff (of *Baywatch* fame) as the replacement Jekyll and Hyde three months before the production folded. The show continues a healthy life-after-Broadway in regular productions worldwide. Heather Long points out that "only 25% of Broadway shows make money." Merely having opened on Broadway helps in getting the show future productions (Long).

6. For the classic taxonomy of melodrama's stock characters, see Booth's *English Melodrama* (15–36). For additional nuance in understanding the complexity of stock characters in melodrama, see Carolyn Williams's "Melodrama and the Realist Novel" (121–215).

7. For discussions of sexuality, see Heath, Linehan, and Halberstam.

8. These scandals include not only President Bill Clinton, whose affair with Monica Lewinsky broke in January of 1998, shortly after the musical's premiere on Broadway, and lending it renewed topicality, but also the covered-up and later revealed affairs of many of the men who called most vociferously for Clinton's impeachment, such as Newt Gingrich (R-GA), Robert Livingston (R-LA), and the serendipitously named Henry Hyde (R-IL).

9. Significantly revised before the New York production, Sullivan's play is not actually the first dramatization of Stevenson's novel, although it is often described as such. The first adaptation identified by Harry M. Geduld is *The Strange Case of a Hyde and a Seekyl,* a burlesque performed in London on May 18, 1886, at L. C. Toole's Theatre (215).

10. Twelve years later, Irving produced an entirely different adaptation with himself as lead.

11. He was born on May 24 either in 1854 or 1857, making him either thirty or thirty-three. See https://www.britannica.com/biography/Richard-Mansfield.

12. Part of creating that contrast involved exploiting the gender divide, which may have exacerbated the letter writer's distress and added to its horror. Remember that he found it particularly unnerving that "in five seconds" an actor could shed and don that symbol of masculinity, his "fine faulse whiskers," secreted in a bag.

13. All three periodical quotations come from Danahay and Chisolm (38).

14. For example, Jules Law points to Hyde's "thingness," invoking Sedgwick's reading of the unnamable in the Gothic. Ed Cohen notes Hyde's somatic transgression as exposing contradictions in male gender identity in late Victorian England. See Arata, Ed Cohen, Halberstam, Heath, Law, Sedgwick, and Walkowitz.

15. For more on Victorian anxiety about identity as performed, see Weltman, *Performing the Victorian.*

16. One comic example of audiences' appetite for virtuoso turns at containing multitudes carried to an extreme is that a single actor plays the entire D'Ysquith family (eight roles) in a single show, the Tony Award–winning *A Gentleman's Guide to Love and Murder* (2013).

17. See Robert Browning's dramatic monologue "Porphyria's Lover," published in *Dramatic Lyrics* (1842) under the title "Madhouse Cells."

18. The 1971 *Dr. Jekyll and Sister Hyde* goes even further than simple association by identifying Jack the Ripper as Dr. Jekyll.

19. This is the title of a Wildhorn-Bricusse song from the show's pre-Broadway tour of *Jekyll and Hyde*.

20. For example, see Wood.

21. The lineage from Mansfield's adaptation is also clear in the appropriation of Carew's daughter, but in addition, as Skal tells us, "Barrymore likely saw Mansfield in the part; the actor was a close friend of his father Maurice" (140).

22. Sullivan expanded the role of Hyde's landlady into a sharp-tongued mercenary servant who is instrumental in bringing him to justice, but she is neither a prostitute nor a love interest for Hyde—and she is not murdered.

23. Sullivan's play designates "Mr. Hyde's chambers in Soho" as "richly furnished but sombre in tone." Yet a contemporary review (*New York Tribune,* September 13, 1887) describes Hyde's Soho apartment as "profuse, disorderly luxury—not that of taste, but that of exuberant sensuality—just as Ben Jonson indicates for *Volpone* and *Sir Epicure Mammon* ("Dr. Jekyll and Mr. Hyde: Richard Mansfield" 118), suggesting that, despite the restrained scene direction, the profligacy figured by the later cinematic Hyde's sexually explicit décor may have sprung from Mansfield's production. Daphne Brooks bases her claim that "Hyde's violent deeds coupled with his material extravagance recall the racist mythology of black dandy discourse in the nineteenth century" on "this sort of scenery" (60).

24. For class, see Danahay, "Dr. Jekyll's Two Bodies"; Brantlinger; and Ed Cohen. For race, see Zieger. For both class and race, see Halberstam.

25. Another Dickensian detail: in this film, Hyde tries to burn the club that he uses to bludgeon Carew to death, just as Sikes tries to burn the club that he uses to brutally murder Nancy.

26. Skal explains that *Variety* states how Mamoulian's film ornamented the script beyond the simplicity of the original novel, changes that they considered to be made for mob appeal, perhaps alluding to the inclusion of women characters (144).

27. Lucy means "light" but also evokes "Lucifer" and thus the devil as a fallen angel. It is the name of the troubled half of the doubled heroines in *Dracula*. Sweeney Todd's wronged wife (the old beggar woman whom he kills before recognizing her) is named Lucy. Since she regularly tries to sell her "muff" to passing sailors, she is also a prostitute.

28. Eder was Wildhorn's wife at the time of the interview, but they were not yet married at the time of the initial productions.

29. One Emma is Emma Porter in *Sketches by Boz:* the other is a minor character in *Pickwick Papers*.

30. This blocking is still available to see on the DVD filmed from a live performance on Broadway in December 2000, featuring the final cast.

31. This number, which I saw at the Saenger Theater in New Orleans in October 1995 during the pre-Broadway Theatre under the Stars tour, was choreographed by Fuller, who previously choreographed *Sweeney Todd* for its initial Broadway run. Once *Jekyll and Hyde* got to New York, the director Robin Phillips substituted "Good 'N' Evil," choreographed by Joey Pizzi. Wildhorn told me that he preferred the song "Bring on the Men," which continued in some productions (personal interview) and

reappeared in the 2013 Broadway revival. Linda Eder also expresses preference for "Bring on the Men," which she refers to as a "great song," "an amazing introduction to my character" (*Greatest Hits,* liner notes), considering its replacement a mistake.

32. This may remind readers of a scene from the 1982 Blake Edwards film *Victor/Victoria* in the nightclub Chez Lui, choreographed by Paddy Stone: "Four performers—two apparently male, two apparently female—dance slowly onstage, facing the audience and the camera. Suddenly, . . . they turn around . . . the males have miraculously become females and the females . . .—they wear masks on the back of their heads to present a different sex than their faces indicate, and their costumes change, front and back, to maintain the illusion" (Luhr and Lehman). The gender-bending jolt is similar, but the Victorian milieu of *Jekyll and Hyde* makes the surprise far more intense than in 1930s Paris introduced by Robert Preston singing about "Gay Paris."

33. Adding and removing glasses and hairdo to change identity goes back at least to Ellen Wood's novel *East Lynn* (1861) and its many stage and screen adaptations.

34. Gollum and Sméagol also duke it out in Peter Jackson's *The Lord of the Rings: The Two Towers* (2002), except that Sméagol succeeds where Jekyll fails, sending Gollum away. An effect similar to the stage actor's head flipping from side to side is managed cinematically by altering the angle of the shot. J. R. R. Tolkien may have thought of Stevenson in creating the dual characters of Gollum and Sméagol for his novels.

35. See "Confrontation (Speeded)" on YouTube: https://www.youtube.com/watch?v=k82I4nq8DMw.

36. See Barish's *Antitheatrical Prejudice.*

8. Broadway's "Jane! Jane! Jane!"

1. Because Stoneman's study has generated multiple examinations of nineteenth-century melodramas based on *Jane Eyre*, I have dispensed with an extended genealogical exploration in this chapter. See Frye (170) and Karen Laird (25–45).

2. *Jane Eyre: The Musical* (sometimes *A Musical Play*) with music by Monty Stevens, lyrics by Hal Sharper, and book by Roy Harley Lewis and Hal Shaper premiered at the Theatre Royal, Windsor, in 1961 and was revived as late as 1973. *Billboard* saw this "rags-to-riches love story" as an attempt to match the success of *Oliver!* (Wedge 19). Never making it to the West End as planned, its chief distinction was to have been seen by the Queen, to whom the cast was presented ("England" 67). *Jane Eyre: The Musical* composed by Bill Kilpatrick, with book and lyrics by Rebecca Thompson-Duvall and Kari Skousen, premiered in Temescal Canyon, California, in August 2000 (a few months before the Caird and Gordon musical opened in New York; both were in development for years before their premieres) and ran off-Broadway in New York at the Wings Theatre for one month in the summer of 2003.

3. Drawing on Genette's ideas about the narrator of the *bildungsroman,* in "Hear Jane Sing" Napolitano argues that the graveside song "The Graveyard" "presents a musical variation on Genette's theories regarding the gradual merger between the heroine and the narrator. . . . The young heroine's journey from abused orphan to

independent woman will be complemented by her developmental journey into the role of the narrator" (38).

4. See, for example, Adrienne Rich's calling it Brontë's "feminist manifesto" (97).

5. Another song finale with a brass conclusion is "Secret Soul."

6. In the Zeffirelli film, Elle McPherson played Blanche, a supermodel choice that more closely resembles the character's figure in the novel.

7. Blanche Devereaux, played by Rue McClanahan, is the Southern belle character on *The Golden Girls*, an American sitcom that ran from 1985 to 1992.

8. This may be an allusion to Arthur Bryant's 1952 history *The Age of Elegance, 1812–1820*, the time period in which some of the novel is set. However, the costuming in the play and in most film versions places most of the action firmly in the Victorian period.

9. Spivak's famous 1985 "Three Women's Texts and a Critique of Imperialism" and Susan Meyer's 1990 reply, "Colonialism and the Figurative Strategy of *Jane Eyre*," have defined the dialogue on gender, race, and colonialism in the novel. Other important essays on this topic are Elsie Michie, "From Simianized Irish to Oriental Despots"; Zonana, "The Sultan and the Slave"; and Mckee, "Racial Strategies in *Jane Eyre*."

10. A triple-decker is a novel in three volumes, as were many Victorian novels, including *Jane Eyre*.

11. Jane never refers to Rochester's soul as "enslaved" either. In fact, her only use of that term involves a teasing threat to Rochester to write a charter that will free women in his hypothetical harem, of which she would be a hypothetical part.

12. Class has generated an abundance of excellent criticism on Brontë's *Jane Eyre*. See Poovey, *Uneven Development;* Sharon Marcus, "Profession of the Author"; Schlossberg, "'Low, Vague Hum'"; Eagleton, *Myths of Power;* Godfrey, "Governess to Girl Bride"; and Vanden Bossche, "What Did Jane Eyre Do?"

13. Yet religion is everywhere in the novel. For a compelling argument that details *Jane Eyre*'s intertextual relationship with the Book of Revelations, see Williams's "Closing the Book."

Conclusion

1. *A Man of No Importance* opened on September 12, 2002, at the Mitzi E. Newhouse Theater at Lincoln Center for a limited run, closing on December 29 of that year. With music by Stephen Flaherty, lyrics by Lynn Ahrens, and book by Terrence McNally, it is adapted from the 1994 film *A Man of No Importance* starring Albert Finney.

2. Jill Santoriello wrote the music, lyrics, and book. The show opened September 18, 2008, at the Al Hirschfeld Theater. After sixty performances (and thirty-three previews), it closed on November 9, 2008. Although reviews were largely negative, it received a nomination for Outstanding New Musical in the 2009 Outer Critics Circle Awards.

3. See Brecht's "A Short Organum for the Theatre," which lays out his notion of an epic theatre that, while still entertaining, defamiliarizes or alienates the audience

from the performance and moves them beyond the opiated state of the "cowed, credulous, hypnotized mass" created by bourgeois drama (188).

4. This occurs when casts also normally address the audience as part of their Broadway Cares/Equity Fights AIDS appeal. For more on the context of Dixon's address to Pence, see Herrera (239–41).

5. An example with millions of hits on YouTube is Miranda's hilarious rewriting of the opening number of *Hamilton,* "Alexander Hamilton," to provide all the information provided in "The Ballad of Sweeney Todd," the opening number of Sondheim's musical; it was performed by the *Hamilton* Broadway cast for the 2016 Easter Bonnet Competition charity.

BIBLIOGRAPHY

Adler, Thomas P. "The Sung and the Said: Literary Value in the Musical Dramas of Stephen Sondheim." In *Reading Stephen Sondheim: A Collection of Critical Essays*. Edited by Sandor Goodhart. New York: Garland Publishing, 2000: 37–60.
Aikin, Roger Cushing. "Was Jud Jewish? Property, Ethnicity, and Gender in *Oklahoma!*" *Quarterly Review of Film and Video*, 22.3 (September 2004): 277–83. http://puffin.creighton.edu/fapa/Bruce/0New%20Film%20as%20Art%20webfiles/all%20texts%20and%20articles/Oklahoma%20essay/property.htm.
Alexander, Christine, and Margaret Smith. *The Oxford Companion to the Brontës*. Oxford: Oxford University Press, 2018.
Almar, George. *Oliver Twist: A Serio-Comic Burletta, in Four Acts*. French's Standard Drama, no. 228. New York: Samuel French, [1864?].
Altick, Richard. *The Shows of London*. Cambridge, MA: Harvard University Press, 1978.
"Amusements." In *Watertown Re-Union* (Wednesday, November 10, 1886): 5. https://nyshistoricnewspapers.org/lccn/sn85054450/1886-11-10/ed-1/seq-5.pdf.
Anglo, Michael. *Penny Dreadfuls and Other Victorian Horrors*. London: Jupiter Books, 1977.
Anna and the King. Directed by Andy Tennant. Starring Jodie Foster and Yun-Fat Chow. Fox, 1999.
Anna and the King of Siam. Directed by John Cromwell. Starring Irene Dunne and Rex Harrison. A Darryl F. Zanuck film. Twentieth Century Fox, 1946.
Anstey, F. (Thomas Anstey Guthrie). *A Long Retrospect*. London: Oxford University Press, 1936.
———. *The Tinted Venus: A Farcical Romance*. London: Harper and Brothers, 1898.
———. *Vice Versâ: A Lesson to Fathers*. New York: D. Appleton, 1893.
Anstey, F. (Thomas Anstey Guthrie), and Ernest Holman Clark. "The Tinted Venus" (film scenario). 1915. Manuscript at the British Library. BL Add. MSS 54308.
"Anything Goes." *Wikipedia*. https://en.wikipedia.org/wiki/Anything_Goes.
Arata, Stephen. "The Sedulous Ape: Atavism, Professionalism, and Stevenson's *Jekyll and Hyde*." *Criticism* 37.2 (1995): 233–59.
Archibald, Diana. "Of all the Horrors . . . the Foulest and Most Cruel." In *Victorian Sensations: Essays on a Scandalous Genre*, edited by Kimberly Harrison and Richard Fantina, 53–63. Columbus: Ohio State University Press, 2006.

Armstrong, Nancy. *Desire and Domestic Fiction: A Political History of the Novel.* Oxford: Oxford University Press, 1987.
Arseneau, Mary. "Incarnation and Interpretation: Christina Rossetti, the Oxford Movement, and *Goblin Market.*" *Victorian Poetry* 31.1 (1993): 79–93.
Atkinson, Rowan. Personal interview with author. Theatre Royal, Drury Lane, London. July 10, 2009.
"At the Theaters." *New York Dramatic Mirror,* May 2, 1891: 2.
Audissino, Emilio. *John Williams's Film Music: "Jaws," "Star Wars," "Raiders of the Lost Ark," and the Return of the Classical Hollywood Music Style.* Madison: University of Wisconsin Press, 2013.
Auerbach, Nina. *Communities of Women: An Idea in Fiction.* Cambridge, MA: Harvard University Press, 1998.
———. "Dickens and Acting Women." In *Dramatic Dickens,* edited by Carol Mackay, 81–86. New York: St. Martin's Press, 1989.
Auslander, Philip. *Liveness: Performance in a Mediatized Culture.* New York: Routledge, 2002.
Bailey, Peter. "Conspiracies of Meaning: Music-Hall and The Knowingness of Popular Culture." *Past and Present* 144.1 (1994): 138–70.
Baker, Joseph E. *The Reinterpretation of Victorian Literature.* Princeton, NJ: Princeton University Press, 1950.
Bakhtin, Mikhail. *Rabelais and His World.* Translated by Hélène Iswolsky. Cambridge, MA: MIT Press, 1968.
Banfield, Stephen. *Sondheim's Broadway Musicals.* Ann Arbor: University of Michigan Press, 1993.
Barish, Jonas A. *The Antitheatrical Prejudice.* Berkeley and Los Angeles: University of California Press, 1985.
Barker, Dennis. "Lionel Bart obituary: Fings ain't wot they used t'be." *The Guardian,* April 4, 1999: 22–23. https://www.theguardian.com/news/1999/apr/05/guardianobituaries1.
Barnes, Clive. "B'way has a Lovely new Musical." *New York Post,* December 11, 2000. http://nypost.com/2000/12/11/bway-has-a-lovely-new-musical.
Barnett, Charles Zachary. *Oliver Twist, or, The Parish Boy's Progress.* London: J. Duncombe, 1838.
Barr, Alan. "Sensuality Survived: Christina Rossetti's *Goblin Market.*" *English Miscellany* 28–29 (1979–80): 279–80.
Barranger, Milly S. *A Gambler's Instinct: The Story of Broadway Producer Cheryl Crawford.* Carbondale: Southern Illinois University Press, 2010.
Barreca, Regina. "'The Mimic Life of the Theatre': The 1838 Adaptation of *Oliver Twist.*" In *Dramatic Dickens,* edited by Carol Mackay. 87–95. New York: St. Martin's Press, 1989.
Bart, Lionel. *Oliver!* (libretto). New York: Tams-Witmark, 1960.
Basch, Françoise. "Dickens's Sinners." *In Relative Creatures: Victorian Women in Society and the Novel, 1837–67,* translated by Anthony Rudolf, 210–28. London: Allen Lane, 1974.

Battiscombe, Georgina. *Christina Rossetti: A Divided Life*. New York: Holt, Rinehart and Winston, 1981.

Baumgarten, Murray. "Seeing Double: Jews in the Fiction of F. Scott Fitzgerald, Charles Dickens, Anthony Trollope and George Eliot." In *Between "Race" and Culture: Representations of "the Jew" in English and American Literature*, edited by Bryan Cheyette, 44–61. Stanford: Stanford University Press, 1996.

Beer, John. "*Edwin Drood* and the Mystery of Apartness." *Dickens Studies Annual* 13 (1984): 143–91.

Behdad, Ali. *Belated Travelers: Orientalism in the Age of Colonial Dissolution*. Durham, NC: Duke University Press, 1994.

Bentley, D. M. R. "The Meretricious and the Meritorious in *Goblin Market*: A Conjecture and an Analysis." In *The Achievement of Christina Rossetti*, edited by David A. Kent, 57–81. Ithaca, NY: Cornell University Press, 1987.

Berlant, Lauren. "Poor Eliza." In *No More Separate Spheres*, edited by Cathy Davidson and Jessamyn Hatcher, 291–323. Durham, NC: Duke University Press, 2002.

Bernardo, Melissa Rose. "Jekyll & Hyde (2013)." *Entertainment Weekly*, April 18, 2013. http://www.ew.com/ew/article/0,,20364394_20692464,00.html.

Billington, Michael. "Wicked: The Musical." *Guardian*, September 28, 2006. https://www.theguardian.com/stage/2006/sep/28/theatre1.

Birdoff, Harry. *The World's Greatest Hit: "Uncle Tom's Cabin."* New York: S. F. Vanni, 1947.

Block, Geoffrey. *Enchanted Evenings: The Broadway Musical From "Show Boat" to Sondheim and Lloyd Webber*. 2nd ed. Oxford: Oxford University Press, 2009.

———. "The Melody (and the Words) Linger On: American Musical Comedies of the 1920s and 1930s." In *The Cambridge Companion to the Musical*, 3rd ed., edited by William A. Everett and Paul R. Laird. 117–31. Cambridge: Cambridge University Press, 2017.

Bluestone, George. *Novels into Film*. Berkeley and Los Angeles: University of California Press, 1957.

Bolton, H. Philip. *Dickens Dramatized*. Boston: G. K. Hall, 1987.

Bond, Christopher. Introduction to *Sweeney Todd: The Demon Barber of Fleet Street*, edited by Stephen Sondheim and Hugh Wheeler, 1–16. New York: Applause Theatre Book Publishers, 1991.

"The BOOK was BETTER than the MOVIE." Listopia. Goodreads.com. https://www.goodreads.com/list/show/429.The_BOOK_was_BETTER_than_the_MOVIE.

Booth, Michael. *English Melodrama*. London: Baker and Taylor, 1965.

———. *English Nineteenth-Century Plays*. Vol. 4. Oxford: Oxford University Press, 1969.

Bordman, Gerald. *American Musical Comedy: From Adonis to Dreamgirls*. Oxford: Oxford University Press, 1982.

Bordman, Gerald, and Richard Norton. *American Musical Comedy: A Chronicle*. 4th ed. Oxford: Oxford University Press, 1982.

Bourdieu, Pierre. *Distinction: A Social Critique of the Judgment of Taste.* Cambridge, MA: Harvard University Press, 1984.

Brantley, Ben. "Grand Guignol, Spare and Stark." Theater. Review of *Sweeney Todd. New York Times,* November 4, 2005. http://www.nytimes.com/2005/11/04/theater/reviews/grand-guignol-spare-and-stark.html.

Brantlinger, Patrick. *The Reading Lesson: The Threat of Mass Literacy in Nineteenth-Century British Fiction.* Bloomington: Indiana University Press, 1998.

Bratton, Jacky. "The Music Hall." In *The Cambridge Companion to Victorian and Edwardian Theatre,* edited by Kerry Powell, 164–82, Cambridge: Cambridge University Press, 2003.

———. *New Readings in Theatre History.* Cambridge: Cambridge University Press, 2003.

Bratton, Jacky, Jim Cook, and Christine Gledhill, eds. *Melodrama: Stage, Picture, Screen.* London: British Film Institute, 1994.

Brecht, Bertolt. "A Short Organum for the Theatre." In *Brecht on Theatre: The Development of an Aesthetic,* edited and translated by John Willett, 179–208. New York: Hill and Wang, 1964.

Brennan, Zoe. *Brontë's Jane Eyre.* London: Continuum International Publishing Group, 2010.

Bridgham, Elizabeth. *Spaces of the Sacred and Profane: Dickens, Trollope, and the Victorian Cathedral Town.* New York: Routledge, 2008.

Bristowe, W. S. *Louis and the King of Siam.* London: Chatto and Windus, 1976.

Brontë, Charlotte. *Jane Eyre.* Edited by Richard J. Dunn. New York: Norton, 2001.

Brooks, Daphne A. *Bodies in Dissent: Spectacular Performances of Race and Freedom, 1850–1910.* Durham, NC: Duke University Press, 2006.

Brooks, Dianne. "The Beautiful English Boy: Mark Lester and *Oliver!*" In *Where the Boys Are: Cinemas of Masculinity and Youth,* edited by Murray Pomerance and Frances Gatewood, 114–30. Detroit: Wayne State University Press, 2006.

Brooks, Peter. *The Melodramatic Imagination: Balzac, Henry James, and the Mode of Excess.* New Haven, CT: Yale University Press, 1976.

Brougham, John. *Jane Eyre, a Drama in Five Acts.* In *Jane Eyre on Stage, 1848–1898: An Illustrated Edition of Eight Plays with Contextual Notes,* edited by Patsy Stoneman. Aldershot, UK: Ashgate, 2007.

Brown, Simon. "Blanche MacIntosh." In *Women Film Pioneers Project,* edited by Jane Gaines, Radha Vatsal, and Monica Dall'Asta. New York: Columbia University Libraries, Center for Digital Research and Scholarship, 2013. https://wfpp.cdrs.columbia.edu/pioneer/ccp-blanche-macintosh/.

Brown, Susan. "Alternatives to the Missionary Position: Anna Leonowens as Victorian Travel Writer." *Feminist Studies* 21.3 (Fall 1995): 587–614.

Brown, T. Allston. *A History of the New York Stage: From the First Performance in 1732 to 1901.* Vol. 2. New York: Dodd, Mead, 1903.

Browning, Elizabeth Barret. "Hiram Powers' 'Greek Slave.'" In *The Poetical Works of Elizabeth B. Browning,* 335. New York: A. L. Burt, 1900.

Browning, Robert. "Porphyria's Lover." In *Robert Browning: The Poems*, edited by John Pettigrew, 380. New Haven, CT: Yale University Press, 1981.
Bryant, Arthur. *The Age of Elegance, 1812–1820*. New York: Harper, 1950.
Buckler, William Earl. *Prose of the Victorian Period*. New York: Houghton Mifflin, 1958.
Buckley, Jerome. Foreword to "Forum on Jerome Hamilton Buckley's *The Victorian Temper and the Shaping of Victorian Studies*." *Nineteenth-Century Studies* 15 (2001): 75–76.
———. *The Victorian Temper*. Cambridge, MA: Harvard University Press, 1951.
Bulwer-Lytton, Edward. *Ernest Maltravers*. Paris: A. and W. Galignani, 1837.
Burgan, Mary. "Heroines at the Piano: Women and Music in Nineteenth-Century Fiction." *Victorian Studies* 30.1 (1986): 51–76.
Burton, Antoinette. *Burdens of History: British Feminists, Indian Women, and Imperial Culture, 1865–1915*. Chapel Hill: University of North Carolina Press, 1994.
"Bustle Fluffah." Music video. Directed by Andy Karl. YouTube, uploaded by Broadway.com, December 20, 2012. https://www.youtube.com/watch?v=TzNcry02Rg4.
Butler, Judith. *Bodies That Matter: On the Discursive Limits of "Sex."* New York: Routledge, 1993.
———. *Notes toward a Performative Theory of Assembly*. Cambridge, MA: Harvard University Press, 2015.
———. "Performing Acts and Gender Constitution: An Essay in Phenomenology and Feminist Theory." In *Performing Feminisms: Feminist Critical Theory and Theatre*, edited by Sue-Ellen Case, 270–82. Baltimore: Johns Hopkins University Press, 1990.
Buzzard, James. "Victorian Women and the Implications of Empire." *Victorian Studies* 36.4 (Summer 1993): 443–53.
Byron, George Gordon. *The Corsair: A Tale*. New York: Eastburn, Kirk, 1814.
Calder, Jenni. *The Robert Louis Stevenson Companion*. Edinburgh: P. Harris, 1980.
Campbell, Bob. "Princeton Rep Introduces Haunting 'Goblin' Fantasy." *Newark Star-Ledger*, August 8, 1989: 46.
Campbell, Elizabeth. "Of Mothers and Merchants: Female Economics in Christina Rossetti's 'Goblin Market.'" *Victorian Studies* 33.3 (1990): 393–410.
Cardwell, Sarah. *Adaptation Revisited: Television and the Classic Novel*. Manchester: Manchester University Press, 2002.
Carpenter, Mary Wilson. "'Eat Me, Drink Me, Love Me': The Consumable Female Body in Christina Rossetti's *Goblin Market*." *Victorian Poetry* 29.4 (1991): 415–34.
Carr, Joseph William Comyns. *Dr. Jekyll and Mr. Hyde*. 1910. In *Jekyll and Hyde Dramatized: The 1887 Richard Mansfield Script and the Evolution of the Story on Stage*, edited by Martin Danahay and Alex Chisolm, 193–225. Jefferson, NC: McFarland, 2005.
Carter, Alison J. *Underwear: The Fashion History*. London: Batsford, 1992.
Case, Sue-Ellen. *Feminism and Theatre*. New York: Methuen, 1988.
———. "Toward a Butch-Femme Aesthetic." In *Making a Spectacle: Feminist Essays on Contemporary Women's Theatre*, edited by Lynda Hart, 294–305. Ann Arbor: University of Michigan Press, 1989.

Casey, Janet Galligani. "The Potential of Sisterhood: Christina Rossetti's 'Goblin Market.'" *Victorian Poetry* 29.1 (1991): 63–78.

Cavenaugh, Jennifer Jones. "A Composer in Her Own Right: Arrangers, Musical Directors, and Conductors." In *Women in American Musical Theatre: Essays on Composers, Lyricists, Librettists, Arrangers, Choreographers, Designers, Directors, Producers and Performance Artists*, edited by Bertram E Coleman and Judith Sebesta, 77–91. Jefferson, NC: McFarland, 2008.

Cecil, Lord David. *Victorian Novelists: Essays in Revaluation.* Chicago: University of Chicago Press, 1958.

Chang, Elizabeth Hope. *Britain's Chinese Eye: Literature, Empire, and Aesthetics in Nineteenth-Century Britain.* Palo Alto, CA: Stanford University Press, 2010.

Chantasingh, Charlermsri Thuriyanonda. "The Americanization of *The King and I*: The Transformation of the English Governess into an American Legend." PhD dissertation, University of Kansas, 1999.

"A Chat with Mr. Richard Mansfield." *Star*, London, July 27, 1888. In *Jekyll and Hyde Dramatized: The 1887 Richard Mansfield Script and the Evolution of the Story on Stage*, edited by Martin Danahay and Alex Chisolm, 104–5. Jefferson, NC: McFarland, 2005.

Clark, Stephenie Brown. "Frankenflicks: Medical Monsters in Classic Horror Films." In *Cultural Sutures: Medicine and Media*, edited by Lester D. Friedman, 129–48. Durham, NC: Duke University Press, 2004.

Clay, Cecil. *Rosina Vokes.* London: Rivington, Percival, 1894.

Clayton, Jay. *Charles Dickens in Cyberspace: The Afterlife of the Nineteenth Century in Postmodern Culture.* Oxford: Oxford University Press, 2006.

Clover, Carol. *Men, Women and Chain Saws: Gender in the Modern Horror Film.* Princeton, NJ: Princeton University Press, 1992.

Clum, John M. *Something for the Boys: Musical Theater and Gay Culture.* New York: St. Martins, 1999.

Cohen, Ed. "Hyding the Subject? The Antimonies of Masculinity in *The Strange Case of Dr. Jekyll and Mr. Hyde*." *Novel: A Forum on Fiction* 37.1–2 (2002–3): 181–99.

Cohen, Jane Rabb. *Charles Dickens and His Original Illustrators.* Columbus: Ohio State University Press, 1980.

Collins, Dick. Introduction to *Sweeney Todd or The String of Pearls*. Hertfordshire, UK: Wordsworth Editions, 2005.

Collins, Philip. *Dickens and Crime.* London: MacMillan, 1962.

"Confrontation (Speeded)." YouTube, uploaded by Crawlfan, April 11, 2007. https://www.youtube.com/watch?v=k82I4nq8DMw.

Connor, Steven. "'Speaking Likenesses': Language and Repetition in Christina Rossetti's *Goblin Market*." *Victorian Poetry* 22.4 (1984): 439–48.

Conrow, Margaret. "Wife-Abuse in Dickens's Fiction." *Dickens Studies Newsletter* 14.2 (June 1983): 43–47.

Courtney, John. *Jane Eyre, or The Secrets of Thornfield Manor. Jane Eyre on Stage, 1848–1898: An Illustrated Edition of Eight Plays with Contextual Notes.* Edited by Patsy Stoneman. Aldershot, UK: Ashgate, 2007.

Covert, Colin. "Bloody Valentine with 'Sweeney Todd.'" *Star Tribune,* December 20, 2007: Entertainment. http://www.startribune.com/entertainment/movies/12672012.html.

Cox, Phillip. *Reading Adaptations: Novel and Verse Narratives on the Stage, 1890–1840.* Manchester: Manchester University Press, 2000.

Crater, Alison. *Underwear: The Fashion History.* London: B. T. Batsford, 1992.

Cunningham, Valentine. *Everywhere Spoken Against: Dissent in the Victorian Novel.* London: Clarendon Press, 1975.

Damico, Diane. *Christina Rossetti: Faith, Gender and Time.* Baton Rouge: Louisiana State University Press, 1999.

Danahay, Martin. "Dr. Jekyll's Two Bodies." *Nineteenth-Century Contexts* 35.1 (February 2013): 23–40.

———. "Nature Red in Hoof and Paw: Domestic Animals and Violence in Victorian Art." In *Victorian Animal Dreams: Representations of Animals in Victorian Literature and Culture,* edited by Martin A. Danahay and Deborah Denenholz Morse, 97–120. Aldershot, UK: Ashgate, 2007.

Danahay, Martin, and Alex Chisholm, eds. *Jekyll and Hyde Dramatized: The 1887 Richard Mansfield Script and the Evolution of the Story on Stage.* Jefferson, NC: McFarland, 2005.

Davidson, James Wood. *The Living Writers of the South.* New York: Carlton, 1869.

Davis, Paul. *The Lives and Times of Ebenezer Scrooge.* New Haven, CT: Yale University Press, 1990.

Davis, Ronald L. *Mary Martin, Broadway Legend.* Norman: University of Oklahoma Press, 2008.

Davis, Tracy C., ed. *The Broadview Anthology of Nineteenth-Century British Performance.* Toronto: Broadview, 2012.

Davison, Carol Margaret. "A Battle of Wills: Solving *The Strange Case of Dr. Jekyll and Mr. Hyde.*" In *Troubled Legacies: Narrative and Inheritance,* edited by Allan Hepburn, 132–62. Toronto: Toronto University Press, 2007.

Dawkins, Marcia Alesan. *Clearly Invisible: Racial Culture and the Color of Cultural Identity.* Waco, TX: Baylor University Press, 2012.

Decker, Todd. *Show Boat: Performing Race in an American Musical.* Oxford: Oxford University Press, 2013.

Dellamora, Richard. *Friendship's Bonds: Democracy and the Novel in Victorian England.* Philadelphia: University of Pennsylvania Press, 2004.

Devlin, Kate. "'Second Wave' of Mad Cow Disease Could Hit Britain, Scientists Warn." *Telegraph,* December 7, 2008. http://www.telegraph.co.uk/health/healthnews/3658886/Second-wave-of-mad-cow-disease-could-hit-Britain-scientists-warn.html.

De Wind, John. "The Empire as Metaphor: England and the East in *The Mystery of Edwin Drood.*" *Victorian Literature and Culture* 21 (1993): 169–89.

Diamond, Elin. *Performance and Cultural Politics.* London: Routledge, 1996.

———. "The Violence of 'We': Politicizing Identifications." In *Critical Theory and Performance,* revised ed., edited by Janelle G. Reinelt and Joseph Roach, 403–12. Ann Arbor: University of Michigan Press, 2007.

Dickens, Charles. *Little Dorrit*. New York: Penguin Classics, 2003.
———. *Martin Chuzzlewit*. New York: Penguin Classics, 2000.
———. *The Mystery of Edwin Drood*. London: Penguin, 1974.
———. *Nicholas Nickleby*. New York: Penguin Classics, 1999.
———. *Oliver Twist*. Edited by Fred Kaplan. New York: W. W. Norton, 1993.
———. *Pickwick Papers*. New York: Penguin Classics, 2000.
———. *Sketches by Boz*. New York: Penguin Classics, 1996.
Dickens, Mamie. *My Father as I Recall Him*. New York: E. P. Dutton, 1900.
Doane, Janice, and Devon Hodges. "Demonic Disturbances of Sexual Identity: The Strange Case of Dr. Jekyll and Mr/s Hyde." *Novel: A Forum on Fiction* 23.1 (1989): 63–74.
Dolan, Jill. *The Feminist Spectator as Critic*. Ann Arbor, MI: UMI Research Press, 1988.
———. "Gender Impersonation Onstage: Destroying or Maintaining the Mirror of Gender Roles?" In *Gender in Performance: The Presentation of Difference in the Performing Arts*, edited by Laurence Senelick, 3–13. Hanover, NH: University Press of New England, 1992.
———. *Presence and Desire: Essays on Gender, Sexuality, Performance*. Ann Arbor: University of Michigan Press, 1993.
Donaldson, Laura. "*The King and I* in *Uncle Tom's Cabin*, or On the Border of the Women's Room." *Cinema Journal* 29.3 (Spring 1990): 53–69.
Dr. Jekyll and Mr. Hyde. Directed by John S. Robertson. Starring John Barrymore. Famous Players-Lasky, 1920.
Dr. Jekyll and Mr. Hyde. Screenplay by Samuel Hoffenstein and Percy Heath. Directed by Rouben Mamoulian. Starring Fredric March. Paramount, 1932.
Dr. Jekyll and Mr. Hyde. Screenplay by John Lee Mahin. Directed by Victor Fleming. Starring Spencer Tracy. Metro-Goldwyn Mayer, 1941.
"Dr. Jekyll and Mr. Hyde." Review. *Boston Post*, May 10, 1887. In *Jekyll and Hyde Dramatized: The 1887 Richard Mansfield Script and the Evolution of the Story on Stage*, edited by Martin Danahay and Alex Chisolm, 108–10. Jefferson, NC: McFarland, 2005.
"Dr. Jekyll and Mr. Hyde: Richard Mansfield as in the Dramatization of Mr. Stevenson's Narrative." Review. *New York Herald*, September 13, 1887. In *Jekyll and Hyde Dramatized: The 1887 Richard Mansfield Script and the Evolution of the Story on Stage*, edited by Martin Danahay and Alex Chisolm, 115–16. Jefferson, NC: McFarland, 2005.
Drury, Richard. *The Annotated Dr. Jekyll and Mr. Hyde: Strange Case of Dr. Jekyll and Mr. Hyde*. Lilan: A. Guerini, 1993.
Dubois, Martin. "Diverse Strains: Music and Religion in Dickens's *Edwin Drood*." *Journal of Victorian Culture*. 16.3 (2011): 347–62.
Duke, Robin. Introduction to *The English Governess at the Siamese Court*, by Anna Harriette Leonowens, 9–17. London: The Folio Society, 1980.
Dunnett, Roderic. "Insignificance, Royal Theatre, Northampton." *Theatre and Dance. Independent*, May 24, 2004. http://www.independent.co.uk/arts-entertainment/theatre-dance/reviews/insignificance-royal-theatre-northampton-564527.html.

Dziemianowicz, Joe. "'Jekyll & Hyde': Theater Review." *New York Daily News,* April 18, 2013. http://www.nydailynews.com/entertainment/music-arts/jekyll-hyde-theater-review-article-1.1319707#ixzz2RounDPgY.

Eagleton, Terry. *Myths of Power: A Marxist Study of the Brontës.* Basingstoke, UK: Palgrave Macmillan, 2005.

Early, Julie English. "A New Man for a New Century: Dr. Crippen and the Principles of Masculinity." In *Disorder in the Court: Trials and Sexual Conflict at the Turn of the Century,* edited by George Robb and Nancy Erber, 209–30. New York: NYU Press, 1999.

Edelstein, David. "It's a Gusher!" *New York* (online edition), December 24, 2007. http://nymag.com/movies/reviews/42087/index1.html.

Eder, Linda. *Greatest Hits.* CD. Rhino Entertainment Group Press, 2007.

Eder, Richard. "Stage: Introducing 'Sweeney Todd.'" Books. *New York Times,* March 2, 1979.

Eigner, Edwin. *The Dickens Pantomime.* Berkeley and Los Angeles: University of California Press, 1989.

Eisenstein, Sergei. "Dickens, Griffith, and Film Today." In *Film Form,* 195–255. 1949. Reprint, New York: Harcourt Brace, 1977.

Eisner, Will. *Fagin the Jew.* New York: Doubleday, 2003.

Ellis, Samantha. "Lionel Bart's Oliver!" June 1960. *Guardian,* June 18, 2003. http://www.guardian.co.uk/stage/2003/jun/18/theatre.samanthaellis/print.

Ellsworth, Elizabeth. "Illicit Pleasures: Feminist Spectators and *Personal Best.*" In *Issues in Feminist Film Criticism,* edited by Patricia Erens, 183–96. Bloomington: Indiana University Press, 1990.

Engel, Lehman. *Words with Music: Creating the Broadway Musical Libretto.* New York: Hall Leonard, 2006.

"England." *The Cash Box* 22.42 (July 1, 1961): 67. https://www.americanradiohistory.com/Archive-Cash-Box/60s/1961/CB-1961-07-01.pdf.

"English Celebrities. Sir Edward Bulwer Lytton and Lord Malmesbury." *New York Times,* April 9, 1859: 9.

"*The English Governess at the Siamese Court: Being Recollections of Six Years in the Royal Palace at Bangkok.*" Review. *Athenaeum,* no. 2252 (December 24, 1870): 836. http://search.proquest.com.libezp.lib.lsu.edu/britishperiodicals/docview/8681926/fulltext/14346CF171CFFC6F6/1?accountid=12154.

"*The English Governess at the Siamese Court.*" Review. *Overland Monthly and Out West Magazine* 6.3 (March 1871): 293. http://quod.lib.umich.edu/cgi/t/text/pageviewer-idx?c=moajrnl&cc=moajrnl&idno=ahj1472.1-06.003&node=ahj1472.1-06.003%3A18&frm=frameset&view=image&seq=289.

Etherington, Norman. Introduction to *The Annotated She: A Critical Edition of H. Rider Haggard's Victorian Romance with Introduction and Notes,* edited by Norman Etherington, xv–xliii. Bloomington: Indiana University Press, 1991.

Everett, William A., and Paul R. Laird, eds. *The Cambridge Companion to the Musical.* 3rd ed. Cambridge: Cambridge University Press, 2017.

"EVERY Charles Dickens adaptation." IMDb (Internet Movie Database). Posted by Basilesque, December 25, 2011. http://www.imdb.com/list/ls006348409.

Faulkner, David. "The Confidence Man: Empire and the Deconstruction of Muscular Christianity in "The Mystery of Edwin Drood." In *Muscular Christianity: Embodying the Victorian Age,* edited by Donald E. Hall, 175–93. Cambridge: Cambridge University Press, 1994.

Felluga, Dino, and Emily Allen. "Now and Forever; or, the Strange Afterlife of Gothic." *RaVoN* 34–35 (2004). http://www.erudit.org/revue/ron/2004/v/n34-35/009439ar.html.

Fitz-Gerald, S. J. Adair. *Dickens and the Drama.* London: Chapman and Hall, 1910.

Fleming, Patrick C. "Dickens, Disney, Oliver, and Company: Adaptation in a Corporate Media Age." *Children's Literature Association Quarterly* 41.2 (2016): 182–98.

Foley, June. "Elizabeth Dickens: Model for Fagin." *Women's Studies: An Interdisciplinary Journal* 30.2 (April 1, 2001): 225–35.

Forbes, Camile. *Introducing Bert Williams: Burnt Cork, Broadway, and the Story of America's First Black Star.* New York: Basic Books, 2008.

Fordin, Hugh. *Getting to Know Him: A Biography of Oscar Hammerstein II.* New York: Da Capo Press, 1986.

Fraiman, Susan. *Unbecoming Women: British Women Writers and the Novel of Development.* New York: Columbia University Press, 1993.

Frederick, Bonnie, and Susan H. McLeod, eds. *Women and the Journey: The Female Travel Experience.* Pullman: Washington State University Press, 1993.

Frederick, Kenneth C. "The Cold, Cold Hearth: Domestic Strife in *Oliver Twist*." In *Readings on Oliver Twist,* edited by Jill Karson, 158–46. San Diego: Greenhaven Press, 2001.

Frye, Doris Raab. "'Vulgarized': Victorian Women's Fiction in Minor Theatres." PhD dissertation, Louisiana State University, 2013.

Furneaux, Holly. *Queer Dickens: Erotics, Families, Masculinities.* Oxford: Oxford University Press, 2010.

Gamerman, Amy. "Theater: A Novel Musical—Broadway's 'Jane Eyre' Puts Trust in the Audience's Intelligence; Big Thrills without Bare Skin." *Wall Street Journal,* December 13, 2000: A.24. https://search-proquest-com.libezp.lib.lsu.edu/docview/398737757/401253A6549A4C91PQ/1?accountid=12154.

Gans, Andrew. "'Letting Go': *Jekyll & Hyde,* Starring Constantine Maroulis and Deborah Cox, Ends Broadway Run May 12." Playbill.com, May 12, 2013. http://www.playbill.com/news/article/177820-Letting-Go-Jekyll-Hyde-Starring-Constantine-Maroulis-and-Deborah-Cox-Ends-Broadway-Run-May-12.

Gänzl, Kurt. *Encyclopedia of the Musical Theatre.* London: Blackwell, 1994.

Garlick, Barbara. "Christina Rossetti and the Gender Politics of Fantasy." In *The Victorian Fantasists: Essays on Culture, Society, and Belief in the Mythopoeic Fiction of the Victorian Age,* edited by Katherine Filmer, 133–52. New York: St. Martin's Press, 1991.

Garnett, Robert. "*Oliver Twist*'s Nancy: The Angel in Chains." *Religion and the Arts.* 4.4 (2000): 491–516.

Garrett, Peter K. *Gothic Reflections: Narrative Force in Nineteenth-Century Fiction.* Ithaca, NY: Cornell University Press, 2003.

Geduld, Harry M., ed. *The Definitive Dr. Jekyll and Mr. Hyde Companion.* New York: Garland, 1983.

Gerould, Daniel. "Larger than Life: Reflections on Melodrama and Sweeney Todd." *New York Literary Forum* 7 (1980): 3–14.

———. "Melodrama and Revolution." In *Melodrama: Stage, Picture, Screen*, edited by Jacky Bratton, Jim Cook, and Christine Gledhill, 185–98. Bloomington: Indiana University Pres, 1994.

Gikandi, Simon. *Maps of Englishness: Writing Identity in the Culture of Colonials.* New York: Columbia University Press, 1996.

Gilbert, Sandra M., and Susan Gubar. *The Madwoman in the Attic: The Woman Writer and the Nineteenth-Century Literary Imagination.* New Haven, CT: Yale University Press, 1979.

Glassmeyer, Danielle. "'A Beautiful Idea': *The King and I* and the Maternal Promise of Sentimental Orientalism." *Journal of American Culture* 35.2 (June 2012): 106–22.

Glavin, John. *After Dickens: Reading, Adaptation and Performance.* Cambridge: Cambridge University Press, 1999.

———. "Dickens and Theatre." In *The Cambridge Companion to Charles Dickens*, edited by John O. Jordon, 189–203. Cambridge: Cambridge University Press, 2001.

———. *Dickens on Screen.* Cambridge: Cambridge University Press, 2003.

Godfrey, Esther. "Jane Eyre, from Governess to Girl Bride." *SEL* 45.4 (Autumn 2005): 853–71.

Golub, Ellen. "Untying Goblin Apron Strings: A Psychoanalytic Reading of 'Goblin Market.'" *Literature and Psychology* 25 (1975): 158–65.

Goodhart, Sandor. "Introduction: Reading Sondheim, The End of Ever After." In *Reading Stephen Sondheim: A Collection of Critical Essays*, edited by Sandor Goodhart, 3–36. New York: Garland, 2000.

Gordon, Joanne. *Art Isn't Easy: The Achievement of Stephen Sondheim.* Carbondale: Southern Illinois University Press, 1990.

———. *Stephen Sondheim: A Casebook.* New York: Garland, 1997.

Gorman, Jack. *Knocking Down Ginger.* London: Caliban Books, 1995.

Gottlieb, Jack. *Funny, It Doesn't Sound Jewish: How Yiddish Songs and Synagogue Melodies Influenced Tin Pan Alley, Broadway, and Hollywood.* Albany, NY: SUNY Press, 2004.

Grant, Mark N. "One Touch of Venus: An Appreciation." Kurt Weill Foundation for Music website. https://www.kwf.org/pages/ww-one-touch-of-venus-an-appreciation.html.

———. *The Rise and Fall of the Broadway Musical.* Boston: Northeastern University Press, 2004.

Green, Laura Morgan. *Educating Women: Cultural Conflict and Victorian Literature.* Athens: Ohio University Press, 2001.

Green, Roger Lancelyn. "A Neglected Novelist: 'F. Anstey.'" *English: Literature, Criticism, Teaching* 11.65 (Summer 1957): 178–81.

Green, Stanley. *Broadway Musicals: Show by Show*. London: Faber and Faber, 1985.
Greer, Germaine. Introduction to *Goblin Market*, vii–xxvi. New York: 1975.
Griswold, A. B. *King Mongkut of Siam*. New York: Asia Society, 1961.
Grossman, Jonathan H. "The Absent Jew in Dickens: Narrators in *Oliver Twist, Our Mutual Friend*, and *A Christmas Carol*." *Dickens Studies Annual* 24 (1996): 37–57.
———. *The Art of Alibi: English Law Courts and the Novel*. Baltimore: Johns Hopkins University Press, 2002.
Grossmith, Weedon. *From Studio to Stage; Reminiscences of Weedon Grossmith*. New York: John Lane, 1913.
Grumet, Madeleine. *Bitter Milk: Women and Teaching*. Amherst: University of Massachusetts Press, 1988.
Guida, Fred. *"A Christmas Carol" and Its Adaptations: A Critical Examination of Dickens's Story and Its Productions on Screen and Television*. Jefferson, NC: McFarland, 2000.
Gussow, Mel. "'Hamelin,' A Musical." Theater. *New York Times*, November 11, 1985. http://www.nytimes.com/1985/11/11/theater/theater-hamelin-a-musical.html.
Hadley, Elaine. *Melodramatic Tactics: Theatricalized Dissent in the English Marketplace, 1800–1885*. Palo Alto, CA: Stanford University Press, 1995.
———. "The Past Is a Foreign Country: The Neo-Conservative Romance with Victorian Liberalism." *Yale Journal of Criticism* 10.1(Spring 1997): 7–38.
Hager, Kelly. *Dickens and the Rise of Divorce: The Failed-Marriage Plot and the Novel Tradition*. Aldershot, UK: Ashgate, 2010.
Haglund, David. "You Can't Handle the Truth about Aaron Sorkin." *The Completist*. Slate.com, June 22, 2012. http://www.slate.com/articles/arts/the_completist/2012/06/the_complete_works_of_aaron_sorkin_from_the_west_wing_to_the_social_network_to_the_newsroom_.html.
Haining, Peter. *Sweeney Todd: The Real Story of the Demon Barber of Fleet Street*. New York: Barnes & Noble Books, 1993.
Halberstam, Judith. *Skin Shows: Gothic Horror and the Technology of Monsters*. Durham, NC: Duke University Press, 1995.
Hammerstein, Oscar. *The King and I*. New York: Random House, 1951.
Hammond, Mary. *Charles Dickens's "Great Expectations": A Cultural Life, 1860–2012*. New York: Routledge, 2016.
Hansen, John Mark. *Gaining Access: Congress and the Farm Lobby, 1919–1981*. Chicago: University of Chicago Press, 1991.
Harnick, Sheldon, Jerry Bock, and Joseph Stein. *Fiddler on the Roof*. New York: Times Square Music Publications, 1964.
Harris, J. J., H. R. Cross, and J. W. Savell. "History of Meat Grading in the United States." Meat Science. Texas A&M University website. https://meat.tamu.edu/meat-grading-history.
Harrison, Rachel. "Review of *Chulalongkorn, Roi de Siam. Itinéraire d'un Voyage à Java en 1896*" by Chanatip Kesavadhana. *Bulletin of the School of Oriental and African Studies* 59.3 (1996): 610–11.

Heath, Stephen. "Psychopathia Sexualis: Stevenson's Strange Case." *Critical Quarterly* 28.1 (1986): 93–108.
Hegeman, Susan. *Patterns for America: Modernism and the Concept of Culture*. Princeton, NJ: Princeton University Press, 1999.
Heilman, Robert. "Charlotte Brontë's New Gothic." In *From Jane Austen to Joseph Conrad*, edited by James Theodore Hillhouse, 118–32. Minneapolis: University of Minnesota Press, 1967.
Helsinger, Elizabeth. "Consumer Power and the Utopia of Desire: Christina Rossetti's "Goblin Market." *ELH* 58 (1991): 903–33.
Herrera, Brian Eugenio. "Looking at *Hamilton* from inside the Broadway Bubble." In *Historians on "Hamilton": How a Blockbuster Musical Is Restaging America's Past*, edited by Renee C. Romano and Claire Bond Potter, 222–45. New Brunswick, NJ: Rutgers University Press, 2018.
Hewison, Robert. *The Heritage Industry: Britain in a Climate of Decline*. London: Methuen, 1987.
Hirsch, David A. H. "Dickens's Queer 'Jew' and Anglo-Christian Identity Politics: The Contradictions of Victorian Family Values." In *Queer Theory and the Jewish Question*, edited by Daniel Boyarin, Daniel Itzkovitz, and Ann Pellegrini, 311–33. New York: Columbia University Press, 2003.
Hirschhorn, Joel. "Wicked." *Variety*, June 23, 2005. https://variety.com/2005/legit/markets-festivals/wicked-5-1200524923.
Hischak, Thomas S. *Through the Screen Door: What Happened to the Broadway Musical When It Went to Hollywood*. Lanham, MD: Scarecrow Press, 2004.
Hoen, Alex. *Terrorism and Modern Literature: From Joseph Conrad to Ciaran Carson*. Oxford: Oxford University Press, 2002.
Holbrook, David. *Charles Dickens and the Image of Women*. New York: NYU Press, 1993.
Holmes, Rupert. *The Mystery of Edwin Drood*. Garden City, NY: Nelson Doubleday, 1986.
Holt, Terrence. "'Men Sell Not Such in Any Town': Exchange in *Goblin Market*." *Victorian Poetry* 28.1 (Spring 1990): 51–67.
Homans, Margaret. "'Syllables of Velvet': Dickinson, Rossetti and the Rhetorics of Sexuality." *Feminist Studies* 11.3 (1985): 569–86.
Horak, Laura. *Girls Will Be Boys: Cross-Dressed Women, Lesbians, and American Cinema, 1908–1934*. New Brunswick, NJ: Rutgers University Press, 2016.
Hornback, Bert. "The Book of Jasper." *Dickens Quarterly* 24.2 (2007): 78–85.
Hoskins, Vicki. "A Whodunit of a Musical." *Smile Politely: Champaign-Urbana's Online Magazine*, April 30, 2013. http://smilepolitely.com/arts/a_whodunit_of_a_musical.
Houghton, Walter E. *The Victorian Frame of Mind*. New Haven, CT: Yale University Press, 1957.
Houghton, Walter Edwards, and George Robert Stange, eds. *Victorian Poetry and Poetics*. New York: Houghton Mifflin, 1959.

Houston, Gail Turley. *From Dickens to Dracula: Gothic, Economics, and Victorian Fiction*. Cambridge: Cambridge University Press, 2005.

Houston, Kerr. "'Siam Not So Small!' Maps, History, and Gender in *The King and I*." *Camera Obscura* 59.20.2 (2005): 73–117.

Howard, Jane. "Earth Mother to the Foodists." *Life*, October 22, 1971: 67–70.

Howe, Marvine. "Irene Sharaff, Designer, 83, Dies; Costumes Won Tony and Oscars." Obituaries. *New York Times*, August 17, 1993. http://www.nytimes.com/1993/08/17/obituaries/irene-sharaff-designer-83-dies-costumes-won-tony-and-oscars.html?mcubz=0.

Huff, Cynthia. "Writer at Large: Culture and Self in Victorian Women's Travel Diaries." *Autobiography Studies* 4.2 (1988): 118–29.

Hustis, Harriet. "Hyding Nietzche in Robert Louis Stevenson's Gothic of Philosophy." *SEL: Studies in English Literature, 1500–1900* 49.4 (2009): 993–1007.

Hutcheon, Linda. *A Theory of Adaptation*. New York: Routledge, 2006.

Ingham, Patricia. *Dickens, Women, and Language*. New York: Harvester Wheatsheaf, 1992.

"The International Exhibition: Twenty-Sixth and Last Notice: Sculpture." *Examiner*, no. 2856 (October 25, 1862): 681.

Isherwood, Charles. "It's Just As If This Man Never Left, Either One of Him: Frank Wildhorn's 'Jekyll & Hyde,' at the Marquis Theater." *New York Times*, April 18, 2013. http://www.nytimes.com/2013/04/19/theater/reviews/frank-wildhorns-jekyll-hyde-at-the-marquis-theater.html?adxnnl=1&smid=fb-share&adxnnlx=1366466575-PPjWUOo2H2hdSCItiTWthw.

Jacobson, Wendy S. "John Jasper and Thugee." *Modern Language Review* 72.3 (1977): 526–37.

James, Louis. *Fiction for the Working Man, 1830–1850*. London: Oxford University Press, 1963.

Jane Eyre: The Musical. Music and lyrics by Paul Gordon. Book by John Caird. Directed by John Caird and Scott Schwartz. Starring Marla Schaffel. Opened at the Brooks Atkinson Theatre, New York City, December 10, 2000. 209 performances.

Jekyll and Hyde: Direct from Broadway. Music by Frank Wildhorn. Lyrics by Leslie Bricusse, Frank Wildhorn, and Steve Cuden. Book by Leslie Bricusse. Starring David Hasselhoff, Coleen Sexton, and Andrea Rivette. Image Entertainment, 2006.

Jekyll and Hyde: The Musical. Music by Frank Wildhorn. Lyrics by Leslie Bricusse, Frank Wildhorn, and Steve Cuden. Book by Leslie Bricusse. Directed by Robin Philips. Starring Robert Cuccioli, Linda Eder, and Christine Noll. Opened at Plymouth Theater, New York City, April 28, 1997. 1,543 performances. Original production at Alley Theatre, Houston, 1990.

Jerden, William. Review of *Essays on Craniology*, by Richard Winter Hamilton (London: Hurst Robinson and Co, 1826). *Literary Gazette and Journal of Belles Lettres, Arts, Sciences, Etc.*, no. 494 (July 8, 1826): 419–22.

John, Juliet. *Dickens and Mass Culture*. Oxford: Oxford University Press, 2011.

———. *Dickens's Villains: Melodrama, Character, Popular Culture.* Oxford: Oxford University Press, 2003.

"John Gibson, R. A." *Athenaeum,* no. 1997 (February 3, 1866): 172. http://search.proquest.com/docview/9429467?accountid=12154.

Johnson, Helen, ed. *Our Familiar Songs and Their Authors: Three Hundred Standard and Popular Songs, Arranged with Piano Accompaniment, and Preceded by Sketches of the Authors and Histories of the Songs.* New York: H. M. Caldwell, 1896.

Jones, John Bush. *Our Musicals, Ourselves: A Social History of the American Musical Theatre.* London: Brandeis University Press, 2003.

Jordan, John O. "*Great Expectations* on Australian Television." In *Dickens on Screen,* edited by John Glavin, 45–52. Cambridge: Cambridge University Press, 2003.

Joseph, Gerhard. "Dickens, Psychoanalysis, and Film: A Roundtable." In *Dickens on Screen,* edited by John Glavin, 11-26. Cambridge: Cambridge University Press, 2003.

———. "Who Cares Who Killed Edwin Drood? Or, On the Whole, I'd Rather Be in Philadelphia." *Nineteenth-Century Literature* 51.2 (1996): 161–75.

Jowitt, Deborah. *Jerome Robbins: His Life, His Theater, His Dance.* New York: Simon and Schuster, 2004.

Kaplan, Caren. "'Getting to Know You': Travel, Gender, and the Politics of Postcolonial Representation in *Anna and the King of Siam* and *The King and I.*" In *Late Imperial Culture,* edited by Roman de la Campa, Ann Kaplan, and Michael Sprinker, 33–52. London: Verso, 1995.

Kaplan, Cora. "The Infinite Disclosed: Christina Rossetti and Emily Dickenson." In *Women Writing and Writing about Women,* edited by Mary Jacobus, 61–79. London: Croom, Helm, 1979.

———. *Victoriana: Histories, Fictions, Criticism.* New York: Columbia University Press, 2007.

Kaplan, Fred. *Dickens: A Biography.* New York: Morrow, 1988.

Keats, John. "Lamia." In *Selected Poems and Letters by John Keats,* edited by Douglas Bush, 212–28. Boston: Houghton Mifflin, 1959.

———. "Ode on a Grecian Urn." In *Selected Poems and Letters by John Keats,* edited by Douglas Bush, 207–8. Boston: Houghton Mifflin, 1959.

Kennedy, George E. "Women Redeemed: Dickens's Fallen Women." *Dickensian* 74.384–86 (1978): 42–47.

Kepner, Susan. "Anna (and Margaret) and the King of Siam." *Crossroads: An Interdisciplinary Journal of Southeast Asian Studies* 10.2: 1–32.

Kerman, Joseph. *Opera as Drama.* Rev. ed. Berkeley and Los Angeles: University of California Press, 1988.

Kermode, Frank. *The Sense of an Ending.* Oxford: Oxford University Press, 1967.

Kincaid, James. *Child-Loving: The Erotic Child and Victorian Culture.* New York: Routledge, 1992.

King, Francis. "Glum-Show." *Sunday Telegraph,* October 13, 1985: 16. The Telegraph Historical Archive. http://tinyurl.galegroup.com/tinyurl/56Riq9.

The King and I. Music by Richard Rodgers. Lyrics and book by Oscar Hammerstein II. Directed by John Van Druten. Starring Gertrude Lawrence and Yul

Brynner. Opened at St. James Theater, New York City, March 29, 1951. 1,246 performances.

Kissell, Howard. "A Ticket to 'Hyde'—Creature Comforts Sell Us on 'Jekyll,' as Musical Supplies the Beast of Both Worlds." New York Now. *New York Daily News*, April 29, 1997: 40.

Kivy, Peter. *Osmin's Rage: Philosophical Reflections on Opera, Drama, and Text, with a New Final Chapter.* Ithaca, NY: Cornell University Press, 1999.

Klein, Christina. *Cold War Orientalism: Asia in the Middlebrow Imagination, 1945–1961.* Berkeley and Los Angeles: University of California Press, 2003.

Knapp, Raymond. *The American Musical and the Formation of National Identity.* Princeton, NJ: Princeton University Press, 2005.

———. *The American Musical and the Performance of Personal Identity.* Princeton, NJ: Princeton University Press, 2006.

"*Knickerbocker Holiday.*" Kurt Weill Foundation for Music website. https://www.kwf.org/pages/ww-knickerbocker-holiday.html.

Kooistra, Lorraine Janzen. *Christina Rossetti and Illustration: A Publishing History.* Athens: Ohio University Press, 2002.

Kornblut, Anne E., Jonathan Weisman, and Paul Kane. "Clinton's Supporters Question Her Strategy." WashingtonPost.com, January 5, 2008: A07. http://www.washingtonpost.com/wpdyn/content/article/2008/01/04/AR2008010404002_pf.html.

Koven, Seth. *Slumming: Sexual and Social Politics in Victorian London.* Princeton, NJ: Princeton University Press, 2004.

Kroller, Eva-Marie. "First Impressions: Rhetorical Strategies in Travel Writing by Victorian Women." *ARIEL: A Review of International English Literature:* 21.4 (October 1990): 87–97.

Krueger, Christine. *Functions of Victorian Culture at the Present Time.* Athens: Ohio University Press, 2002.

Kucich, John, and Dianne Sadoff. *Victorian Afterlife: Postmodern Culture Rewrites the Nineteenth-Century.* Minneapolis: University of Minnesota Press, 2000.

Kurnick, David. *Empty Houses: Theatrical Failure and the Novel.* Princeton, NJ: Princeton University Press, 2011.

Laird, Karen. *The Art of Adapting Victorian Literature, 1848–1920: Dramatizing "Jane Eyre," "David Copperfield," and "The Woman in White."* Farnham, UK: Ashgate, 2015.

Laird, Paul R. "Choreographers, Directors, and the Fully Integrated Musical." In *Cambridge Companion to the Musical,* 3rd ed., edited by William A. Everett and Paul R. Laird, 247–63. Cambridge: Cambridge University Press, 2017.

Lamb, John B. "Faces in the Window, Stains on the Rose: Grimaces of the Real in *Oliver Twist.*" *Dickens Studies Annual* 34 (2004): 1–16.

Landon, Brooks. *Science Fiction after 1900: From the Steam Man to the Stars.* New York: Routledge, 2002.

Landon, Margaret. *Anna and the King of Siam.* New York: John Day, 1943.

Langland, Elizabeth. *Nobody's Angels: Middle Class Women and Domestic Ideology in Victorian Culture.* Ithaca, NY: Cornell University Press, 1995.

Law, Graham. *Serializing Fiction in the Victorian Press*. London: Palgrave, 2000.
Law, Jules. "There's Something about Hyde." *Novel: A Forum on Fiction* 42.3 (2009): 504–9.
Leavis, F. R. *The Great Tradition*. New York: New York University Press, 1963.
Ledger, Sally. *Dickens and the Popular Radical Imagination*. Cambridge: Cambridge University Press, 2007.
Lehman, Peter. "Looking at Ivy Looking at Us Looking at Her: The Camera and the Garter." *Wide Angle* 5.3 (1983): 59–63.
Leitch, Thomas. *Film Adaptation and Its Discontents*. Baltimore: Johns Hopkins University Press, 2007.
———. "Twelve Fallacies in Contemporary Adaptation Theory." *Criticism* 45.2 (Spring 2003): 149–71.
Leonowens, Anna. *The English Governess at the Siamese Court*. Oxford: Oxford University Press, 1988.
———. *The Romance of the Harem*. Charlottesville: University Press of Virginia, 1991.
Levine, Caroline, and Marion Ortiz-Robles. Introduction to *Narrative Middles: Navigating the Nineteenth Century British Novel*, edited by Caroline Levine and Mario Ortiz-Robles, 1–24. Columbus: Ohio State University Press, 2011.
Levine, George. *The Realistic Imagination: Fiction from Frankenstein to Lady Chatterley*. Chicago: University of Chicago Press, 1983.
[Lewes, George Henry]. "Recent Novels: French and English." *Fraser's Magazine* 36 (December 1847): 686–95.
Lewin, David. *Studies in Music with Text*. Oxford: Oxford University Press, 2006.
Lewis, C. S. *On Stories: And Other Essays on Literature*. New York: Houghton Mifflin Harcourt, 2002.
Lewis, Reina. *Gendering Orientalism: Race, Femininity, and Representation*. New York: Routledge, 1996.
Lewis, Wyndam, et al. "Manifesto." *Blast: Review of the Great English Vortex* 1 (June 1914): 11–21.
Liberatori, Victoria J. Personal interview with author. McCarter Theatre, Princeton, NJ. August 1989.
Library of Congress Copyright Office. *Dramatic Compositions Copyrighted in the United States, 1870 to 1916*. Vol. 1. U.S. Government Printing Office, 1918. https://books.google.com/books?id=H6I5A43IKVwC&pg=PA79&lpg=PA79&dq=aphrodite+play+thomas+addison+charles+blake&source=bl&ots=6IqcFLr-wY&sig=ACfU3UomWJySZmIrFsuQKb6dn3garH_w2Q&hl=en&ppis=_c&sa=X&ved=2ahUKEwic2fSEzIHmAhUPDKwKHYEVCGgQ6AEwC30ECAkQAQ#v=onepage&q=aphrodite%20play%20thomas%20addison%20charles%20blake&f=false.
Linehan, Katherine Bailey. "'Closer than a wife': The Strange Case of Dr. Jekyll's Significant Other." In *Robert Louis Stevenson Reconsidered*, 85–100. Jefferson, NC: McFarland, 2003.
Litvak, Joseph. *Caught in the Act: Theatricality in the Nineteenth-Century Novel*. Berkeley and Los Angeles: University of California Press, 1992.

Lodge, Mary Jo. "From Madness to Melodramas to Musicals: The Women of *Lady Audley's Secret* and *Sweeney Todd*." *Theatre Annual: A Journal of Performance Studies* 56 (Fall 2003): 78–96.
Long, Heather. "Investing in Broadway: How We Actually Made Money." CNN Money: Investing Guide, June 12, 2016. http://money.cnn.com/2016/06/11/investing/fun-home-broadway-investors/index.html.
Lord, Donald C. "The King and the Apostle: Mongkut, Bradley, and the American Missionaries." *South Atlantic Quarterly* 46:3 (Summer 1967): 326–40.
Lott, Eric. "Blackface and Blackness: The Minstrel Show in American Culture." In *Inside the Minstrel Mask: Readings in Nineteenth-Century Blackface Minstrelsy*, edited by Annemarie Beau, James Hatch, and Brooks McNamara, 3–34. Hanover, NH: Wesleyan University Press, 1996.
Lovensheimer, Jim. *South Pacific: Paradise Rewritten*. Oxford: Oxford University Press, 2010.
Lucas, E. V. "F. Anstey [Thomas Anstey Guthrie]." *English Illustrated Magazine* 29 (1903): 544–45.
Luhr, William, and Peter Lehman. "'Crazy World Full of Crazy Contradictions,' Blake Edwards' *Victor/Victoria*." *Wide Angle* 5.4 (1983): 4–13. http://www.screeningthepast.com/2011/04/%E2%80%9Ccrazy-world-full-of-crazy-contradictions%E2%80%9D-blake-edwards%E2%80%99-victorvictoria.
"Lyceum Theatre." Review. *Sunday Times*, London, August 5, 1888. In *Jekyll and Hyde Dramatized: The 1887 Richard Mansfield Script and the Evolution of the Story on Stage*, edited by Martin Danahay and Alex Chisolm, 122. Jefferson, NC: McFarland, 2005.
"Lyceum Theatre." Review. *Daily Telegraph*, August 6, 1888. In *Jekyll and Hyde Dramatized: The 1887 Richard Mansfield Script and the Evolution of the Story on Stage*, edited by Martin Danahay and Alex Chisolm, 123–26. Jefferson, NC: McFarland, 2005.
Lynch, Jesse. *Why Marry?* New York: Scribner, 1918.
MacDonald, Dwight. "Masscult and Midcult." In *Masscult and Midcult: Essays against the American Grain*, 3–75. New York: New York Review Books Classics, 2011.
Mack, Robert. Introduction to *Sweeney Todd: The Demon Barber of Fleet Street*, edited by Robert Mack, vii–xxviii. Oxford: Oxford University Press, 2007.
———. *The Wonderful and Surprising History of Sweeney Todd: The Life and Times of an Urban Legend*. London: Continuum International Publishing Group, 2007.
Malik, Rachel. "Stories Many, Fast and Slow: *Great Expectations* and the Mid-Victorian Horizon of the Publishable." *ELH* 79.2 (Summer 2012): 477–500.
Mank, Gregory William. *Hollywood Cauldron: 13 Horror Films from the Genre's Golden Age*. Jefferson, NC: McFarland, 2001.
"Mansfield's Triumph. 'Dr. Jekyll and Mr. Hyde' Win Plaudits Loud, and Long Continued, from a Brilliant Throng. A Great Piece of Character Acting at the Boston Museum." *Boston Globe*, May 10, 1887. In *Jekyll and Hyde Dramatized: The 1887 Richard Mansfield Script and the Evolution of the Story on Stage*, edited by Martin Danahay and Alex Chisolm, 110–13. Jefferson, NC: McFarland, 2005.

Mara, Miriam O'Kane. "Sucking the Empire Dry: Colonial Critique in *The Mystery of Edwin Drood.*" *Dickens Studies Annual* 32 (2002): 233–46.

Marcus, Sharon. *Between Women: Friendship, Desire, and Marriage in Victorian England.* Princeton, NJ: Princeton University Press, 2007.

———. "The Profession of the Author: Abstraction, Advertising, and *Jane Eyre.*" *PMLA* 110.2 (March 1995): 206–19.

Marcus, Steven. "Who is Fagin?" In *Oliver Twist,* edited by Fred Kaplan, 478–95. New York: W. W. Norton, 1993.

Margolotti, Jaime. "The Mystery of Edwin Drood." In *Dickens at 200: 1812–2012: An Exhibition in Special Collections.* University of Delaware Library. http://www.lib.udel.edu/ud/spec/exhibits/dickens/drood.html.

Marsh, Joss. "Dickens and Film." In *The Cambridge Companion to Charles Dickens,* edited by John O. Jordan, 204–23. Cambridge: Cambridge University Press, 2001.

Marshall, Gail. *Actresses on the Victorian Stage: Feminine Performance and the Galatea Myth.* Cambridge: Cambridge University Press, 1998.

Massey, Doreen. *Space, Place, and Gender.* Minneapolis: University of Minnesota Press, 1994.

Mast, Gerald. *Can't Help Singin': The American Musical on Stage and Screen.* New York: Overlook Press, 1987.

Mayberry, Katherine J. *Christina Rossetti and the Poetry of Discovery.* Baton Rouge: Louisiana State University Press, 1989.

Mayer, David. "Encountering Melodrama." In *The Cambridge Companion to Victorian and Edwardian Theatre,* edited by Kerry Powell, 145–63. Cambridge: Cambridge University Press, 2004.

Mayer, Jed. "'Come Buy, Come Buy!': Christina Rossetti and the Victorian Animal Market." In *Animals in Victorian Literature and Culture: Contexts for Criticism,* edited by Laurence W. Mazzeno and Ronald D. Morrison, 213–31. London: Palgrave Macmillan, 2017.

McAllister, David. "'Subject to the sceptre of imagination': Sleep, Dreams, and Unconsciousness in *Oliver Twist.*" *Dickens Studies Annual* 38 (2007): 1–17.

McConachie, Bruce. "The 'Oriental' Musicals of Rodgers and Hammerstein and the U.S. War in Southeast Asia." *Theatre Journal* 46.3 (October 1994): 385–98. http://www.jstor.org/stable/3208614.

McFarlane, Brian. "David Lean's *Great Expectations*—Meeting Two Challenges." *Film/Literature Quarterly* 20 (1992): 68–76.

———. *Novel to Film: An Introduction to the Theory of Adaptation.* Oxford: Oxford University Press, 1996.

McGann, Jerome J. "Christina Rossetti's Poems: A New Edition and a Revaluation." *Victorian Studies* 23.2 (1980): 237–54.

Mckee, Patricia. "Racial Strategies in *Jane Eyre.*" *Victorian Literature and Culture* 37.1 (2009): 67–83.

McKibben, Gordon. *Cutting Edge: Gillette's Journey to Global Leadership.* Boston: Harvard Business School Press, 1998.

McMillin, Scott. *The Musical as Drama*. Princeton, NJ: Princeton University Press, 2006.

McNulty, Charles. "Fleet Street Blues." Theater. *Village Voice*, March 9, 2004. http://www.villagevoice.com/2004-03-09/theater/fleet-street-blues/1.

McWilliam, Rohan. "Melodrama." In *A Companion to Sensation Fiction*, edited by Pamela K. Gilbert, 54–66. Malden, MA: Wiley-Blackwell, 2011.

Meer, Sarah. *Uncle Tom Mania: Slavery, Minstrelsy, and Transatlantic Culture in the 1850s*. Athens: University of Georgia Press, 2005.

Meisel, Martin. *Realizations: Narrative, Pictorial, and Theatrical Arts in Nineteenth-Century England*. Princeton, NJ: Princeton, 1983.

Menke, Richard. "The Political Economy of Fruit: Goblin Market." In *The Culture of Christina Rossetti: Female Poetics and Victorian Contexts*, edited by Mary Arseneau, Antony H. Harrison, and Lorraine Janzen Kooistra, 104–36. Athens: Ohio University Press, 1999.

Merchant, Peter. Introduction to *Vice Versâ*, by F. Anstey, edited by Peter Merchant, 5-13. Brighton, UK: Victorian Secrets, 2011.

———. "Thomas Anstey Guthrie's Madhouse Shuffle: Steps toward a Nightmare Scenario." *Nineteenth Century Theatre and Film* 42.2 (2015): 146–63.

Mermin, Dorothy. "Heroic Sisterhood in *Goblin Market*." *Victorian Poetry* 21.2 (1983): 107–18.

Meyer, Susan L. "Colonialism and the Figurative Strategy of *Jane Eyre*." *Victorian Studies* 33.2 (Winter 1990): 247–68.

Michie, Elsie. "From Simianized Irish to Oriental Despots: Heathcliff, Rochester, and Racial Difference." *Novel: A Forum on Fiction*. 25.2 (1992): 125–40.

Michie, Helena. "'There Is No Friend like a Sister': Sisterhood as Sexual Difference." *ELH* 56.2 (1989): 401–21.

Mighall, Robert. "Dickens and the Gothic." In *A Companion to Charles Dickens*, edited by David Paroissien, 81–96. Malden, MA: Blackwell, 2008.

Miller, D. M. *[Place for Us]*. Cambridge, MA: Harvard University Press, 1998.

Miller, Edmund. "'The Mystery of Edwin Drood': The Deconstructionist Musical of Rupert Holmes." *Clues: A Journal of Detection* 13.2 (1992): 47–59.

Miller, J. Hillis. *Charles Dickens: The World of His Novels*. Cambridge, MA: Harvard University Press, 1965.

———. *Victorian Subjects*. Durham, NC: Duke University Press, 1991.

Milligan, Barry. *Pleasures and Pains: Opium and the Orient in Nineteenth-Century British Culture*. Charlottesville: University Press of Virginia, 1995.

M.M.B. "Rebel Art in Modern Life." Interview with Wyndham Lewis. *Daily News and Leader,* April 7, 1914: 14.

Moers, Ellen. *Literary Women*. Garden City, NY: Doubleday, 1976.

Moffat, A. L. *Mongkut, the King of Siam*. Ithaca, NY: Cornell University Press, 1961.

Mordden, Ethan. *Beautiful Mornin': The Broadway Musical in the 1940s*. Oxford: Oxford University Press, 1999.

———. *Coming Up Roses: The Broadway Musical in the 1950s*. New York: Oxford University Press, 1998.

———. *Open a New Window: The Broadway Musical in the 1960s.* London: Macmillan, 2002.
Morley, Malcolm. "Dickens's Contributions to Sweeney Todd." *Dickensian* 58.337 (Spring 1962): 92–95.
Morgan, Susan. *Bombay Anna: The Real Story of the English Governess Who Went to Siam.* Berkeley and Los Angeles: University of California Press, 2008.
———. "Chinese Coolies, Hidden Perfume, and Harriet Beecher Stowe in Anna Leonowens's *The Romance of the Harem.*" In *White Women in Racialized Spaces: Imaginative Transformation and Ethical Action in Literature,* edited by Samina Najmi and Rajini Srikanth, 243–56. Albany: SUNY Press, 2002.
———. Introduction to *The Romance of the Harem,* by Anna Leonowens, ix–xxxix. Charlottesville: University Press of Virginia, 1991.
———. "An Introduction to Victorian Women's Travel Writings about Southeast Asia." *Genre* 20 (Summer 1987): 189–208.
Moss, Robert. *The Films of Carol Reed.* New York: Columbia University Press, 1987.
Most, Andrea. *Making Americans: Jews and the Broadway Musical.* Cambridge, MA: Harvard University Press, 2004.
Muir, John Kenneth. *Singing a New Tune: The Rebirth of the Modern Film Musical from "Evita" to "De-Lovely" and Beyond.* New York: Applause, 2005.
Murphy, Jacqueline Shea. "Unrest and Uncle Tom: Bill T. Jones/Arnie Zane Dance Company's *Last Supper at Uncle Tom's Cabin/The Promised Land.*" In *Bodies of the Text: Dance as Theory, Literature as Dance,* edited by Ellen W. Goellner and Jacqueline Shea Murphy, 81–105. New Brunswick, NJ: Rutgers University Press, 1994.
"The Mystery of Edwin Drood." *Nassau Literary Magazine (1848–1908)* 38, no. 1 (1882): 1-7.
Naden, Corinne. *The Golden Age of American Musical Theatre: 1943–1965.* Lanham, MD: Scarecrow Press, 2011.
Napolitano, Marc. "Disneyfying Dickens: *Oliver & Company* and *The Muppet Christmas Carol* as Dickensian Musicals." *Studies in Popular Culture* 32.1 (Fall 2009): 79–102.
———. "Hear Jane Sing: Narrative Authority in Two Musical Versions of *Jane Eyre.*" *Studies in Musical Theatre.* 2.1 (2008): 11–50.
———. *Oliver!: A Dickensian Musical.* Oxford: Oxford University Press, 2014.
———. "'Reviewing the Situation': *Oliver!* and the Musical Afterlife of Dickens's Novels." PhD dissertation, University of North Carolina, 2009.
———. "'This garish parish called the music hall'. Rupert Holmes's *Drood* as Dickensian Adaptation." *Neo-Victorian Studies* 3.2 (2010): 118–44.
Naremore, James. *Film Adaptation.* New Brunswick, NJ: Rutgers University Press, 2000.
Nathan, John. "This is how you play Fagin, Rowan." *Jewish Chronicle Online,* December 18, 2008. https://www.thejc.com/culture/theatre/this-is-how-you-play-fagin-rowan-1.6705.

Nesvet, Rebecca. "Growing an Audience for Penny Bloods: The James Malcolm Rymer Collection." Paper presented at the Research Society for Victorian Periodicals Conference, University of Missouri, Kansas City, September 9, 2016.

Nicoll, Alardyce. *A History of English Drama, 1660–1900.* Vol. 5. Cambridge: Cambridge University Press, 1975.

Nichols, Lewis. "One Touch of Venus." *New York Times,* October 17, 1943: section 2, XI.

"The Nightmare at the Lyceum." *Pall Mall Gazette,* August 7, 1888. In *Jekyll and Hyde Dramatized: The 1887 Richard Mansfield Script and the Evolution of the Story on Stage,* edited by Martin Danahay and Alex Chisolm, 126–27. Jefferson, NC: McFarland, 2005.

Nord, Deborah Epstein. *Walking the Victorian Streets: Women, Representation, and the City.* Ithaca, NY: Cornell University Press, 1995.

Nuechterlein, Donald E. *Thailand and the Struggle for Southeast Asia.* Ithaca, NY: Cornell University Press, 1965.

O'Farrell, Mary Ann. "Sister Acts." *Women's Studies Quarterly* 34.3/4 (2006): 154–73.

"*Oliver!* Creator Dies after Cancer Battle." BBC (online), April 3, 1999. http://news.bbc.co.uk/2/hi/uk_news/311100.stm.

Olsen, Vickie. "The Subordination of Gender to Race Issues in the Film Musical *South Pacific.*" In *Gender, I-deology: Essays on Theory, Fiction, and Film,* edited by Chantel Cornut-Gentille D'Arcy and Jose Angel Garcia Landa, 345–57. Amsterdam: Rodopi, 1996.

"The Only Jones." *Judy, or the London Serio-Comic Journal,* May 14, 1884: 232.

Oxford English Dictionary. Oxford: Oxford University Press, 1971.

Pace, Eric. "Lionel Bart, 68, Songwriter; Created the Musical 'Oliver!'" *New York Times,* April 5, 1999: A19. http://www.nytimes.com/1999/04/05/theater/lionel-bart-68-songwriter-created-the-musical-oliver.html?sec=&spon=.

"panties, n." *OED Online.* Oxford University Press. https://www-oed-com.libezp.lib.lsu.edu/view/Entry/137008?redirectedFrom=pantie#eid.

Panyarachun, Anand. "Chulalongkorn." *Time Asia Online* 154.7/8 (August 23–30, 1999). http://www.cnn.com/ASIANOW/time/asia/magazine/1999/990823/rama1.html.

Park, Hyungji. "'Going to Wake Up Egypt': Exhibiting Empire in 'Edwin Drood.'" *Victorian Literature and Culture* 30.2 (2002): 529–50.

Paroissien, David. *The Companion to Oliver Twist.* Edinburgh: Edinburgh University Press, 1992.

Pascal, Julia. "Time to Bury Fagin." *Guardian,* January 16, 2009. https://www.theguardian.com/commentisfree/2009/jan/17/jewish-stereotypes-fagin-shylock.

Pater, Walter. *The Renaissance: Studies in Art and Poetry.* Mineola, NY: Dover Publishing, 2005.

Patten, Robert. "When Is a Book Not a Book? *Oliver Twist* in Context." New York Public Library's Online Exhibition Archive. http://web-static.nypl.org/exhibitions/booknotbook/2magazines.html.

Pen, Polly. Personal interview with author. Author's home, New Paltz, NY. September 22, 2014.
Perelman, S. J., and Ogden Nash. *One Touch of Venus*. Boston: Little, Brown and Company, 1944.
"Phantom of the Opera, Musical vs. Book." Message Board. Broadwayworld.com. https://www.broadwayworld.com/board/readmessage.php?thread=695794.
Pinkston, C. Alex. "The Stage Premiere of *Dr. Jekyll and Mr. Hyde*." *Nineteenth Century Theatre Research* 14.1–2 (1986): 21–44.
Pleon, Harry. *A Vision of Venus; or, A Midsummer-Night's Nightmare*. Dicks Standard Plays, no. 1025. London: John Dicks, 1893.
Poovey, Mary. *Uneven Developments: The Ideological Work of Gender in Mid-Victorian England*. Chicago: University of Chicago Press, 1988.
Preston, Katherine. "American Musical Theatre before the Twentieth Century." In *The Cambridge Companion to the Musical*, 2nd ed., edited by William A. Everett and Paul R. Laird, 1–28. Cambridge: Cambridge University Press, 2008.
Radway, Janice. *A Feeling for Books: The Book-of-the-Month Club, Literary Taste, and Middle-Class Desire*. Chapel Hill: University of North Carolina Press, 1997.
Rappoport, Jill. *Giving Women: Alliance and Exchange in Victorian Culture*. Oxford: Oxford University Press, 2012.
Rastogi, Pallavi. *Afrindian Fictions: Diaspora, Race, and National Desire in South Africa*. Columbus: Ohio State University Press, 2008.
"'The Real Dr. Jekyll and Mr. Hyde': An Interview with Mr. Richard Mansfield." *Pall Mall Gazette*, London, July 24, 1888. In *Jekyll and Hyde Dramatized: The 1887 Richard Mansfield Script and the Evolution of the Story on Stage*, edited by Martin Danahay and Alex Chisolm, 102–3. Jefferson, NC: McFarland, 2005.
Reiff, Marija. "The Musical of *The Mystery of Edwin Drood*." Paper presented at the Interdisciplinary Nineteenth-Century Studies Conference, "Adaptations" panel, University of Virginia, Charlottesville, March 15, 2013.
Review of *The English Governess at the Siamese Court: Being Recollections of Six Years in the Royal Palace at Bangkok*. *Athenaeum*, no. 2252 (December 24, 1870): 836. http://gateway.proquest.com/openurl?url_ver=Z39.88-2004&res_dat=xri:bp-us:&rft_dat=xri:bp:article:e932-1870-000-52-142361:1.
Review of *The English Governess at the Siamese Court*. *Overland Monthly and Out West Magazine* 6.3 (March 1871): 293. http://quod.lib.umich.edu/cgi/t/text/pageviewer-idx?c=moajrnl&cc=moajrnl&idno=ahj1472.1-06.003&node=ahj1472.1-06.003%3A18&frm=frameset&view=image&seq=289.
Review of *The Romance of Siamese Harem Life*. *Athenaeum*, no. 2364 (February 15, 1873): 205–7. http://gateway.proquest.com/openurl?url_ver=Z39.88-2004&res_dat=xri:bp-us:&rft_dat=xri:bp:article:e932-1873-000-64-136675:3.
Review of *Romance of the Harem*. *Princeton Review* 2.6 (April 1873): 378. http://quod.lib.umich.edu/cgi/t/text/pageviewer-idx?c=moajrnl&cc=moajrnl&idno=acf4325.2-02.006&node=acf4325.2-02.006%3A12&frm=frameset&view=image&seq=380.
Rhys, Jean. *Wide Sargasso Sea*. New York: W. W. Norton, 1982.

Rich, Adrienne. "*Jane Eyre:* Temptations of a Motherless Woman." In *On Lies, Secrets and Silence: Selected Prose, 1966–1978*. 89-106. New York: Norton, 1979.

"Richard Mansfield: Actor." *Encyclopædia Britannica Online.* https://www.britannica.com/biography/Richard-Mansfield.

"Richard Mansfield as Dr. Jekyll and Mr. Hyde." *New York Tribune,* September 13, 1887. In *Jekyll and Hyde Dramatized: The 1887 Richard Mansfield Script and the Evolution of the Story on Stage,* edited by Martin Danahay and Alex Chisolm, 116–20. Jefferson, NC: McFarland, 2005.

Richards, Jeffrey. "Tod Slaughter and the Cinema of Excess." In *The Unknown 1930s: An Alternative History of the British Cinema, 1929–39,* edited by Jeffrey Richards, 139–60. New York: IB Tauris, 1998.

Richardson, Robert D. *Literature and Film.* Bloomington: Indiana University Press, 1970.

Rigby, Elizabeth [Lady Eastlake]. "*Vanity Fair* and *Jane Eyre.*" *London Quarterly* 84 (1848): 153–85.

Roach, Rebecca. *Literature and the Rise of the Interview.* Oxford: Oxford University Press, 2019.

Robson, Catherine. *Men in Wonderland: The Lost Girlhood of the Victorian Gentleman.* Princeton, NJ: Princeton University Press, 2001.

Rodgers, Richard. *Musical Stages: An Autobiography.* New York: Random House, 1975.

Rogin, Michael. *Blackface, White Noise: Jewish Immigrants in the Hollywood Melting Pot.* Berkeley and Los Angeles: University of California Press, 1998.

Romano, John. *Dickens and Reality.* New York: Columbia University Press, 1978.

Romano, Renee C., and Claire Bond Potter, eds. *Historians on "Hamilton": How a Blockbuster Musical Is Restaging America's Past.* New Brunswick, NJ: Rutgers University Press, 2018.

Roper, David. *Bart!: The Unauthorized Life and Times, Ins and Outs, Ups and Downs of Lionel Bart.* New York: Pavilion, 1994.

Rose, Brian A. *Jekyll and Hyde Adapted: Dramatizations of Cultural Anxiety.* Westport, CT: Greenwood Press, 1996.

Rosenberg, Edgar. *From Shylock to Svengali: Jewish Stereotypes in English Fiction.* Palo Alto, CA: Stanford University Press, 1960.

Rosenthal, Jesse. *Good Form: The Ethical Experience of the Victorian Novel.* Princeton, NJ: Princeton University Press, 2016.

Rossetti, Christina. "Goblin Market." In *The Complete Poems of Christina Rossetti,* edited by Rebecca W. Crump and Betty Sue Flowers, 5–20. London: Penguin, 2001.

Rosso, Martha. "Philadelphia's Great Drood Trial." *Pennsylvania Magazine of History and Biography* 105.1 (January 1, 1981): 99–104.

Rowell, George. *The Victorian Theatre: A Survey.* Oxford: Oxford University Press, 1956.

Rubens, Alfred. "Jews and the English Stage, 1667–1850." *Transactions and Miscellanies* (Jewish Historical Society of England) 24 (1970–73): 151–70.

Rubin, Gayle. "The Traffic in Women: Notes on the 'Political Economy' of Sex." In *Toward an Anthropology of Women,* edited by Regina R. Reiter, 157–210. New York: Monthly Review Press, 1975.

Rubin, Joan Shelley. *The Making of Middlebrow Culture.* Chapel Hill: University of North Carolina Press, 1992.

Ruskin, John. *The Works of John Ruskin.* Edited by E. T. Cook and Alexander Wedderburn. 39 vols. London: George Allen; Longmans Green, 1903–12.

Russell, Kathy, Midge Wilson, and Ronald Hall. *The Color Complex: The Politics of Skin Color in a New Millennium.* Rev. ed. New York: Random House, 2013.

Sadoff, Dianne F. *Victorian Vogue: British Novels on Screen.* Minneapolis: University of Minnesota Press, 2010.

Sanders, Julie. *Adaptation and Appropriation.* London: Routledge, 2005.

Sandoval-Sanchez, Alberto. *José Can You See? Latinos On And Off Broadway.* Madison: University of Wisconsin Press, 1999.

Savran, David. "Class and Culture." In *The Oxford Handbook of the American Musical,* 239–50. Oxford: Oxford University Press, 2011.

———. *Highbrow/Lowdown: Theater, Jazz, and the Making of the New Middle Class.* Ann Arbor: University of Michigan Press, 2009.

———. *A Queer Sort of Materialism: Recontextualizing American Theater.* Ann Arbor: University of Michigan Press, 2003.

Schlicke, Paul. *A Christmas Carol.* In *The Oxford Companion to Charles Dickens: Anniversary Edition,* edited by Paul Schlicke, 102. Oxford: Oxford University Press, 2012.

Schlossberg, Linda. "'The Low, Vague Hum of Numbers': The Malthusian Economies of *Jane Eyre.*" *Victorian Literature and Culture* 29.2 (2001). 489–506.

Schoch, Richard W. Introduction to *Victorian Theatrical Burlesques,* edited by Richard W. Schoch, xi–xlii. Aldershot, UK: Ashgate, 2003.

Schoeser, Mary, Julien Macdonald, and Bruno Marcandalli. *Silk.* New Haven, CT: Yale University Press, 2007.

Schor, Hilary. *Dickens and the Daughter of the House.* Cambridge: Cambridge University Press, 1999.

Scott, A. O. "Murder Most Musical." Movies. *New York Times,* December 21, 2007. http://www.nytimes.com/2007/12/21/movies/21swee.html?ref=movies.

Scott, Heidi. "Subversive Ecology in Rossetti's "Goblin Market."" *Explicator* 65.4 (2007): 219–22.

Sears, Ann. "The Coming of the Musical Play: Rodgers and Hammerstein." In *The Cambridge Companion to the Musical,* edited by William A. Everett and Paul R. Laird, 2nd ed., 1–28. Cambridge: Cambridge University Press, 2008.

Sedgwick, Eve Kososfky. *Between Men.* New York: Columbia University Press, 1985.

———. *Epistemology of the Closet.* Berkeley and Los Angeles: University of California Press, 1990.

———. "Queer Performativity: Henry James's *The Art of the Novel.*" *GLQ* 1.1 (1993): 1–16.

Shakespeare, William. Sonnet 18. In *The Riverside Shakespeare*, edited by G. Blakemore Evans, 1752. Boston: Houghton Mifflin, 1974.

Shaw, George Bernard. *Pygmalion.* In *Complete Plays with Prefaces,* vol. 1. New York: Dodd, Mead, 1963.

Shelley, Percy Bysshe. "Ode to the West Wind." In *Shelley's Poetry and Prose,* edited by Donald H. Reiman and Sharon B. Powers. New York: Norton, 1977.

Shurbutt, Sylvia Bailey. "Revisionist Mythmaking in Christina Rossetti's 'Goblin Market': Eve's Apple and Other Questions Revised and Reconsidered." *Victorian Newsletter* 82 (Fall 1992): 40–44.

Sinyard, Neil. "Dickens on Television." *Screen Online.* British Film Institute. http://www.screenonline.org.uk/tv/id/1420996.

Skal, David. *The Monster Show: A Cultural History of Horror.* New York: W. W. Norton, 1993.

Slater, Michael. *Dickens and Women.* Stanford: Stanford University Press, 1983.

Smith, Alison. *The Victorian Nude: Sexuality, Morality, and Art.* Manchester: Manchester University Press, 1996.

Smith, Grahame. *Dickens and the Dream of Cinema.* Manchester: Manchester University Press, 2003.

Smith, Helen. *Sweeney Todd, Thomas Peckett Prest, James Malcolm Rymer and Elizabeth Caroline Grey.* London: Jarndyce Books, 2002.

Sod, Ted. "Ladies and Gentlemen, Mister Rupert Holmes!" In *UPSTAGE: The Mystery of Edwin Drood,* 4–6. New York: Education Department at the Roundabout Theatre Company, 2012. https://res.cloudinary.com/roundabout-theatre-company/image/upload/v1545236575/PDFs-and-FORMS/UPSTAGE/Drood_Upstage2.pdf.

Sollers, Werner. *Neither Black nor White yet Both: Thematic Exploration of Interracial Literature.* Cambridge, MA: Harvard University Press, 1999.

Sondheim, Stephen. *Finishing the Hat: Collected Lyrics (1954–1981) with Attendant Comments, Principles, Heresies, Grudges, Whines and Anecdotes.* New York: Alfred A. Knopf, 2010.

———. *Look, I Made a Hat: Collected Lyrics (1981–2011), With Attendant Comments, Amplifications, Dogmas, Harangues, Digressions, Anecdotes and Miscellany.* New York: Alfred A. Knopf, 2011.

———. Personal recorded interview for author. December 22, 2012.

———. "Re: From Stephen Sondheim." Email correspondence received by Sharon Aronofsky Weltman, December 15, 2013.

Sondheim, Stephen, and Hugh Wheeler. *Sweeney Todd: The Demon Barber of Fleet Street.* New York: Applause, 1991.

Spingarn, Adena. *Uncle Tom: From Martyr to Traitor.* Stanford: Stanford University Press, 2018.

Spivak, Gayatri Chakravorty. "Three Women's Texts and a Critique of Imperialism." *Critical Inquiry* 12.1 (1985): 243–61.

Stacey, Jackie. *Star Gazing: Hollywood Cinema and Female Spectatorship.* London: Routledge, 2013.

Starobinski, Jean. "The Style of Autobiography." In *Autobiography: Essays Theoretical and Critical,* edited by James Olney, 73–83. Princeton, NJ: Princeton University Press, 1980.

Stephens, Walter. *Lost: A Drama in Two Acts.* London: J. W. Last, 1871.

Stern, Rebecca F. "'Adulterations Detected': Food and Fraud in Christina Rossetti's "Goblin Market.'" *Nineteenth-Century Literature* 57.4 (March 2003): 477–511.

Sternfeld, Jessica. *The Megamusical.* Bloomington: Indiana University Press, 2006.

———. "'Pitiful Creature of Darkness': The Subhuman and the Superhuman in *The Phantom of the Opera.*" In *The Oxford Handbook of Music and Disability Studies,* edited by Blake Howe, Stephanie Jensen-Moulton, Neil Lerner, and Joseph Straus, 795–813. New York: Oxford University Press, 2016.

Stevenson, Robert Louis. *The Strange Case of Dr. Jekyll and Mr. Hyde.* Edited by Martin A. Danahay. Petersborough, Ontario: Broadview, 1999.

Steyn, Mark. *Broadway Babies Say Goodnight.* London: Faber and Faber, 1997.

Stone, Harry. "Dickens and the Jews." *Victorian Studies* 2 (1959): 223–53.

Stoneman, Patsy. *Brontë Transformations: The Cultural Dissemination of Jane Eyre and Wuthering Heights.* London: Prentice Hall, 1996.

———. *Jane Eyre on Stage, 1848–1898: An Illustrated Edition of Eight Plays with Contextual Notes.* Aldershot, UK: Ashgate Press, 2007.

Stowe, Harriet Beecher. *Uncle Tom's Cabin, or, Life among the Lowly.* New York: Airmont Publishing, 1967.

Stowe, Judith A. *Siam Becomes Thailand: A Story of Intrigue.* Honolulu: University of Hawaii Press, 1991.

Strachey, Lytton. *Eminent Victorians.* London: Chatto and Windus, 1918.

Stratford, Jenny. "F. Anstey." *British Museum Quarterly* 33.1/2 (Autumn 1968): 85n17.

The String of Pearls: A Romance [perhaps by Malcolm Rymer, Thomas Peckett Prest, and others]. *The People's Periodical and Family Library.* Edited by Edward Lloyd. November 21, 1846–March 20, 1847, in 18 numbers.

Sullivan, T. R. *Jekyll and Mr. Hyde.* In *Jekyll and Hyde Dramatized: The 1887 Richard Mansfield Script and the Evolution of the Story on Stage,* edited by Martin Danahay and Alex Chisolm, 47–79. Jefferson, NC: McFarland, 2005.

Suskin, Steven. *Broadway Yearbook 2001–2002.* Oxford: Oxford University Press, 2003.

Swain, Joseph P. *The Broadway Musical: A Critical and Musical Survey.* Lanham, MD: Scarecrow Press, 2002.

Sweeney Todd, or The String of Pearls. Edited by Dick Collins. Hertfordshire, UK: Wordsworth Editions, 2005.

Sweeney Todd: The Demon Barber of Fleet Street. Directed by Tim Burton. Starring Johnny Depp, Helena Bonham Carter, Alan Rickman, Sacha Baron Cohen, and Laura Michelle Kelly. Paramount Pictures, December 2007. DVD, Paramount Home Entertainment, April 2008.

Sweeney Todd: The Demon Barber of Fleet Street. Music and lyrics by Stephen Sondheim. Book by Hugh Wheeler. Directed and designed by John Doyle. Starring

Michael Cerveris and Patti LuPone. Opened at Eugene O'Neill Theatre, New York City, November 2005. 384 performances.

Sweeney Todd: The Demon Barber of Fleet Street. Music and lyrics by Stephen Sondheim. Book by Hugh Wheeler. Directed by Harold Prince. Starring Angela Lansbury and Len Cariou. Opened at Uris Theater, New York City, March 1, 1979. 557 performances.

Taruskin, Richard. *The Danger of Music and Other Anti-Utopian Essays.* Berkeley and Los Angeles: University of California Press, 2008.

Tatum, Karen Elizabeth. "'Something Covered with an Old Blanket': Nancy and Other Dead Mothers in Oliver Twist." *American Journal of Psychoanalysis* 65.3 (September 2005): 239–60.

Taylor, Diana. "Saving the 'Live': Re-performance and UNESCO's Intangible Cultural Heritage." Public lecture, Louisiana State University, Baton Rouge, LA, March 6, 2013.

Taylor, Millie. "Lionel Bart: British Vernacular Musical Theatre." In *The Oxford Handbook of the British Musical,* edited by Robert Gordon and Olaf Jubin, 484–506. Oxford: Oxford University Press, 2016.

Terwiel, B. J. *A History of Modern Thailand, 1767–1942.* St. Lucia, Australia: University of Queensland Press, 1983.

Toppman, Lawrence. "5 Years Ago, Lin-Manuel Miranda Was Pondering 'Hamilton'—but Not the Way You Think." *Charlotte Observer,* June 7, 2016. http://www.charlotteobserver.com/entertainment/ent-columns-blogs/lawrence-toppman/article82286737.html.

Tracy, Robert. "Jasper's Plot: Inventing the *Mystery of Edwin Drood.*" *Dickens Quarterly* 23.1 (2006): 29–38.

———. "'Opium Is the True Hero of the Tale': De Quincey, Dickens, and *The Mystery of Edwin Drood.*" *Dickens Studies Annual* 40 (2009): 199–214.

Tromp, Marlene. *The Private Rod: Marital Violence, Sensation, and the Law in Victorian Britain.* Charlotte: University of Virginia Press, 2000.

———. "Victorian Murder: Complex Problems and Academic Interdisciplinarity." *Literature Compass* 10 (May 2013): 582–91.

Twain, Mark. "Model Artists." In *The American Stage: Writing on Theater from Washington Irving to Tony Kushner,* edited by Laurence Senelick, 82–84. New York: Library of America, 2010. Reprinted from the San Francisco *Daily Alta,* March 28, 1867.

Vallance, Tom. "Obituary: Lionel Bart." *Independent,* April 5, 1999. https://www.independent.co.uk/arts-entertainment/obituary-lionel-bart-1085282.html.

Vanden Bossche, Chris. "What Did Jane Eyre Do? Ideology, Class, Agency, and the Novel." *Narrative* 14.1 (2005): 46–66.

Van Esterik, Penny. "Anna and the King: Digesting Difference." *South East Asia Research* 14.2 (2006): 289–307.

Veeder, William, and Gordon Hirsch, eds. *Dr. Jekyll and Mr. Hyde after One Hundred Years.* Chicago: University of Chicago Press, 1988.

Vidal, Belén. *Heritage Film: Nation, Genre and Representation.* New York: Columbia University Press, 2012.
Vincentelli, Elisabeth. "Run & 'Hyde' from Ridiculous Revival of 'Jekyll & Hyde.'" *New York Post,* April 19, 2013. http://nypost.com/2013/04/19/run-hyde-from-ridiculous-revival-of-jekyll-hyde.
Viswantahan, Gauri. *Masks of Conquest: Literary Study and British Rule in India.* New York: Columbia University Press, 1989.
Voskuil, Lynn. *Acting Naturally: Victorian Theatricality and Authenticity.* Charlottesville: University of Virginia Press, 2004.
Wald, Gayle. *Crossing the Line: Racial Passing in Twentieth-Century U.S. Literature and Culture.* Durham, NC: Duke University Press, 2000.
Walker, Lenore. *The Battered Woman Syndrome.* 2nd ed. New York: Springer, 2000.
Walkowitz, Judith R. *City of Dreadful Delight: Narratives of Sexual Danger in Late-Victorian London.* Chicago: University of Chicago Press, 1992.
Ward, Rachel. "Northern Ballet's New 'Jane Eyre' Is a Beautiful and Expressive Tribute to Brontë—Review." Culture. Dance. *Telegraph,* June 1, 2016. https://www.youtube.com/watch?v=-NKXNThJ6I0.
"Was Dr. Crippen Innocent of His Wife's Murder?" *BBC News Magazine,* July 2010. http://www.bbc.com/news/magazine-10802059.
Watson, Jeanie. "'Men Sell Not Such in Any Town': Christina Rossetti's Goblin Fruit of Fairy Tale." *Children's Literature 12.* New Haven, CT: Yale University Press, 1984.
Weber, Bruce. "Theater Reviews: *Jane Eyre.*" *New York Times,* December 11, 2011: D11, E1: 1. http://www.nytimes.com/2000/12/11/theater/theater-review-an-arsonist-in-the-attic-a-feminist-in-the-making.html.
Wedge, Don. "New British Musical Promising." *Billboard Music Week,* June 26, 1961: 19.
Weitzel, Edward. "Barrymore Does Amazing Transformation in Paramount's 'Dr. Jekyll and Mr. Hyde.'" *Moving Picture World,* April 3, 1920: 63.
Weliver, Phyllis. "Tom-Toms, Dream-Fugues and Poppy Juice: East Meets West in Nineteenth-Century Fiction." In *Music and Orientalism in the British Empire, 1780s–1940s Portrayal of the East,* edited by Bennett Zon, 257–74. Aldershot, UK: Ashgate, 2007.
———. *Women Musicians in Victorian Fiction, 1860–1900: Representations of Music, Science, and Gender in the Leisured Home.* Aldershot, UK: Ashgate, 2000.
Welsh, Alexander. *The City of Dickens.* Cambridge, MA: Harvard University Press, 1986.
Weltman, Sharon Aronofsky. "Adopting and Adapting Dickens since 1870: Stage, Film, Radio, Television." In *Oxford Handbook to Charles Dickens,* edited by John Jordan, Bob Patten, and Cathy Waters, 738–55. Oxford: Oxford University Press, 2018.
———. "Boz versus Bos in *Sweeney Todd:* Dickens, Sondheim, and Victorianness." *Dickens Studies Annual* 42 (2011): 55–76.

———. "Dickens and Musical Theatre." In *Edinburgh Companion to Dickens and the Arts,* edited by Juliet John and Claire Wood. Edinburgh: Edinburgh University Press, forthcoming 2020.

———. "Editorial: Investigating Early Film and the Nineteenth-Century Theatre." *Nineteenth Century Theatre and Film* 42.1 (2015): 119–23.

———. Introduction to *Sweeney Todd: The String of Pearls, or The Fiend of Fleet Street,* by George Dibdin Pitt. Special issue, *Nineteenth-Century Theatre and Film* 38.1 (June 2011): 1–22.

———. "Melodrama and the Modern Musical Theatre." In *Cambridge Companion to Melodrama,* edited by Carolyn Williams, 262–76. Cambridge: Cambridge University Press, 2018.

———. "Melodrama, *Purimspiel,* and Jewish Emancipation." *Victorian Literature and Culture* 47.2 (June 2019): 305–45.

———. *Performing the Victorian: John Ruskin and Identity in Theater, Science, and Education.* Columbus: Ohio State University Press, 2007.

———. "Sondheim's *Sweeney Todd* on Stage and Screen." *Victorian Literature and Culture* 26.6 (2009): 301–10.

———. "Theater, Exhibition, and Spectacle in the Nineteenth Century." In *Companion to British Literature,* edited by Robert DeMaria Jr., Heesok Chang, and Samantha Zacher, 68–88. London: Wiley Blackwell, 2014.

———. "Victorians on the Contemporary Stage." *Journal of Victorian Culture* 13.2 (October 2008): 303–9.

Whelehan, Imelda. "Adaptations: The Contemporary Dilemmas." In *Adaptations: From Text to Screen, Screen to Text,* edited by Deborah Cartmell and Imelda Whelehan, 3–20. London: Routledge, 1999.

"When Stars Are in the Quiet Skies." The LiederNet Archive. http://www.lieder.net/lieder/get_text.html?TextId=3288.

Wilde, Oscar. *The Complete Works of Oscar Wilde: Stories, Plays, Poems, and Essays.* 1966. Reprint, New York: Harper and Row, 1989.

———. *The Picture of Dorian Gray.* New York: Penguin, 2000.

Wildhorn, Frank. Personal phone interview with composer. February 17, 2000.

Williams, Carolyn, ed. *Cambridge Companion to Melodrama.* Cambridge: Cambridge University Press, 2018.

———. "Closing the Book: The Intertextual End of *Jane Eyre.*" In *Victorian Connections,* edited by Jerome J. McGann, 60–87. Charlottesville: University Press of Virginia, 1989.

———. *Gilbert and Sullivan: Gender, Genre, Parody.* New York: Columbia University Press, 2010.

———. "Melodrama and the Realist Novel." In *Cambridge Companion to Melodrama,* edited by Carolyn Williams, 209–23. Cambridge: Cambridge University Press, 2018.

Wills, Gary. "The Loves of Oliver Twist." In *Oliver Twist,* edited by Fred Kaplan, 593–608. New York: W. W. Norton, 1993.

Wilson, Edmund. *The Wound and the Bow.* New York: Riverside Press, 1939.

Winer, Linda. "A Smaller Bite of 'Sweeney,' but It's Bloody Good." Theater & Arts: Broadway Review. *Newsday,* November 4, 2005. http://archive.li/ipd1C.

———. "A Touch of the Original." Entertainment. *Newsday,* November 4, 2008.

Wolf, Stacy. *A Problem Like Maria: Gender and Sexuality in the American Musical.* Ann Arbor: University of Michigan Press, 2002.

———. *Changed for Good: A Feminist History of the Broadway Musical.* Oxford: Oxford University Press, 2011.

———. "Musical Theatre Studies." *Journal of Drama and the Theatre* 28.1 (Winter 2016). http://jadtjournal.org/2016/03/23/musical-theatre-studies.

Wolff, Larry. "'The Boys Were Pickpockets and the Girl Is a Prostitute': Gender and Juvenile Criminality in Early Victorian England from *Oliver Twist* to *London Labour.*" *New Literary History* 22.2 (1996): 27–49.

Woll, Allen L. *Black Musical Theatre: From Coontown to Dreamgirls.* Baton Rouge: Louisiana State University Press, 1989.

Wollman, Elizabeth. *Hard Times: The Adult Musical in 1970s New York City.* Oxford: Oxford University Press, 2013.

———. *The Theatre Will Rock: A History of the Rock Musical, from Hair to Hedwig.* Ann Arbor: University of Michigan Press, 2009.

"The Woman's Angle." *Variety,* January 5, 1932: 19.

Wood, Bret. "The Many Faces of Jekyll/Hyde." In Supplemental Features: "An Illustrated Essay on the Story's Origins and Incarnations." *Dr. Jekyll and Mr. Hyde* (1920). Directed by John S. Robertson. Kino Video, 2001.

Woolf, Virginia. "Middlebrow." In *The Death of the Moth, and Other Essays,* 176–86. New York: Harcourt, Brace, 1942.

———. "Professions for Women." In *The Death of the Moth, and Other Essays,* 235–42. New York: Harcourt, Brace, 1942.

Yeazell, Ruth. *Harems of the Mind: Passages of Western Art and Literature.* New Haven, CT: Yale University Press, 2000.

Zemka, Sue. "The Death of Nancy 'Sikes,' 1838–1912." *Representations* 110.1 (Spring 2010): 29–57.

Zieger, Susan. *Inventing the Addict: Drugs, Race, and Sexuality in Nineteenth-Century British and American Literature.* Amherst: University of Massachusetts Press, 2008.

Zlotnick, Susan. "Jane Eyre, Anna Leonowens, and the White Woman's Burden: Governesses, Missionaries, and Maternal Imperialists in Mid-Victorian Britain." *Victorian Institutes Journal* 24 (1996): 27–55.

———. "'The Law's a Bachelor': *Oliver Twist,* Bastardy, and the New Poor Law." *Victorian Literature and Culture* 34 (2006): 131–46.

Zonana, Joyce. "The Sultan and the Slave: Feminist Orientalism and the Structure of *Jane Eyre.*" *Signs* 18.3 (Spring 1993): 592–617.

INDEX

Italicized page numbers refer to illustrations, and characters, songs, and musicals are indexed separately from composers and lyricists..

abolitionism, 56–77, 240n36, 242n6, 247n12
ACT UP, 181
adaptation theory, 6–12
Addison, Thomas, 238n21
adultery/sexual infidelity, 71, 195, 242n7
Ahrens, Lynn, 235n25, 260n1
Aibel, Douglas, 253n1
AIDS crisis, 4, 162, 164, 168, 181
Aiken, George L., 70
Aikin, Robert Cushing, 236n9
Ainsworth, William Harrison, 81, 108
Aladdin (Disney, 1992), 89
Albee, Edward, 14
Alceste (Gluck and Calzabigi, 1767), 234n15
Alcott, Louisa May, 63, 180
"Alexander Hamilton" (*Hamilton*), 261n5
Allen, Emily, 226
Alloula, Malek, 60
"All Ripe Together" (*Goblin Market*), 169
All the Year Round (Dickens), 160, 197
"All through the Night" (*Red, Hot, and Blue*), 29
Almar, George, 81–82
American Slave, The (Bell, 1862), 240n36
alter egos, 182–209

alternative endings, 132–33, 142–43, 150–60, 252nn22–23
alternative fiction, 132–60
Altick, Richard, 35, 40–41
American beef boycott, 20, 123–24
American Civil War, 67
American Idol, 153, 183, 256n4
Americanization, 14, 53, 71, 214, 217
American musical theater, history of, 25–33
Anatomy of Melancholy (Burton), 38
Anderson, Mary, 39
Anderson, Maxwell, 28
Angel in the House, The (Patmore, 1854), 33, 75
Angel in the House trope, 33, 57, 75–78, 99, 107, 200, 224
Angels in America (Kushner), 168, 201
animal magnetism, 252n28
animated adaptations, 88–89, 242n2, 245n20
Anna and the King (CBS), 242n2
Anna and the King (Tennant, 1999), 242n2
Anna and the King of Siam (Cromwell, 1946), 241n2
Anna and the King of Siam (Landon, 1944), 241–42n2
Annie (character), 199, 203
Annie Get Your Gun (Berlin), 256n1

Anstey, F., 9, 18, 25–54, 122, 238n22, 239nn25–26
anti-communism, 56–57
anti-Semitism, 3, 18, 79–107. *See also* racism
anorexia, 161
Anything Goes (Porter), 28–29, 236n6
Aphrodite, 53, 238n21
Aphrodite (Addison and Blake), 238n21
Arabian Nights, 60, 134, 146–48
Archibald, Diana, 99–100
Arnold, Matthew, 15
Arseneau, Mary, 253n2
Artful Dodger (character), 82, 100, 102–3, 106, 119–20
Arthur, Joseph, 128, 191
arts funding, 162
Ashman, Howard, 89
"As Long as He Needs Me" (*Oliver!*), 245n21
Assassins (Sondheim and Weidman), 134
Atkinson, Rowan, 20, 97, 104–5, 244n1, 245n19, 245n23
Atlas, Leopold, 251n18
"At the Piano" (*Edwin Drood* illustration by Fildes), *140*
Auerbach, Nina, 61, 168
Auslander, Philip, 194
Austen, Jane, 34, 237n16
Australia, 125, 248n29

Babes in Arms (Rodgers and Hart), 250n11
Bailey, Peter, 160
Baker, Joseph E., 237n18
Bakhtin, Mikhail, 230
Balanchine, George, 31–32
Balderston, John L., 251n18
"Ballad of Sweeney Todd, The" (*Sweeney Todd*), 206, 261n5
ballet, 19, 23, 26–27, 31–32, 41, 50–51, 57, 67–73, 111, 134, 148–50, 210, 236n33; dream, 32, 50, 57, 134, 148–51

Bamford, Beadle (character), 17, 88, 109, 120
Barabas (character), 93
"Barber and His Wife, The" (*Sweeney Todd*), 125
barber shave, 121–23
barbers/hairdresser characters, 20, 37, 41–47, 51–52, 111–31, 239n24, 249n34
Barbour, James, 211
Barker, Wayne, 252n23
Barnaby Rudge (Dickens), 116
Barnes, Clive, 211–13
Barnett, Zachary, 82, 84
Barney (character), 95
Barras, Charles M., 26–27
Barrie, J. M., 84–85
Barrymore, John, 186, 203, 258n21
Barrymore, Lionel, 3
Bart, Lionel, 3, 8, 19–20, 79–107, 113–14, 119–20, 132–33, 136, 184, 199–200, 244n13
Bassey, Shirley, 245n20
battered women, 99–100, 245n21
Battiscombe, Georgina, 253n2
Baudrillard, Jean, 169
Baum, L. Frank, 228
Baumgarten, Murray, 93
BBC, 34, 95, 135, 137, 141, 211, 245n20, 249n4
Beane, Sawney, 247n15
Beauty and the Beast (Split Britches, 1983), 176
Beauty and the Beast (Disney film, 1991), 89
Beauty and the Beast (Menken and Ashman, 1994), 202, 211, 235n25
"Be Back Soon" (*Oliver!*), 104
Bedwin, Mrs. (character), 104
Beggar's Opera, The (Gay, 1728), 246n6
"Begone, Dull Care" (*Drood*), 137
Behind the Mask (Alcott), 180
"Believe Me, If All Those Endearing Young Charms" (Moore), 141

Bells, The (Lewis), 106
Bennett, Michael, 135
Bennett, Robert Russell, 132
Bennett, Rodney, 135
Berenger, Clara, 196
Bergman, Ingrid, 198, 203
Berlin, Irving, 28, 91, 174
Bernardo, Melissa, 203
Bernstein, Leonard, 9, 149
Bet (character), 199, 248n24
bildungsroman, 259n3
Billington, Michael, 228
Bird, Isabella, 59
Birdoff, Harry, 70
Birth of a Nation (Griffith), 235n22
Bizet, Georges, 73
Black Adder, The (BBC), 244n7
Black Crook, The (Barras), 26–27
blackface minstrelsy, 19, 29, 68–71, 236n8, 243n19, 252n25
Bleak House (BBC, 1985), 135
Bleak House (Dickens, 1852–53), 117, 135, 201
Bligh, Betty, 85
Blitz! (Bart), 90
Block, Geoffrey, 27–29, 50, 233n3
Blue Angel, The (Sternberg), 241n42
Blue Jeans (Arthur), 128, 191
blues, 28–29
Bluestone, George, 2
Blum, Galen, 252n23
Bock, Jerry, 7, 71, 97, 106
Bolton, Philip, 81, 83, 85, 87, 153
Bombay (India), 58, 60, 78
Bond, Christopher, 9, 108–10, 164, 207, 264n8
bondage, 203
Bonham-Carter, Helena, 129
book musical, 26, 28–30
Booth, Michael, 41
Bordman, Gerald, 27, 233n3
Bos, 111, 113. *See also* Prest, Thomas Peckett
Bosetti, Carlo, 250n13

Boublil, Alain, 256n2
Bourdieu, Pierre, 12–13, 15–16, 46, 211
bourgeoisie. *See* middle class
Bowman, Nellie, *84,* 84
Boz, 15, 111, 113, 228, 258n29. *See also* Dickens, Charles
Brahms, Johannes, 172–74, 255n17
Bram Stoker's Dracula (Coppola), 7
Branagh, Kenneth, 7
Brantley, Ben, 78
Bratton, Jacky, 154, 209
"Brave Enough for Love" (*Jane Eyre*), 225
Brecht, Bertolt, 109, 127, 184, 229, 260–61n3
Brechtian, 20, 126–27, 156, 183, 246n5, 248n22
Bricusse, Leslie, 3, 22, 183–209, 258n19
Brigadoon (Lerner and Loewe), 237n12
"Bring on the Men" (*Jekyll and Hyde*), 201–3, 258n31
Britishness, 49, 189, 200
Brocklehurst, Rev. (character), 210, 214, 221
Broken Blossoms (Griffith), 235n22
Brontë, Charlotte, 2, 7, 23, 59, 210–36, 260n4, 260n12
Brontë, Emily, 7
Brooke, Norman, 253n3
Brooks, Daphne, 258n23
Brooks, Dianne, 9, 93, 244n7
Brooks, Mel, 96
Brooks, Peter, 183
Brougham, John, 223–24
Brown, Georgia, 92
Brown, Simon, 37
Brown, Susan, 61–62, 64, 77
Brown, T. Allston, 36
Browning, Elizabeth Barrett, 240n36
Browning, Robert, 253n3, 257n17
Brownlow, Mr. (character), 104–6
Brown v. Board of Education, 74
Brynner, Yul, 241n2, 243n17
Buckley, Betty, 155, 164

Buckley, Jerome, 34
Bud, Rosa (character), 3, 21, 133–34, 137–52, 158, 250n6, 250n12, 251n14, 252n28
Buddhism, 60–61
Bulwer-Lytton, Edward, 144, 251n16
Bumble, Mr. (character), 17, 79, 88, 120
Bumble, Mrs. (character), 20, 79, 118–19, 129
Bunyan, Paul, 102
"Burlington Bertie," 155
Burne-Jones, Edward, 39, 43
Burne-Jones, Georgiana, 39
Burney, Frances, 239n26
Burns, Helen (character), 215, 221–22, 225
Burton, Robert, 38
Burton, Tim, 88, 109–10, 127–31, 239n22, 248n23, 248n30, 249n37
"Bustle Fluffah," 159
butch-femme aesthetic, 176
Butler, Judith, 164–65, 229, 253n5, 254n6, 255n19
Byatt, A. S., 256n3
Byron, George Gordon, 15, 34, 248n26

Cable, Lt. Joe (character), 74
Cage, John, 158
Caird, John, 23, 210, 256n2, 259n2
Calhoun, Jeff, 203, 205, 256n4
Caliban (character), 200
Calzabigi, Ranieri de', 234n15
Campbell, Bob, 168, 253n2
campiness, 11, 54, 132, 136
cannibals/cannibalism, 20, 108–13, 206, 246n5, 247n15, 247n17, 247n20
"Can't Help Loving Dat Man" (*Show Boat*), 30
Cantor, Eddie, 70, 236n8
Cariou, Len, 245n1
Carlisle, Kitty, 241n42
Carpenter, Bridget, 238n20
Carpenter, Mary, 253n2
Cardwell, Sarah, 3, 138

Carew, Agnes (character), 187–88, 258n21
Carew, MP (General/Sir) Danvers (character), 187–89, 199, 198, 200, 256n4, 258n25
Carew, Emma (character), 200, 256n4
Carew, Sir George (character), 196, 202
Carew, Lady (character), 195
Carew, Lisa (character), 199–200
Carew, Millicent (character), 196
Carew, Muriel (character), 198
Carey, Peter, 256n3
Carlyle, Warren, 149–50
Carmen (Bizet, 1875), 73
Carmen Jones (Hammerstein), 73
Carousel (Rodgers and Hammerstein, 1945), 211; 1994 revival, 211
Carr, J. Comyns, 83, 195
Carter, Alison, 49
Case, Sue-Ellen, 169, 171, 176, 254n6
Casey, Janet Galligani, 253n2
casting, 30, 218, 220, 257n5; cross-gender, 88, 154, 171, 176, 202; cross-race, 230, 245n20; Hispanic or Filipino actors to play non-whites, 243n17; race-blind, 245n20; race-conscious, 220, 230; racially integrated, 30
Cats (Lloyd Webber, 1980), 10, 87, 135, 163, 210, 253n3
Cavenaugh, Jennifer, 70
CBS, 135
Cecil, David, 212
Cezanne, Paul, 45
Chadwick, George Whitefield, 251n17
Chairman (character), 154–59, 251n15, 252n25
Chaney, Lon, 85
Chapman, Annie, 191, 199
Chartism, 222
Chernow, Ron, 7
Chesterton, G. K., 153
children's literature, 161, 168

Chiodo, Tom, 252n23
Chisolm, Alex, 187, 190–91, 195, 197, 207–8
Choose Your Own Adventure books, 153
choreography, 8, 18–19, 23, 31–32, 50–51, 57, 66–82, 106, 149, 158, 175, 201–9, 230, 243n18, 258n31, 259n32
Chorus Line, A (Hamlisch and Kleban), 135
Christian allegory, 161
Christianity, 21, 60, 64, 71, 102, 161, 177–78, 214, 222, 260n13; fundamentalism, 221
Christie, Agatha, 155–56
Christmas, 149, 235n25
Christmas Carol, A (Dickens, 1843), 16, 19–20, 89, 135, 159, 199, 235nn24–25
Christmas Carol, A (Donner, 1984), 135
Christmas Carol, A (Menken and Ahrens, 1994), 244n9
Chodorov, Jerome, 236n2
Chulalongkorn, King, 73
Chulalongkorn, Prince (character), 56, 59, 73, 243n19, 243n22
City of Women, 58–67, 77
"City on Fire" (*Sweeney Todd*), 206
civil rights movement, the, 19, 57, 73
Clark, Ernest Holman, 238n22
class, 11, 45, 55–131, 184–209, 214, 260n12; conflict, 107–31, 222; hierarchy, 61, 117, 199, 218, 222; racialization of, 197
Clinton, Bill, 257n8
Clooney, Rosemary, 174
Clue (Blum, Barker, Martucci, and Chiodo, 1997), 252n23
Clue (Lynn, 1985), 153, 252n23
Cohan, George M., 27, 55
Cohen, Ed, 257n14
Cold War, 4, 56
collective action, 124
Collins, Charles Allston, 250n10; *Edwin Drood* wrapper (with Luke Fildes) by, *143*

Collins, Dick, 246n10
Collins, Phil, 244n7
Collins, Wilkie, 34, 159–60, 250n10
Collum, Matilda (character), 37, 239n24
Colonel Jeffrey (character), 112, 247n18
colonialism/imperialism, 19, 45, 52–53, 56, 59, 60, 67, 77–78, 146–47, 158, 188–89, 198–99, 220, 231n1, 241n1, 242n6, 251n20, 260n9
comic opera, 27–28, 53; British dominance of, 53
"community of women," 61–62
Company (Sondheim and Furth), 20, 134
competing discourses, 230
concept albums, 182–83
concept musicals, 4, 20, 134–35, 163
conceptual set, 127
concubines, 59, 61–64, 67–68, 76
"Confrontation, The" (*Jekyll and Hyde*), 204–5
Connor, Steven, 253n2
Conrad, Joseph, 34, 237n16
conservative romanization of Victorians, 135–36
"Consider Yourself" (*Oliver!*), 100, 103, 106
consumer consciousness, 123–24
Coogan, Jackie, 85
Copland, Aaron, 32
Copperfield (Kasha and Hirschhorn, 1981), 244n9
Coppola, Francis Ford, 7
copyright protection, lack of, 16–17, 81
Corney, Widow (character). *See* Bumble, Mrs. (character)
Corpse Bride, The (Burton, 2005), 239n22
Corsair, The (Byron), 248n26
costume drama. *See* heritage film and television
counterpoint, 10, 32, 175, 230
Courtney, John, 210, 223–24
Covert, Colin, 109
Coward, Noël, 90

Cox, Deborah, 256n4
Cox, Philip, 15, 81–82
Craft, Kinuko, 22. See also *Playboy*
Crawford, Cheryl, 44, 236n11, 241n42
criminals as characters, 79–107
Crimson Petal and the White, The (Faber), 256n3
Crippen, Hawley Harvey, 52, 241n43
Crisparkle, Mrs. (character), 141
Crisparkle, Septimus (character), 137, 141, 143–44, 250n6
Cromwell, John, 241n2
Crosby, Bing, 174
Cross, Beverley, 8
cross-gender casting, 176
cross-gender performance/performativity, 22, 70–72, 161–81, 201–20, 254n6, 255n19, 259n32
Cruikshank, George, 20, 81, 85, 87
Crummles, Mrs. (character), 115–16, 152
Crump, Rebecca W., 254n7
Cuccioli, Robert, 204
cultural uplift, 14–15, 46
culture text, 16, 195, 207, 209, 230, 240n38
culture moyenne. See middlebrow culture
Cunningham, Valentine, 247n19
Curtis, Jamie Lee, 36
Curtiz, Michael, 174

Dahmer, Jeffrey, 206
Daly, Augustin, 128, 190
Dame role, male actor in, 202
Danahay, Martin, 187, 190–91, 195, 197, 207–8
dance hall entertainer characters, 196–99
Danielle, Graciella, 149–50
Datchery, Dick (character), 142, 147, 151–52, 155–56, 249n6, 251n20
David Copperfield (BBC, 1986), 135
David Copperfield (Dickens, 1850), 15, 135, 187, 197

Davidson, James Wood, 144–45
Davis, Adele, 124, 248n28
Davis, Eliza, 93, 95
Davis, Paul, 16, 230
Davis, Ronald, 52
Davis, Tracy, 209
Death of Nancy Sykes (Lumière, 1897), 17, 82
DeGeneres, Ellen, 201
DeGrazia, Elizabeth, 219
Dellamora, Richard, 102, 245n22
"Delovely" (*Red, Hot, and Blue*), 29
DeLuise, Dom, 88–89
de Mille, Agnes, 31–32, 50
Demme, Jonathan, 201, 206
Democratic National Convention (1996), 184
DePietro, Peter, 252n23
Depp, Johnny, 110, 126–31
Deputy (character), 137, 155, 249n6
desegregation, 74
Devereaux, Blanche (character), 219, 260n7
Devlin, Kate, 130
Dewhurst, George, 239n23
Diamond, Elin, 169
Dickens, Charles, 3, 6, 8–9, 15–21, 33–34, 38, 54, 57, 75–76, 79–107, 109–11, 113–14, 116–20, 132–60, 169, 186, 197–201, 212, 218, 224, 228, 230, 235nn24–25, 244n9, 247n20, 250n8, 250n10, 251n18, 251n20; illustrations of his work, 20, 85–87, *140, 143,* 184, 250n10; musical adaptations of his work, 79–107, 132–60, 235nn24–25
Dickens, Mamie, 18
Dickensian, 2, 16–18, 21, 57, 75–76, 88, 106–31, 135–36, 159, 185, 197–201, 212–14, 231, 250n12, 258n25
"Die Schwestern" (Brahms), 172–74, 255n17
Dietrich, Malena, 240–41n42
Disney, 88–89, 135, 202, 235n25, 238n20, 244n12, 254n10

Disraeli, Benjamin, 85
disrobing on stage, 170–71. *See also* nudity on stage/appearance of nudity on stage
divided self/dual self, 161–209
Dixon, Brandon, 228–29, 261n4
Dolan, Jill, 169, 171, 254n6, 255n20
Dombey and Son (BBC, 1983), 135
Dombey and Son (Dickens, 1848), 135, 239n28
domesticity, 38, 57, 75–79, 99–103, 107, 188–89, 200; domestic catastrophe, 189; domestic space, 62, 77–78, 100, 102
Donaldson, Laura, 68, 72, 242n6
Donner, Clive, 135
"Don't Quit While You're Ahead" (*Drood*), 156
Doolittle, Eliza (character), 103–4, 111, 164
doppelgänger, 200. *See also* divided self/dual self
Doro, Marie, 83–84
Dorrit, Amy (character), 75, 135
doubled protagonists, 197, 199–201
"double I," 215, 218, 236n36
double voicing, 230
Douglas, Kirk, 199, 203
Dow, Bruce, 213–14
Doyle, Richard, 109–10, 126–31, 249n37
Dracula (character), 207, 209
Dracula (Stoker), 7, 128, 247n11, 258n27
drag performance, 174, 201–3, 254n6, 255n20. *See also* cross-gender performance/performativity; transvestite performance
Drama Desk Award, 211, 242n2
dreams, 32, 50, 57, 134, 137, 147–51
"Dr. Crippen" (*One Touch of Venus*), 51–52
Dr. Fogg (character), 112, 117, 121, 126
drinking, 100–104
Dr. Jekyll and Mr. Hyde (Carr, 1910), 195

Dr. Jekyll and Mr. Hyde (Flemming, 1941), 198–99
Dr. Jekyll and Mr. Hyde (Mamoulian, 1932), 197–98, 200
Dr. Jekyll and Mr. Hyde (Robertson, 1920), 3, 185–86, 196–97, 207
Dr. Jekyll and Mr. Hyde (Sullivan, 1887), 185–91, 195–97, 200, 257n9
Dr. Jekyll and Mr. Hyde (Winters, 1973), 199
Dr. Jekyll and Sister Hyde (Baker, 1971), 257n18
Drood (Holmes, 1985), 4, 17, 21, 54, 132–64, 173, 177, 200, 202, 228, 244n9, 249n1, 250n12, 251n20, 252nn23–24, 256n3
Drood, Edwin (character), 132–60, 249n6, 250n12, 251n20
DuBarry Was a Lady (Porter), 29
DuBois, Blanche (character), 219
Dubois, Martin, 137
Duncan, Sandy, 85
Dunne, Irene, 241n2
Dunnett, Roderic, 109, 246n3
Durdles (character), 137, 147, 152, 155, 157, 250n6
Dust Bowl, 30–31
Dziemianowicz, Joe, 205

Early, Julie English, 52
Eastlake, Lady. *See* Rigby, Elizabeth
East Lynn (Wood), 259n33
Eddowes, Catherine, 191
Eder, Linda, 199, 258n28, 259n31
Edgar, E. F., 251n14
Ed Sullivan Show, The, 13
education as a tool of colonialism, 67, 241n1, 242n6
Edwards, Blake, 259n32
Edzard, Christine, 135
Eigner, Edwin, 148
Eisenhauer, Peggy, 211
Eisenstein, Sergei, 17
Eisner, Will, 245n16

Elgin Marbles, 53
Eliot, George, 34, 237n16
Eliot, T. S., 10, 135, 163
Elizabeth II, Queen, 259n2
Ellis, Samantha, 79, 88, 91, 93, 201
Ellsworth, Elizabeth, 254n14
Elmore, Belle, 52, 241n43
embodiment, discourses of, 192–93
Emery, Beatrix (character), 198
Emery, Sir Charles (character), 198
Enfield (character), 192, 208
Engel, Lehman, 233n3
English Governess at the Siamese Court, The (Leonowens), 19, 57, 61, 72, 77, 241n2
equality, 214, 222–24
Ernest Maltravers (Bulwer-Lytton), 144, 251n17
Ernotte, Andre, 253n1
escapism/escapist, 3, 15–16, 136, 184, 229
Etherington, Norman, 239n25
Evita (Lloyd Webber and Rice), 87
Expresso Bongo (Norman and Heneker), 244n15
eyewitness accounts, 194, 207
Eyre, Jane (character), 210–26, 243n12, 259n3, 260n11

Faber, Michael, 256n3
"Façade" (*Jekyll and Hyde*), 206–7
Fagin (character), 3, 18, 20, 79–107, 113–15, 119, 130, 244n1, 245nn16–17, 245nn22–23
"Fagin's Political School" (*Punch* cartoon by Tenniel), 85, *86*
Fagin the Jew (Eisner), 245n16
Fairfax, Mrs. (character), 218–19
"Fair Harvard" (Gilman), 141
fairy tale, 161
fallen woman character, 195, 197, 258n27
Falsettos (Finn), 168, 201
Family Guy, 79, 230
Famous Players, Lasky Production Company, 185

fantastic fiction, 9, 18, 25–54,122, 239n25
farce, 36–38, 41–42
"Farewell, Good Angel" (*Jane Eyre*), 224
Faust (Goethe), 47
féerie extravaganzas, 26
Felluga, Dino, 226
Felski, Rita, 235n27
female actors playing boys' roles, *84*, 84–85, 154–55, 202
female impersonators, 201–2
femininity, 55–67, 72–78, 99–107, 161–209, 224, 255n24
feminism, 23, 40, 56–77, 161, 214–18, 221, 242n6; first wave, 40, 57, 59–60, 80, 235n20; second wave, 124; third wave, 180
feminist criticism, 33, 59, 64, 75–76, 161–81, 214, 216, 242n6, 243n11, 248n22, 260n4
Fenton, James, 256n2
Ferber, Edna, 29
Fiddler on the Roof (Bock and Harnick, 1964), 71, 97, 106
fidelity theory, 7–9, 234n11
Fields, Joseph, 236n2
Fifty Million Frenchmen (Porter, 1929), 29
Fildes, Samuel Luke, 139–40, 250n10; *Edwin Drood* illustration by, *140*; *Edwin Drood* wrapper (with Charles Collins) by, *143*
film adaptations, 6, 19–20, 23, 36–37, 39, 45, 52, 62–63, 66, 68–70, 79, 82–83, 85–86, 88–89, 91, 93–95, 97–98, 100–101, 109–11, 123, 127–31, 135–37, 141–42, 147–48, 151, 158, 161, 164, 173–74, 184–86, 193, 196–201, 206–7, 210, 218, 234nn10–11, 238n20, 238n22, 239n29, 241n2, 242n6, 243n13, 243nn17–18, 244n7, 245n20, 247n17, 248n23, 248n30, 249n34, 249n37, 249n40, 252n23, 256n3, 258nn25–26, 260n6, 260n8, 260n1.

See also silent film adaptations; television adaptations
"Finer Things, The" (*Jane Eyre*), 219
Fingersmith (Waters, 2002), 256n3
Fings Ain't Wot They Used T'Be (Bart), 90
Finian's Rainbow (Lane and Harburg), 237n12
Finishing the Hat (Sondheim), 9
Finn, William, 168, 201
Finney, Albert, 260n1
Fiorello! (Bock and Harnick), 8
Fisher, Jules, 211
Fitz-Gerald, S. J. Adair, 155
Flaherty, Stephen, 260n1
Flaubert, Gustave, 34
Fleming, Patrick C., 89
Fleming, Victor, 198–99
folk elements, 10, 30, 32, 106, 237n12
Follies (Sondheim and Goldman), 20, 134
Fontaine, Joan, 11, 218
"Food, Glorious Food" (*Oliver!*), 106
food supply 108–31, 248n28. *See also* meat
Forbush, Nellie (character), 241n42
Fordin, Hugh, 74
"Forgiveness" (*Jane Eyre*), 225
"fortunate fall," 254n12
"Forty Minutes for Lunch" (*One Touch of Venus*), 50
Foster, Jodie, 206, 238n20, 242n2
Fouche, Joseph, 247n15
"4'33'"" (Cage), 158
fourth-wall realism, 127, 156, 180, 252n27
Fowles, John, 256n3
Frankenstein (Shelley), 7, 247n11
Freaky Friday (Disney, 2018), 238n20
Freaky Friday (Kitt and Yorkey, 2016), 238n20
Freaky Friday (Nelson, 1976,) 36, 238n20
Freaky Friday (Rodgers, 1972), 36
Freaky Friday (Waters, 2003), 36

Frears, Stephen, 185
freedom, 214–18, 242n6
French Lieutenant's Woman, The (Fowles), 256n3
French Revolution, 128, 184
Freud, Sigmund/Freudian, 48, 119, 129, 148, 183–84, 198
Friedman, Monroe, 123–24
"Friendship" (*DuBarry Was a Lady*), 29
Friml, Rudolf, 27
From Hell (Albert and Allen Hughes), 129
Frozen (Disney), 254n10
Fry, Jud (character), 30, 50
Fuller, Larry, 201, 203–4, 258n31

Gacy, John Wayne, 206
Gainsborough, Thomas, 46
Gainsbourg, Charlotte, 218
Galatea myth, 37–39, 41, 43–44, 47
Galatea, or Pygmalion Re-Versed (Stephens, Webster, and Lutz), 39
Gamerman, Amy, 214
Gänzl, Kurt, 36
Gardner, Ava, 240n39
Garland, Judy, 90
Garlick, Barbara, 253n2
Gaskell, Elizabeth, 34
Gaugin, Paul, 45
Gay, John, 246n6
Geduld, Harry M., 257n9
Geffen, David, 129
gender, 55–78, 80, 99–107, 136, 161–81, 260n9; bending, 22, 259n32; coding, 174–78; dichotomy, 165, 190, 257n12; dynamics, 189; fluidity, 201; as performative/performance, 2, 22–23, 58, 161–209, 253n5, 254n6, 255n19; roles, 57–67, 99–107, 222, 224, 257n12. *See also* sexual politics
Genette, Gerard, 259–60n3
Gentleman's Agreement (Kazan), 45
Gentleman's Guide to Love and Murder, A (Freedman and Lutvak), 257n16

George, Susan, 199
Gerould, Daniel, 184
Gershwin, George, 13, 27–29, 91
Gershwin, Ira, 29, 91
"Getting to Know You" (*The King and I*), 66
Gibson, John, 39–43, 240n36
Gilbert, Sandra, 253n2
Gilbert, W. S., 27, 38–39, 41, 55, 152, 240n31
Gilman, Rev. Samuel, 141
Gina (character,) 196, 198
Gingrich, Newt, 136, 257n8
Girl in Pink Tights, The (Romberg and Robin), 27, 236n2
Gissing, George, 33, 180
"Give My Regards to Broadway" (*Little Johnny Jones*), 27
Glassmeyer, Danielle, 56
Glavin, John, 152–53
Glee (Fox), 203
Gluck, Christoph Willibald, 14, 234n15
Goblin Market (Pen and Harmon, 1985), 4, 21, 161–81, 253nn1–3
Goblin Market (Rossetti, 1859), 4, 161–81, 253n2, 254n7, 254n10, 254n12, 255nn16–17; illustrations of, 22, 255n16
God, 221–26; sexual union with, 255n23
Goddess of Love (Drake) 239n22
Goethe, Johann Wolfgang von, 47
Golden Age of Broadway, the, 4, 134, 233n3
Golden Girls, The, 219, 260n7
Gollum (character), 259n34
Golub, Ellen, 253n2
governess/teacher as character, 55–78, 210–26
"Good 'N' Evil" (*Jekyll and Hyde*), 202–3, 258n31
Gordon, Joanne, 248n21
Gordon, Paul, 23, 210, 259n2
Gothic, 23, 117, 129, 188, 200, 214, 221–26, 257n14

Gottlieb, Jack, 92
Grainger, Edmund, 251n18
Grand Guignol, 127–28, 248n33
Grant, Amy, 210
Grant, Mark 44, 50
Grant, Molly (character), 48, 237n11
Grapes of Wrath, The (Steinbeck), 31
Graves, C., 239n25
"Graveyard, The" (*Jane Eyre*), 259n3
Gray, Dorian (character), 193, 196
Gray, Steven, 253n3
"Great Exhibition, The" (*Punch* cartoon by Leach), 40
Great Expectations (BBC, 1981), 135
Great Expectations (Disney, 1989), 135
Great Expectations (Dickens, 1861), 23, 135, 248n29
Great Expectations: The Untold Story (Australian Broadcasting Company, 1987), 249n4
Greek and Roman mythology, 37–39, 41, 43–44, 47, 92, 104, 239n24, 240n31, 240n37, 247n15
Greek Slave (Powers, 1844), 240n36
Green, Kathe, 85
Green, Roger Lancelyn, 37, 239n25
Green, Stanley, 87
Greenberg, Stanley, 247n17
"Green Finch and Linnet Bird" (*Sweeney Todd*), 121
Grewgious, Hiram (character), 250n6
Griffith, D. W., 17, 235n22
Grossman, Jonathan, 103
Grossmith, Weedon, 238n21
Gubar, Susan, 253n2
Guest, Al, 135
Guettel, Adam, 238n20
Guinness, Alec, 20, 85–86, 94–95, 97–98
Gussow, Mel, 253n3
Guthrie, Thomas Anstey. *See* Anstey, F.

Hadley, Elaine, 136, 212
Hager, Kelly, 75

Hakim, Ali (character), 30
Half a Sixpence (Cross), 8
Hamburger, Richard, 254n11
Hamelin: A Musical Tale from Rats to Riches (Jarboe and Shield), 253n3
Hamilton (Miranda, 2015), 2, 7, 228–31, 233n1, 261n5
Hamilton, Alexander, 7, 229
Hamilton, Richard Winter, 248n27
Hamlet (Shakespeare), 46, 67
Hammerstein, Dorothy, 74, 241n2
Hammerstein, Oscar, 4, 12, 14, 19, 29–32, 50–80, 87, 89, 91, 202, 233nn3–4, 241nn1–22
Hampshire, Susan, 199
Hanks, Tom, 201
Hansberry, Lorraine, 14
Harburg, E. Y., 237n12
Hard Times (Dickens, 1854), 15, 34, 117, 137
Hardy, Thomas, 34
harem, 55–77, 201, 242n6, 242n8, 260n11
Harlot's Progress, A (Hogarth, 1732), 102
Harmon, Peggy, 4, 21, 161–81
Harris, Barbara, 238n20
Harris, J. J., 124
Harris, Lucy (character), 17, 199–201, 203, 206, 256n4, 258n27
Harrison, Harry, 247n17
Harrison, Rex, 241n2
Hart, Charles, 256n2
Hart, Gary, 249n39
Hart, Lorenz, 12, 29–32, 141, 236n3, 250n11
Hasselhoff, David, 192, 204, 257n5
Hatch, Rodney (character), 45, 47–48, 50–52
Haynes sisters (characters), 174
Hazleton, Frederick, 247n20
Heart of Darkness (Conrad), 237n16
"Heaven Hop" (*Paris*), 29

Hegeman, Susan, 14–15
Heilman, Robert, 226
helicopter moment, 191
Hellman, Lillian, 14
Helsinger, Elizabeth, 253n2
Heneker, David, 244n15
Hepworth, Cecil, 36
heritage film and television, 10–12, 15, 136, 234n16
Herman, Jerry, 168
Hero and Leander myth, 38
heteronormativity: Hollywood's normalization, of 11; subversion of, 11–12
Hewison, Robert, 10–11, 136
Heyward, Dorothy, 236n7
Heyward, DuBose, 236n7
Higgins, Henry (character), 164, 253n4
high art/high culture. *See* highbrow culture
highbrow culture, 12, 15–16, 25–54, 235n20
"Hiram Powers' 'Greek Slave'" (E. B. Browning, 1851), 240n36
Hirsch, David A., 27, 102
Hirschhorn, Joel, 228
Hischak, Thomas, 87
Hobart, Rose, 198, 200
Hobson, Valerie, 147
Hogarth, William, 102
Hollingshead, John, 240n31
Holloway, Stanley, 111, 199, 247n13
Holmes, Rupert, 3, 21, 132–60, 163–64, 250n12, 251n15, 251–52n20, 252n24
Holocaust, the, 57, 80, 86, 96
Holt, Terrence, 253n2, 255n24
Holzman, Winnie, 228
homoeroticism, 22, 161–81, 202
homosexuality, 168, 201; acceptance of, 201
Hope, Anthony (character), 121
Hope-Wallace, Philip, 93
Hopkins, Anthony, 206
Hopkins, Miriam, 197–98

horror film/horror genre, 127–29, 246n5, 248n26
Hoskins, Vicki, 152
Houghton, Walter E., 35
Howard, Jane, 124
Hughes, Albert and Allen, 129
Hugo, Victor, 184, 256n2
Hurst, Brandon, 196
Hutcheon, Linda, 9, 80
Hyde, Edward (character), 22–23, 182–209, 251n20, 257n5, 257n14, 258nn22–23, 258n25
Hyde, Henry, 257n8

"I'd Do Anything" (*Oliver!*), 102, 119–20
identity performance, 187, 191–95, 257n15
"I'm a Stranger Here Myself" (*One Touch of Venus*), 47–48, 50
imperialism. *See* colonialism/imperialism
Importance of Being Earnest, The (Wilde), 46–47
incest, 21, 161, 173–74
individualism, 214, 217
industrial revolution, brutality of, 116–17, 127, 137
Ingestrie, Mark (character), 112–13, 115, 117, 121
Ingram, Blanche (character), 214, 218–20, 260n6
"In His Eyes" (*Jekyll and Hyde*), 200
integrated cast, 73, 236n8
integrated musicals, 4, 8, 12, 30–31, 48, 50–54, 80, 87, 233n4
integration, 57–58
Intolerance (Griffith), 235n22
invert, 201. *See also* homosexuality
Irving, Henry, 187, 195, 257n10
Iseri, Michiko, 69
"I Shall Scream" (*Oliver!*), 118
Isherwood, Charles, 205
Islam, 53, 60

Isobel (character), 199
"It's a Fine Life" (*Oliver!*), 100–101, 199
"I've Grown Accustomed to Her Face" (*My Fair Lady*), 164
Ives, Charles, 251n17
Ivy (character), 197–98, 203

Jack Maggs (Carey), 256n3
Jack Sheppard (Ainsworth), 108
Jackson, Peter, 259n34
Jack the Ripper, 52, 128, 185–86, 191–95, 198, 201, 205, 207–9, 257n18
Jacobson, Wendy S., 251n20
James, Henry, 34, 237n16
Jane Eyre (Brontë, 1847), 7, 23, 63, 160, 210–26, 235n28, 259n1, 260n4, 260nn9–10, 260nn12–13
Jane Eyre (Brougham, 1849), 223
Jane Eyre (Marston, 2016), 236n33
Jane Eyre (Stevens, 1943), 11, 218
Jane Eyre (Williams, 1971), 236n33
Jane Eyre (Zeffirelli, 1996), 7, 218, 260n6
Jane Eyre or the Secrets of Thornfield Manor (Courtney, 1848), 210, 223
Jane Eyre: The Musical (Caird and Gordon, 2000), 4, 11, 23, 210–26, 228, 234n12, 259n2; playbill, *213*
Jane Eyre: The Musical (Kilpatrick, Thompson-Duvall, and Skousen, 2000), 259n2
Jane Eyre: The Musical (Stevens, Shaper, and Lewis, 1961), 259n2
Jarboe, Richard, 253n3
Jasper, John (character), 21, 133–34, 137–42, 144–51, 153, 155, 158–59, 197, 249n6, 250n7, 250n9, 250n12, 251n14, 251n20, 252n28
"Jasper's Vision" (*Drood*), 134, 148–51
jazz, 9, 13, 27–28, 50
Jekyll, Henry (character), 22, 182–209, 251–52n20, 257n5, 257n18; transformation into Hyde, 194–95, 203–5, 207–8

Jekyll and Hyde: The Musical (Wildhorn and Bricusse, 1997), 2, 4, 8, 17, 22–23, 75, 182–209, 211–13, 218, 228, 234n12, 256n4, 257n5, 258n19, 258n31, 259n32; playbill, *186*
Jessy Ashton; or, The Adventures of a Barmaid (Young), 128
Jesus Christ Superstar (Lloyd Webber and Rice), 87, 183
Jewish: actors, 70, 92; audiences, 6, 82; authors, 82, 90–92, 245n16; characters, 20, 71, 79–107; composers, 90–92; Jewish-American experience, 70–71; liturgical and secular music, 96; politicians, 85–86
Jewishness, 3, 20, 57, 71, 79–107, 245n19
Jew of Malta, The (Marlowe,) 93
John, Juliet, 94–95
"Johnny One Note" (*Babes in Arms*), 141, 250n11
Johnson, Helen, 144
Jones, Bill T., 71
Jones, Davy, 244n7
Jones, John Bush, 211, 246n4
Jones, Maria B., 251n14
Jones, Quincy, 210
Joseph, Gerhard, 94
Jowitt, Deborah, 69
justice, social and economic, 130–31, 136, 184

Kabuki drama, 69
Kaplan, Caren, 68, 242n6
Kaufman, George S., 236n4
Kaye, Danny, 174
Kazan, Elia, 45, 50, 53, 236n11
Kean, Charles, 152–53
Keats, John, 34, 240n37, 240n41
Keckley, Elizabeth, 243n16
Kelly, Mary Jane, 191
Kenny, Sean, 88
Kern, Jerome, 29, 233nn3–4
Kerr, Deborah, 58
keynote, 137–38, 140, 150, 157–60

Kikuchi, Yuriko, 69
Kilpatrick, Bill, 259n2
King, Bradley, 251n18
King, Francis, 184
King, George, 123, 129
King and I, The (Lang, 1956), 58, 243n17
King and I, The (Rich, 1999), 242n2
King and I, The (Rodgers and Hammerstein, 1951), 2, 4, 19, 23–24, 35, 53–80, 87, 132, 211, 214, 217, 222, 224, 228, 230, 241n44, 241nn1–2, 243n17; revivals of, 55–56
King of Siam. *See* Mongkut, King
Kingsley, Charles, 34
Kingsley, Henry, 34
Kingsley, Mary, 59
Kirk, Roger, 242n2
Kissell, Howard, 183–84
Kiss Me Kate (Porter), 9, 240n40
Kitt, Tom, 238n20
Klausner, Terri, 253n1
Klean, Sonn, 65, 72
Klein, Christina, 56, 73–74
klezmer music and instrumentation, 20, 96
Knapp, Raymond, 26–27, 29
Knickerbocker Holiday (Weill and Anderson), 28
Knopflmacher, U. C., 168
Koppelberg (Gray and Brooke), 253n3
Kosminsky, Peter, 7
Kramer, Gloria (character), 47–48, 52
Kramer, Larry, 181
Kretzmer, Herbert, 256n2
Krieger, Barbara Zinn, 253n1
Kurnick, David, 18, 138
Kushner, Tony, 14, 168, 201

LaBelle, Patti, 210
La Biche au Bois, 26
La Cage aux Folles (Herman), 168
Lady in the Dark (Weill and Gershwin), 237n11
"Lady or the Tiger?, The" (Stockton), 9

Laemmle, Carl, Jr., 251n18
LaGuardia, Fiorello, 8
Laird, Paul F., 32
"Lamia" (Keats, 1819), 240n37
Landless, Helena (character), 139–47, 150, 250n12, 251n20, 253n28
Landless, Neville (character), 139–40, 142–43, 146–47, 150, 152, 250n12, 251n14
Landon, Brooks, 38
Landon, Margaret, 241n2
Lane, Anthony, 182
Lane, Burton, 237n12
Lang, Andrew, 245n18
Lang, Walter, 58
Langtry, Lillie, 41–43
Lansbury, Angela, 118, 129, 245n1
Larry the Lobster, 153
La Strada (Bart), 90, 92
"Last Supper at Uncle Tom's Cabin/The Promised Land" (Jones), 71
La Traviata (Verdi), 13
Laubenstein, Linda, 181
Laura (character), 21–22, 162–81, 254n9, 254n12, 255n15, 256n24
Laurence, Paula, 236n11
"Laurey Makes Up Her Mind" (*Oklahoma!*), 32, 149
"La Vénus d'Ille" (Mérrimée), 239n27
La Verne, Julie (character), 30
Lawrence, Gertrude, 58, 241n2
Lanyon, Dr. (character), 189, 194, 207
Lanyon, Mrs. (character), 188, 197
Leach, John, 40; *Punch* cartoon by, *40*
Lean, David, 82, 85, 93–95
Leavis, F. R., 15, 34–35
Ledger, Sally, 117
Leeford, Edward "Monks" (character), 94
Le Fantôme de l'Opéra (Leroux), 256n2
Lehár, Franz, 27
Lehman, Peter, 259n32
Leitch, Thomas, 3, 196
LeNeve, Ethyl, 52

Leonowens, Anna, 19, 55–78, 86, 241n2, 242n3, 242nn6–8, 243n11, 243n19
Lerner, Alan Jay, 91–92, 164, 237n12
Leroux, Gaston, 256n2
Les Misérables (Hugo, 1862), 184, 256n2
Les Misérables (Schönberg, Boublil, and Natel, 1980), 22, 88, 182, 184, 210–11, 256n2
Lester, Marc, 85
"Let's Misbehave" (*Paris*), 29
"Let's Step Out" (*Fifty Million Frenchmen*), 29
Levine, Caroline, 156
Levine, George, 38
Lewes, George Henry, 212
Lewinsky, Monica, 257n8
Lewis, C. S., 38, 239n25
Lewis, Leopold, 106
Lewis, Ron Harley, 259n2
Lewis, Wyndham, 33
Liberace, Władziu Valentino, 90
Liberatori, Victoria J., 254n14
liberty, 215–17, 221, 242n6, 243n14. *See also* freedom
Light, Derry, 254n9
Light in the Piazza (Lucas and Guettel), 238n20
Li'l Emily (character), 197
Lincoln, Abraham, 68
Lion King, The (Elton John and Rice), 202, 235n25
Little Dorrit (Dickens, 1855–57), 117, 247n20
Little Dorrit (Edzard, 1987), 135
Little Johnny Jones (Cohan), 27, 55
Little Mermaid, The (Disney), 89
Little Night Music, A (Sondheim and Wheeler), 233n3
"Little Priest, A" (*Sweeney Todd*), 126, 131
Little Shop of Horrors (Geffen), 129
Little Women (Alcott,) 63
Litvak, Joe, 79
Livingston, Robert, 257n8

Lizzie (character), 21–22, 162–81, 254n9, 254n12, 255n15, 255n24
Llana, Jose, 243n17
Lloyd, Edward, 110–11, 129, 246n10
Lloyd, Frank, 82, 85
Lloyd Webber, Andrew, 10, 87–88, 135, 163, 210–12, 228, 256n2
Loesser, Frank, 91
Loewe, Frederick, 91–92, 164, 237n12
Lohan, Lindsay, 36
London International Exhibition (1862), 39, 41–42
Long, Heather, 257n5
Long Retrospect, A (Anstey), 38
Look Back in Anger (Osborn, 1956), 245n15
Lord of the Rings, The: The Two Towers (Jackson, 2002), 259n34
Lost (Stephens), 21, 133–34, 141–45, 147–48, 153–54
Lott, Emmeline, 242n8
love-interest character, 21, 121, 195–97, 258n22
Lovett, Mrs. Nellie (character), 20, 88, 112–13, 117–31, 206, 241n44, 245n1, 246n2, 248n22
lowbrow culture, 34, 46, 128–29, 239n24
Lowood Academy, 23, 210, 216–18
Lucas, E. V., 37
Luhr, William, 259n32
Lumière brothers, 82
Lun Tha (character), 62, 68, 243n17
Lupin, Reverend Mr. (character), 116
LuPone, Patti, 88
Lutz, Wilhelm Meyer, 39, 239n30
Lynn, Jonathan, 153

MacDonald, Dwight, 5, 12–14
Macfarren, George, 111, 246n10
MacIntosh, Blanche, 37
Macintosh, Cameron, 90, 97, 210
MacIntyre, Marguerite, 220
Mack, Robert, 116, 246n10, 247n18
Mackintosh, Laird, 256n4
mad cow disease, 130
"Madhouse Cells" (R. Browning, "Porphyria's Lover"), 257n17
Maggie May (Bart), 90
Maguire, Gregory, 228
Magwitch (character), 248n29
male impersonators, 155, 202
Malik, Rachel, 81
Malkovich, John, 185
Mamet, David, 14
Mamoulian, Rouben, 197, 200
"Man Could Go Quite Mad, A" (*Drood*), 151
Mank, Gregory, 198
Mannequin (Gottlieb), 52
Man of La Mancha (Leigh and Darion), 252n26
Man of No Importance, A (Flaherty, Ahrens, and McNally, 2002), 228, 260n1
Man of No Importance, A (Krishnamma, 1994), 260n1
Mansfield, Martha, 196
Mansfield, Richard, 23, 187–93, 198, 200, 203–4, 207–8, 257n11, 258n21, 258n23
Mapplethorpe, Robert, 162
March, Fredric, 197
Marcus, Steven, 96
Margaret, Princess, 90
Margolyes, Miriam, 228
Marlowe, Christopher, 93
Maroulis, Constantine, 205, 207–8, 256n4
marriage, 60, 101, 121, 134, 152, 217, 219–20, 235n20; failed marriage plot, 75, 189, 224; feminist critique of, 63–76; interracial, 30, 58, 73–74, 143–44, 147–48
Marryat, Frederick, 34
Mary Reilly (Frears, 1995), 185
Mary Reilly (Martin, 1990), 185
Mary Shelley's Frankenstein (Branagh), 7

Marsten, Cathy, 236n33
Martin, Mary, 47, 51, 85, 237n11, 240–41n42
Martin, Valerie, 185
Martin Chuzzlewit (Dickens), 116
Martineau, Harriet, 59
Martucci, Vinnie, 252n23
masculinity, 161–209, 257n14
Mason, Bertha (character), 160, 214, 218–20
Massey, Doreen, 78
Matisse, Henri, 45–46
Maugham, Somerset, 198
Mayer, David, 189
Mayer, Jed, 253n2
Maylie, Rose (character), 22, 75, 93, 99–100, 106–7, 119, 197
Mazeppa (Byron), 254n13
McClanahan, Rue, 260n7
McClintock, Anne, 60
McConachie, Bruce, 241n1
McDonalds, 124–25
McFarlane, Brian, 2
McKibben, Gordon, 122–23
McLain, Curly (character), 30, 50, 236n10
McMillin, Scott, 3, 233n2
McNally, Terrence, 228, 260n1
McNulty, Charles, 109, 246n3
McPherson, Elle, 260n6
McWilliam, Robin, 184
meat, 20, 123–26, 130, 248n28; tainted, 130, 248n28
Medici Venus (Cleomenes, 1st century BCE), 240n36
megamusical, 4–5, 22, 182–87, 191, 198, 202–3, 206, 211–12, 256n1
Meisel, Martin, 85
melodrama, 3–5, 19, 21–22, 26–27, 29, 41, 43, 69–70, 81–85, 91, 106, 108, 110–11, 115–17, 121–22, 126–31, 133–34, 141–42, 145, 154, 182–210, 212, 228, 233n4, 244n14, 245n1, 247n12, 247n18, 249n34, 257n6, 259n1

Menke, Richard, 253n2
Menken, Adah, 254n13
Menken, Alan, 89, 205, 235n25, 244n9
Merchant, Peter, 238n21, 239nn28–29
Merchant of Venice, The (Shakespeare), 93
Mermin, Dorothy, 253n2
Merrick, David, 87, 96, 244n8
Mérrimée, Prosper, 239n27
Merry Widow, The (Lehár), 27
meta-text/meta-textuality, 3, 136
meta-theatricality, 136, 151–60, 230
Meyer, Susan, 260n9
Michener, James, 74
Michie, Elsie, 252n21, 252n23
Michie, Helena, 171, 253n2
midcult, 5. *See also* middlebrow culture.
"Middlebrow" (Woolf), 15, 18, 25, 33–54
middlebrow culture, 5–7, 12–16, 25–54, 91, 117, 129, 180, 211–12, 229–30
middle class, 10–15, 38, 46, 58, 91, 100, 104, 117–18, 189, 234n19, 235n20
Midler, Bette, 210
Mielziner, Jo, 241–42n2
Mighall, Robert, 200–201
Millais, John Everett, 46
Miller, Edmund, 153, 156
Miller, J. Hillis, 81, 245n22
Milligan, Barry, 197
minstrelsy/minstrel shows, 19, 27, 29, 70, 252n25
Miranda, Lin-Manuel, 2, 7, 228–29, 261n5
miscegenation, 29, 73. *See also* marriage: interracial
Miss Prism. *See* Prism, Letitia (character)
Miss Saigon (Schönberg, Boublil, and Maltby), 182, 191, 210, 230
Modernism, 5, 15, 32–33, 45–48, 55; rejection of Victorians, 18, 33–36, 45–48, 76
Moers, Ellen, 253n2

Mondale, Walter, 249n39
Mongkut, King, 56, 58–59, 68–69, 71, 73, 78, 243n17
Monks character. *See* Leeford, Edward "Monks" (character)
Monro, Matt, 90
Montgomery, Douglas, 147
Moody, Ron, 92, 96–97, 105
"Moonfall" (*Drood*), 146, 173, 250n12
Moonstone, The (Collins), 159
Moore, Dickie, 244n6
Moore, Thomas, 141
Mordden, Ethan, 47, 87
Moreno, Rita, 243n17
Morgan, Susan, 58–59
Morissette, Alanis, 211
Morley, Malcolm, 247n12
Morris, Jane, 39
Morris, William, 39
Morrison, Ann, 253n1
Most, Andrea, 57, 70–71, 74
Mother Courage (character), 248n22
Motion Picture Production Code, 198
murder/murderers, 17, 20, 23, 43, 50, 52, 79–82, 89, 94, 99, 101, 105, 108–32, 146–48, 150–52, 155–59, 185–98, 205–9, 246n5, 247n15, 248n30, 251n20, 252n27, 258n25
"Murder, Murder" (*Jekyll and Hyde*), 205–6
Murder on the Orient Express (Christie), 155–56
Murphy, Donna, 242n2
Murphy, Eddie, 153
Murphy, Jacqueline Shea, 72
Murphy, Marguerite, 239n27
musical comedy, 4–5, 26–32, 38, 48, 51–52, 54, 174; definition of, 28–29; revivals of, 29
musicality, 21, 134, 137, 163, 219–20
musicalizing, 9–10
music hall, Victorian, 21, 41, 91, 133, 154–60, 197, 200, 202
"My Country 'Tis of Thee" (Smith), 217

"My Heart Belongs to Daddy" (*Leave It to Me!*), 241n42
My Fair Lady (Lerner and Loewe), 92, 104, 164
mystery genre, 134, 155–56
Mystery of Edwin Drood, The (Dickens, 1870), 3, 17, 21, 54, 132–60, *140*, *143*, 197, 212, 249n3, 250n10, 251n20
Mystery of Edwin Drood, The (Holmes). *See Drood* (Holmes, 1985)
Mystery of Edwin Drood, The (Lawrence, 2012), 137, 141–42, 149
Mystery of Edwin Drood, The (MacDermott, 1872), 154–55
Mystery of Edwin Drood, The (Stephens, 1871), 21, 133–34, 141–45, 147–48, 251n17
Mystery of Edwin Drood (Walker, 1935), 137, 141–42, 147–48, 151, 251n18
Mystery of Edwin Drood, mock trials, 153
"Myth That Threatens America, The" (Hammerstein), 73

Naden, Corrine, 233n3
Naldi, Nita, 186, 196
Napier, John, 210–11
Napolitano, Marc, 89, 91, 96, 160, 259n3
Naremore, Paul, 7
Nash, Ogden, 9, 18–19, 24–26, 32, 35–36, 44–55, 79–80, 86, 87, 149, 211
Natel, Jean-Marc, 256n2
Nathan, John, 96
National Endowment for the Arts, 162
Neo-Victorian fiction, 3, 182, 187, 206, 211, 256n3
Nesvet, Rebecca, 247n10
Neville, Henry, 251n14
Newgate novel, 81, 106, 108, 111, 113
Newley, Anthony, 90
Newsies (Menken and Feldman), 205, 252n26
New Yorkers, The (Porter), 29

New York Shakespeare Festival, 249n1, 252n23
Next to Normal (Yorkey and Kitt), 238n20
Nicholas Nickleby (Dickens, 1838–39), 111
Nicholas Nickleby (Royal Shakespeare Company, 1980–81), 116–17, 135, 152
Nichols, Lewis, 51
Nichols, Mary Ann, 191
Nickelas Nicklebery (Prest, 1839), 111
"Night and Love" (Bulwer-Lytton), 144
Night Governess, The (Pen), 180
Nightingale, Florence, 59
Night of January 16th (Rand), 252n22
Nixon, Richard, resignation of, 122
Noh drama, 69
Normal Heart, The (Kramer), 181
Norman, Monty, 244n15
Norton, Caroline, 141, 233n3
"Not While I'm Around" (*Sweeney Todd*), 119, 129
novel, privileging of in Victorian literary studies, 5
nudity on stage/appearance of nudity on stage, 26–27, 170–71, 240–41n42, 254n13
Nunn, Trevor, 256n2
Nutcracker, The (Tchaikovsky), 235n25
Nutting, Miss (character), 154–55, 164, 251n15

Oakley, Annie (character), 256n1
Oakley, Johanna (character), 112, 115–17, 126–27, 130, 248n22, 249n40
Ockrent, Mike, 235n25
"Ode to the West Wind" (Shelley), 253n31
"Odd Women" (*The Night Governess*), 180
Odd Women, The (Gissing), 180
"Ode on a Grecian Urn" (Keats), 240n41
Oedipal fantasy, 119–20, 129

"Of Queens' Gardens" (Ruskin), 74
Of Thee I Sing (George and Ira Gershwin), 28, 236n4
O'Hara, Kelli, 242n2
O'Hara, Scarlett (character), 219
"Oh, What a Beautiful Mornin'" (*Oklahoma!*), 30
Oklahoma! (Rodgers and Hammerstein), 4, 12, 26, 29–32, 50–52, 55, 75, 149, 233n4
Okonedo, Sophie, 245n20
Old Beggar Woman (character). *See* Harris, Lucy (character)
Old Curiosity Shop, The (Dickens), 115
"Old Fashioned Wedding, An" (*Annie Get Your Gun*), 256n1
Old Possum's Book of Practical Cats (Eliot), 10, 135, 163
Oliver! (Bart, 1968), 3–4, 8–9, 17–20, 79–107, 109–10, 113–14, 118–20, 132, 136, 169, 198–200, 218, 224, 230, 235n24, 244n7, 244nn9–10, 245n15, 245n20, 259n2; playbill from Baton Rouge Little Theater revival, *98*
Oliver! A Dickensian Musical (Napolitano, 2014), 89, 91
Oliver & Company (Disney, 1988), 88–89, 244n12, 245n20
Oliver Twiss (Prest, 1838), 111
Oliver Twist (BBC, 2008), 245n20
Oliver Twist (Carr, 1905), 83; playbill, *83*
Oliver Twist (Cowan, 1933), 244n6
Oliver Twist (Dickens, 1837–39), 3, 8–9, 17–20, 79–107, 109–10, 113–14, 118–20, 132, 136, 169, 198–200, 218, 224, 230, 235n24, 244n7, 244nn9–10, 245n22, 259n2
Oliver Twist (Donner, 1982), 135
Oliver Twist (Lean, 1948), 82, 85, 93–95
Oliver Twist (Lloyd, 1922), 82, 85
Oliver Twist (Young, 1916), 84
Oliver Twist: A Serio-Comic Burletta (Almar, 1838), 81–82

Oliver Twist, or, The Parish Boy's Progress (Barnett, 1838), 82, 84
"Ol' Man River" (*Show Boat*), 30
Once upon a Mattress (Rodgers and Barer, 1959), 238n20
Ondrejka, Malia, 254n9
O'Neill, Rebecca Gorman, 244n11
One Thousand and One Nights. See *Arabian Nights*
"One Touch of Venus" (*One Touch of Venus*), 48, 240n42
One Touch of Venus (Weill and Nash, 1948), 4, 9, 18–19, 24–55, 79–80, 86–87, 149, 211, 236n11, 238n22, 240n39
One Touch of Venus (Seiter, 1948), 52, 240n39
On the Town (Bernstein, Comden, and Green), 149
On Your Toes (Rodgers and Hart), 31–32, 236n3
"Oom-Pah-Pah" (*Oliver!*), 100–102, 200
opera, 6–10, 14, 21, 29, 41, 73, 108, 126, 128–29, 182, 210, 230, 233n2, 234n15, 246n2, 253n3
operetta, 27–29, 53, 55; Continental dominance of, 53, 55
opium, 134, 137–38, 146–51, 158, 196–97
opium dream ballet. See "Jasper's Vision" (*Drood*)
Oprah, 200
Orientalism, 46, 53, 56–77, 146–49, 251n20
"Orphan, The" (*Jane Eyre*), 217–18
orphans, 94, 118–19, 129, 139, 142–47, 217, 259n3
Osborn, John, 244–45n15
Oscars, 201, 241n2, 243n17, 244n7
"Out on a Limerick" (*Drood*), 152

Pace, Eric, 87
Pal Joey (Rodgers and Hart, 1940), 12, 233n3

Palmer, Beth, 256n3
Pan, Peter (character), 241n42
pantomime, 68, 84, 134, 137, 148–50, 154, 202
pants roles, 175–76
Panyarachun, Anand, 243n22
Papp, Joseph, 132, 135, 181
Paradise Lost (Milton), 255n15
Paris (Porter), 29
Park, Hyungji, 147
Pascal, Julia, 98
Pater, Walter, 9
Patmore, Coventry, 33, 75
Patten, Robert, 81
pedophilia, 102, 199
Peller, Clara, 124–25
Pen, Polly, 21–22, 161–81
Pence, Mike, 228–29
Penny Pickwick, The (Prest), 111
Perelman, S. J., 9, 18–19, 32, 35–36, 44–55
performativity, 136; racial, 57, 68; in Victorian novels, 138. *See also* cross-gender performance/performativity
Peter Pan (Barrie), 84–85
Phantom of the Opera (Lloyd Webber and Hart), 184, 234n13
Philadelphia (Demme), 201
Philips, Lou Diamond, 243n17
Phillips, Robin, 258n31
Picasso, Pablo, 45
Pickwick (Ornadel, 1965), 244n9
Pickwick Papers, The (BBC, 1985), 135
Pickwick Papers, The (Dickens, 1836), 16–17, 111, 116, 247n12, 258n29
Picture of Dorian Gray, The (Wilde), 3, 128, 185–86, 193, 195–97, 205
Pied Piper of Hamelin, The (R. Browning), 253n3
Pilgrim's Progress, A (Bunyan), 102
Pinky (Kazan, 1949), 45
Pinky (Seiter, 1948), 45
Pirates of the Caribbean trilogy, 129

Pitt, George Dibdin, 43, 110–11, 122–23, 129, 245n1, 247n12, 247n18, 248n20, 249n34
Pizzi, Joel, 258n31
Playboy, 22, 255n16
play-within-a-play device, 67–72, 133, 136, 152, 154
Pleon, Harry, 36
poetry, 8, 10, 21, 81, 135, 162–64, 253n31, 253n3
Pointillist, 85, 211–12
Poirot, Hercule (character), 155–56
polygamy, 60, 78, 243n10
polyphony, 230
Poole (character), 189, 199
Poore, Benjamin, 256n3
Porgy (Heyward, 1927), 236n7
Porgy and Bess (Gershwin, Gershwin, and Heyward, 1935), 236n7
"Porphyria's Lover" (R. Browning). *See* "Madhouse Cells" (R. Browning, "Porphyria's Lover")
Porter, Cole, 9, 28–29, 240n40, 241n42
Porter, Emma (character), 258n29
Possession (Byatt), 256n3
postcolonial criticism, 59–60, 137, 249n3
Pound, Ezra, 33
poverty, 17, 89–91, 94, 105, 115, 117, 120, 131, 184, 197, 222–23
Powers, Hiram, 240n36
Poynter, Agnes, 39
Poynter, Edward, 39
Pratt, Mary Louise, 60
Pre-Raphaelite artists, 39
Prest, Thomas Peckett, 20, 110–11, 246n10
Preston, Robert, 259n32
Prince, Harold, 17, 109, 127, 245n1
Principal Boy role, female actor in, 154, 202
Prism, Letitia (character), 46–47
Procne, myth of, 247n15
Producers, The (Brooks), 96

"Professions for Women" (Woolf), 33, 76
"Proposal, The" (*Jane Eyre*), 223–24
prostitutes as characters, 17, 22, 52, 77, 90, 94, 99–102, 195, 197–200, 248n30, 258n22, 258n27
Pryce, Jonathan, 96–97
Puffer, Princess (character), 137, 150, 155–56, 250n6
Pulitzer Prize, 14, 28, 31, 168, 201, 236n4, 238n20
Pygmalion (Shaw), 92, 104, 164, 253n4
Pygmalion and Galatea (Gilbert), 38–39
Pygmalion myth, 37–39, 41, 43–44, 92, 104, 240n37

queerness, 102, 245n17
Quilp (character), 200, 115

race, 42–43, 45, 57–78, 93, 144, 220–21, 240n36, 241n1, 252n20, 260n9; class, racialization of/racial passing, 29, 45, 58, 67–72, 242n3; racial performativity, 57
racism, 29, 45, 57, 73–74, 79–102, 235n22, 241n1, 242n6. *See also* anti-Semitism; xenophobia
Radway, Janice, 15, 212
Ragg, Tobias (character), 112–14, 117–20, 128–29
ragtime, 28–29
Ralph, Sheryl Lee, 245n20
Rand, Ayn, 252n22
Rastogi, Pallavi, 60
rape, 125, 166, 175–81, 197, 241n44
Rappoport, Jill, 253n2
Reade, Charles, 34
Reagan-era United States, 135–36
realism, 38, 169, 244n15
Redgrave, Michael, 199
Red, Hot, and Blue (Porter), 29
Reed, Carol, 94, 244n7, 245n20
Reed, Mrs. (character), 221

Rembrandt (Rembrandt Harmenszoon van Rijn), 46, 220
Renoir, Pierre-Auguste, 46
retrospective narrator, 214–15
revenge, 20, 47, 108, 116, 119, 125, 130–31, 207
"Reviewing the Situation" (*Oliver!*), 96, 103–4, 106
Revill, Clive, 96–97
revue, 16–18, 27–28, 134, 236n8
Rhapsody in Blue (Gershwin), 13
Rhys, Jean, 23, 160, 220, 256n3
Rich, Adrienne, 260n4
Richard, Don, 214
Richards, Cliff, 90
Richards, Jeffrey, 129
Rigby, Cathy, 85
Rigby, Elizabeth, 222
ring placed on wrong finger trope, 38, 239n22, 239n27
Rittman, Trude, 70
Rivas, Carlos, 243n17
Rivers, St. John (character), 221, 224, 225
Road Show (Sondheim and Weidman), 1
Robbins, Jerome, 19, 66, 68–71
Roberts, Julia, 185
Robertson, John S., 3, 185–86, 196–97, 207
Robin, Leo, 236n2
Robin Hood (character), 90–91
Robinson, Smokey, 210
Robinson, Tony, 244n7
Rochester, Edward Fairfax (character), 24, 210–12, 219–26, 243n12, 260n11
Rocky Horror Picture Show (Sharman and O'Brien), 129, 234n10
Rodeo (Copland), 32
Rodgers, Dorothy, 241n2
Rodgers, Mary, 9, 36, 238n20
Rodgers, Richard, 4–5, 12, 14, 19, 55–78, 87, 89, 91, 132, 141, 202, 233n3, 236n3, 241nn1–2, 250n11
Rogin, Michael, 70

Romance of the Harem, The (Leonowens), 19, 57, 59, 61, 64–65, 72, 241n2
Roman mythology. *See* Greek and Roman mythology
Romano, John, 94
romantic love, 27, 47–50, 187, 189, 211–26, 242n2
Romberg, Sigmund, 27, 236n2
Romeo and Juliet (Shakespeare), 152
Romney, George, 46
Roper, David, 89–91, 244n13
Rosalie (Gershwin and Romberg), 27–28
Rose, Brian, 189
Rose, Edward, 239n25
Rose-Marie (Friml and Harbach), 27
Rossetti, Christina, 4, 161–81, 253n2, 254n7, 254n10, 254n12, 255nn16–17, 255n24
Rosso, Martha, 153
Rothschild, Lionel de, 85
Rowell, George, 237n18
Rubin, Gayle, 254n8
Rubin, Joan, 14–15
RuPaul's Drag Race (2009–), 203
Ruskin, John, 46, 75
Rymer, Malcolm, 110, 246n10
Ryskind, Morrie, 236n4

sadism, 196, 198–99, 203
Sadoff, Dianne, 4, 7, 10–11, 15, 136
safety razors, 122–23
Saidy, Fred, 237n12
Salome (Wilde), 228
Sanders, Julie, 7, 9, 16, 79, 136, 227
Santoriello, Jill, 260n2
Sapsea, Thomas (character), 249n6, 250n9
Saturday Night Live, 153
Savory, Whitelaw (Whitefield; character), 45–48, 50–52
Savran, David, 5, 14–15, 234n19
Schaffel, Martha, 210–11, 218–19
Scheherazade (Rimsky-Korsakov), 13

Schlicke, Paul, 117
Schoenberg, Arnold, 158
Schönberg, Claude-Michel, 182, 191, 212, 230, 256n2
Schwartz, Scott, 210
Schwartz, Stephen, 228
science fiction. *See* speculative fiction
Scott, A. O., 109
Scott, George C., 135
Scott, Heidi, 253n2
Scott, Walter, 34, 121
Seacole, Mary, 59
Sears, Ann, 30–31
"Secret Soul" (*Jane Eyre*), 260n5
Sedgwick, Eve Kosofsky, 14, 136, 249n5, 254n8
seduction and abandonment, 196–97
Seiter, William A., 45
sentimentalism/sentimentality, 12, 15, 115, 136, 145–46, 159, 184, 202
serial killers, 23, 43, 51–52, 108–31, 185–87, 191–95, 198, 201, 205, 207–9, 257n18
Seurat, Georges, 85, 211
sex scandals, 23, 187, 257n8
sexual content, explicit or implicit, 140–46, 149–50, 161–62, 165–68, 172, 176, 197–98, 202, 245n22, 249n2, 253n28, 255n15
sexual double standards, 187, 199
sexuality, 161–81, 257n7; fluid, 203; repressed, 47, 166–72, 180, 183, 198, 209; Victorian, 161–81
sexual politics, 49, 185
Shakespeare, William, 5, 9, 15, 34, 152–53, 159, 193, 237n14, 247n15, 251n15, 253n31
"Shall I Tell You What I Think of You?" (*The King and I*), 63
"Shall We Dance" (*The King and I*), 65
Shaper, Hal, 259n2
Sharaff, Irene, 237n11, 241n2
Sharman, Jim, 129

Shaw, George Bernard, 5, 54, 92, 104, 153, 164, 253n4
She (Haggard), 239n25
Shelley, Mary, 7
Shelley, Percy Bysshe, 159, 253n31
Shepard, Sam, 14
Sher, Bartlett, 242n2
Sheridan, Richard Brinsley, 5
Shield, Harvey, 253n3
Shorthouse, Joseph Henry, 34
Show Boat (Ferber, 1926), 29
Show Boat (Kern and Hammerstein, 1927), 29–31, 73, 233n4
Shulman, Milton, 88
Shurbutt, Sylvia Bailey, 253n2
Shylock (character), 93
Siam, 55–77. *See also* Thailand
sibling rivalry, 22, 162, 171–74
Sidney, W., 239n25
Sikes, Bill (character), 17, 79, 82, 89, 94–95, 99–101, 104, 119–20, 128, 199, 258n25
Sikes, Nancy (character), 17, 22, 79, 82, 92, 99–107, 119–20, 245nn20–21, 248n24; murder of, 17, 79, 81–82, 94–95, 119–20, 128, 197–200, 245nn20–21, 258n25
Silence of the Lambs, The (Demme), 206
silent film adaptations, 3, 17, 36, 39, 82, 84–85, 185–86, 196, 238n22
Sinyard, Neil, 135–36
sisterhood, 161, 166–71, 242n6
"Sisters" (Berlin), 173
"Sisters, The" (*Goblin Market*), 172–74, 179
Skal, David, 196–97, 258n21, 258n26
Sketches by Boz (Dickens), 15, 258n29
Skousen, Kari, 259n2
slasher film. *See* horror film/horror genre
Slaughter, Tod, 111, 123, 249n38
Slaughter on Tenth Avenue (*On Your Toes*), 31–32

slavery, 56, 62–63, 67–73, 78, 240n36; African chattel, 19, 45, 57, 64–65, 68–70, 72–73. 78, 240n36, 243n16

"Small House of Uncle Thomas, The" (*The King and I*), 19, 57–58, 67–71, 74, 241n44

Sméagol (character), 259n34

Smith, Alison, 39

Smith, Grahame, 17

Smith, Helen, 246n10

Smith, Samuel Francis, 217

social criticism, 17, 111, 116–17, 122, 136, 138, 181, 184, 199, 221, 230, 250n8

"Something Wonderful" (*The King and I*), 73

Sondheim, Stephen, 1, 4–5, 9, 16–17, 20–21, 85, 88–89, 91, 108–31, 132, 134, 163–64, 183–84, 211–13, 227–28, 245n1, 246n2, 246n8, 247n16, 248n33, 249n35, 261n5

"Sonnet 18" (Shakespeare), 253n31

"Sonnet 130" (Shakespeare), 251n15

Sound of Music, The (Rodgers and Hammerstein), 252n26

Southern belle, 219, 260n7

South Pacific (Rodgers and Hammerstein), 12, 73–74

Soylent Green (Fleischer), 247n17

Spall, Timothy, 95, 109

special effects, 202; lack of, 192, 198

spectacle, 2, 14, 22, 133, 148, 182, 184, 191, 229

speculative fiction, 38, 239n25. *See also* fantastic fiction

Spewack, Bella, 44–45, 240n40

spirituals, 29

Spivak, Gayatri Chakravorty, 260n9

Split Britches Theatre Company, 176

spoken drama, 5

Stacey, Jackie, 254n14

stage Jew (racist stock character), 93, 95, 106

Starobinski, Jean, 215, 218

Statue at Large, A (Anstey), 238n22

Steele, Tommy, 90

Stein, Dick, 247n13

Stein, Joseph, 71, 97, 106

Steinbeck, John, 31

Stephens, Henry Pottinger, 39, 239n30

Stephens, Walter, 21, 133–34, 141–45, 147–48, 251n17

Stern, Rebecca F., 253n2

Steuer, Gary, 253n1

Stevens, Monty, 259n2

Stevenson, Robert, 11, 142–44

Stevenson, Robert Louis, 3, 17, 22, 128, 182–209, 212, 239n25, 257n9

Steyn, Mark, 87–88, 90, 96

Stilgoe, Richard, 256n2

stock characters, 93, 95, 106, 131, 183, 188, 252n25, 257n6

Stockton, Frank R., 9

Stoker, Bram, 7, 128

Stone, Harry, 93

Stone, Paddy, 259n32

Stoneman, Patsy, 259n1

Stop the World, I Want to Get Off (Bricusse and Newley), 244n8

Stothart, Herbert, 27

Stowe, Harriett Beecher, 19, 57, 59, 65, 67–68, 70–72

Strachey, Lytton, 33–35

Strange Case of a Hyde and a Seekyl, The (Geduld), 257n9

Strange Case of Dr. Jekyll and Mr. Hyde, The (Stevenson, 1886), 3, 17, 22, 128, 182–209, 212, 239n25

Streetcar Named Desire, A (Williams), 13

Streisand, Barbra, 132

Stride, Elizabeth, 191

String of Pearls, The (Anonymous/Prest), 20, 88, 108–21, 129–30, 212, 245n1, 246n10, 248n20, 248n26, 248n29, 249n34

student-teacher relationship, 139–42, 145–46

Stuyvesant, Peter, 28

subjectivity, 193, 202
Sullivan, Arthur, 27, 55, 152, 240n31
Sullivan, Thomas Russell, 3, 23, 185–91, 195–97, 200, 257n9, 258nn22–23
Summers, Julia, 154–55
Summerson, Esther (character), 75, 99
Sunday Afternoon on the Island of La Grande Jatte, A (Seurat), 85, 211
Sunday in the Park with George (Sondheim and Lapine), 85, 211
Suskin, Steven, 211
Swain, Joseph, 4
Sweeney Todd (Burton, 2007), 88, 108–10, 126–31, 248n23, 248n30, 249n37
Sweeney Todd: A Musical Thriller (Sondheim and Wheeler, 1979), 4, 9, 17, 20–21, 23, 41, 51, 75, 88, 108–32, 134, 163–64, 183, 206–7, 212–13, 224, 228, 230, 240n38, 241n44, 244n10, 245n1, 246n2, 246nn4–6, 246n8, 246n10, 248n20, 248n33, 256n3, 258n31, 261n5
"Sweeney Todd: The Barber" (Holloway, 1956), 111, 247n13
Sweeney Todd, The Barber of Fleet Street: or, The String of Pearls (Hazelton, 1865), 248n20
Sweeney Todd: The Demon Barber of Fleet Street (Bond, 1973), 108–10, 164, 207, 264n8
Sweeney Todd: The Demon Barber of Fleet Street (King, 1936), 123, 129
Sweeney Todd: The Fiend of Fleet Street (Pitt, 1847), 43, 110, 154, 247n12, 247n18, 248n20, 249n34
Sweeney Todd hair salons, 111, 247n14
Sweet, Matthew, 191
"Sweet Liberty" (*Jane Eyre*), 216–17
Sykes, Nancy. *See* Sikes, Nancy (character)

Tabram, Martha, 191
"Take Me Back to Manhattan" (*The New Yorkers*), 29
Tale of Two Cities, A (BBC, 1980), 135
Tale of Two Cities, A (CBS, 1980), 135
Tale of Two Cities, A (Dickens, 1859), 135, 228, 244n9
Tale of Two Cities, A (Santoriello, 2008), 244n9
Tales of the South Pacific (Michener), 74
Taylor, Alma, 239n23
Taylor, Diana, 184, 194
Taylor, Millie, 89, 244n15
teacher as character. *See* governess/teacher as character
television adaptations, 9, 23, 85, 111, 135, 155, 199, 210, 238n20, 242n2, 256n3
"Tell Me, Shepherds" (*Drood*), 137
Tenniel, John, *Punch* cartoon by, *86*
Tennyson, Alfred Lord, 33
Tevye (character), 71
Thackeray, William, 38, 100, 239n26
Thailand, 19, 55–68, 242n3, 243n19, 243n22. *See also* Siam
Thatcher-era England, 135–36, 234n16
theatricality, 18, 69; intertheatricality, 209; meta-theatricality, 136, 151–60, 230; musical-theatricality, 2–3, 36, 42, 163–64, 187, 194; of novels, 137, 209, 227
Thespis, or the Gods Grown Old (Gilbert and Sullivan), 240n31
Thiang, Lady (character), 56, 65–67, 73, 78
"This Is the Moment" (*Jekyll and Hyde*), 183–84
Thompson, Emma, 246n2
Thompson-Duvall, Linda, 259n2
Thomson, Brian, 242n2
Thornfield Hall, 23, 210, 212, 216–17, 223
Thornhill, Mr. (character), 112, 247n18, 248n26
Threepenny Opera, The (Weill and Brecht), 109, 246nn5–6
Thugee theory, 251–52n20
Tillotson, Kathleen, 35
Tilly, Vesta, 155

Tinted Venus (Gibson, 1851–56), 39–40, 42–43, 237n11
Tinted Venus, The (Hepworth, 1921), 36–37
Tinted Venus, The (W. Wilde, 1885), 36
Tinted Venus, The: A Farcical Romance (Anstey, 1885), 9, 18, 25–54, 122, 237n11, 239nn25–26
Tipping the Velvet (Waters), 256n3
Titus Andronicus (Shakespeare), 247n15
Todd, Lucy (character), 119–20, 125, 130, 241n44, 248n30, 258n27
Todd, Sweeney (character), 41, 43, 51–52, 108–31, 207, 209, 245n1, 247n18, 249n34, 249n40
Tolkien, J. R. R., 239n25, 259n34
Tony Awards, 87–88, 126, 132, 168, 201, 210–11, 234n12, 238n20, 241n2, 243n17, 245n1, 249n1, 257n16
Toppman, Lawrence, 231
"To Russia with Love" (*To Russia with Love*), 90
touring productions, 202
Tracy, Spencer, 192, 198, 203
Tragic Mulatta trope, 245n20
transvestite performance, 255n19. *See also* cross-gender performance/performativity
travel narratives, 55–79
Tree, Herbert Beerbohm, 84
Trollope, Anthony, 34, 36
Tromp, Marlene, 205
Trotwood, Betsey (character), 76
Truman, Harry, 74
Trump, Donald, 228–29
Tupenny (character), 199
Tuptim (character), 59, 61–52, 64, 67–68, 71–72, 241n44, 241n2, 242n7, 243n17
Turner, Lana, 198, 200
Turpin, Judge (character), 119–20, 125–26
Twain, Mark, 26, 254n13
Twang!! (Bart, 1965), 90–91

Tweddle, Leander (character), 37–47, 122, 238n21, 239n24, 240n37
Twinkleton, Miss (character), 141, 144
twins, 139, 142–43, 146–47
Twist, Oliver (character), 79–107, 114, 119, 129, 245n22, 248n24
Tynan, Kenneth, 88

Uncle Tom (character), 70, 243n20
Uncle Tom's Cabin (Aiken, 1852), 70
Uncle Tom's Cabin (Stowe, 1852), 19, 57, 64–65, 67–72, 78
Under the Gaslight (Daly), 128, 190
Unger, Gladys, 251n18
unrequited love, 37, 41–42, 132–60
upward mobility, 118, 127, 248n23
Utah, 60, 243n10
Utterson, John (character), 202–3, 256n4

vampirism, 127
Van Dyck, Anthony, 46
Vane, Sybil (character), 193, 198
van Esterik, Penny, 59
Van Gogh, Vincent, 45–46
Vanity Fair (Thackery), 239n26
vaudeville, 27, 70
Venus (character), 25–54, 237n11, 238n21, 239n24, 240n42
"Venus in Ozone Heights" (*One Touch of Venus*), 50
Venus myth, 37, 241n42
Vera-Ellen (Vera-Ellen Rohe), 174
Verdi, Giuseppe, 13
Vice Versâ (Anstey), 36, 238nn19–20
Victorian dress, 66–67, 243n15
Victorian gender roles, 57
Victorian literature, elevation of, 53–54
Victor/Victoria (Edwards), 259n32
video games, 153–54
Vietnam War, 241n1
Vincentelli, Elizabeth, 205
Vineyard Theater (New York), 161

violence, 182–209; against women, 79–107, 182–209, 245n21
visibility, discourses of, 192
Vision of Venus (Pleon), 36
Viswanathan, Gauri, 241n1
Vokes, Rosina, 36, 238n21
von Selheim, Mara, 69
von Trapp, Maria (character), 241n42
Vorticist manifesto, 33

Walker, Stephen, 137, 141–42, 147–48
Walkowitz, Judith, 191
Wallis, Shani, 89
Wandering Jew, The (Lewis), 106
Wandering Jew trope, 106
Wasserstein, Wendy, 14
Watanabe, Jerry, 74, 244n23
Watanabe, Ken, 242n2
Waters, Mark, 36
Waters, Sarah, 256n3
Watson, Jeanie, 253n2
Weber, Bruce, 210–12
Webster, W., 29, 239n30
Weill, Kurt, 18, 28, 32, 35–36, 45, 47, 50, 52, 109, 236n5, 237n11, 240n39, 246n5
Weitzel, Edward, 203
Weliver, Phyllis, 137, 158
Weller, Sam (character), 116
Welles, Orson, 11
Wells, Matthew, 253n3
Welsh, Alexander, 99
Weltman, Jerry, 253n29
Weltman, Sharon Aronofsky, 5, 233n4, 247n12
Wendy's, 124–25
West Side Story (Bernstein, Laurents, and Sondheim), 9
"West Wind" (*One Touch of Venus*), 50, 253n31
Wheeler, Hugh, 20, 108–10, 245n1
Whelehan, Imelda, 7

"When the Stars Are in the Quiet Skies" (*Lost*), 141, 143–45, 251n16
"Where Are the Men?" (*Anything Goes*), 29
White, George, 28
White, Richard, 256n4
White, Vanna, 238n22
White Christmas (Curtiz), 174
"Who Will Buy?" (*Oliver!*), 169
Why Marry? (Williams), 235n20
Wicked (Maguire, 1995), 228
Wicked (Schwartz and Holzman, 2003), 228
Wickfield, Agnes (character), 75–76, 187
Wicks, Teal, 256n4
Wide Sargasso Sea (Rhys, 1966), 23, 160, 220, 256n3
Wilde, Oscar, 3, 22, 33, 46–47, 128, 185–86, 196–97, 205, 228
Wilde, Willie, 36
Wildhorn, Frank, 3, 22, 182–209, 258n19, 258n28, 258n31
Will and Grace, 201
Williams, Allison, 85
Williams, Bert, 70, 236n8
Williams, Carolyn, 225, 249n5
Williams, Jesse Lynch, 235n20
Williams, John, 236n33
Williams, Laurey (character), 30, 50, 236nn9–10
Williams, Tennessee, 13
Williams, William Smith, 210
Wilson, August, 14
Wilson, Edmund, 138, 158, 250n8, 251n20, 252n28
Winer, Linda, 109
Winters, David, 199
Winter's Tale, The (Shakespeare), 153
Wizard of Oz, The (Baum), 228
Wolf, Stacy, 5, 14, 233n3
Wolff, Larry, 102
Wollstonecraft, Mary, 59

Woman in White, The (Lloyd Webber, Zippel, and Jones), 211, 228
women: as homosocial conduit for men, 254n8; including in adaptations, 184–84, 189; subjugation of, 55–77, 214–18
women's independence, 62, 76
women's professions, 55–78
women's rights, 55–78, 181, 214–16, 235n20
Wood, Ellen, 259n33
Woolf, Virginia, 15, 18, 25–54, 76–78, 212
Woolverton, Linda, 211
working class/underclass, 79–107, 184–209
World War I, 27, 33, 123
World War II, 47, 69, 73–74, 90
"Worst Pies in London, The" (*Sweeney Todd*), 124
Wotton, Lord Henry (character), 196, 202
"Would I Were with Thee!" (Norton), 141

Wuthering Heights (Brontë, 1847), 7

xenophobia 147, 158. *See also* racism

"Yankee Doodle Boy, The" (*Little Johnny Jones*), 27
Yellen, Sherman, 199
Yiddish, 95–96
Yorkey, Brian, 238n20
Young, Mrs. Henry, 128
Young, James, 84
Younge, Charlotte, 34
"You've Got to Be Carefully Taught" (*South Pacific*), 73–74
"You've Got to Pick a Pocket or Two" (*Oliver!*), 18, 82, 96, 106
Yun-Fat, Chow, 242n2

Zanuck, Darryl F., 241n2
Zeffirelli, Franco, 7, 218, 260n6
Zemka, Sue, 82
Ziegfeld's Follies, 27, 236n8

CPSIA information can be obtained
at www.ICGtesting.com
Printed in the USA
LVHW111029051022
730021LV00003B/160